Shaping Immigration News

This book offers a comprehensive portrait of French and American journalists in action as they grapple with how to report and comment on one of the most important issues of our era. Drawing on interviews with leading journalists and analyses of an extensive sample of newspaper and television coverage since the early 1970s, Rodney Benson shows how the immigration debate has become increasingly focused on the dramatic, emotion-laden frames of humanitarianism and public order. Yet, even in an era of global hypercommercialism, Benson also finds enduring French-American differences related to the distinctive societal positions, professional logics, and internal structures of each country's journalistic fields. In both countries, less commercialized media tend to offer the most in-depth, multiperspectival, and critical news. Benson challenges classic liberalism's assumptions about state intervention's chilling effects on the press, suggests costs as well as benefits to the current vogue in personalized narrative news, and calls attention to journalistic practices that can help empower civil society. This book offers new theories and methods for sociologists and media scholars and fresh insights for journalists, policymakers, and concerned citizens.

Rodney Benson is associate professor in the Department of Media, Culture, and Communication and an affiliated faculty member in the Department of Sociology at New York University. Benson's research lies at the intersection of the sociology of culture, comparative media systems, political communication, and journalism studies. His articles have appeared in the *American Sociological Review*, *Journal of Communication*, *European Journal of Communication*, *Press/Politics*, *Political Communication*, *Le Monde Diplomatique*, and many other publications. Benson is also co-editor of *Bourdieu and the Journalistic Field* (with Erik Neveu, 2005) and co-author of the Free Press policy report *Public Media and Political Independence: Lessons for the Future of Journalism from Around the World* (with Matthew Powers, 2011).

Communication, Society and Politics

Editors

W. LANCE BENNETT, University of Washington
ROBERT M. ENTMAN, The George Washington University

Politics and relations among individuals in societies across the world are being transformed by new technologies for targeting individuals and sophisticated methods for shaping personalized messages. The new technologies challenge boundaries of many kinds – between news, information, entertainment, and advertising; between media, with the arrival of the World Wide Web; and even between nations. Communication, Society and Politics probes the political and social impacts of these new communication systems in national, comparative, and global perspective.

Other Books in the Series

(continued after Index)

Shaping Immigration News

A French-American Comparison

RODNEY BENSON

New York University

CAMBRIDGE
UNIVERSITY PRESS

CAMBRIDGE
UNIVERSITY PRESS

32 Avenue of the Americas, New York NY 10013-2473, USA

Cambridge University Press is part of the University of Cambridge.

It furthers the University's mission by disseminating knowledge in the pursuit of
education, learning and research at the highest international levels of excellence.

www.cambridge.org
Information on this title: www.cambridge.org/9780521715676

First published 2013
First paperback edition 2014

A catalogue record for this publication is available from the British Library

Library of Congress Cataloguing in Publication data
Benson, Rodney.
Shaping immigration news : A French-American comparison / Rodney Benson, New York
University.
pages ; cm
Includes bibliographical references and index.
ISBN 978-0-521-88767-0
1. Mass media and immigrants – United States. 2. Mass media and
immigrants – France I. Title.
P94.5.I482U654 2013
070.404930482–dc23 2012048874

ISBN 978-0-521-88767-0 Hardback
ISBN 978-0-521-71567-6 Paperback

Additional resources for this publication at http://rodneybenson.org/

Portions of Chapter 6 previously appeared in "What Makes News More Multiperspectival? A
Field Analysis," *Poetics* 37, 5–6 (fall 2009): 402–418, © Elsevier and are reprinted by
permission. Portions of Chapter 7 previously appeared in "What Makes for a Critical Press?
A Case Study of French and U.S. Immigration News Coverage," *International Journal of
Press/Politics* 15, 1 (winter 2010): 3–24, © Sage Publishing and are reprinted by permission.

Contents

Tables and Figures

FIGURES

APPENDIX TABLES

ONLINE APPENDIX TABLES

Acknowledgments

In the process of researching and writing this book, I have benefited from the encouragement and comments of many esteemed colleagues and friends. I feel fortunate to be part of the growing and vibrant community of comparative media and culture researchers and to be able to engage with so many scholars whose work I admire, such as Dan Hallin, Paolo Mancini, Jay Blumler, James Curran, Michèle Lamont, Sonia Livingstone, Frank Esser, Silvio Waisbord, Toril Aalberg, Thomas Hanitzsch, Jesper Strömbäck, Cyril Lemieux, Myra Marx Ferree, David Levy, and Rasmus Kleis Nielsen. Cross-national comparative research is continually challenging the conventional wisdom based on single-nation studies and in so doing is revitalizing and transforming our disciplines. Even so, cross-national comparative projects face continuing epistemological, explanatory, and normative challenges in taking account of new technologies, transnational as well as cross-national dimensions of culture, and comparisons that go beyond North America and Western Europe. While this book is an ambitious attempt to paint a portrait of the French and U.S. journalistic fields and to offer a model for other cross-national studies, it certainly cannot fully transcend its temporal and spatial limitations; I can only hope that its shortcomings will be just as helpful in orienting and improving future research as its successes.

For generously taking the time to read through draft chapters and offer extremely helpful constructive critiques, I want to express my gratitude to Michael Schudson, Steve Reese, Mark Pedelty, Ron Jacobs, Marty Schain, Tim Dowd, Susanne Janssen, Bill Kunerth, Eric Klinenberg, Abby Saguy, Kjersti Thorbjørnsrud, Elizabeth Hanauer, Max Benavidez, and two anonymous Cambridge reviewers. My thinking and writing have also been enriched by the productive dialogues about theories and methods that I have had with Hartmut Wessler, Nick Couldry, Aeron Davis, John Thompson, Herbert Gans, David Swartz, Tore Slaata, Ida Willig, Barbie Zelizer, Jay Rosen,

Sandrine Boudana, Michael Palmer, Sarah Stroup, Dalton Conley, Steven Lukes, David Folsom, Ed Berenson, Herrick Chapman, Frédéric Viguier, and James Graff.

In France, I have been helped immeasurably in my understanding of French society and media (although I am still and always hope to be learning more) and of sociological theory and methodology in general (likewise) by my colleagues at the Centre de sociologie européenne established by Pierre Bourdieu, especially Dominique Marchetti, Julien Duval, Patrick Champagne, Julie Sedel, and Gisèle Sapiro. I also have benefited greatly from and enjoyed every minute of my ongoing intellectual collaborations with Erik Neveu in Rennes and Eric Darras and Olivier Baisnée in Toulouse. Philippe Juhem generously shared his own interview transcripts (for his excellent research on antiracism associations and the media), some of which I have cited in this book.

A host of distinguished immigration scholars have helped me navigate the ins and outs of French and U.S. immigration history and policy, including Smaïn Laacher, Patrick Weil, Adrian Favell, Erik Bleich, Elaine Thomas, Virginie Guiraudon, Denis Lacorne, Michel Wieviorka, Farhad Khosrokhavar, Catherine Wihtol de Wenden, Gérard Noiriel, and my NYU colleague Marty Schain. Given its focus on news media, this book cannot fully capture the immense complexities of immigration in France and the United States so ably documented by these scholars. Building on their work, however, I hope that my research on the news media's role in shaping the immigration debate can add an important new dimension to our understanding of contemporary immigration politics. For the insights that come from firsthand experiences of immigration politics and news media work, I am also immensely grateful to the many journalists and activists in France and the United States who took time from their busy schedules to share something of their professional worlds with me.

Colleagues at Yale, Erasmus University–Rotterdam, the University of Oslo, and the Toulouse Institut d'Études Politiques invited me to share my work-in-progress on this book and provided useful and cogent critical feedback. I also received helpful comments when I presented papers drawing on material from the book at conferences hosted by Connecticut College (on Undocumented Hispanic Immigration) and by the International Communication Association. In addition, I want to thank Thibault Chareton of the French-American Foundation, Ted Glasser of Stanford University's Department of Communication, and Giovanna Dell'Orto of the University of Minnesota School of Journalism and Mass Communication (working with Vicki Birchfield of the Georgia Institute of Technology) for inviting me to present my research to diverse groups that included many journalists and activists as well as scholars.

Shaping Immigration News is substantially based on a large corpus of discourse and image data gathered and analyzed over the past few years; its theoretical and methodological framework draws not only on this study of immigration news, but also on additional comparative studies I have conducted, many of them collaborative, of other topics, regions, and dimensions of media. It also builds upon earlier research conducted under the outstanding guidance of Loïc Wacquant, along with Neil Fligstein, Todd Gitlin, and Allan Pred, at the University of California–Berkeley. Loïc and Neil first sparked my interest in field theory and encouraged me to extend and develop it for cross-national research. Todd's early writings on hegemony motivated me to pursue an academic career; I continue to try to emulate his open-minded exploration of new theories and methods. Michael Schudson was also an early and important supporter of this project. Whether or not I always provided sufficient responses to his devil's advocate critiques, the effort to do so has made this a better book. The pioneering work of Dan Hallin and Paolo Mancini (in particular, their landmark 1984 essay in *Theory and Society*) inspired me to try to bring together critical theory with rigorous quantitative and qualitative discourse analysis. In some ways, this book is an attempt to elaborate, complicate, and update Dan and Paolo's findings in their empirically condensed – but theoretically rich and methodologically generative – case study comparison of the Italian and U.S. public spheres.

A number of talented graduate students have worked closely with me on this project; this book could not have been completed without their assistance. Sarah Stonbely and Kathryn Kleppinger ably helped me conduct most of the content coding. Matt Powers, Burcu Baykurt, and Jane Mabe also provided crucial research support. In addition, the book benefited from research conducted by Luke Stark, Jason Stanley, Emily Nickerson, Ann Kosseff, Elly Hanauer, Jill Campaiola, Lin Zhang, and Beth Harris. In Paris, Nathalie Le Dinh Bao, Sara Dezalay, Nicolas Jaoul, and Gaia Fisher helped me construct complete newspaper and TV news samples. Tim Wood provided thorough and thoughtful help in the final stages of fact checking, copyediting, proofing, and indexing.

Throughout the research process, Frank Lopresti of the NYU Statistics Lab was my indispensable advisor for statistical analysis. In Paris, Christine Barbier-Bouvet guided me in making full use of the impressive French INA television archives; in Nashville, Marshall Breeding deftly managed my request for newscast DVDs from the Vanderbilt Television News Archives.

At New York University, I want to thank my department chairs Ted Magder and Marita Sturken for always going to bat to provide me with the time and resources that I needed for this project. As director of graduate studies of NYU's Department of Media, Culture, and Communication over the past four years, I would never have been able to finish this book if it were not for Mary Taylor, the extremely capable and affable graduate advisor who made sure I stayed on top of all my responsibilities rather than being buried by them. Dove Pedlosky generously helped refine the design of the figures of the U.S. and French journalistic fields in Chapter 2. Alison Garforth ensured that all my copyright permissions were in order. Brett Gary, Victor Pickard, Charlton McIlwain, Mark Crispin Miller, and Helen Nissenbaum always helped me to see the bigger picture, in life as much as in scholarship. I am fortunate to work with so many talented colleagues in my department and across NYU. I am grateful for the financial support I have received for this book from the New York University Challenge Grant, NYU Steinhardt Challenge Fund, and NYU Humanities Initiative Grants.

As editors of the Cambridge series on communication, society, and politics, Bob Entman and Lance Bennett championed this book from the start and encouraged me to think big; it goes without saying that their work as scholars has also been an inspiration to me. At Cambridge, it has been a pleasure to work with Lew Bateman, Shaun Vigil, Mark Fox, and Cherline Daniel.

My deepest and most heartfelt appreciation goes to Kelly Benson. As to the book, she was patient and knew how to balance no-nonsense critique with just the right amount of motivating encouragement. As to everything else, she and our two sons – Thomas and Peter – always gave me plenty of reasons to keep going and even more reasons to wrap it up.

I

Why Study Immigration News?

In recent years, immigration has become a hot-button political issue in virtually every major Western democracy, raising complex policy questions and prompting strong emotional responses. Globally, migration is on the rise, with positive and negative effects on the fabric of daily life in both sending and receiving nation-states. Immigration is reshaping our lives, yet much of what we know about immigration is limited by the information and analyses we receive from the news media. Are the media up to the task?

From this perspective, the ongoing debate about whether news coverage is pro-immigrant or anti-immigrant misses the point. Rather, the test for journalism is how well it helps citizens and policymakers understand the causes and consequences of immigration, as well as the backlash against it. My claim in this book is straightforward: we are more likely to get a clearer picture of this complex reality when the "journalistic field" is shaped more by civic-cultural ends than by commercial or instrumental political ends. This is a not a question of ethics, it is a question of social structure: the challenge is to find the best ways to institutionally secure "quality" journalism, in all senses of the term.

So, how have news media covered immigration? And how has this coverage varied in relation to journalistic ownership, funding, audiences, and professional practices? I try to answer these questions in two ways. First, I look at immigration coverage over time, from the early 1970s through 2006, and explore how changes in news treatment of immigration are related to structural transformations of the journalistic field. This is a period when commercial pressures inside the U.S. journalistic field increased considerably. Do we then see changes in news content that accord with the structural changes in the U.S. journalistic field? Second, I bring in a comparison with the French journalistic field and its immigration coverage during the same period. As I document in this book, the French journalistic field continues to be less market-driven than its American counterpart. A U.S.-French comparison allows us to see what difference in news coverage these and other structural variations make.

In fact, the U.S. and French media have both at various times successfully served as a democratic public forum for debating immigration. Over the past forty years, U.S. news coverage has often examined immigration in a serious, in-depth manner. American journalism at its best offers compelling close-up examinations of the immigrant experience and hard-hitting investigative reports about the agencies that administer immigration policy. Looking abroad, French media show another way of funding, regulating, and presenting the news. As I demonstrate throughout this book, this French approach has the virtue of making more room for multiple, often critical, perspectives, diverse civil society voices, and in-depth expert analyses. The French approach may or may not be replicable in the United States, but it reminds us that there are alternatives. In an ideal world, citizens in all democracies would benefit from some combination of these – and other – national models.

This book is a careful response to the many and varied criticisms of the American media's coverage of immigration. But it is more than that – because if there is room for improvement, that improvement is more than a matter of individual initiative. As with other cultural professions, journalists work under a series of institutional constraints. All knowledge is constructed. The question is, what are the social conditions underlying the production of *journalistic* knowledge? My aim is to use historical and international comparative analysis to fully describe these constraints and conditions and thus provide the first precondition for their potential transformation. Or, to put it another way, I explore the French case to illuminate the American experience, and vice versa, while at the same time drawing general lessons for the sociology of news and political communication.

Admittedly, any number of issues or sampling methods could be used to compare news media systems. Immigration, however, provides a number of advantages over other potential content samples. A case study focusing on a single issue allows for a focused and detailed analysis. Immigration is an especially multifaceted and complex social phenomenon; rhetorically, immigration can be (and has been) discussed in a range of ways, from thoughtful analyses to simplistic polemics. Describing the challenge and appeal of covering immigration, one journalist writes: "Immigration stories have everything – history, languages, economics, statistics, class conflict [and] picaresque narratives."[1] If such an array of "angles" makes the issue interesting for journalists, it also ensures that the media sociologist will have plenty of variation in the "dependent variable" to analyze and try to explain.

Although France and the United States have their own distinct immigration histories, the structural characteristics and politics of immigration in the two

---

[1] Christopher Caldwell, "After Londonistan," *New York Times Sunday Magazine*, June 25, 2006, p. 6.

countries are similar in many ways (see Appendix C: Immigration Context). France and the United States are among the top migrant-receiving countries worldwide, and, until 2000, France actually had a higher proportion of foreign-born residents than the United States. Research shows similar economic costs and benefits for the host society and similar struggles for immigrants. In both countries, a plethora of well-established immigrant rights associations and restrictionist groups vie for influence over immigration policy, and periodically the immigration issue has become an important stake in political party struggles for power. Thus, there are enough similarities that a comparison of media coverage of immigration can tell us something about the media in the two countries and not just about the particularities of their respective immigration experiences.

Likewise, immigration reporting occupies a similar location in the French and U.S. journalistic professional hierarchies: the issue generally concerns disadvantaged populations, but the "beat" carries a certain prestige because of its societal and political importance. Immigration reporting is no more specialized than most beats (Gans 1979/2005). At many newspapers, a few reporters have special, but not exclusive, responsibility for the immigration issue.[2] Most eventually move on to cover other issues. Immigration reporters tend not to have any expertise on the issue beyond that learned on the job. The majority of immigration reporters are men, but the number of women journalists has risen steadily in both countries since the 1970s[3]; they are not particularly ethnically diverse in either country (see Chapters 3 and 4). French and American immigration reporters tend to share similar social class and educational backgrounds. Compared to their colleagues, it may be that immigration reporters are more reflexive and internationally informed. Since the 1990s, numerous national and international conferences have been held on immigration reporting. Many of the reporters I interviewed for this book took part in such conferences or other international exchanges.[4] Thus, if this study finds ongoing cross-national differences, it will not be because French and U.S.

---

[2] At the three agenda-setting newspapers in France (*Libération*, *Le Figaro*, and *Le Monde*) and the United States (*Los Angeles Times*, *New York Times*, *Washington Post*) whose coverage I examine between the 1970s and 2000s, one-quarter or less of front-page immigration coverage from 2002–2006 can be attributed to specialized reporters (defined simply as the top three reporters whose bylines appear most often).

[3] My byline analysis shows that the proportion of female immigration reporters increased in the United States from 12 percent in the 1970s to 33 percent in the 2000s, and in France from 14 to 41 percent during the same period.

[4] For instance, I leaned from Diane Lindquist, a reporter for the *San Diego Union-Tribune*, that she had met Philippe Bernard of *Le Monde* in the mid-1990s as part of a German Marshall Fund program on immigration. In 2009 and 2010, I participated in conferences (in Paris and Miami) on immigration reporting sponsored by the French-American Foundation; in April 2012, I participated in a similar multinational conference sponsored by the University of Minnesota. Numerous noninternational immigration reporting conferences have been held in both countries, beginning in the 1980s and increasingly in recent years.

immigration reporters have been insulated from global influences – in fact, quite the contrary.

For all these reasons, immigration reporting presents an excellent case study to describe, understand, and evaluate the democratic performance of news media in two leading democracies.

DESCRIBING IMMIGRATION NEWS

What are the dominant tendencies in news about immigration? There seems to be no consensus in either the scholarly or popular literature. For instance, political scientist Peter Skerry (1993, 320) has argued that U.S. news organizations, such as the *Los Angeles Times*, have adopted a "civil rights mindset" in the way that they cover Latino immigration, racializing the Mexican-American experience in a way that many Mexican Americans themselves reject. Journalist William McGowan (2002, 181) criticizes the media for being "all too ready to celebrate immigration's relationship to America's increasing cultural diversity ... in the process, [leaving] important questions unanswered and dismiss[ing] legitimate concerns as 'nativism.'"

Coming from a completely different direction, linguist Otto Santa Ana (1999, 217) locates racist metaphors in *Los Angeles Times*'s coverage that contribute, even if unwittingly, to "demeaning and dehumanizing the immigrant worker." Similarly, anthropologist Leo Chavez (2008, 16) argues that U.S. news media have exaggerated a "Latino threat" narrative, according to which "Mexicans (and other Latin American immigrants) are unable or unwilling to integrate into U.S. society, preferring to remain linguistically and socially isolated, and in the narrative's more sinister renditions ... [engaging in] a conspiracy to take over the southwestern United States." For Aviva Chomsky (2007), immigrants are wrongly accused by the media of taking jobs and driving down wages, whereas, for Kitty Calavita (1996), the dominant discourse beginning in the 1990s emphasized immigrants' abuse of welfare benefits.[5]

Who is correct? Actually, all of them are, to a degree. As my research will show, most news items mention multiple "frames" rather than just one, although the dominant frames vary over time and across types of media outlets. Framing is about selective perception. Confronted with the world in all its buzzing complexity, all of us – not just journalists – must focus our attention to accomplish even the simplest tasks. A linguistic frame – like a window frame – focuses our attention on a particular vista to the exclusion of others. At its most basic, a frame defines the "problem" (or the "success"), and that is how I use the term.[6] The language of framing also reminds us that some element of truth is

---

[5] Other recent content analyses of U.S. immigration coverage include Branton and Dunaway (2008; 2009), Suro (2008), and Kim, Carvalho, Davis, and Mullins (2011).

[6] Robert Entman (1993, 52) defines framing as consisting of four "functions," beginning with the selection and emphasis of "some aspects of a perceived reality ... in such a way as to promote a

usually present in the different ways of looking at an issue or event. Rather than searching for "bias," this approach suggests new kinds of questions, such as: How many of the diverse ways of looking at an issue are presented? Which perspectives are emphasized or de-emphasized? And, how does this selection of a complex reality differ across time, types of news outlets, and countries?

As I will show, journalists have indeed called attention to the concerns of some that immigrants threaten national cohesion, take jobs, or abuse welfare benefits. Many newspaper articles and television news segments have decried racism against immigrants, and others have celebrated the virtues of cultural diversity. However, additional frames, not mentioned by these critics, have also risen and fallen in the mediated immigration debate. Again, it must be emphasized, no single frame has completely dominated the news.

If this is so obvious, why the sharply competing claims about immigration coverage? Some of the divergent findings may be chalked up to differences in time periods or media outlets studied. Arguments, in some cases, are based more on anecdotes than systematic evidence. Other scholars, such as Leo Chavez, employ subtle qualitative methods that nevertheless risk overinterpretation. For Chavez (2008, 3), the "Latino Threat Narrative is pervasive even when not explicitly mentioned. It is the cultural dark matter filling space with taken-for-granted 'truths' in [media] debates over immigration." Even if some researchers see this "dark matter," that doesn't mean that most audiences will see it or be influenced by it.

What we do know is that news media play an important role in setting the public agenda (McCombs 2004). In their choices of which events and trends to highlight and which to downplay or ignore, media do not simply reflect social reality but actively shape it. Experimental studies have shown that media frames shape audience frames (Iyengar 1991; Dunaway, Abrajano, and Branton 2007) and can even affect audience members' sense of civic empowerment (Chong and Druckman 2007; Porto 2007). Although latent frames may well exist, my approach is to analyze frames at the manifest level, where they exert their first and most uncontested level of influence. Manifest frames can be identified by the presence of particular words or phrases. With careful training and testing, coding can be conducted in a consistent way to help ensure that a finding is not simply one researcher's idiosyncratic interpretation.

---

particular *problem definition*" (my emphasis); in similar fashion, Snow and Benford (1988) refer to the most basic task of framing as "diagnostic." Such "problem definition," issue-specific frames are often used in media content analysis (see, e.g., Hallin [1994]; Jasperson and El-Kikhia [2003]), and this usage best suits the purposes of this study. My approach thus differs from attempts to identify fully developed, coherent frame "packages" that also incorporate causal claims, moral evaluations, and/or proposed solutions (e.g., Gamson and Modigliani 1989; Ferree et al., 2002); one rarely discovers such fully developed frames in news articles. For other discussions of framing methodology, see Gitlin (1980), Ryan (1991), Reese et al. (2003), and D'Angelo and Kuypers (2010).

After reading through dozens of policy papers, activist manifestos, and academic studies,[7] as well as numerous news articles and editorials in a range of alternative and mainstream media outlets in both France and the United States, I arrived at a list of ten broad immigration frames. Each immigration frame suggests a distinct answer to the question: What kind of problem (or positive phenomenon) is being attributed to immigration or immigrants?[8] These frames are "culturally available" (Beckett 1996) for use by policy advocates, ordinary citizens, and media alike in both France and the United States, and thus provide a common ground for comparative analysis. Here, I build on the work of comparative cultural sociologists Michèle Lamont and Laurent Thévenot (2000) who conceive of national cultural differences within the Western world – including those between France and the United States – largely as divergences in the hierarchical ordering and emphasis of shared sets of ideas (or repertoires) rather than fundamentally different worldviews.[9]

Three broad frames portray immigrants as victims. Of these, the "global economy" frame emphasizes problems of global poverty, underdevelopment, and inequality, of which migration from the Global South to North is only one symptom. The "humanitarian" frame highlights the economic, social, and political suffering and hardships of immigrants in their everyday lives. The "racism/xenophobia" frame brings attention to individual assaults or systematic discrimination against immigrants on the basis of their ethnicity, culture, or religion.

Three additional frames portray immigrants as heroes. The "cultural diversity" frame emphasizes positive aspects of the differences that immigrants bring to society. The "integration" frame puts a positive spin on immigrants adapting and fitting into their host society, either civically or culturally. The "good worker" frame refers to the claim that immigrants "perform work that others won't do" (without acknowledging the low wages or poor working conditions that can dissuade nonimmigrants).

Finally, there are four frames that portray immigrants or immigration as a threat. These are the "jobs" frame, which accuses immigrants of taking jobs from or lowering the wages of domestic workers; the "public order" frame, which emphasizes law-breaking of any kind by immigrants, as well as the health

---

[7] In addition to those already mentioned, see Benoît (1980), Craig (1981), Bilderback (1989), Bonnafous (1991), Crawford (1992), Silverman (1992), Battegay and Boubeker (1993), Noiriel (1996; 2007), Sassen (1999), Fetzer (2000a), Gastaut (2000), and Lamont (2000; 2004).

[8] In the coding, a frame would be indicated by any empirical (or normative) reference to relevant aspects, whether made by a journalist or named or unnamed source. All newspaper page-one or television evening newscast "news packages" were coded for presence or absence of each type of frame. A package includes all closely related news items from a sample day's coverage. Any given newspaper/TV package may include more than one frame type and usually does; thus, the total percentage scores of frame mentions (presence in a package) will far exceed 100.

[9] Of course, some cultural differences are qualitative. However, enough of the important French-American differences are of degree rather than fundamental type that quantitative analysis is useful and appropriate.

or environmental threats posed by unlimited immigration; the "fiscal" frame, which is concerned with the costs to taxpayers of public health and educational services offered to immigrants; and finally, the "national cohesion" frame, which portrays immigrant cultural differences (customs, religion, language) as a threat to national unity and social harmony.

The six victim and hero frames correlate roughly with pro-immigration advocacy, whereas the four threat frames correlate with anti-immigration advocacy. Some scholars have grouped victim and threat frames together as both contributing to a "negative" image of immigrants and immigration (e.g., Branton and Dunaway 2008, 1011), although, if this is true, one could say the same for coverage of virtually any other social group commonly in the news. Most news coverage focuses on conflicts and problems (Tuchman 1978; Gans 1979; Shoemaker and Cohen 2006). Certainly, the immigration lawyers who promote "victim" coverage and the reporters who follow these leads do not perceive themselves as promoting anti-immigration attitudes, although it is possible that some readers predisposed to such attitudes will find evidence in such coverage to reinforce their worldviews.

It is also important to note the ways that typical categories of left and right are scrambled in immigration politics, producing a number of "strange bedfellows" alliances (Teitelbaum 2006; Zolberg 2006). On the pro-immigration side are left progressives (global economy), civil libertarians (humanitarian), and laissez-faire capitalists (good worker)[10]; on the anti-immigration side are some labor unions and African-American groups (jobs), as well as various tribes of conservatives, sometimes (but not always) overlapping, concerned with balanced budgets (fiscal threat), cultural unity (national cohesion), or law and order (public order) (see Table 1.1).

Some of these frames concern immigration in general; others emphasize to a greater extent the problem of illegal or undocumented immigration. Because it is a matter of ongoing debate whether legal and illegal immigration should be distinguished – immigrant advocates generally do not want to differentiate them, whereas restrictionists do – I do not sort them out in advance. I generally use the term "restrictionist" or "anti-immigration" rather than "anti-immigrant" by design. Although some restrictionist activists may be nativist or racist, I try to avoid these and other labels that can unfairly presume "guilt" in advance of adequate evidence.

---

[10] Sometimes, the affinity between civil libertarian and laissez-faire capitalist positions is not directly made but is obvious from the lack of critical interrogation of the economic system. See, e.g., Leo Chavez's list of recommended policies (2008, 185), including "a comprehensive approach to labor market needs and immigration policy" in order to "reduce the tendency to blame Latino immigrants as 'the problem' when they come to the United States to satisfy its labor needs." My point is not that immigrants should, in fact, be blamed, but rather that Chavez takes "labor needs" as given by the neo-liberal capitalist system, without critiquing this system's race to the bottom in wages and social benefits, both domestically and globally.

TABLE 1.1. *Immigration frames*

Frames (10)	Discursive Indicators
Victim Frames	
Global economy	Immigration is a subset of the larger problem of laissez-faire economic globalization and unjust North-South relations; problems of economic insecurity affect domestic workers as well as immigrants
Humanitarian	Immigrants are victims of unjust government policies (violations of human rights, fair legal process) or business practices; they suffer from poverty, lack of access to health care, dangers related to border crossing, etc.; or they have difficulties in adapting to their host society
Racism/ Xenophobia	Immigrants are victims of racist or xenophobic slurs or hate crimes, or discrimination based on national origin, race/ethnicity, religion, or culture
Hero Frames	
Cultural diversity	Immigrants bring positive differences to a society, from new cuisines to the unique contributions of immigrant artists, musicians, and writers
Integration	Immigrants enthusiastically adopt mainstream cultural mores or civic obligations
Good worker	Immigrants work hard, take jobs that citizens or legal residents will not or cannot do, or contribute to economic prosperity and growth
Threat Frames	
Jobs	Immigrants take nonimmigrants' jobs or depress wages
Public order	Illegal immigrants break the law in coming into this country; once here, immigrants – legal or illegal – are more likely than others to commit crimes, use drugs, and carry diseases; immigrants are coming in such numbers that they threaten overcrowding and environmental degradation
Fiscal	Immigrants (especially illegal) abuse government social services programs (health, education, etc.), imposing an unfair burden on taxpayers
National cohesion	Immigrants bring foreign customs and values that threaten to undermine the host country's culture or national identity; immigrants are inassimilable

To assess who "speaks" in news media coverage of immigration, articles and television transcripts were also coded for individuals or organizations quoted or paraphrased. In total, forty-two specific categories were used, distinguishing groups according to both political leaning, when appropriate, and institutional affiliation (e.g., center left political party vs. center right political party). For purposes of analysis, the categories are sometimes compressed; for example, "center legislative" includes legislators from both center left and center right parties. Table 1.2 presents the sixteen broad speaker categories used in Chapter 6 to capture the institutional diversity of voices in the news. Depending on the purposes of my analyses, at other points I disaggregate or combine these categories in other ways. For instance, I sometimes group

TABLE 1.2. *Speaker categories*

Institutional fields (16)	Description
Executive/Bureaucratic	Elected executives (president, governor, mayor), appointed officials (cabinet ministers, etc.), civil service bureaucrats, military, and police
Judicial	Court decisions, judges, lawyers (advocates for individual clients)
Center legislative	Elected legislators from dominant left or right political parties
Center political parties	Dominant left or right political parties (Democratic and Republican in the United States; Socialist and centrist Right parties in France)
Peripheral political party and legislative	Peripheral left or right political parties and/or elected legislators (Communist, Green, Libertarian, National Front, etc.)
Trade unions	Specific labor unions and broad labor federations
Religious	Churches, synagogues, mosques, and religiously oriented associations
University/Research	Universities, "think tanks," and other research centers
Associations	Humanitarian, antiracist, pro-immigration, anti-immigration, and diverse other voluntary associations
Journalistic	News and commentary-oriented media, whether newspapers, magazines, television, radio, or websites (coded if presenting new information or promoting a viewpoint, not when serving as a venue for other institutional field voices)
Arts and entertainment	Musicians, singers, actors, comedians, writers, artists
Business	Publicly traded and privately owned businesses, and business lobbying organizations (e.g., Chamber of Commerce)
Foreign and international	Foreign governments, foreign political or civil society organizations, international regulatory or governmental bodies (United Nations, European Commission, World Trade Organization, etc.)
Immigrant individuals	Immigrants or their direct descendants, of both European and non-European origin
Nonimmigrant individuals	Long-term residents or citizens, of both European and non-European origin
Public opinion	Polling agencies or categories of poll respondents (male vs. female, racial-ethnic, age, educational or income level, regional location, etc.)

together labor unions, university/research, nonprofit associations, religious organizations, arts/entertainment, and news media into a single "civil society" category; I also create a category of "unaffiliated individuals and polls" to capture efforts by reporters to represent nonorganized public opinion either anecdotally or by statistical aggregations (e.g., men, women, Latinos,

Democrats, Republicans).[11] Each speaker category is meant to capture the particular logic of a field or subfield, although there may be important differences within as well as across these speaker fields, whether they are government agencies, political parties, or differentially socially located individuals. Nevertheless, these sixteen speaker categories provide one measure of the diversity of voices in the public sphere.

As will be detailed later in the book, other aspects of coverage were also coded, such as indicators of rational-critical discourse and news generation (from the initiative of the political, civil society, or journalistic fields). A multi-step process was used to assure that the sampling method provided a fair indicator of news coverage. First, based on searches of electronic databases, as well as on data provided by other news content studies, I identified peak years of media attention to immigration – roughly adjacent in France and the United States – during the 1970s (1973 in France, 1974–75 in the United States), the 1980s (1983 in France, 1986 in the United States), the 1990s (1991 in France, 1994 in the United States), and the post-9/11 period (2002, 2004, and the first half of 2006 in both France and the United States). During such critical discourse moments (Gamson 1992, 26), public debate is likely to be especially intense and wide-ranging, thus providing roughly equivalent news content samples for comparison. Second, only prominent immigration news packages, defined as a given day's page-one articles and related inside articles (including editorials and op-eds) or closely related news segments on the main evening news broadcasts, were selected. Research has shown that the front section of the newspaper plays a key role in attracting audiences and is the most read (Graber 1988; Bogart 1989; Weldon 2008; Hubé 2008). The samples only included domestic immigration-focused coverage (migration to France in French media, migration to the United States in U.S. media).

To control for the bias of any particular media outlet, a range of media outlets in both countries was included in the sample. For the entire 1970s–2000s period, I analyze texts or transcripts of national agenda-setting newspapers and national television news: for the United States, the *New York Times*, the *Washington Post*, the *Los Angeles Times*, and the main evening news programs for the national commercial networks ABC, CBS, and NBC; for France, *Le Monde*, *Le Figaro*, *Libération*, and the main evening news programs for the two leading national channels France 2 (public) and TF1 (the most-watched private channel, public until 1987). Throughout the book, I refer to this as my "core" media

[11] Critics of survey methodologies have also called attention to the ways in which polls do not represent authentic public opinion but rather often superimpose onto the surveyed public the concerns of media or policy-making elites (Bourdieu 1979; Ginsberg 1986; Champagne 1990). For this reason, I count immigrants, nonimmigrants, and poll respondents as separate categories for purposes of creating an index of institutional (speaker) diversity (see Chapter 6). As a broad measure of populist tendencies to highlight nonorganized public opinion, however, it makes sense to group individuals and poll respondents together. In any case, mentions of public opinion polls make up only a very small percentage of citations in both France and the United States.

sample.[12] For 2002–2006, I expanded the sample to include public channels Arte in France and PBS in the United States, and added additional elite, mass market, and financial newspapers with direct or indirect national reach, representing roughly equivalent national cross-sections of class-segmented newspaper reading audiences: for France, *Les Echos* (financial), *La Croix*, *L'Humanité*, and the national edition of the mass market or "popular" *Le Parisien* (*Aujourd'hui en France*); for the United States, the *Wall Street Journal*, the *Christian Science Monitor*, *USA Today*, and the mass market New York *Daily News* and *New York Post*.[13] These French and U.S. media outlets also differ in their forms of ownership and funding, thus providing the kind of variation needed to test hypotheses about the effects of such structural factors on news content.

Given that cable television, even today, is not nearly as widespread or important in France as it is in the United States, in order to maintain roughly equivalent national samples I did not include cable in my already large corpus. Certainly, MSNBC, CNN (especially via Lou Dobbs's outspoken restrictionist views during the years when his program aired), and Fox Cable News are important venues for immigration commentary (less so, probably, for original reporting). Even so, it should be kept in mind that cable news audiences are still much smaller than network evening news audiences. In 2011, total prime-time news program viewers were 2.2 million for Fox, 0.95 million for MSNBC, and 0.77 million for CNN, versus 9.2 million for NBC, 8.1 million for ABC, and 6.0 million for CBS.[14]

Other notable exclusions from my sample are weekly or monthly magazines and regional newspapers. Including magazines would highlight the existence of influential (Entman 2012), high-quality, analytical, opinion-oriented journalism in the United States quite similar to that practiced in France. Moreover, on the web, temporal distinctions become less clear. Many "weekly" or "monthly" print publications continually update their websites no less than "daily" outlets.

---

[12] In addition to their relatively large audiences, these six newspapers have accumulated the greatest amount of symbolic capital, via professional awards and other indicators of journalistic and public prestige, and thus exert an outsized influence in their respective national fields. *Libération* is only included in the study from the 1980s onward; in 1973, the year of its founding, *Libération* published intermittently and was more closely associated with the French political field (small far-left parties) than the journalistic field.

[13] In constructing the two national "fields," I sought a relational, "system-to-system" comparison (Bourdieu 1998, 6), taking into account how the actors (the journalists themselves) understand who is or is not in the field. Thus, given the much more marginal place of the far left in the U.S. political and media spectrum, it would *not* be appropriate to balance France's communist *L'Humanité* with the U.S. *People's Weekly World*, the official newspaper of the Communist Party USA. In terms of structural location in the field, *L'Humanité* is close to the Catholic *La Croix* in France, and both are in some ways comparable to the *Christian Science Monitor*. Although more openly ideological and serving less elite audiences than the *Monitor*, *La Croix* and *L'Humanité* are similar to the *Monitor* in their low reliance on advertising revenues, as well as in their reputations for serious, in-depth analysis and commentary.

[14] Nielsen ratings are as reported on TheWrap TV (http://thewrap.com) on June 28, 2011.

For the immigration issue, regional U.S. newspapers such as the *Arizona Republic*, the *Houston Chronicle*, and the *Miami Herald* often provide quality news coverage and can sometimes play a leading role in bringing issues to national attention. In France, the Normandy-based *Ouest-France* has the highest print readership in the country, although its reach is mostly limited to its region. However unwieldy, it would have been ideal to include magazines and regional newspapers – as well as online-only news media – to provide a truly comprehensive mapping of the U.S. and French journalistic fields. Conversely, my limited sample was carefully constructed to provide the historical and structural variation necessary to test competing explanatory theories in the sociology of news. I hope that my theoretical and methodological framework will be useful for future researchers who wish to study other types of media.

Going beyond accurate description, I now turn to the explanatory and evaluative purposes of this study: Why has coverage followed certain patterns and not others? Why do France and the United States make for a good comparison, in relation both to their media systems and their experiences of immigration? And how can we explain and assess their respective news coverage of immigration in relation to various democratic ideals?

EXPLAINING IMMIGRATION NEWS

Surprisingly, in their explanations of news coverage, many immigration scholars skip over the media entirely to emphasize broad macro-societal factors such as contingent political realignments and the shift to a post-Fordist global economy (Calavita 1996; Chavez 2001), or, in the words of Santa Ana (1999, 217), the "foundational racism of American society." Yet, clearly, the media do more than simply "reflect" the society of which they are a part. Although contextual factors related to immigration conditions and political contestation are never far from mind, my focus throughout this book is on showing how news media specifically contribute to the shaping of public debate.

This is where I draw on the concept of "field" – the mezzo-level organizational and professional space inside of which external constraints are mediated. Contemporary societies are composed of a number of competing and semi-autonomous institutional orders or fields (Fligstein 1990; DiMaggio and Powell 1991; Bourdieu 1993; Martin 2003). Journalism is a field in most if not all Western democratic nation-states, in that it has developed some limited amount of autonomy from the state and the capitalist market and that it is an arena of contestation and struggle operating according to "rules of the game" consciously or unconsciously enacted by actors in the field.

French sociologist Pierre Bourdieu (1995) argues that, at this historical moment, social struggle tends to be organized around an opposition between two forms of power – economic and cultural – that take specific forms inside each field. According to Bourdieu, economic power, allied to political power, constitutes an external "heteronomous" form of power exerted inside fields of cultural production. In contrast, cultural power is synonymous with "autonomous" power and takes particular forms depending on the field (e.g., methodological rigor and theoretical sophistication in scientific fields, mastery of aesthetic techniques and historical precedents in artistic fields, etc.). Although a powerful heuristic, this basic dichotomy is inadequate to explain the complex dynamics of the ongoing journalistic mediation of public discourse, especially as these processes differ cross-nationally.

First, as I have argued elsewhere, political power and economic power are not necessarily aligned as part of a single heteronomous "pole."[15] Sometimes they are allied (as when governments pass "deregulating" laws favored by powerful businesses); sometimes they are not (as when governments pass laws helping workers organize unions). Indeed, we may live in an era when big corporations get their way more often that not, but concluding in advance that the game is rigged is not only cynically destructive of democracy but empirically incorrect. In addition, sometimes governments act neither for nor against business, but purely to protect and extend their own prerogatives (Runciman 1989; Garnham 2000). This is the kernel of wisdom in the American First Amendment tradition that deeply distrusts state power. Second, Bourdieu's terminology of cultural and economic power can be misleading. It can be useful sometimes to analytically separate these forms of power (Alexander and Smith 1993), but it is important to remember that any effective power is simultaneously material and symbolic. Third, heteronomous power is not by definition a destructive force, as is often implied in Bourdieu's work. In the long term, autonomy from the market is only possible if it is materially secured by someone or something else (philanthropists, foundations, voluntary political, religious, or civic associations, the state), in other words, an opposing heteronomous pole. This is especially the case for a public, mediating arena such as the journalistic field. Contra Bourdieu, I conceive of the journalistic field as organized around a basic opposition between two heteronomous poles – a civic, nonmarket pole and a market pole. Some forms of journalistic excellence – for instance, investigative journalism – seem to be located in the unstable hybrid space in which competing heteronomous powers simultaneously overlap and are balanced against one another (see Figures 2.1 and 2.2). This space in the middle could rightly be called the "space of autonomy," but it should not be privileged as the sole locus of journalistic excellence. Many forms of "quality" journalism, such as mobilizing or deliberative journalism, may be the product of proximity rather than distance to a heteronomous power, such as the external logic of democratic civil society (supported by the state and/or nonprofit associations and political parties).

After reconceptualizing the journalistic field's external "position" in this way, I identify two theoretically significant internal elements of the field: logic and structure. Logic refers to historically shaped dominant forms of practice.

---

[15] See an early development of this critique in Benson (1999) and earlier iterations of my international comparative field theory framework in Benson (2005; 2006).

Structure refers to class-based hierarchies and the structural ecology of organizational competition.

Although heteronomous fields provide most of the symbolic and financial resources operative in the journalistic field, journalists and journalistic organizations react to, translate, and combine these resources (primarily civic vs. market) to meet demands to produce content in a given period of time while simultaneously managing relations with their information sources and their audiences. In Bourdieu's terms (1998, 39), a field is a "microcosm with its own laws ... [which is to say] that what happens in it cannot be understood by looking at only external factors." Yet there is much we do not yet know about how field logics and dynamics shape the production of news content. For example, to what extent do these rules or logics serve simply as "mechanisms" of external influence, as opposed to a means of resisting such pressures? Social class background correlates with attitudes, tastes, and beliefs, but how do such class-related factors shape both news gathering (e.g., reporter–source relations) and news presentation (certain types of news and opinion for certain types of audiences)? Finally, the structural organizational ecology of the field – an aspect largely ignored by Bourdieu – calls attention to the relative directness and intensity of competition among journalists and media outlets. To what extent does such competition contribute to either ideological diversity (Bagdikian 2004), homogenization of news content (Boczkowski 2010), or sensationalism (Fenton 2010)?

To answer such questions, I use a range of primary and secondary data sources on news media management, funding, employment, and professional practice. I also draw on more than eighty interviews that I conducted between 1995 and 2012 with French and American journalists, activists, scholars, and politicians in the two countries (most of the journalist and activist interviews are listed in Appendix B; scholars I spoke with are noted in the acknowledgments). Where appropriate, I quote from these interviews. Throughout the book, these interviews inform my understanding and analysis of journalism and immigration in the two countries.

In sum, cross-national research allows us to see more clearly the discursive effects of variable system properties. By simultaneously analyzing field position, logic, and structure, my field theory approach builds on the classic sociology of news while offering a more comprehensive systems-level framework. I now turn to a brief consideration of similarities and differences between the French and U.S. journalistic fields and the subfield of immigration reporting. It is because of these systemic similarities and differences that a comparative case study offers potentially rich theoretical rewards.

French and U.S. Journalistic Fields

In both France and the United States, the journalistic field is situated in the larger field of power and serves to mediate among various elites and between these

elites and broader publics. National journalists come from increasingly privileged backgrounds and have higher levels of education than the public at large.
The media outlets they work for, especially newspapers, tend to be produced for
audiences with above-average levels of education and income.

At the same time, the French and American journalistic fields differ in
systematic ways. For many scholars, they represent opposite "ideal types"
(Alexander 1981; Albert 2004; Neveu 2009; Boudana 2010b), embodying
distinct professional traditions, structural ecologies, and relations with the
state and the market. For these reasons, as I will argue throughout this book,
the two cases allow for testing of common assumptions about the effects of
state intervention, market pressures, and professional and organizational factors. Documentation of these structural differences will be provided in
Chapter 2.

The American news media system is substantially more commercialized than
its French counterpart. French newspapers rely on advertising far less than
American newspapers, and French news media companies are less likely
than American companies to be listed on the stock market. Although the
economic success of U.S. news organizations has certainly diminished in recent
years, they remain more reliant on advertising and more oriented toward maximizing profits than do French news outlets.

Conversely, the state intervenes in the French journalistic field to a greater
extent than is the case in the United States. French "restrictive" policies extend
political power over the journalistic field through tough defamation laws and
restrictions on access to government documents. In the United States, by contrast, the legal tradition of First Amendment supremacy strongly limits restrictive regulation. Journalists in both countries, however, rely on government
officials as authoritative sources or "primary definers" (Hall et al. 1978) of the
news, providing government with a certain power over the media regardless of
specific laws or regulations.

The French state also actively promotes diverse, reasoned discourse in the
journalistic field. Overall, in raw terms, French state aid to the press is second
in Europe only to Italy (Nielsen and Linnebank 2011) and includes targeted
subsidies to help keep alive newspapers that add to the ideological diversity of
public discourse. State aid to the press in the United States, by contrast, is
quite limited. With the exception of modest support for public television and
radio, the U.S. government has done very little to provide a civic counter-
weight to market pressures. Although foundation and individual philanthropic donations in support of civic-oriented media are higher in the
United States, the total amount of money deployed is far less than French
government contributions.

Differing relations to political, market, and civic power have helped shape
distinctive logics of practice – or forms of news – within the French and U.S.
journalistic fields. The stereotype is that U.S. journalism is objective and fact-
oriented whereas French journalism is partisan and interpretive. Even if there is

some truth in these characterizations (Chalaby 1996), I will show that the major difference between U.S. and French newspapers lies in the "form" of news (Schudson 1995; Barnhurst and Nerone 2001), both at the level of the individual article and in the overall presentation of news and opinion. In the United States, personalized "dramatic narrative" has become a dominant journalistic form, producing a tendency toward both investigative reports and human interest profiles.[16] In contrast, in France, a "debate ensemble" format is oriented primarily toward facilitating reasoned if often polemical debate and presenting multiple, diverse viewpoints – a standard that goes beyond the American notion of "balancing" two sides.

Because the French and American journalistic fields differ systematically in these ways – in their relations to market and nonmarket power and in their internal logics (professional traditions and practices) – there is good reason to suspect that their respective coverage of immigration will also differ in systematic ways. But how?

Indeed, many claims have been made about the distinctive characteristics of French and U.S. news. American journalists sometimes dismiss the French press as being too intellectual, too partisan, and, without a First Amendment to protect it, not critical enough of government (Hunter 1997; Stanger 2003). Former *New York Times* executive editor Abe Rosenthal offered this backhanded compliment to France's famed *Le Monde*: "It's the best something in the world, but whatever it is, it's not a real newspaper" (cited in Padioleau 1985, 39). Conversely, French journalism is sometimes idolized by critics of the American media. Ben Bagdikian admires French and other European newspapers for presenting "news [not] as a series of isolated facts and public events but rather in a context of political and social meaning" (1992, 204). Likewise, Thomas Frank (2002, 313) praises the "wide open debates ... [that] routinely sweep across the newspapers of countries like France" in contrast to the "extremely narrow range of opinion represented" in U.S. newspapers.

Which perspective is correct? Surprisingly, there has been very little cross-national content analysis of news coverage that could test these long-held assumptions about U.S. versus French and other European national media systems. As Daniel Hallin and Paolo Mancini (2004, 304) write in their pathbreaking work, *Comparing Media Systems*: "There is a need ... for more case studies of the interaction of media with other social actors in the coverage of particular kinds of events or issues ... This kind of study would make it possible

---

[16] At a metaphoric level, much if not all of human knowledge can be characterized as narrative. Even structural accounts can be analyzed in relation to classical narrative forms such as tragedy, comedy, romance, and irony (White 1981; Jacobs 2000). My use of the term "narrative" is narrower. I aim to call attention to journalistic construction of articles as "human interest stories" told about nonelite individuals, generally beginning with the lead paragraphs, whose form tends to work against substantial structural analysis or juxtaposition of opposing viewpoints.

to explore which points of view are able to enter the public sphere, which actors and institutions are able to shape the process of debate, and how these processes are affected by the structural characteristics of media systems." *Shaping Immigration News* takes up this challenge, going beyond the stereotypes to provide in-depth portraits of two actually existing national media systems – one, the U.S. system, which falls within Hallin and Mancini's "liberal" model; the other, the French media system, an example of their "polarized pluralist" model.[17] These are the two Western democratic models most clearly opposed in the media's relationship to the state and market; they are also important to study because of their enduring and sometimes competing influences on other national media systems around the world.[18]

At the same time, my model of journalistic field position, logic, and structure aims to improve on Hallin and Mancini's "four dimensions" of media systems, which they list as: (1) historical development of a strong or weak mass circulation press; (2) political parallelism, or the extent to which the media system reflects the major political currents; (3) journalistic professional training and tradition; and (4) type and extent of state intervention in the media sector. Hallin and Mancini's first dimension does not exhaust the range of relevant commercial constraints. Their second and fourth dimensions are both types of political constraints, although the fourth factor is very broad and does not adequately emphasize the crucial role of the state in influencing the relative power of market versus nonmarket logics of action. Finally, their third dimension is certainly one aspect of the journalistic field – what I would term the "logic of the field" – but, as noted, there are other important field dynamics as well, chiefly the class relations that structure journalist–source and media outlet–audience relations.

Hallin and Mancini (2004, 80–83) discuss field theory in their book, but their "four dimensions" model does not integrate field theory as effectively as it might. Although there is great analytical value in Hallin and Mancini's approach, what is needed is an integrated *explanatory* model that links both dominant traits of national systems and variations inside those systems to discursive outcomes. The position-logic-structure model of the journalistic field developed in this book aims to provide such a framework.

---

[17] Hallin and Mancini (2004) demonstrate the persistence of three distinct media models within Europe and North America that result in markedly different relations between journalism, politics, and the larger society: the (laissez-faire) "liberal" model of the United States, Canada, and the United Kingdom versus the more state-dominated "polarized pluralist" model of France and southern Europe and the "democratic corporatist" model of Germany, Scandinavia, and other central and northern European countries (which is portrayed as combining characteristics of the liberal and polarized pluralist models).

[18] For instance, Waisbord (2000) shows how Latin American journalism has been shaped by the distinctive influences of the French and Spanish versus U.S. journalistic traditions. See also Hallin and Mancini (2012).

EVALUATING IMMIGRATION NEWS

In addition to description and explanation, I seek to highlight the normative dimension that is ever present but often submerged in media studies. As James Carey (1995) has argued, journalism is important not so much in itself but because it directly affects the health of our democracies. To what extent do the French and U.S. news media, in their coverage of one of the major issues of our day, achieve the ideal of the democratic "public sphere"?

Habermas's concept of "public sphere" concerns two broad ideals – usefully characterized by Craig Calhoun (1992) as "quantity" and "quality" – that condense and make explicit the diverse array of normative concerns that have long motivated empirical sociological research on the news. The first ideal (quantity) concerns broad inclusion and diverse representation of a wide range of voices and viewpoints. The second ideal (quality) concerns the extent to which public discourse is reasoned and critical. Interpreted broadly (as in Habermas's [1996] more recent conceptualization), these ideals make room for marginal speakers and diverse writing and speaking styles. As measured in this study, quantity and quality of public discourse do not capture the entirety of Habermas's concerns (e.g., the need to achieve consensus) nor those of all other normative theories of the press, but they do, it seems to me, represent the core of the normative literature and thus provide a helpful compass for comparative research.[19]

Thus, in addition to analyzing the use of specific immigration frames in news coverage, I also develop several original content indicators designed to measure aspects of pluralist or multiperspectival news: frame and speaker diversity, balancing of opposing frames, and external pluralism of the journalistic field as a whole (see Chapter 6). In line with recent "constructionist" critiques (see Ferree, Gamson, Gerhards, and Rucht 2002, 222–228), I am particularly interested in the visibility of voices and viewpoints from the social or intellectual margins, including strong critiques of neo-liberal economic orthodoxy (global economy frame). Critical discourse is measured by discrete critical statements, categorized according to type (e.g., policy vs. strategic) and target (left vs. right political actors, business, etc.), as well as by the use of genres such as investigative reports (see Chapter 7). I also draw attention to persistent qualitative aspects of texts relevant to multiperspectival or critical ideals. And, for television news, I analyze images for their dramatic and emotional properties.

Normatively guided empirical research (Habermas 2006) is highly relevant for both media policy and journalistic practice. Because the French media have historically received substantial government subsidies whereas the American media have been more commercially driven, a comparison of journalism in the two countries allows us to directly engage with long-running debates about the

---

[19] For other discussions of democratic normative models for the news media, see Baker (2002), Ferree et al. (2002), Benson (2008), and Christians et al. (2009).

relative merits (or demerits) of public- versus market-supported media. And, because news formats also differ in the two countries, we can assess the democratic pluses and minuses of various types of journalistic practice.

PLAN OF BOOK

In Chapter 2, I elaborate my field position-logic-structure model and use this framework to provide a historical and structural comparison of U.S. and French journalism. Chapters 3 and 4 offer a close look at changes over time in immigration news coverage in the United States and France from the early 1970s through 2006. How did journalistic framing of immigration change or remain the same? Who were the dominant speakers in the public debate? And how did patterns of news coverage relate to structural shifts in the journalistic and political fields? Chapter 5 pulls together the empirical strands of U.S. and French immigration news since the 1970s to begin to make sense of the theoretical puzzle of field continuity and change.

Chapter 6 compares the degree to which press coverage of immigration is "multiperspectival" in France and the United States. Chapter 7 compares the "critical" qualities of immigration reports in French and U.S. newspapers. Chapter 8 raises the question of medium effects by assessing the degree to which French and U.S. television news follow the same patterns as newspaper coverage. In the final chapter, I synthesize the descriptive, explanatory, and normative findings of this book, address potential criticisms and directions for future research, and assess the implications for journalistic practice and media policy.

To preview some of the key findings, across the four decades, the humanitarian and public order frames have predominated in both countries. The critical global economy frame has remained common in French newspapers while declining in the U.S. press. Overall, individualist market-oriented frames (fiscal, jobs, good worker) have been more common in U.S. news coverage, whereas civic solidarity frames (especially national cohesion) have been more common in France. Other frames have risen and fallen across the decades as political parties, activist groups, and journalistic organizations have vied to use the issue in ongoing material and symbolic struggles. I show that, in many ways, the French news media as a whole are more multiperspectival, more supportive of civil society mobilization, more oriented toward structural explanations, and more substantively critical of government and the leading political parties. American journalism, however, does more to investigate bureaucratic incompetence and corruption, to highlight the hypocrisy of anti-immigrant politicians, and to trace the diverse "narratives" of individual immigrants and the immigrant experience.

Although the two countries have converged somewhat in overall frame and speaker diversity, French-American differences in the dominance of particular frames, types of speakers cited, news event generation, news design formats, narrative structure of stories, and prevalence of investigative reporting have largely remained the same. Thus, even in the contemporary period of global hypercommercialism and supposed cross-national convergence and homogenization, the French and U.S. news media continue to be marked by distinctive styles, formats, and content.

My research generally confirms one of the more dire predictions of critical political economy – that commercialism is inversely related to ideological diversity in the news – while challenging liberal assumptions about state intervention's chilling effects on press criticism of government. At the same time, I am able to show how the intervening variable of the journalistic field, and, in particular, the "form of news" as an expression of field logic, crucially adds to our understanding of news media performance.

Given rapid technological change, any attempt to write about news media may seem doomed to being outdated almost as soon as it is written. It is worth noting, however, that past predictions of epochal change initiated by new technologies have generally been overstated. This study cannot speak authoritatively about all French and U.S. news media. It can, hopefully, say something worthwhile about a particular subset of media organizations, during a particular historical period. Going beyond the historical particularities, the theories and methods employed are not limited to this case study and can certainly be used to analyze a variety of old and "new" media.

Ultimately, I hope that this book will be interesting and useful not only for scholars of media and immigration but also for journalists, activists, and policymakers on both sides of the Atlantic. Although acknowledging the evident historical and structural complexities, an important purpose of comparative research, in my view, is to draw lessons that might actually be used to make journalism and political communication better. If certain state policies help promote ideological diversity in the press, why not consider adopting them? If some ways of practicing journalism do more than others to deepen analysis and critique, why not try them? Of course, there are always hurdles and sound reasons why what works in France may not work in the United States, and vice versa. But the comparison at least shows that we do have a choice, and such knowledge is an important step toward any meaningful reform. A press that is multiperspectival, that is reasoned and contextual, that is critical cannot, of course, guarantee wise policies toward immigration or any other contemporary social problem, but it is surely part of the solution for any democracy that seeks to engage the public. It is one place to start.

2

The French and U.S. Journalistic Fields

Position, Logic, and Structure

Although the sociology of news literature is vast, it is dominated by research in the United States and Great Britain that too often assumes that what is specific to these milieus automatically holds for the rest of the world. On the one hand, this tradition tends to be focused on commercial factors largely to the exclusion of the state, except as a constraining and censoring force; on the other hand, often rooted in newsroom studies, it highlights micro-organizational practices without adequately connecting these back to broader market, civic, and governmental institutional influences. In this chapter, after assessing the strengths and weaknesses of previous approaches, I develop an alternative field model and show how it can be used to map relevant historical and structural features of French and U.S. journalism.

SOCIOLOGY OF NEWS: MACRO- AND MICRO-APPROACHES

Among macro-structural approaches, two competing schools of thought have tended to dominate research on news media. The first approach posits the existence of a singular commercial "media logic" (Altheide and Snow 1979; Mazzolini 1987; Castells 1997; Bagdikian 2004) that makes news superficial, sensationalist, and ideologically narrow.[1] This approach comes close to the Frankfurt School's totalizing critique of capitalist commercial culture. Although Jürgen Habermas's (2006) analysis is ultimately less pessimistic than that of Horkheimer and Adorno, the public sphere theorist likewise has consistently

---

[1] Media logic arguments are often associated with the growing "mediatization" school of research. However, at least one leading proponent of this approach, Knut Lunby (2009, 117) argues, as I do, that "it is not viable to speak of an overall media logic: it is necessary to specify how various media capabilities are applied in various patterns of social interactions." Other mediatization scholars, such as Rawolle and Lingard (2010), explicitly draw on field theory.

raised concerns about how advertising and profit pressures undermine the press's capacity to serve as a forum for rational-critical debate.

Many social constructionist studies have adopted wholesale this notion of a universal media logic or set of media practices (e.g., Gamson and Modigliani 1989; Ryan 1991; Oliver and Myers 1999). There is more than a grain of truth in such claims, especially as a description of large, general-audience commercial media. However, the media logic approach fails to see how commercialism varies in quantity and quality and downplays the potential for market-driven media to sometimes add diverse and critical perspectives (see Benson 2003; Hesmondhalgh 2006). Just as problematic, this approach ignores the potential positive alternative offered by noncommercial "public" media, which might operate according to a different logic. Dismissing Herbert Gans's (1979) advocacy of state subsidies to support multiperspectival news, Charlotte Ryan (1991, 13) expresses the frequently heard cynical view of American activist scholars: "After the experience of the Reagan-era manipulation of television and radio, [allowing state funding of media] seems neither likely nor desirable." Wholesale dismissal of public policy solutions is a blind spot, likewise, in Herman and Chomsky's (1988) propaganda model.

From another direction – the liberal philosophical tradition – state intervention is ignored or lambasted based on the assumption that it will ultimately lead to press censorship. This liberal view received its most powerful, lasting endorsement in the classic text *Four Theories of the Press* (Siebert, Patterson, and Schramm 1956). *Four Theories* celebrated the nonregulated "Libertarian" and self-regulated "Social Responsibility" models, reviled the "Authoritarian" and "Soviet Communist" alternatives, and simply ignored the possibility of anything in between – namely, the democratic nation-states of western Europe with news media partially or wholly publicly funded. The liberal tradition remains strong in the United States, especially among journalists: this was certainly evident in the many negative reactions to a Columbia University Journalism School-sponsored report authored by Leonard Downie, Jr. and Michael Schudson (2009) advocating modest government support for public affairs journalism. Liberal state-phobia manifests itself indirectly in work that uncritically celebrates the liberating potential of new technologies (Jarvis 2009) or pessimistically dismisses government action as politically unrealistic (Christians, Glasser, McQuail, Nordenstreng, and White 2009); it is less common in western Europe, but has its proponents there (De Tarlé 1980; Eveno 2003). Perhaps the most prominent scholar of French media to take this position is Jean Chalaby, who argues that an ongoing "connivance between journalists and politicians" to hide corruption at the highest levels of French government can be attributed to "the limited role played by market forces" independent of the state (2005, 287).

Almost on a separate track from such broad critiques of the market or the state is a large body of micro-organizational newsroom research. The U.S. literature, based on ethnographies of mainstream commercial news organizations, has identified a laundry list of generalized "media practices": time and space pressures, technological constraints, bureaucratic division of labor, reliance on government agencies as sources, and so on.[2] Some notable exceptions to American- and British-dominated research are Jean Padioleau's (unfortunately untranslated) comparative study of *Le Monde* and the *Washington Post* (1985) and Frank Esser's (1998) portrait of German and British regional newspaper newsrooms. A growing body of global, single-nation or comparative ethnographic and organizational research is bringing to light differences across newsrooms in journalistic practices and formats.[3] Consistent with this research, this book will show that the presentation of immigration news and opinion differs in consistent ways at French and U.S. news organizations. But, if this is so, the origin of such cross-national differences does not derive simply from the individual newsrooms involved. Rather, the source lies with the societal structural configuration of fields that regulate, fund, and provide normative legitimation of distinctive national journalistic practices.

FIELD ANALYSIS

Going beyond the individual newsroom, the concept of field brings attention to a broader mezzo-level social and professional space – indeed, to the entire universe of journalists and news organizations relevant to a particular geographical region or political decision-making apparatus. When we analyze specific fields of cultural production, we simultaneously bridge the macro- and the micro-, the social and the semiotic.

As Pierre Bourdieu (2005, 33) has argued:

[B]etween an internal reading of the text [in this case journalistic] which consists in considering the text in itself and for itself, and an external reading which crudely relates the text to the society in general, there is a social universe that is always forgotten, that of the producers of the works. To speak of the field is to name this microcosm, which is also a social universe, but a social universe freed from a certain number of the constraints that characterize the encompassing social universe, a universe that is somewhat apart, endowed with its own laws, its own nomos ... without being completely independent of the external laws.

Paying attention to fields thus helps one avoid both a semiotic analysis devoid of the social and a crude political-economy that reduces journalistic (or other cultural) texts to broad social determinations. Bourdieu (2005) sees journalism as a "weakly autonomous field," but one which nevertheless "refracts" rather than simply reflects the play of external forces. Refraction is a scientific term that refers to any change in direction of a light or sound wave, usually due to the

---

[2] See the important studies of Epstein (1973), Tuchman (1978), Gans (1979), Fishman (1980), Boczkowski (2004), and Klinenberg (2005), as well as Shoemaker and Reese (1996) and Schudson (2011) for critical overviews of the literature.

[3] See Waisbord (2000), Hasty (2005), Hughes (2006), and Bird (2010).

passage from one medium to another (e.g., air, water). Rainbows, for instance, are the result of the refraction of light waves through moist air. Just as environmental media (e.g., air, water) have particular properties, social fields shape action within their boundaries according to their own distinct logics.

As noted in the introduction, I take issue with Bourdieu's basic premise that all fields are structured around a basic opposition between an autonomous (internal cultural) and heteronomous (external economic *and* political) pole. Bourdieu refers to a "political/economic" heteronomous pole (1998, 38; 2005, 41) when, in fact, the political and economic may be at least partially at odds. Bourdieu's conception ignores the possibility of multiple, competing external influences. Schudson (2005) argues against the normative ideal of complete autonomy for journalism, given that its democratic raison d'être is to be open to all elements and aspects of society. I would concur. My point, however, is ontological: focusing only on the struggle for autonomy draws attention from the ways in which heteronom(ies) can be productive. The particular balance of power between competing heteronomous forces also shapes practice within the field.

In relation to the journalistic field, Bourdieu's emphasis on heteronomous forces as largely economic stems no doubt from the dramatic and rapid commercialization of television and radio in France beginning in the 1980s. Limited by his dichotomous framework and also lacking a comparative perspective, Bourdieu downplayed the ways in which the state continues to insulate (or might further insulate) the French journalistic field from commercial pressures.[4] Even in the United States, as Timothy Cook (1998, 60) demonstrated, government has crucially shaped the character of the media system via "policies designed with the presumption on the part of policymakers that the news media performed governmental and political functions and needed to be assisted in doing so properly." In many cases, these policies operated in explicit contradiction of market principles, as in the case of "joint operating agreements" between directly competing metropolitan newspapers. In democracies across the globe, states are serving as civic counterforces to market power. Similar themes have been taken up by leading historical and international comparative media policy scholars, such as James Curran (2011), Robert McChesney (2000), Peter Golding and Graham Murdock (2000), C. Edwin Baker (2002), Des Freedman (2008), and Victor Pickard (2011). This research has been pathbreaking – at least in the Anglo-American academic world, in which either

---

[4] In a book he co-authored with artist Hans Haacke, Bourdieu called for "reinforcing both state assistance . . . and [cultural producers'] controls on the uses of that assistance" [in order to] escape the alternative of statism and liberalism" (Bourdieu and Haacke 1995, 73). Politically, he played an important insider role in helping create the fully state-funded French-German cultural channel Arte (Clément 2011, 32–43). Toward the end of his life, Bourdieu increasingly viewed the state as a necessary bulwark against encroaching neo-liberalism. However, in his texts directly focused on news media (Bourdieu 1998; 2005), he does not call for government media policies to correct the deficiencies of journalism as he sees them.

cynical or antagonistic views of the state have predominated – in identifying the range of ways that proactive government policies have historically helped compensate for the market failure of commercial media.

The theoretical framework I develop here is in substantial sympathy with this scholarly tradition but seeks to expand and deepen it by using the concept of "journalistic field" to analyze the complex interplay of market, civic, class, and organizational ecological dynamics. In contrast to the chasm that often separates political economy, organizational studies, and news content analyses, I seek to bring these strands together to provide a more complete account of how and why news is produced as it is and what it might take to produce it in different and better ways.

Institutional field structuring of news can be conceptualized as involving three analytically distinct levels: field *position* (relative "proximity" to either nonmarket or market power, as mediated by the state); field *logic* (dominant news practices and formats, which are hybrid translations or refractions of external field influences); and field *structure* (distinctions inside the field, related to class habitus of news workers and news audiences; hierarchically organized differences across media outlets, news desks, or beats; and the organizational ecology of competition).

Analysis of field *position* locates the journalistic field within the field of power, situated in relation to the nonmarket or civic field and the capitalist market field. A two-dimensional representation is inadequate to express the complexity of field relations. Fields overlap, and yet remain distinct (since they are partially autonomous), in a kind of three-dimensional space. The state, in the form of lawmaking and regulatory bodies, extends its reach over both nonmarket and market actors in the field of power. Thus, although sometimes used in shorthand, it is misleading to suggest any necessary dichotomy between state and market: the state enables and constrains both market and nonmarket activity.

Likewise, both civic and market logics are simultaneously material and symbolic. Organizing society according to competitive, individualistic market principles is no more "natural" than organizing it according to communitarian civic solidarity principles, and within these two competing models there are also multiple ways to allocate resources and define the rules of the game. Field position provides a rough graphical representation of the relative power of these external logics within the journalistic field. Analysis of field position helps us to see that symbolic and material resources operative within the journalistic field are multiple, sometimes opposed, and sometimes allied in unstable hybrid formations (as with commercial media outlets at least partially oriented toward civic ends). (See Figures 2.1 and 2.2, p. 38.)

Analysis of field *logic* begins by tracing the unique historical formation of the field and its subsequent trajectory. A field's rules of the game are established when the field is founded and, once routinized, tend to persist over time. The dominant internal field logic may thus continue even after conditions external to the field change. In such cases, what seemed before to be a mechanism of hegemony (internal logic harmony with external pressures) comes to be seen as a tool of resistance (internal-external mismatch). But how do we identify the dominant logic of the field? A field's logic is not fully captured in the words people self-consciously use to express their beliefs or aspirations. One has to dive below the surface discourse to locate a deeper logic consisting of taken-for-granted assumptions and habitual practices. As Paolo Mancini (2000) has shown for Italy, just because Italian journalists use U.S.-style terms like "objectivity" or "balance" does not mean that they attach the same meaning to them or that the terms have much relation to actual practice. Likewise, in France, I found that many French journalists had great admiration for the U.S. press, which they often associate with Watergate, the Pulitzer Prizes, and the Columbia School of Journalism. Yet, as I observed firsthand and will systematically demonstrate in this book, the way these French journalists wrote their articles and packaged the news tended to be quite different from typical U.S. practices.

Building on earlier theorizing and research on the "form of news" or "news formats,"[5] I argue that distinct "forms" of news – modes of article construction, mixing of genres, design formats – reveal most fully a field's underlying logic of practice. In the United States, "dramatic narrative" has become a dominant way of organizing the news. As a result, political news is often about clashing personalities, and even thematic, trend stories are often constructed around highly emotional narrative accounts of individuals, both obscure and prominent. In other countries, other forms predominate. For instance, Ferree et al. (2002, 273) show that German news privileges "emotionally detached, disembodied argumentation"; Hallin and Mancini (1984) found that Italian public television news emphasized the presentation of opposing party viewpoints. Likewise, I find that the form of news in France – at least in newspapers – is quite distinct from that of the United States. Instead of personalized narratives, a French multiarticle, multigenre "debate ensemble" approach facilitates a contextualized, multiperspectival approach to the news. My analysis concurs with that of Simon Cottle (1995, 279), who has argued that news formats can "play a critical role in either enabling or disabling the range of viewpoints and discourses sustained by vying social interests."

Finally, analysis of field *structure* takes into account multiple aspects of the social hierarchical organization of competition within the field and emphasizes variation among media outlets. Analysis of class is one of the biggest omissions in the Anglo-American sociology of news.[6] A field analysis situates the position of each media outlet in relation to other media outlets in the class stratification of audiences and operates with the working hypothesis that different social locations (effectively,

---

[5] See, especially, Altheide (1987), Schudson (1995), Cottle (1995), Golding and Murdock (2000), Barnhurst and Nerone (2001), and Broersma (2007).

[6] For some notable exceptions that do analyze class, see Crossley (2004), Heider (2004), and Kendall (2011).

one's stake and resources in nonmarket vs. market logics) produce different discourses.[7] Demonstrating such connections, French sociologist Julien Duval's (2005) analysis of French business news showed that economic orthodoxy or heterodoxy were related to the structural position of the news outlet in the subfield of business journalism. Field analysis also points to the "habitus" gap between journalists and their sources. Habitus refers to an individual's habitual way of being – encompassing ideological predispositions, judgments of taste, and physical bearing – shaped by family, education, and profession (Bourdieu and Wacquant 1992, 115–140). Given the singularity of any biographical trajectory, each individual habitus is unique. Nevertheless, those with similar habitus are likely to share a confluence of interests and tastes. One might expect habitus affinities to contribute to more (and more positive) news coverage of some groups, whereas habitus disaffinities could contribute to less (and less positive) news coverage of other groups.

Inside media outlets, structural hierarchies – such as those between news departments or beats – partially determine the amount and type of coverage devoted to a given topic. In addition, comparative research calls attention to ecological features of fields, such as the degree to which they are centralized or decentralized, and their mode of distribution (e.g., through subscriptions or daily street sales), which can shape the form or intensity of competition among journalists and media outlets.

I now turn to a closer consideration of the specific positions, logics, and structures of the U.S. and French journalistic fields, with an eye toward uncovering substantial historical changes (and continuities) and cross-national differences (and similarities). This historical and structural mapping of the French and American news media provides essential background context for the chapters to follow.

HISTORIES OF FIELD FORMATION

Field theory posits that the rules of the game that are established at a field's founding tend to endure. These logics of practice are not inviolable and can be modified over time. Even so, there is a tendency for early contingencies to become routinized and naturalized, thus establishing a difficult to modify "path dependency" (Powell 1991, 191–194). Analysis of the formation and partially contingent transformations of a national journalistic field thus adds an important historical, contextual explanation often missing from political economy or organizational studies of news production.

Early Histories

In both France and Great Britain's North American colonies, the earliest newspapers (Theophraste Renaudot's *Gazette* in 1631, Benjamin Harris's Boston

---

[7] As Bourdieu (1993, 87–89) has argued, "the structured space of discourses reproduces, in its own terms, the structured space of the newspapers [or other media outlets] and of the [audiences] for whom they are produced..."

Publick Occurrences Both Forreign and Domestick in 1690) emerged under monarchical rule and were subject to strict political censorship (Leonard 1986, 18–32; Palmer 1994, 118–126). With the political upheavals of the late eighteenth century, newspapers in both France and the United States became much more openly politicized and played an important role in the formation and consolidation of their respective democratic republics. In France, however, this politicization was joined to a more literary and explanatory approach to journalism. The full title of a prominent early and enduring journal testifies to this two-fold allegiance: *Le Journal des débats politiques et littéraires* (Newspaper of Political and Literary Debates) (Ferenczi 1993, 27). In contrast to the American First Amendment, which prohibits Congress from "abridging the freedom of speech, or of the press," the eleventh article of the French Declaration of the Rights of Man and Citizen positively affirms the right to the "the free communication of thoughts and opinions." Thus, in the French case, freedom of the press was, from the beginning, justified and defended as the right to opinions rather than "mere" information (Barbrook 1995, 10–11).

After the French Revolution, the paths of the French and American press began to diverge more sharply. With the 1799 coup d'état of Napoleon Bonaparte and the subsequent restoration of the monarchy in France, overt state censorship of the press became the norm over the next eight decades. Thus, the particular French notion of journalistic autonomy was crucially influenced by this long formative period during which the early journalistic heroes were of necessity also political dissidents, some of whom were imprisoned or killed for attempting to exercise their *métier*. If most of the American press also remained highly partisan through the nineteenth century, the stakes were not nearly as high. In the 1830s, some American newspapers became significantly more populist, information-oriented, and commercially profitable (Schudson 1978; Kaplan 2002). These developments did not go unnoticed in France. Émile de Girardin, France's first media mogul who dominated the country's newspaper industry from 1828 until his death in 1881, saw in America's so-called penny press a model to follow. He figured, rightly, that a sensationalist but apolitical press could thrive even under the cloud of monarchical censorship. Girardin's politically opportunistic advocacy of information-oriented newspapers only led many French journalists and intellectuals to celebrate all the more the virtues of a literary, opinionated, and politically engaged press (Palmer 1994, 146–158; see also Ferenczi 1993, 12).

If this American-French distinction between a U.S. popular journalism of "fact-centered discursive practices" (Chalaby 1996) and a more stylized French "political-literary" journalism was thus established early on, a distinctive American conception of journalistic "objectivity" was not consolidated until at least the 1920s. Partly, new reporting practices can be linked to the tendency of an advertising-supported newspaper market to produce monopolies in all but the biggest markets (Schiller 1981). In order to hold their politically diverse mass audiences, the surviving "omnibus" papers had every incentive to cover the news in a more neutral, balanced way. Michael Schudson (1978) also convincingly links the rise of objectivity in journalism to the early twentieth-century Progressive political and intellectual movement, which stressed the value of rationalized social scientific and public administrative expertise.

With the launching of journalism schools and professional awards, such as the Pulitzer prizes, American journalists increasingly sought to rationalize their professional practice, set standards for journalistic excellence, and raise their public prestige (Weaver 2003; Krause 2011). The first journalism courses were offered at the University of Pennsylvania business school in 1893; subsequently, degree programs were established at the University of Missouri-Columbia in 1908 and at Columbia University in New York in 1912 (Becker et al. 2001). In contrast, although the first French journalism school was launched in 1899 by the American Dick May (Delporte 1999, 280), professional education did not gain widespread legitimacy in France until the founding of the Paris Center for Journalism studies (CFJ) in 1946 (Charon 2003).

The political climates at the time of founding of the dominant U.S. and French journalism schools were dramatically different. Whereas the media industry has always been a crucial supporter and monitor of journalism education in the United States, the CFJ was started by the politically engaged journalists of the French resistance who sought to develop journalism in contradistinction to the corrupt commercial news industry that had collaborated with the pro-Nazi Vichy regime during World War II (Charon 2003, 142–143). Thus, at their origins, professional education in the United States and France primarily reinforced preexisting cross-national differences in professional practices – toward a more commercially adaptable informational journalism in the former and a more politically engaged essayistic journalism in the latter. Recent critical investigations of French journalism schools suggest that they increasingly emphasize factual reporting, especially about "breaking" news, over the literary essay or political commentary (Ruffin 2003). Yet it is telling that the top French journalistic prize – the Albert Londres Prize – is named after a journalist known for his naturalistic writing style rather than classic, hard-nosed investigative reporting *à l'américaine*. The French prize tends to be awarded to journalists who exhibit prodigious "writing talent" and offer "fresh perspectives" on current events (Albert 2004, 51; Gatien 2007; Mulhlmann 2008, 79–94).

Another factor influential at the moment of field formation is the level of elite political consensus. In the United States, political opposition – especially after the systematic crushing of pre-World War I radical socialist and populist movements – historically has been relatively well maintained within a broad ideological acceptance of the governmental system and the capitalist economy.[8]

---

[8] Although the U.S. socialist left has never recovered, the early twenty-first century has witnessed a revival of the antigovernment far right. This right-induced polarization of the American polity has facilitated the growth of partisan media, notably on cable and radio, but most leading news organizations still hold on at least to the pretence of neutrality.

This helped create the conditions for American-style "objective," nonpartisan (which is not to say nonideological[9]) journalism. In France, however, a highly "polarized pluralistic" political system (Hallin and Mancini 2004, 59–63) made adopting a neutral position outside and above the fray virtually impossible. When it was finally granted a measure of autonomy from the state during the Third Republic with passage of a new press law in 1881, the French press found itself on the shaky ground of a tenuous political consensus still very much threatened by antidemocratic currents on both the right (monarchists and later fascists) and, to a lesser extent, the left (communists, after 1920). Among these factions there was very little mutual trust, and the press continued to be seen as an appropriate means (whether through lies, bribes, or scandal) to attain mutually exclusive political ends. Because the parties themselves differed so fundamentally, the press was not allowed to avoid choosing sides and thus remained politicized even as it became more commercialized.[10]

Radio's emergence in both countries was marked by an ongoing struggle between commercial and noncommercial uses. French radio initially imitated the German approach, in which the state "retained control over the transmission of radio signals, but allowed private control over program-making" (Thomas 1976, 1–3; Barbrook 1995). As the Third Republic moved leftward in its policies during the 1930s, private radio stations became increasingly allied with far right and neo-fascist domestic interests, which launched vicious attacks on the government. Thus, in 1933, the state established a regulatory agency (PTT) that took direct control of Radio Paris, the nation's leading commercial station; halted any further expansion of the commercial sector; and, inspired by the British approach, established a license fee funding system for the expanding national radio system. As the threat of war with Germany increased in the late 1930s, the government, now in the hands of the conservatives, increased direct control over both state and commercial radio stations. In the United States, the emerging radio system did not experience this level of political upheaval, but, as Robert McChesney (1993) has documented, the commercialization of radio was far from a foregone conclusion. During the 1920s, many leading politicians, including Herbert Hoover, favored a noncommercial radio system similar to the British Broadcasting Corporation (BBC). The consolidation of a largely

---

[9] As Mark Pedelty observes (1995, 8) in his trenchant analysis of U.S. foreign correspondents, "In the North American vernacular, 'ideology' is considered the antithesis of objectivity . . . [However] [i]n claiming to be objective, media organizations shield their close affinity for and incorporation with dominant institutions and ruling class structures."

[10] In purely economic terms, the early twentieth century has often been called the "golden age" of the French press. In 1915, for instance, *Le Petit Parisien*'s circulation of 1.5 million was the highest in the world (Kuhn 1995, 19). Even so, cross-national differences persisted. As Thogmartin (1998, 94) nicely summarizes: "Economic determinists might think that the pressures of industrialization and mass marketing would make newspapers in all the industrialized countries converge in form and content, but the French mass newspapers of the nineteenth century persisted in following their own distinct line of development." See also Ferenczi (1993), Delporte (1999), and Charles (2004).

commercial system under the control of the fledgling networks of the Columbia Broadcasting System (CBS) and the National Broadcasting Corporation (NBC) in the 1930s was achieved through an intensive lobbying and public relations campaign. Even so, civic demands on radio were not entirely abandoned. Broadcasting licenses for CBS and NBC were linked to public service require-ments, however flimsy, and the scattered noncommercial network of educational radio stations maintained a foothold in many parts of the country.

Post-World War II through the Early 1980s

After World War II, the postwar government prevented most of the major French newspapers from reopening because of their collaboration with the pro-Nazi Vichy regime. Thus, the very notion of a commercial press was once again discredited, strengthening the noncommercial, civic pole of the journalistic field. In the immediate postwar years, Paris had more than twenty-five daily newspapers, with the largest circulation belonging to the communist *L'Humanité* (Kuhn 1995, 24–27). *Le Monde* came into being in December 1944, when General Charles de Gaulle recruited respected journalist and resist-ance fighter Hubert Beuve-Méry to direct a new "newspaper of reference." In return, de Gaulle may have expected Beuve-Méry to be his ally, but *Le Monde* was often critical of de Gaulle during his presidency (from 1958 to 1969) (Thibau 1996).

Even though most of the new postwar papers eventually closed, the high prestige accorded to a noncommercial, engaged, and politicized press continued for nearly three decades and was revitalized by Jean-Paul Sartre's founding of *Libération* in 1973 (Samuelson 1979; Guisnel 2003). *Libération* was explicitly praised that year by the Gaullist party newspaper *La Nation* for helping to keep alive the French tradition of a politically engaged press (Perrier 1994).

Postwar legislation sought to protect the French print and audio-visual media's independence against capitalist concentration and commercial pressure, laying the groundwork as well for an entirely state-owned television sector that endured, more or less in the same form, until the early 1980s (Kuhn 1995). The first French state-owned television channel began broadcasts shortly after the end of World War II, followed by a second channel in 1964 and a third region-oriented channel in 1972. After de Gaulle founded the Fifth Republic in 1958, he consolidated state control over radio and television (Chalaby 2002). During the Pompidou and Giscard d'Estaing administrations, state controls were gradually loosened and advertising was introduced, but the politically appointed directors of information continued to play a decisive role in determining what could or could not "pass" on television (Miège 1986, 22). It would be left to the socialist government of François Mitterrand, elected in 1981, to shift television further toward the market pole of the field of power. The first private channel, the subscription Canal-Plus, began operating in November 1984. With the election of a conservative parliamentary majority in 1986, new prime minister Jacques

Chirac extended Mitterrand's tentative steps by officially privatizing France's leading public channel, TF1, in 1987 (Péan and Nick 1997).

Many French intellectuals and media scholars, including Pierre Bourdieu in his short book *On Television* (1998), see the privatization of TF1 as the single most important contemporary transformation of the French journalistic field, introducing "pure" market logic into a field historically shaped much more by the political and intellectual fields. The historical timing of the change, however, mitigated its effects. Market power, even if ascendant, would have to overcome the institutional inertia of the long-established "public service" tradition.

In the United States, the notion of public service broadcasting has not been entirely absent, but it is weaker. Once the policy battle was settled in favor of private interests in the 1930s, the commercial model was transferred without effective opposition from radio to television in the 1940s. In principle, both radio and television broadcast licenses could be revoked by the Federal Communications Commission (FCC, established in 1934) if licensees failed to serve an ill-defined "public interest"; but they rarely were. Scattered educational and public television channels were only consolidated into a loosely organized and underfunded Public Broadcasting Service (PBS) in 1967 (Shorenstein and Veraldi 1989; Hoynes 1994).

Increasing U.S. commercialization, at least for a time, was accompanied by widespread acceptance of the professional ideal of "objective," information-oriented journalism. In contrast to France, the history of the American press beginning in the 1920s and 1930s is in part one of increasing professional autonomy through a process of "differentiation" from the political field (Alexander 1981) or, at least, particular political parties. At the same time, American journalism's relationship to the state – the elected executive and legislative branches and the civil service bureaucracy – was not severed and was perhaps even strengthened. Daniel Hallin (1996, 246) has called this the period of "high modernism" in American journalism. Sharing the ethos of the high modernist period in art and architecture, journalism of the era entailed a "belief in progress, rationality and universal truths or standards, as well as a conviction that it is possible to be part of the 'establishment,' with wealth, access and prestige, and simultaneously independent – an avant-garde in art, a watchdog in the media." Over the course of the 1960s and 1970s, investigative journalism became increasingly prominent, exemplified in the now mythic "Pentagon Papers" and "Watergate" episodes. U.S. commercial network television, which came of age in the 1960s, did not substantially challenge this public service ethos. In part, this was due to television's own economic prosperity but also because, in the wake of the quiz show scandals of the late 1950s, it willingly submitted to government regulation and even increased its commitment to news programming in order to shore up its legitimacy (Barnouw 1977).

Historically, as Schudson (1978) notes, reliable, even dry information was the calling card of quality newspapers such as the *New York Times*, whereas emotional story-telling marked the popular press. During the 1970s, this dichotomy began to break down. Elite newspapers (Darnton 1975) and national television news (Hallin and Mancini 1984) alike increasingly presented the news as dramatic narrative. Yet such changes were not perceived, at least inside the journalistic field, as antithetical to public service. Good journalism was seen as good business, and vice versa. For a time, there was some truth in such claims, although it must be remembered that even in this "golden age," the U.S. news media mostly failed to challenge business power or provide much attention to socially or ideologically marginal groups.

By the late 1980s, both the American and French journalistic fields were poised for change – in both cases toward more market-driven logics – yet, as we will see, patterns established from earlier periods would continue.

CONTEMPORARY FIELD POSITION: BETWEEN CIVIC
AND MARKET POWER

French and American journalism can thus be understood in part as products of different historical struggles, through which different conceptions of good journalism have emerged: journalism as ideologically diverse analysis and debate of ideas in France, and journalism as information, investigation, and personalized narrative in the United States. Of course, the contrast is not black and white. Just as national cultures are not unitary, neither are intermediary institutional fields such as journalism. As I argue throughout this book, national culture is best understood as a "repertoire" of logics, with some more dominant than others. Michèle Lamont and Laurent Thévenot (2000) find that market logics (individualist emphasis on profits and wealth as the measure of success) and civic solidarity logics (egalitarian, nonmaterialist orientation to community) both exist in France and the United States. The difference between the two societies lies in the relative dominance of one or the other: market logics are dominant (but not exclusively so) in the United States, whereas civic solidarity logics are dominant (but not exclusively so) in France. Put another way, what is considered "alternative" in the United States is much closer to the "mainstream" in France, and vice versa.

My argument about enduring differences between French and American journalism is rooted in this conception of national culture but places a greater emphasis than Lamont and Thévenot on the financial and bureaucratic support of organizational actors, from state agencies and political parties to philanthropies and voluntary associations. In particular, government elected and administrative bodies play a crucial role coercively (through laws and regulations), symbolically (through public discourses and rituals), and financially (by distributing resources either indirectly through tax exemptions or directly through subsidies) in reproducing or transforming the balance of power among the existing repertoires of cultural logics. Thus, it is not a question of state or no state, of repressive policies or no policies at all. It is a question of how the state will choose to act, or not to act, to favor various market or nonmarket logics. In short, if French and American journalism continue to be different, it is *not* because the state is supposedly more involved in one system (France) than in the other (United States); it is because the states in these respective societies maintain different mixes of policies that enable or constrain different types of journalism.

Standard liberal accounts of "press freedom" emphasize the laws and regulations that limit journalistic freedom to report about certain kinds of government information, as well as penalties to journalists who overstep these lines. Along with informal social relations between politicians and journalists, which may be more or less intimate and friendly, these factors affect the proximity of the journalistic field to the state, what Hanitzsch (2007, 373) refers to as "power distance."

In the United States, First Amendment protections, as interpreted by the Supreme Court over the past several decades, give the American press wide latitude to investigate and criticize politicians. U.S. journalistic freedom to investigate and report on government officials, and increasingly, a broader category of "public figures," took a giant leap forward in 1964, with the Supreme Court's decision in *New York Times v. Sullivan*, in which the press was no longer required to prove that it had avoided falsehood but only that it had acted without "actual malice." The Freedom of Information Act, first passed in 1966 and bolstered by additional legislation in 1974, required more government agencies to make available internal documents to the press and public. In 1971, the Supreme Court upheld the prohibition against "prior restraint" (the state's intervening to stop publication of sensitive information), ruling in favor of the *New York Times*'s right to publish classified documents about the government's involvement in the Vietnam War, the so-called "Pentagon Papers." The "right-of-reply" for individuals criticized by the press was explicitly prohibited by the U.S. Supreme Court in 1974 (*Miami Herald v. Tornillo*).[11]

In contrast, France has no direct equivalent to the First Amendment or the Freedom of Information Act. Neither truth nor "absence of malice" constitute a defense from criminal prosecution if journalists publish restricted government information. There has not and probably never will be a French equivalent of the Pentagon Papers or Watergate: one major exception, *Le Monde*'s investigation of the Greenpeace *Rainbow Warrior* affair during the early years of the Mitterrand government, was technically legal because it concerned events taking place outside of French territory.[12] In addition, France maintains hate speech

---

[11] For overviews of U.S. press law, see Howard (1989) and Kirtley (2005).

[12] In 1985, *Le Monde* reporters Edwy Plenel and Bertrand Le Gendre reported that high government officials had planned the bombing of the Greenpeace boat *Rainbow Warrior* that had come to New Zealand to protest French nuclear tests in the region. The coverage led to the dismissal of the defense minister. For histories and analyses of investigative journalism in France, see Hunter (1997), Marchetti (2000), Lemieux (2001), and Chalaby (2004).

laws (in particular, prohibiting racist or Holocaust-denying public remarks); laws protecting the privacy of public officials that, if violated, can apply criminal penalties against journalists; and a "right of reply" for officials who have been criticized in the press.[13]

Television is regulated in both countries by agencies with public service mandates: the FCC and Corporation for Public Broadcasting (CPB, for public television and radio) in the United States, and the Conseil supérieur de l'audiovisuel (CSA, Supreme Audiovisual Council) in France. The CSA monitors television programs to see that they fulfill public service obligations – such as a degree of "pluralism and equity" in news coverage of all political parties during election periods – but only issues reports and recommendations after a program has been aired. Just as with the American FCC, the CSA has no legal right to censor (Kuhn 2010). In both instances, the regulatory agencies are at least partially insulated from political pressures, although in the French case this insulation was undermined in 2008 when President Sarkozy restored direct presidential appointment of the directors of French public television and radio (FCC 2010; Levy 2010).

In sum, American reporters have laws and regulations on their side to facilitate in-depth, critical, and investigative reporting. One recent example of this kind of legally enabled reporting is *New York Times*' reporter Nina Bernstein's damning investigation of government mistreatment of immigrant detainees (and officials' subsequent lies about their actions), which was crucially supported by documents obtained through the Freedom of Information Act.[14] But how often do American reporters engage in such critical reporting? Or, put another way, to what extent does the legal right to engage in investigative reporting actually coincide with (or trump) the commercial imperative to attract audiences? Research suggests that the answer is "less and less" (Greenwald and Bernt 2000).

Likewise, regardless of French-U.S. cross-national differences in information access laws, it is debatable whether any substantial difference exists between the two countries in reporters' reliance on official "sources" as "primary definers" of issues in the news (Hall, Critcher, Jefferson, Clarke, and Roberts 1978). To the extent that the French government places tighter restrictions on the release of sensitive documents, French reporters may rely more on officials to directly provide information.[15] However, numerous U.S. studies have shown that U.S. reporters are also heavily reliant on press releases and interviews with officials and that they "index" their coverage closely to political elite actions

---

[13] For a comprehensive overview of French press law, see Derieux (2001); for solid English-language accounts, see Barbrook (1995), Kuhn (1995), and Thogmartin (1998).
[14] See, e.g., Nina Bernstein, "Officials Hid Truth of Immigrant Deaths in Jail," *New York Times*, p. 1, January 10, 2010.
[15] This point was made by *Le Monde* reporter Elise Vincent at a 2012 University of Minnesota conference ("Covering the Southern Borders") in response to a U.S. journalist's question.

and debates (Hallin 1994; Pedelty 1995; Entman 2004; Bennett, Lawrence, and Livingston 2007). Conversely, because French journalists tend to be less wed to the convention of "sourcing" every fact and opinion in a news article, they may actually have greater autonomy from the government to shape the news as they see fit.[16] Thus, the *effective* differences in relations between government officials and journalists in France and the United States are not as great as is sometimes claimed (for instance, U.S. elite journalists – Bob Woodward is a good example – are not nearly as antagonistic toward politicians as is sometimes imagined or hoped for). And for many types of news coverage that are about civil society and business actors as much or more than political actors – immigration would seem to be one of them – proximity or political power distance may not be all that decisive in shaping everyday news coverage. Thus, rather than portraying government purely in terms of its statutory restrictive or partisan instrumental power over the news, it is important to also highlight its role in either promoting or inhibiting market- or nonmarket-oriented logics of action.[17]

Using the terminology of field position, the structural differences between U.S. and French journalism can be portrayed as follows (see Figures 2.1 and 2.2): In both France and the United States, the journalistic field is part of the field of power, that is, it possesses a relatively high volume of financial and symbolic resources. Likewise, in both countries, nonmarket (civic) and market logics of worth and excellence vie for dominance. In France, however, the civic field, funded largely by the state, extends its reach over a larger portion of the field of power and encompasses more of the journalistic field. This is evident in the fact that state subsidies provide a substantial portion of funding of both civil society associations (Veugelers and Lamont 1991; Baumgartner 1996) and the media. Because of more extensive state regulations oriented toward noncommercial or anticommercial purposes, the French market field itself does not operate according to "pure" market principles as much as is the case in the United States (thus, in Figure 2.1, the French market field's "market" pole is further left, closer to the civic pole, than in Figure 2.2, representing the United States). Conversely, in the United States, the market field occupies a larger space within the field of power, including the journalistic field. Given its lesser dependence on state funding as compared to France, the U.S. civic field does not extend so far in the direction of the civic pole of the field of power (i.e., toward a pure antimarket orientation, in part because the civic field is dominated by capitalist or donor-based philanthropies) (Baumgartner 1996). In each case, nonmarket and market logics are constructed historically and relationally.

---

[16] See Ruellan (1993, 202). In my study with Dan Hallin of political news coverage in the French and U.S. press during the 1960s and 1990s (Benson and Hallin 2007, 38), we found that French news articles were substantially more likely to offer unattributed interpretations and opinions.

[17] This conception of field position is compatible with Hanitzsch's variable of "market orientation" (2007, 374). The difference is that I emphasize more the state's role in promoting such an orientation. See Thomas Streeter (1996) for a demonstration of how state intervention, rather than neglect, created the dominant commercial logic of U.S. television.

The political field or state traverses these oppositions: it might be conceived of as a specialized field in its own right, such as a governmental bureaucratic field, or more expansively as an ensemble of fields including the judicial field. It is not represented in Figures 2.1 and 2.2, but may be imagined in a three-dimensional representation to be hovering above and partially parallel to the journalistic field. As opposed to a totalizing notion of "governmentality," this model preserves both the potential and actuality of modes of action not consonant with or even in opposition to neo-liberal market logic (as well as cross-national variation in the relative power of these potentially dissonant logics).

One final cross-national difference needs to be noted: in both countries, a hybrid space exists in which the seemingly opposed civic and market logics are brought together. In the United States, civic ends have been financed by profit-driven news companies whose owners nevertheless retain a public service orientation. In France, some subsidized, public service–oriented newspapers have worked hard to expand their audiences and revenues. It is generally in this hybrid space that we find the forms of professional practice richest in the symbolic capital of prestige: in the United States, investigative and other types of narrative, long-form daily journalism; in France, elegantly written, in-depth analysis and evaluation of ideas and social issues. Contra Bourdieu, this "autonomous" journalism is not strictly opposed to the market but rather represents a variety of fragile, ongoing attempts to balance market and civic demands.

Proximity to the Civic Pole

The nonmarket or civic field consists of the organized sector of society oriented toward a variety of normative ends, united, however, by a shared distance from the immediate demands of the marketplace (even in those cases in which a group may advocate "free market" policies). In the United States, this is often referred to as the "nonprofit" sector. Government media policy intersects with the civic field most directly when it "promotes" forms of speech not otherwise provided for by the market (Baker 2002). States can provide tax breaks or subsidies to media that provide news relevant to individuals and organizations that lie outside the desired audience demographics of commercial media. They can also take an ownership stake in "public service" media, such as the BBC, investing in the kind of in-depth treatment of issues that may seem too risky or "boring" to commercial media oriented toward maximizing short-term profits.

During the early years of the nation, the U.S. government actually took a far more interventionist role in promoting the press and democratic civic life than did governments in France or most other European nation-states. Cheap postal rates for newspapers were the most direct form of aid, but support for public schools (raising literacy rates) and transportation networks also indirectly supported a vibrant press (John 1995; Starr 2004). In recent years, as U.S. advertising revenues have plummeted and commercial news operations have been forced to scale back considerably (and, in some cases, close altogether),

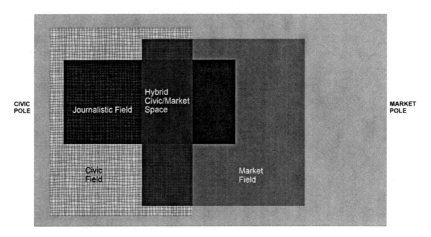

FIGURE 2.1. The French field of power.

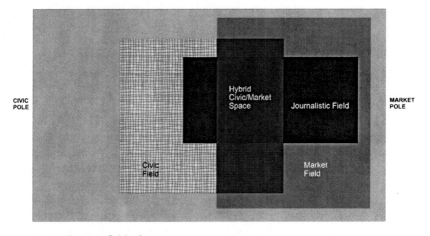

FIGURE 2.2. The U.S. field of power.

major foundations – Ford, Carnegie, Pew Charitable Trusts, Knight, and others – have contributed an estimated $180 million to news operations, mostly small-scale ventures. However, this amount is dwarfed by the amount of advertising funding lost since the early 2000s and the resulting $1.6 billion cut from newsroom budgets (Waldman 2011, 16). Much of this U.S. foundation funding, moreover, is targeted at start-up online media with small audiences and is oriented toward providing a temporary boost to the creation of "new business models" (Grueskin, Seave, and Graves 2011) rather than supporting ongoing nonmarket-oriented news media.

In contrast, French indirect and direct government subsidies to the press are among the highest in the Western world, constituting between 10 and 15 percent of total press revenues, a range that has remained relatively constant to this day

(Nielsen and Linnebank 2011). A variety of direct aid is available to all French press outlets, such as reimbursements for telephone and fax expenditures, shipping of newspapers and the return of unsold copies (Charon 2005). In addition, targeted subsidies in "defense of political pluralism" were initiated during the 1970s for politically oriented newspapers with low advertising revenues and circulations. Publications having received such subsidies at various times, contributing from 1 to 4 percent of their total revenues, include *Libération*, *La Croix* (left-Catholic), *L'Humanité* (communist), and *Présent* (linked to the far right National Front party) (Charon 1996, 61). Among the newspapers in this study, only *La Croix* and *L'Humanité* received the pluralism subsidy during the 2002–2006 sampled years. (Albert 2004, 105). Indirect aid to the French media includes tax breaks for individual journalists and for the press enterprises themselves, lower postal charges, and the "39 bis" provision of the Import code that allows newspapers to recover up to 80 percent of their expenses on equipment.

Also helping ensure widespread French public access to a diversity of press voices is the legal requirement that all French national general information newspapers and magazines be made available for sale through the unionized kiosk distribution network (*Nouvelles messageries de la presse Parisienne*) (Balle 2001, 319–320; Hubé 2008). In addition, the France 2 public television midday news, the public radio channel France-Inter, and the cable channel France 24 offer daily "press reviews" (*revues de presse*) that broadcast for the benefit of both journalists and the general public the news and views of a broad range of newspapers. The pluralist orientation of these government initiatives is expressed well in this remark by the retiring host of the France-Inter radio press review program:

It was my duty to help the alternative press (*presse minoritaire*). I often cited *La Croix* which is a remarkably well-done small newspaper and I often cited *L'Humanité* because it would be a catastrophe if *L'Humanité* were to one day disappear, an ecological catastrophe, in the sense of ecology of ideas.[18]

These and other French government policies thus help ensure that the public will have access to a wide array of viewpoints, even those perspectives that are inconsistent with the demands of commercial enterprises and their upper-middle-class audiences.

Political parties and religious organizations provide another institutional support for civic logics to operate in the journalistic field. Although party-owned newspapers have existed in both the United States and France, the tradition continued much longer in France and, as noted, was revived during the immediate post-World War II period, as well as in the decade following the protests of May 1968. *L'Humanité*, founded in 1904 by socialist leader Jean Jaurès, served as the official newspaper of the French Communist Party (PCF)

---

[18] Quoted in Charles Silvestre, "Ivan Levaï n'en finit pas de passer la presse en revue." *L'Humanité*, November 16, 1996. All translations are by author.

beginning in 1920 (Thogmartin 1998, 246–248). Since 2000, the paper no longer has official ties to the PCF, but it continues to receive some funding from the party, and most of its editors and readers remain members of the PCF or other far left political parties (Eveno 2004).[19] At a day-long conference on the "challenge of pluralism for today's press" held in June 2003, *L'Humanité* editors, leaders of the Confédération Générale du Travail (CGT) labor union, and other sympathetic journalists and activists positioned the newspaper at the forefront of a campaign to strengthen France's tradition of a diverse "press of opinion."[20] The Catholic *La Croix* is published by the nonprofit religious publisher Bayard Press, owned in turn by the Roman Catholic Assumptionist religious order; it operates at a loss, which is covered by Bayard's other profitable operations, as well as by the aforementioned government subsidies.[21] During the early 1970s, a new generation of left newspapers emerged, including the socialist party-sponsored *Le Matin* (founded in 1977 and closed in 1987) and, most durably, *Libération*, founded in 1973 and originally linked to Maoist and other far left parties, but, by the 1980s, entirely independent of any political party although still left-leaning (Freiberg 1981; Thogmartin 1998). In France, a nonprofit "press of opinion" has some prominent supporters. When *L'Humanité* was facing a financial crisis in 2001, the CEO of the private and largest television channel, TF1, stepped in to make a major donation.[22] During the 2009 Etats généraux de la presse écrite (Estates General of the Print Press, a national conference convened by the French president), former *Le Monde* editor and current editor-in-chief of *La Croix* Bruno Frappat spoke forcefully in favor of a noncommercial, public service–oriented press.

In the United States, the most prominent nonprofit newspaper is the *Christian Science Monitor*, owned by the publishing arm of the Christian Scientist church (Usher and Layser 2010, 1340–1341; Christian Science Monitor 2008).[23] *Christian Science Monitor* immigration reporter Alexandra Marks, who had also worked for other news organizations, defined the *Monitor* "difference" as follows:

---

[19] Pascale Egré (interview 2009), currently a reporter at *Le Parisien*, told me that when she worked at *L'Humanité* during the 1990s, she was one of the rare journalists there who was not a PCF member. Interviews conducted for this book are listed in Appendix B.

[20] Author field notes, Saint-Denis, France, June 14, 2003.

[21] See the Bayard press website: http://www.groupebayard.com/index.php/fr/articles/rubrique/id/3. *La Croix*'s early years were marred by its vitriolic anti-Semitic attacks on Captain Dreyfus, but in its post-World War II reincarnation, it is generally considered "progressive, tolerant, and thought-ful" (Thogmartin 1998, 246).

[22] Michel Delberghe, "Des entreprises privées s'engagent dans le sauvetage de *L'Humanité*," *Le Monde*, May 17, 2001, p. 19.

[23] Two other church-owned newspapers are the Salt Lake City *Deseret News* (Mormon) and the *Washington Times* (Unification church). The *St. Petersburg* (Florida) *Times* is also often presented as an example of nonprofit journalism when, in fact, it is a "private, for-profit" subsidiary of the nonprofit, tax-exempt Poynter Institute. This hybrid model lessens profit pressures, compared to a publicly traded company, without entirely removing it from the market.

Every news organization has its underlying criteria. I used to work for NBC and their underlying criteria was the profit motive, it was to produce news that attracts as many eyeballs as possible. [The *Monitor*'s] underlying criteria is offering good, balanced news ... to shed new light ... to put [the news] in perspective.[24]

Even so, the church-subsidized *Christian Science Monitor* has aggressively moved to become more profitable in recent years. The dominant U.S. "market" definition of success is evident in recent remarks by editor John Yemma (who had previously spent many years at the *Boston Globe*): "I'd love to get to the point where we could actually return some money to the church. That would do wonders psychologically for everyone because it would show that *Monitor* journalism isn't just a good thing to do, but it's a successful thing" (Kennedy 2009, 37). *Monitor* managing editor Marshall Ingwerson described to me how he traveled to New York to attend seminars at Columbia University's Sulzberger Institute to "find a business model that works" and discover better ways "to monetize" *Monitor* content, both online and offline, "same as everybody else."[25]

As for U.S. television, FCC regulation has long had the purpose of ensuring that television news stations that benefit from free licenses to use the publicly owned airwaves allot a certain portion of their broadcasting day to "public interest" programs. However, beginning in the early 1980s, the FCC began loosening even these vague requirements, with the spirit of these "reforms" captured well in the remark by then FCC chairman Mark Fowler: "Public interest is that which interests the public" (Auletta 1992). The "Fairness Doctrine" (instituted in 1949) – a sort of right-of-reply regulation that allowed organizations or individuals criticized by a television station to be given air time to offer their response – was ended in 1987 (Aufderheide 1990).

Other than the Voice of America (prohibited from broadcasting inside the United States), the only national audio-visual news outlets in which the American federal government is directly involved are PBS and National Public Radio (NPR), but, in these cases, far from exclusively. The 1967 Public Broadcasting Act created the private, nonprofit Corporation for Public Broadcasting (CPB) to provide quasi-independent, limited coordination of the hundreds of pre-existing local public channels. The federal government's main link to public television and radio has been via small biannual congressional appropriations to CPB. PBS's signature national news program (broadcast by more than 300 member television stations, as well as online), the "NewsHour," receives 40 percent of its funding from the federal government (including

---

[24] Alexandra Marks interview (2008). Marks, not a member of the Christian Science church, added that the *Monitor*'s commitment to truth stems from church founder Mary Baker Eddy's belief that "God is truth" so "there has to be a place to find out what is actually happening in the world." The only restricting influence of church beliefs is on medical news: "Christian Scientists don't believe you're ill, it's a spiritual malady. So you don't say someone's ill, you say, 'doctor's say.' You attribute it to doctors." But Marks quickly added, "I have no qualms about that ... to work for a newspaper with integrity, that is a small sacrifice."

[25] Marshall Ingwerson interview (2011).

National Science Foundation grants), 35 percent from business underwriting (including Chevron, BNSF Railway, Bank of America, Intel, and Monsanto), and 25 percent from foundations (such as the John S. and James L. Knight Foundation, Atlantic Philanthropies, and the William & Flora Hewitt Foundation) (PBS 2010; PEJ 2010b). "Member" stations that broadcast the NewsHour rely heavily on viewer contributions, as well as on state and local government (including university) support, and relatively less as a whole on business and federal government funding (Hoynes 1994; Waldman 2011). Total public funding (federal, state, and local governments combined) for both PBS and NPR amounted to less than $4 per person in the United States versus $52 per person for public television in France (Benson and Powers 2011).

All French television, until 1983, was state-owned. Through the 1970s, at least, it was often used in subtle and not-so-subtle ways to support the government in power (Kuhn 1995). At the same time, this "public service" television system represented a limited bulwark against the commercial colonization of the public sphere. French public television, unlike the British BBC, has a mixed funding system: from the early 1970s onward, at least a quarter of its funding has come from advertising and, by the late 1990s, this had risen to more than 40 percent for France 2, the main national public channel (Lecomte 1999, 51; Open Society Institute 2005). The French-German channel Arte relies mostly on the annual license fee and other government funding (Mathien 2003, 216; Clément 2011). French advertising limitations are stricter than European Union policies which, as of 2008, allowed an average of 12 minutes per hour of advertising: for both French private and public channels, the total amount of advertising is limited by the government to an average of just 6 minutes per hour, with a maximum of 12 minutes in any given hour, whereas Arte is only allowed an average of 4 minutes per hour, with a maximum of 9 minutes in any given hour (Anderson 2005, 7). This compares to an average of 15 minutes per hour on U.S. commercial television (Lowrey, Shrum, and McCarty 2005, 123). French state policy also limits advertising to contained periods *between* (rather than during) programs on all channels, both public and private (with the exception of allowing a single commercial break in the middle of long films on the private TF1) (Balle 2001).[26]

In sum, civic logics tend to be more extensive – and, due to state support, more purely nonmarket – in the French journalistic field, with little French-U.S. structural convergence over the past four decades. In the face of increasing commercial pressures on newspapers, the French government

---

[26] See, e.g., Angelique Chrisafis, "France Bans Adverts on State TV during Primetime," *The Guardian*, January 6, 2009. As of 2009, subsequent to the sample of television news items analyzed in this study, the French government banned all advertising after 8 p.m. on the French public channels 2 and 3. Ostensibly enacted to move French public service television closer to the British BBC model and to free it up to be more creative and risk-taking, the ban would also result in an increase in advertising and profits at TF1, M6, and private cable channels.

implemented in 2009 a $950 million package of subsidies, more than twice the U.S. federal budget for public television (Etats généraux de la presse écrite 2009; Wauters 2009). In contrast, as the economic crisis has worsened in the United States, no new government subsidies for newspapers have been offered, and government appropriations for public television and radio have at best remained steady even as there have been intensified conservative campaigns to cut or even eliminate funding (McChesney and Nichols 2010; Benson and Powers 2011).

Proximity to the Market Pole

As with other cross-national comparisons, French-U.S. differences in degree of commercialization are relative, not absolute. France's economy consists of a vibrant mix of small- and large-scale capitalist enterprises, its urban public spaces are dominated by advertising billboards, and the French are avid consumers, like their American counterparts. French newspapers are privately owned, even if partially publicly subsidized. Privately owned television channels garner a majority of the French audience. Both newspapers and television news closely monitor the demographics and sizes of their audiences (Bourdon 1994; Chaniac 2009).

Nevertheless, there are ongoing cross-national differences in both quantity and quality of media commercialization. At the macro-societal level, France is less advertising-saturated than the United States; as a percentage of gross domestic product, total advertising expenditures are less than half as high in France as in the United States (Kuhn 1995; Benson 2005). In relation to journalism, especially telling are cross-national differences related to advertising funding, type of ownership, and profit expectations.

In an international comparison compiled by the World Association of Newspapers (WAN 2007, 8), U.S. newspapers were at the top of the list, with 87 percent of revenues earned from advertising (averaging 2002 and 2004), and French newspapers were near the bottom, at 39 percent (averaging 2002 and 2003), percentages that are roughly consistent with their respective long-term averages (Baker 1994, 16; Mathien 2003, 92). Leading French dailies, such as *Libération* and *Le Monde*, have earned less than 30 percent of their revenues from advertising some years (Albert 1998, 83); the conservative *Le Figaro* is the only major French newspaper to approach the American advertising average (Albert 2004, 97). Even as U.S. newspaper advertising has declined due to the migration of advertising to the Internet and the worldwide financial crisis, the relative reliance on advertising remains greater in the United States than in France (Santhanam and Rosenstiel 2011). On television, this difference seems to be widening as French public television (France 2 and 3, in addition to Arte) move toward greater reliance on license fee funding. These public channels reach more than 40 percent of the French television audience, compared to PBS's average audience reach of less than 5 percent. As noted, although PBS does not accept advertising, it does receive substantial funding from business "sponsors." Overall, the U.S. television space is the most advertising-saturated in the world.[27]

It is important to acknowledge that the market enables as well as constrains: it helps create capacity. When advertising declines during a recession, journalists as well as owners see this as a problem because they know it will inevitably lead to cuts in newsroom budgets. When President Sarkozy announced his plan to eliminate advertising on public television – long a goal of the left – public television journalists staged protests because they feared the lost advertising dollars would not be replaced with public funding.[28] Although smaller newspapers like the communist *L'Humanité* or the Catholic *La Croix* know that they will never attract substantial advertising, more mainstream papers like *Le Monde* are eager to increase their advertising revenues, as a managing editor for the newspaper told me.[29] Partly because of lower advertising revenues, editorial staffs at the leading French national newspapers have numbered around 300, less than half the number at the *Washington Post* and *Los Angeles Times* and less than one-third the total at the *New York Times*.[30] One obstacle to obtaining more advertising is the content of many leading French newspapers. As a journalist for the French media industry magazine *Stratégies* remarked, "Advertisers don't like their products next to starving children in Africa, and *Le Monde* has a lot of that kind of content."[31] The other obstacle is the persistence of a national newspaper market with multiple titles: in the competition for advertising, only a few newspapers are likely to win. In fact, advertising expenditures are concentrated at *Le Figaro* and the financial newspaper *Les Echos*, followed by *Le Monde*, and then, at some distance, *Le Parisien*, *Libération*, *La Croix*, and *L'Humanité* (Albert 2004, 98).

Another important factor influencing the level and intensity of market pressures is type of ownership (Baker 2007). The publicly traded corporation is the dominant organizational form in the United States for the 80 percent of newspapers that are chain-owned, as well as radio and television channels, both network-affiliated and "independent" (Cranberg, Bezanson, and Soloski 2001; Klinenberg 2007). In this study's sample of newspapers, the two main exceptions are the *Daily News*, privately owned by New York investor Mortimer

---

[27] According to a September 12, 2006 report in *MediaWeek* (U.K. edition, p. 8), the United States has "the most cluttered TV market in the world ... where adults are exposed to 789 ads per week, 62 percent higher than the global average."

[28] Chrisafis, "France bans adverts ...," 2009, op cit.

[29] Anne Chaussebourg interview (2002).

[30] According to Weldon (2008, 165), citing Bacon's 2005 *Newspaper Directory*, editorial staff sizes in 2005 were 920 at the *New York Times*, 696 at the *Washington Post*, and 588 at the *Los Angeles Times*. The French statistic of 300 is based on Padioleau (1985), Thogmartin (1998), and author interviews. Although newsroom employment has fallen in both France and the United States in recent years, the French-U.S. proportion has remained about the same. See, e.g., John Tagliabue, "Le Monde Strike Stops Presses," *New York Times*, April 15, 2008; Brian Stelter, "New York Times Plans Staff Reductions," Media Decoder, nytimes.com, October 13, 2011.

[31] Amaury de Rochegonde interview (2002).

Zuckerman and, as noted, the *Christian Science Monitor*, owned by the non-profit Christian Science Publishing Company in Boston. Some newspapers have developed hybrid forms of commercial ownership explicitly aimed at lessening profit pressures. The Ochs-Sulzberger and Graham families controlling the *New York Times* and the *Washington Post*, respectively, have created two classes of stock ownership, reserving a clear majority of the class A voting stock for family members. During the period examined in this book, through 2006, this form of ownership also held for the *Wall Street Journal*, majority owned and controlled by the Bancroft family (but since 2007, part of Rupert Murdoch's News Corporation). Of the other U.S. newspapers in this study, the *Los Angeles Times*, founded by the Chandler family–controlled Times-Mirror Co., has been owned since 2000 by the now bankrupt Tribune Company (also publisher of the *Chicago Tribune* and *Baltimore Sun*); *USA Today* is the flagship national newspaper of the aggressively profit-maximizing, publicly traded Gannett newspaper chain; and the *New York Post* is owned by the publicly traded News Corporation.

In contrast, a wide variety of ownership models are used by French national newspapers (Albert 2004). *Le Parisien/Aujourd'hui en France* is part of the private Amaury group. As described previously, *L'Humanité* and *La Croix* are owned by nonprofit publishing companies. Until 2010, when it was sold to a group of investors with ties to the socialist party, *Le Monde* was majority owned by its journalists and other employees, and journalists elected the director (a position combining prerogatives of both editor and publisher) every six years. *Libération* had a similar arrangement through the early 1990s, with journalists effectively controlling 55 percent of the newspaper. Although it is now owned and controlled by investor Edouard de Rothschild, journalists retain a 20 percent share of the stock and retain the right to elect their editor-in-chief (Guisnel 2003; Rimbert 2005).[32] This level of journalist involvement in the business side of operations represents a very different approach from that of the "benevolent dictator" publisher arrangement at America's comparable "quality" newspapers, such as the *New York Times* and the *Washington Post*.[33]

---

[32] The current editor-in-chief, Nicolas Demorand, was elected in 2011 with 57 percent of the journalists' votes (http://www.liberation.fr/medias/01012318518-nicolas-demorand-elu-directeur-de-la-redaction-de-liberation, posted February 7, 2011). Despite such continuities, today's *Libération* has drifted far from its early organizational form, which included an open partisan engagement; a cooperative ownership structure, including equal pay for all employees; and an absolute refusal of advertising (Samuelson 1979; Veronique Brocard interview 1997; Juhem 2001).

[33] Informed of these arrangements at *Le Monde* and *Libération* by an American journalist, *Washington Post* publisher Katherine Graham is reported to have replied "You mean to say that the journalists vote? That they are the owners? They must be out of their minds. How can you run a paper like that?" (Quoted in Edward Behr, "L'ami américain: si je racontais Libération," *Libération*, June 5–6, 1993, p. 21).

Only a handful of the leading French media outlets, such as the national private channels TF1 and M6, and the subscription channel Canal-Plus are owned by companies listed on the French stock market. Public stock ownership of French media companies has been hindered by a 1986 law that limits the amount of foreign investment, as well as a provision that specifically prohibits a newspaper company from being publicly listed (Ramonet 2001). Despite these restrictions, two French newspapers in this study are effectively owned by publicly traded companies: *Le Figaro* is owned by the U.S.-NASDAQ–traded arms manufacturer and aeronautics company Dassault, and, from 1988 through 2006, *Les Echos* was owned by the British publicly traded publishing company Pearson PLP (in 2007 it was sold to the French publicly traded luxury goods company LVMH). At least in the case of *Le Figaro*, however, ownership by a publicly traded company has not led to an exclusive focus on maximizing profits. After purchasing the newspaper, company head Serge Dassault remarked: "For me, it's important to own a newspaper in order to express my opinion as well as to be able to respond to certain [critical] journalists."[34] Indeed, this attitude is similar to News Corporation head Rupert Murdoch's approach to journalism at the *New York Post* and Fox Cable News (Morris 2005; Wolff 2010) but such overt instrumentalization has earned Murdoch the scorn of many U.S. media owners and journalists and is further from the norm in the United States than in France.

The introduction of private television in France in the 1980s is often argued to have transformed the entire French journalistic field (Champagne and Marchetti 2005); in fact, as noted, French media policies continue to limit the degree and reach of commercialization in both television and the press. French newspaper companies continue to be less profit-driven and less profitable than their American counterparts, at best attaining 5 to 7 percent profit margins (Eveno 2008, 192).

In contrast, in the United States, an already commercial system has become even more hypercommercialized. The 1980 presidential election of the laissez-faire Ronald Reagan ushered in a series of tax and other regulatory policies that dramatically intensified market pressures across the U.S. field of power. A new spirit of media capitalism was embodied by the Gannett newspaper chain, which routinely earned 25 to 35 percent profits, setting a new Wall Street standard that other publicly owned media companies were expected to follow (Bagdikian 1992, 74). Challenging ideas that quality journalism was to be defined by journalists according to civic, public service criteria (as for instance, with the Pulitzer prizes), Gannett sought to redefine journalistic excellence in purely market terms as whatever worked to maximize profits (Squires 1993, 126; Underwood 1995, 40). At the same time, mergers and acquisitions of news outlets initiated by chains and other publicly traded companies were often accompanied by significant debt loads, payment of which has only been made

---

[34] See *Le Monde*, "Dassault prend le contrôle de la Socpresse," March 11, 2004.

possible by substantial cuts in news-gathering budgets (O'Shea 2011). A similar debt-driven downsizing has long been at work in the television news sector of the U.S. journalistic field (Hallin 1994; Kurtz 2007; Friedman 2012).

As a result of this long-term intensification of market pressures, when the financial crisis hit in 2008, American journalism was far more vulnerable than its counterparts in other countries. Numerous studies are finding that continental European news media are suffering less financially than American media because of the latter's greater dependence on advertising, greater likelihood of being traded on the stock market, greater involvement in mergers and acquisitions, and lesser access to public subsidies that might cushion the shock.[35]

Admittedly, the dominant ownership and funding models in both France and the United States have faced domestic challenges, but, to date, these have not gained traction. During the early 2000s, *Le Monde* sought to expand its commercial holdings, increase profits, and sell shares on the French stock exchange. Against *Le Monde* founder Hubert Beuve-Méry's insistence in the 1960s that only a "poor" press could be independent, some leading French journalists and academics in the 2000s looked to the United States (before the current crisis) and argued that editorial independence could only come from increased advertising and profitability (see, e.g., Eveno 2001). To date, however, this push to emulate the "American model" has been unsuccessful: the Le Monde group never did "go public" (Benson 2004), and there has been no indication that this effort will be revived. In the United States, the economic crisis has led to a recent flowering of alternative ownership and funding schemes (Pickard, Stearns, and Aaron 2009; Usher and Layser 2010), but most of these remain small in scale. Public funding, despite gaining endorsements from the Columbia and USC-Annenberg journalism schools (Downie, Jr. and Schudson 2009; Cowan and Westphal 2010) and the Association for Education in Journalism and Mass Communication (AEJMC), has so far not gained widespread journalistic or public support. Finding new "business models" remains the mainstream preoccupation and preference (Grueskin et al. 2011).

The question remains: what is the relationship between journalistic field position and journalistic practice? There are many ways to translate a given mix of market and civic incentives and constraints into a set of professional practices. The field-specific logics that emerge are at least partly the result of accident, competition, and tradition. Distinctive news formats embody historically shaped conceptions of good journalism, mediating between social structural constraints and news content.

---

[35] See recent reports from the Pew Center (Santhanam and Rosenstiel 2011) and the Reuters Institute (Levy and Nielsen 2011). Similar conclusions by the German Newspaper Publishers' Association are reported in Eric Pfanner, "For U.S. Newspaper Industry, an Example in Germany?," *New York Times*, May 16, 2010.

FIELD LOGIC: THE FORM OF NEWS

The logic of the journalistic field refers to the tacit "rules of the game" that organize competition and provide a standard of excellence and achievement. Many news practices are shared by journalists around the world, given their common organizational demands, work routines, and time and space constraints. In the words of one *Le Monde* editor, "Good journalism is universal ... Precise, right to the point, well-written, not too specialized."[36] Yet French newspapers clearly are not the same as American newspapers. Wherein lies the difference? Emphasizing an aspect of news largely ignored by Bourdieu and other field researchers, I suggest that the most basic expression of a journalistic field's distinctive logic lies in the "form of news." By this, I mean the presentation and organization of news, both externally (in the mix of genres on the page) and internally (in the discursive structural composition of articles). Barnhurst and Nerone (2001, 3) define the form of news as "the persisting visible structure of the newspaper, the things that make the *New York Times*, for example, recognizable as the same newspaper day after day although the content changes ... [such as] layout and design and typography ... habits of illustration, genres of reportage, and schemes of departmentalization." Further, they posit that "the form [of news] reenacts and reinforces patterns of deference" and that "the form of a medium encodes a system of authority [with] some forms always allow[ing] for more democracy than others" (Barnhurst and Nerone 2001, 9). This is an important insight, but I would modify it slightly: different forms of journalism are produced by and help produce different *types* of democracy, each with their unique civic advantages and disadvantages.

In his comparative study of *Le Monde* and the *Washington Post* during the 1970s and early 1980s, French sociologist Jean Padioleau (1985, 92–98) contrasts two very different forms of journalism. *Le Monde* favored a "pluralist" assemblage of multiple discursive genres and perspectives, anchored by its twin commitments to thoroughly "document" (via publication of diverse original source materials) and "comment" on the issues of the day, with the two facets in close proximity to one another. *Le Monde*'s "editor's association" (*société des rédacteurs*), the vehicle of journalistic ownership of the newspaper, described their journalistic approach in 1978: "It isn't enough to inform – one also has to do the groundwork to get ahead of events, to find ways to shed new light, to give voice to the voiceless" (cited in Padioleau 1985, 97). In contrast, the *Washington Post* focused on "breaking" new information, providing new "insight" (although not making evaluative comments), and constructing "vivid narratives" (Padioleau 1985, 255). Although less likely to mix news and commentary on news pages, the *Post* was more likely to shape the raw events of the news into coherent, compelling "stories."

This contrast suggests how the particular mix of historically shaped civic and market logics is refracted inside the French and American journalistic fields at

---

[36] Eric Le Boucher interview (2002). For a ten-country study that stresses cross-national similarities in news – a shared focus on deviance and/or social significance – see Shoemaker and Cohen (2006).

news organizations with high symbolic capital. In line with a French field of power dominated by nonmarket rather than market forces, materially as much as symbolically, *Le Monde*'s format is first and foremost pedagogical and pluralist. In contrast, in a U.S. market-driven field of power, the *Washington Post*'s format privileges breaking news and narrative as means to attract paying audiences and advertisers. Both formats are simultaneously civic and commercial. The difference lies in the enduring influence of history and the relative power of civic and market capital inside the two national fields.

It is important to stress that *Le Monde* and the *Washington Post* do not exhaust the actuality or potentiality of French and U.S. journalism. Rather, with their high prestige and influence, they embody the center of gravity within their respective fields. In France, other newspapers – *La Croix* perhaps – or certainly monthly publications such as *Le Monde Diplomatique* or the various intellectual reviews (*Les Temps Modernes*, *L'Esprit*, *Politix*, etc.) – lie closer to the civic pole; at the other end of the spectrum, especially after the mid-1980s, television news is driven more fully by market imperatives. As we will see in Chapter 8, narrative has a stronger pride of place among French TV journalists than it does for their newspaper colleagues. In the United States, closer to the nonmarket civic pole, policy rather than personality-driven news has been offered by specialist publications like *The National Journal*, various weekly and monthly political magazines, and PBS. At the other end of the spectrum (local commercial TV news, supermarket tabloids), narrative is not only more dominant, but qualitatively distinct from that offered by elite newspapers like the *Washington Post*: here the search for "insight" is almost completely overshadowed by the quest to elicit strong emotions. Narrative, thus, should not be understood as a single phenomenon, but as a general orientation toward story-telling that can – in varying degrees and in different ways – be personalized, emotional, insightful, and even structural. However, as I demonstrate throughout this book, there seems to be a generalized tension between narrative and structural analysis that makes it difficult to fully integrate the two, even for elite journalists who are consciously trying to do so.

Narrative has a long pedigree in both American newspapers (Darnton 1975; Schudson 1995; Pedelty 1995) and television (Hallin and Mancini 1984). Again, by narrative, in this broad sense, I mean simply the shaping of information as a "story" with clear characters and plot. Both breaking news and timeless feature articles may share these narrative tendencies. Even news with a classic "inverted pyramid" format that proceeds from most important to least important information may contain elements of narrative. To the extent that American page-one coverage is dominated by breaking news and feature articles – as opposed to other genres such as analyses, commentaries or interview transcripts – it is more narrative-driven than French news, as Padioleau (1985) found to be the case even in the 1970s.

Concurrent with the intensifying commercialization of the U.S. journalistic field and the rise of Internet news, however, an increasingly emotional, personalized form of narrative news has become more prestigious and predominant. During the early 2000s, Weldon (2008) documents an increase in the use of human interest feature articles and an increase in the use of the "anecdotal lead" (beginning the article with an individual profile) for all types of articles on the front pages of twenty leading American newspapers. *Arizona Republic* immigration reporter Dan Gonzalez described to me how the newspaper shifted from the classic "inverted pyramid" style to an overt "story-telling" approach[37]: story-telling was introduced into the newspaper in the early 2000s, shortly after its purchase by the Gannett chain, with the help of a "writing coach" who also "trained" journalists at other Gannett newspapers.

> We have a very specific structure in how we write stories. . . . The whole idea now is that when we write a story, we want the reader to read the entire story. So it's written very deliberately and consciously in story form. We break up the story into chapters, so each element of the story has its own chapter and its specific theme.

Personalized narrative journalism has even received the public stamp of approval from a *New York Times* executive editor, who gave a keynote speech to a national conference on narrative journalism, and from the prestigious Pulitzer Prizes. Rather than the dispassionate search for objective news, a recent study by Karin Wahl-Jorgensen found that Pulitzer Prize-winning journalism in the United States is increasingly characterized by "emotional story-telling."[38] Professionally, daily journalism thus associates itself with the prestige of narrative nonfiction in book publishing. Commercially, compelling narratives provide a reason for readers to still turn to newspapers, online or off, in an age when the Internet provides constantly updated information. Normatively, narrative approaches are conducive to the morally charged investigative journalism valued by elite democrats and the recuperation of ordinary lives at the margins valued by constructionist and radical pluralist democrats (Baker 2002; Ferree et al. 2002). As we will see, American news coverage of immigration often lives up to these aspirations, even as it falls short in other ways.

Implicit in discussions of the American narrative approach is that a news story is singular. When the story is big enough – an election result, a terrorist attack, a weather disaster, or the like – multiple news reports may be produced. But these are the exceptions: the usual impulse is to expand the story rather than divide it into parts and to keep the focus on information rather than opinion. In France, organizing news into multiarticle – and multigenre – ensembles is the rule.

Just as a long-standing U.S. narrative approach to news has intensified since the 1970s, this well-established French multigenre format has been solidified over the past few decades. The French newspaper *Libération* took it to a new level beginning

---

[37] Dan Gonzalez interview (2012).

[38] See Wahl-Jorgensen (2012, 13) and Beth Macy, "*New York Times* Editor Bill Keller on Narrative's Future," Harvard Nieman Journalism Lab, April 27, 2010, available at http://www.niemanstoryboard.org/2010/04/27/new-york-times-editor-bill-keller-on-the-future-of-narrative-journalism-and-three-threats-to-it-he-doesnt-buy/. See also Mark Kramer, "Narrative Journalism Comes of Age," Nieman Reports, October 1, 2001, available at http://www.nieman.harvard.edu/reports/article/101828/Narrative-Journalism-Comes-of-Age.aspx.

in 1981, with the launch of its *événement* format [literally, "today's big news"].
Événement highlights a single event or trend on the cover and first few inside pages,
regardless of the gravity of the day's events. As one senior *Libération* journalist told
me, "The *événement* format always includes the same elements: breaking news,
analysis, background information, interviews, [and] editorial."[39] *Événement* thus
crystallizes and amplifies a preexisting French tradition of a journalism of ideas. As a
kind of "daily magazine," it provides a means of both "reflecting upon" and
"conveying the emotion" of the news (Perrier 1994, 123–124, 202). Accompanied
by powerful images and headlines, it is a format also well-suited to enticing readers
to purchase newspapers at newsstands, the main mode of distribution for most of the
French press. Instead of talking about "stories," French reporters generally speak of
"papers" (*papiers*). Instead of referring to individual articles, they think in terms of
"pages." From a French perspective, it is not fair to critique an individual article's
fairness or comprehensiveness. What matters is the entire "page," consisting of
multiple articles[40] and multiple genres of articles. Feature articles are part of the
mix, but they tend to be shorter. As a result, narrative structuring is less fully
developed: there is simply no room to adequately develop a storyline.[41]

There continues to be a greater mixing of news and opinion on the same page
in France than in the United States, with editorials or commentaries often
appearing alongside news articles in the front portion of the newspaper. At *Le
Monde*, the topic and stance of the day's editorials are decided at the same
meeting in which page-one decisions are made; at the *New York Times*, the
news and opinion editors work on different floors and conduct their own
separate meetings to choose the day's top news stories and editorials.[42] As
Times editor Bill Keller said at a Columbia Journalism school event in 2011:
"The editorial page is not my domain. . . .. The editorial page answers to a
different boss. I'm not aware of what they're doing."[43] (See Figure 2.3.)

---

[39] Gilles Bresson interview (1998). Since 1981, *Libération* has modified its *événement* formula in
various ways, but the basic elements remain the same. See Blin (2002), Guisnel (2003), and
Aeschimann (2007).

[40] Boudana (2010a, appendix I, viii) notes that Rémy Ourdan (*Le Monde* foreign editor and former
war correspondent) took issue with the methodological approach of analyzing the content of
individual articles: "You mustn't isolate the article, but rather try to consider the page as a whole."
Likewise, Patrick de Saint-Exupéry (*Le Figaro* international reporter) told her, "You shouldn't
analyze each article separately, but as a set of papers." "In their view," Boudana writes, "each
article only represents a piece of the puzzle. For instance, Ourdan argues that no article can
pretend to completeness, each one offers an angle . . . completeness should emerge from a corpus
of texts considered as a whole."

[41] Jean-Jacques Rouche interview (2008).

[42] These conclusions are based on my own observations and interviews at *Le Monde* and the *New
York Times*. I observed similar nation-specific tendencies at *Libération*, the *Los Angeles Times*,
and the *Orange County Register*. See also Padioleau (1985, 215), Diamond (1994), Clayman and
Reisner (1998), Hubé (2004), Sedel (2004), and Saïtta (2005).

[43] Bill Keller, executive editor of the *New York Times*, remarks at Columbia School of Journalism
event on Wiki-leaks, February 3, 2011. Author notes.

FIGURE 2.3. The French "debate ensemble" form of news. (A) *Libération*'s "*événement*" of May 18, 2006 focuses on Interior Minister Nicolas Sarkozy's visit to Africa shortly after passage of his proposed legislation to make it easier for highly skilled immigrants (*immigration choisie*) to come to France. The first two inside pages include breaking news, analyses, background context, national and international "reactions," and the official editorial. (Main articles are by Vanessa Schneider and Catherine Coroller and editorial is by Pierre Haski; reproduced with permission of *Libération*.)

LIBÉRATION
JEUDI 18 MAI 2006

3

«Cette notion d'immigration choisie, cet apartheid migratoire renvoient au temps des esclaves où les marchands choisissaient les plus vigoureux, ceux qui avaient les meilleures dents, pour les faire venir en Occident.»
Alpha Blondy, chanteur ivoirien et messager pour la paix de l'ONU, interrogé dimanche par l'AFP

«Je dépense de l'argent pour former les jeunes. Je ne connais pas un pays au monde qui fasse autant de sacrifices pour l'éducation. Et, pendant ce temps-là, tous ceux qui terminent leurs études, on va les prendre ici en France. Je ne suis pas d'accord.»
Le président sénégalais, Abdoulaye Wade, mardi sur RTL

Cartes de séjour
La loi Sarkozy prévoit la création de «cartes compétences et talents» de trois ans renouvelables pour attirer les étrangers étudiants, valables quatre ans pour les plus diplômés. Pour les autres migrants, trois cartes de séjour temporaires sont créées: «salarié», «temporaire» et «saisonnier».

DÉBARQUE EN AFRIQUE

editorial
Par PIERRE HASKI

L'immigration «choisie» entérinée par les députés
PCF et PS ont voté contre le texte, la moitié de l'UDF s'est abstenue.

Les députés ont adopté hier par 367 voix contre 164 le projet de loi Sarkozy sur l'immigration. L'UMP a voté pour. Le PC et le PS contre. L'UDF était, sur ce sujet, aussi divisée que la veille lors du vote de la motion de censure socialiste: 13 pour et 13 abstentions dont François Bayrou. Chaque groupe avait auparavant rappelé ses positions sur un texte censé permettre à la France de passer d'une immigration «subie» à une immigration «choisie». Serge Blisko (PS, Paris) l'a jugé «inacceptable et intolérable», Patrick Braouezec (PCF, Seine-Saint-Denis) «inacceptable et inefficace».

A quelques heures du départ de Sarkozy pour l'Afrique, les porte-parole de chaque groupe ont également commenté la création de la carte Compétences et talents. Ce nouveau titre de séjour, d'une durée de trois ans, est censé attirer vers la France l'élite des pays en voie de développement. Serge Blisko (PS, Paris) et Nicolas Perruchot (UDF, Loir-et-Cher) ont parlé tous deux de «pillage des cerveaux». «Extraire les gens – médecins, ingénieurs, informaticiens – de leur pays d'origine sans contrepartie, c'est l'inverse du codéveloppement», a déclaré Blisko. Cet-

te politique «ne correspond pas à la tradition républicaine de notre pays», a affirmé Perruchot qui a toutefois voté ce projet de loi. Patrick Braouezec a assuré que l'immigration choisie aurait des «conséquences dramatiques pour les hommes, les femmes et les États» du Sud.
CATHERINE COROLLER

Une aide au retour peu prisée
Giscard avait inventé le «million» (d'anciens francs) pour inciter les immigrés à rentrer dans leur pays d'origine. Sans succès. Trente ans plus tard, Sarkozy croit dur comme fer à l'aide au retour. Lors d'un premier voyage au Mali, en février 2003, il avait doublé le montant de l'incitation (porté à 7 000 euros), destinée aux Maliens désirant rentrer au pays pour investir. En 2002, année de lancement, et 2003, seuls 10 à 20 retours avaient été enregistrés. «Aujourd'hui, nous sommes presque à 150 par an», se félicite un conseiller du ministre de l'Intérieur. Et d'égrener les projets, dont «80% sont viables»: 60 taxis à Bamako, une boulangerie, une buvette, une épicerie, etc. Nicolas Sarkozy, qui devait poser pour une photo avec les taxis payés par la France, visitera finalement une crèche.
C.A.

Un ministre indésirable en Afrique
Les Africains reprochent à Sarkozy ses positions extrémistes.

«Un racisme dans nos mœurs.» La manchette du quotidien privé malien, Infomatin, donne la mesure de la popularité de Nicolas Sarkozy en Afrique en général et au Mali en particulier. Ce dernier pays, qui compte l'une des plus importantes diasporas africaines en France, est évidemment très sensible au durcissement de la nouvelle loi sur l'immigration, en matière de mariages mixtes et de regroupement familial.

Au Bénin non plus, deuxième étape de sa minitournée, Sarkozy n'a pas la cote. Pour Roger Gbégnonvi, de l'ONG Transparency international-Bénin, «il ne saurait être le bienvenu au Bénin et nulle part ailleurs en Afrique». Sarkozy, poursuit-il, «aurait dû prendre le temps de se refaire une virginité vis-à-vis de nous». Les propos musclés sur le «Kärcher» et la crise de

banlieues ont laissé des traces. Tous les Africains ont suivi les émeutes de novembre à la télé ou la radio. Les débats sur le «rôle positif» de la colonisation ont parachevé le tableau. Le chanteur ivoirien Alpha Blondy, connu pour une bonne partie de sa carrière en France, est évidemment dans le camp de ceux qui lui sont hostiles.

Les propos musclés de Nicolas Sarkozy sur le «Kärcher» et la crise des banlieues en novembre ont laissé des traces.

«Monsieur Sarkozy joue les Le Pen.»
Pourtant, le candidat déclaré à la présidentielle avait une carte à jouer auprès des Africains. Douze ans de Chiraquie et le silence de la gauche lui ont valu un boulevard. Les maladresses françaises en Côte-d'Ivoire, le soutien à une succession plus que contes-

table au Togo, et l'aide militaire apportée sans contrepartie au président tchadien Idriss Déby ont découragé bien des Africains. La «rupture» préconisée par Sarkozy est attendue avec impatience par beaucoup en Afrique.

Dans ce contexte actuel, le discours que doit prononcer le patron de l'UMP sur la politique africaine de la France, ce, dans lequel il précédais «la fin du paternalisme», et des relations «adultes» entre Paris et ses partenaires africains, risque fort d'être perçu comme un nouveau lâchage. Valère, un étudiant malien interrogé par l'AFP, résumait hier avec fatalisme: «C'est sûr que quand Sarkozy deviendra président de la République, tout dépendra du pour nous autres Africains.»
C.A.

et les rebondissements quotidiens dans l'affaire Clearstream, le ministre ne souhaitait pas s'absenter trop longtemps de Paris», dit un proche. Il a aussi failli renoncer au Gabon, envisagé un temps, à cause du «veto» de Chirac, qui considère ce pays comme un «fief», selon l'entourage du chef de l'UMP. Outre la restauration de son image écornée par sa politique en matière d'immigration, le numéro 2 du gouvernement se fixe pour objectif avec ce voyage de jeter les bases d'une nouvelle politique à l'égard de l'Afrique. Il a ainsi l'intention de proclamer

la «fin du paternalisme». «La France doit garder des relations privilégiées avec notamment l'Afrique francophone, mais elles doivent évoluer vers un véritable partenariat. On doit définitivement considérer les pays africains comme des pays majeurs», explique son directeur de cabinet. En matière d'aide au développement, Sarkozy devait se prononcer en faveur de l'augmentation des investissements productifs et va appeler à ne pas se contenter d'une augmentation en volume des aides, comme le proclame Chirac.
VANESSA SCHNEIDER

Belles paroles
S'il est un domaine où le terme de «rupture» cher à Nicolas Sarkozy pourrait s'appliquer avec bonheur, c'est bien celui de la politique africaine. Jacques Chirac incarne le souhait un mode de relation avec le continent noir instauré par le général de Gaulle dès la décolonisation du début des années 60, un modèle suivi, à quelques nuances près, par tous les présidents de la Ve République, de droite comme de gauche. Un mélange pas toujours subtil de paternalisme et de coups fourrés, d'aide au développement et d'exploitation éhontée. Le président de l'UMP a pour lui d'appartenir à une nouvelle génération politique qui pourrait se dégager de la rhétorique de l'amitié franco-africaine, qui somme creux depuis bien longtemps. Mais il a cru bon de s'envoler pour Bamako le jour où est adoptée à Paris sa loi contestable sur l'immigration «choisie», prise comme une claque par de nombreux Africains. C'est, au mieux, une maladresse déconcertante; au pire, un signe d'arrogance peu rassurant. De quoi rendre inaudible son discours annoncé sur sa «nouvelle politique africaine»: sur ce plan, les Africains sont peu de belles paroles rarement suivies d'effets. Que la politique africaine de la France soit en mal de redéfinition est clair qu'une évidence, et il est urgent d'y procéder avant que le désamour ne se transforme en rejet pur et simple. Lionel Jospin avait défini un slogan fort vis-à-vis de l'Afrique: «Ni ingérence, ni indifférence.» Mais en pleine cohabitation avec Jacques Chirac, il ne s'était pas battu pour le mettre en œuvre. Une «autre» politique africaine reste à inventer, et surtout à appliquer: en enfourchant le cheval de bataille de la République pour pêcher des voix à l'extrême droite, Sarkozy n'en prend toutefois pas le chemin.

FIGURE 2.3.(A) (cont.)

Although differences in journalistic formats seem to be strongly related to national traditions, they are not entirely limited to them. As we will see, French and U.S. news organizations with similar types of audiences and relations to the civic and market poles may sometimes adopt similar journalistic approaches. Thus, the *Christian Science Monitor* and PBS, less constrained by market pressures than other U.S. media, are closer in some ways to the "French" model.

FIGURE 2.3. (B) *Le Monde*'s "dossier" on January 21, 2006 examines France's colonial history and its links to contemporary immigration politics. In addition to contextual analyses written by *Le Monde* journalists (Gérard Courtois, above), the dossier includes a lengthy interview by Philippe Bernard with immigration scholar Emmanuelle Saada. (Reproduced with permission of *Le Monde*.)

VIII

Le Monde
Samedi 21 janvier 2006

LES BLESSURES DE LA COLONISATION

PARCOURS

EMMANUELLE SAADA a 36 ans. Historienne et sociologue, elle travaille sur les thèmes de la colonisation, l'immigration et l'identité.

Maître de conférences à l'Ecole des hautes études en sciences sociales, elle enseigne aussi à la New York University.

Elle publie en 2006 *Les Enfants de la colonie. Les métis de l'Empire français entre sujétion et citoyenneté* (La Découverte).

EMMANUELLE SAADA « Il faut distinguer travail historique et positions militantes »

Pourquoi, après une longue période de refoulement de l'histoire coloniale, la société française relance-t-elle la polémique ?

Ce passé resurgit sous la forme d'une revendication de mémoire, mais celle-ci a été précédée par un renouveau de la recherche. Depuis dix ans, de nombreuses publications ont mis en avant les aspects sociaux et culturels du fait colonial, là où dominait le récit politique et militaire de l'histoire dite « traditionnelle ».

Sous la pression de l'actualité, l'histoire de l'immigration a émergé dans les années 1980 et c'est d'abord développée sans intégrer le fait colonial. A cette époque, les historiens refusaient de distinguer l'immigration postcoloniale pour ne pas tomber dans le piège de l'extrême droite qui justifiait l'exclusion des immigrés issus des anciennes colonies par le caractère irréductible de leurs différences raciale et religieuse.

Par ailleurs, l'analyse a pâti des changements de l'histoire coloniale : on est passé de l'hagiographie du début du XXe siècle, à un récit dénonciateur au moment de la décolonisation. Puis on a fait l'histoire des grandes cultures du monde, en longue durée. C'est une avancée essentielle, mais qui a relégué le rapport colonial au statut d'épiphénomène.

Pourquoi surgit-il maintenant ?

Les enfants ou petite-enfants d'immigrés coloniaux ou postcoloniaux cherchent à se réapproprier une histoire que leurs parents ont tuée, vivant souvent leur immigration comme une trahison.

Ces silences se dissipent avec l'émergence d'une génération nouvelle qui arrive à maturité politique avec un bagage culturel important : cette génération accède à l'université avec de grandes interrogations. Elle est en train de produire de jeunes chercheurs brillants sur ces questions. Mais cette volonté de savoir ne distingue pas toujours travail historique et positions militantes.

Considérez-vous la pétition des « indigènes de la République » comme une manifestation de cette confusion ?

Certes, un programme antiuniversaliste l'histoire coloniale en utilisant des raccourcis contestables, par exemple en assimilant le statut des « sujets indigènes » à celui des immigrés et de leurs descendants dans la France d'aujourd'hui. Mais sans céder sur les faits historiques, il faut reconnaître que cette initiative a le mérite d'ouvrir un débat politique sur les implications actuelles du passé colonial de la France. Elle fait pendant aux pressions exercées par le lobby des nostalgiques de la colonisation qui a réussi à faire voter la loi du 23 février 2005.

Comment expliquer la polémique suscitée par ce texte qui entend consacrer dans les programmes scolaires « le rôle positif de la présence française outre-mer » ?

Le vote de cet article révèle la puissance des groupes militants liés à l'extrême droite qui se posent en représentants des rapatriés. Mais la polémique qui a suivi peut faire avancer le débat plus général sur les rapports entre histoire et mémoire. La mobilisation des historiens, l'intervention de Jacques Chirac, vont dans ce sens.

Comment les professionnels de l'histoire peuvent-ils participer à ce débat sur enjeux très actuels ?

Les historiens n'ont pas toujours contribué à dissiper les malentendus. Une remise en cause de la capacité de l'histoire à tenir un discours vrai. Scientifiquement très utiles, ces critiques ont aussi ouvert la voie aux prises de position militantes : si l'histoire n'est qu'un récit parmi d'autres, pourquoi ne pas plutôt mettre en avant les mémoires ? Comme de nombreux collègues, je crois que l'on doit défendre l'autonomie de l'histoire, qui est un métier, avec ses règles à la fois scientifiques et déontologiques : si elle ne produit pas de vérité absolue, elle possède des procédures d'objectivation contre les distorsions de la mémoire : critique des sources, lecture croisée des documents...

Partagez-vous la revendication de vos collègues qui militent pour l'abrogation des lois en référant à l'histoire ?

Je suis opposée à la revendication d'une telle « libération » par l'histoire : la suppression des lois Taubira et Gays-

La perception positive des Asiatiques vient aussi du fait qu'ils ont été accueillis comme de « bons » immigrés

sot et celle de 2005. On ne peut pas mettre tous les discours sur le même plan : fliquement très utiles, le traite des Noirs, le génocide des juifs et la souffrance des rapatriés d'Algérie. L'historien peut dire que ce n'est pas la même chose !

Que vous révèlent les recherches récentes sur le colonialisme « républicain » français ?

La réflexion sur les rapports entre la République et le colonialisme permet de remettre en cause l'existence d'un « modèle républicain » unique, idée très en vogue depuis les années 1980. Le prétendu modèle a produit deux interprétations contradictoires : pour certains, il aurait été en contradiction avec la réalité coloniale ; d'autres affirment au contraire que la « mission civilisatrice » accomplie dans les colonies fournit la preuve de la solidité du modèle.

D'ailleurs, où chercher LE modèle républicain ? Dans l'abolition de l'esclavage par la IIe République, ou, dans la répression féroce des indigènes organisée par la IIIe ? Dans l'idéal d'assimilation prôné au début du XIXe siècle au nom de l'universalisme, ou dans son abandon à la fin du même siècle sous l'influence du racisme évolutionniste ?

En réalité, le mode de gouvernement colonial a beaucoup varié selon les lieux et les époques, et l'idée d'un « empire » n'est apparue que dans les années 1930, peu avant son effondrement.

Que reste-t-il dans la France actuelle des rapports de domination qui prévalaient dans l'Empire français ?

Institutionnellement, ce grand-chose : le statut spécifique des immigrés algériens a pratiquement disparu. Ce qui subsiste est plus diffus. D'une part, c'est la façon de penser l'appartenance nationale et donc l'altérité. Ainsi la notion d'assimilation forgée dans le rapport colonial reste-t-elle une condition de la naturalisation des étrangers.

C'est ainsi un lien subjectif fait par les acteurs eux-mêmes. Les anciens colonisés savent qu'ils ont été dépossédés, constamment humiliés, et ils considèrent leur immigration comme le prolongement de cette dépossession. Leurs enfants et petits-enfants se heurtent souvent à un soupçon quant à leur pleine appartenance à la nation. Que les violences urbaines de

novembre aient été interprétées comme un « problème de l'immigration » est à cet égard révélateur, comme l'a été la loi sur le foulard à l'école. Du temps des colonies déjà, on excluait les musulmans de l'espace public au nom de leur incapacité à distinguer religion et politique.

Certains descendants de colonisés dénoncent une perpétuation du rapport colonial. Ce parallèle vous semble-t-il recevable ?

Mon métier ne consiste pas à juger du bon usage des mémoires. Mais sur le plan de l'histoire, la réponse est négative : les indigènes étaient soumis à un statut discriminatoire, le code de l'indigénat, inscrit dans le droit, alors qu'aujourd'hui, c'est la lutte contre la discrimination et le racisme qui est la loi. Et c'est bien ce cadre juridique qui rend possibles les revendications. Par ailleurs, ramener tout à la colonisation risque de rendre invisibles les enjeux politiques et sociaux fondamentaux, par exemple le problème des inégalités ou celui du maintien de l'Etat dans les banlieues.

En quoi le petit-fils d'un immigré est-il plus lourdement handicapé que celui d'un ouvrier français ?

Il me semble assez illusoire d'établir un palmarès en la matière... Mais on peut souligner que certains handicaps collectifs d'origine coloniale se reproduisent dans l'immigration. Les grands-parents ont été spoliés et maintenus dans l'ignorance. On a fait venir les parents pour travailler dans la grande industrie et on les a logés dans des bidonvilles. Ils ont vécu dans le « temporaire qui dure » et ont eu bien du mal à construire leur histoire familiale dans une France qui leur enjoignait de s'intégrer tout en menaçant longtemps de les expulser. La différence est là : dans ce constant déni d'appartenance.

Les Asiatiques, présentés comme des modèles d'intégration, ne constituent-ils pas l'une des stigmatisation spécifique aux populations issues des ex-colonies ?

Cette contradiction apparente correspond à la réactivation de modèles coloniaux et notamment de l'échelle d'évolution raciste de la fin du XIXe siècle : au sommet se trouvaient les Européens et au plus bas les Kanaks. Entre les deux, les « barbares » algériens. Mais les Asiatiques suivaient près de près les Européens : ils étaient considérés comme les héritiers d'une noble civilisation. La perception positive des Asiatiques vient aussi du fait qu'ils ont été accueillis comme de « bons » immigrés : réfugiés, anticommunistes et souvent catholiques.

La colonisation a-t-elle généré une « dette » des anciennes puissances impériales ?

S'il existe une dette, elle est intellectuelle. Nous nous devons de mieux comprendre ce que le rapport colonial et de faire connaître nos résultats à celles et ceux dont l'histoire personnelle et familiale a été marquée par la colonisation.

PROPOS RECUEILLIS PAR PHILIPPE BERNARD

Une foule manifeste sa joie en brandissant des drapeaux algériens le 3 juillet 1962 dans le quartier européen d'Alger, devant la grande poste. C'est ce jour-là que, au terme du processus des accords d'Evian, la France reconnaît l'indépendance de l'Algérie. AFP

FIGURE 2.3.(B) (cont.)

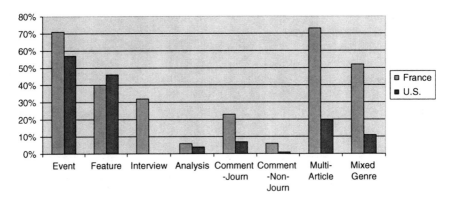

FIGURE 2.4. French and U.S. journalistic genres (fourteen-newspaper sample, 2002–2006). Percentages are of page-one immigration news packages (France $n = 379$; U.S. $n = 471$); because packages sometimes include multiple genres, the sum of genre percentages exceeds 100 percent.

Conversely, the major French and U.S. national television news programs oriented toward comparably large omnibus audiences are similarly narrative-driven (although the precise shape of these narratives differs). Such findings remind us once again that cross-national differences often tend to be of degree, not basic type (Lamont and Thévenot 2000; Lemieux 2004).

At least for newspapers, however, cross-national differences in news format tend to be substantial and consistent. As Figure 2.4 shows, 73 percent of French immigration news content in this study consists of multiarticle ensembles versus just 20 percent of U.S. news.[44] Fifty-two percent of the sampled French daily news content incorporates genres that go beyond factual information. Only 11 percent of the U.S. sample offers noninformational as well as informational genres.

Event news articles are more common in French coverage, whereas feature (background, profile, or other non-timely) articles are more common in U.S. coverage. However, most of the French event news is joined together with other genres: just under one-third (31 percent) of French daily coverage consisted of *only* event articles, whereas almost one-half (47 percent) of U.S. daily coverage did (figures not shown in tables).

News analyses (written by journalists) appeared with roughly equal frequency in the French (6 percent) and U.S. (4 percent) coverage. Demonstrating the ongoing mixing of news and opinion in the French press, journalist-authored

[44] All French newspapers are substantially more likely than their U.S. counterparts to offer multi-article and multigenre page-one coverage, with the partial exception of the financial newspaper *Les Echos*, which is also distinct but much closer to the American pattern. Although this sample concerns only immigration news, a quick perusal of any week's worth of French newspapers would illustrate that this format is used for all types of news.

commentaries – in the form of unsigned editorials or signed essays – appeared in 23 percent of the French sample versus 7 percent in the United States. Non–journalist authored commentaries appeared in about 6 percent of French coverage versus slightly less than 1 percent in the United States. Although op-ed articles written by nonjournalists are, of course, a staple of U.S. editorial pages, this finding emphasizes that they only rarely appear alongside related breaking news or even in the same day's issue, as is more often the case in France.

Perhaps the greatest genre difference between the French and U.S. press, however, is the frequent appearance of interview transcripts in the former and their almost complete absence in the latter.[45] The interview as a reporting technique is an American "invention" that was originally exported to France (Schudson 1995; Chalaby 1996). Interviews published in their entirety have now become a staple of French newspapers.[46] On average, interviews appeared in 32 percent of French news packages in the 2002–2006 newspaper sample; only in the business newspaper *Les Echos* did they appear in less than 20 percent of packages (figures not shown in tables). Interviews are common in French newspapers, of course, not only for beneficent democratic reasons. They are also a relatively cheap form of news gathering. Moreover, politicians and other French elites, who have grown accustomed to articulating their views at length via such formats – even editing their remarks prior to publication, which many journalists still allow them to do – often agree to be interviewed only on condition that the interview will be published as a transcript. However, Table 2.1 clearly shows that French interview transcripts are not simply "soapboxes" for already powerful political elites. At *Libération* and *Le Monde*, academics and other experts were the most frequently interviewed persons; at *L'Humanité* and *La Croix*, other civil society actors were most prominent; and at *Le Parisien*, unaffiliated individuals were highlighted. Only at *Le Figaro* were politicians the dominant interviewee group.

These examples show that the multigenre format is used to varying degrees by all of the French national newspapers (the *événement* at *L'Humanité*, *le fait du jour* [fact of the day] at *Le Parisien*, etc.) (Guisnel 2003; Hubé and Kaciaf 2006; Hubé 2008).[47] Eugénie Saïtta's (2005, 198–201) recent updating of Padioleau's

---

[45] Not a single interview transcript appeared in the U.S. immigration news samples drawn for this study. I have since discovered, on a nonsystematic basis, occasional transcripts of interviews in the *Los Angeles Times* on its op-ed, general news, and business pages (including, on one occasion, a transcript of an interview with the head of the U.S. immigration service), as well as in other newspapers, but the practice is clearly less common than in France.

[46] The importance of interviews at both national and regional newspapers and their editing procedures were explained to me by Jean-Jacques Rouche of *La Dépêche du Midi* (interview 2008) and Elise Vincent of *Le Monde* (interview 2012). See also Lemieux (2000).

[47] *Le Monde*'s 1995 and 2002 graphic redesigns were not only influenced by *Libération* but carried out by advisors who were former *Libération* editors (Jean-François Fogel interview 2002; see also Poulet 2003, 129–132).

TABLE 2.1. *Types of Interviewees in Individual French Newspapers*

Media Outlet (N interviews)	% Political Officials	% Academic/ Other Experts	% Other Civil Society	% Unaffiliated Individuals	% Business	% Foreign
L'Humanité (46)	21.7	13.0	47.8	10.9	0.0	6.5
La Croix (40)	30.0	7.5	60.0	0.0	0.0	2.5
Libération (22)	22.7	45.5	22.7	4.5	0.0	4.5
Le Monde (14)	28.6	57.1	7.1	0.0	0.0	7.1
Le Figaro (17)	41.2	29.4	11.8	5.9	0.0	11.8
Les Echos (3)	0.0	66.7	0.0	0.0	33.3	0.0
*Le Parisien** (77, 43)	19.5 (34.9)	10.4 (18.6)	14.3 (25.6)	53.2 (16.3)	1.3 (2.3)	1.3 (2.3)

From 2002–2006 sample. * Many of *Le Parisien*'s interviews take the form of extended quotes (50–60 words) from ordinary citizens or immigrants appearing in the frequent "Voix Express" rubric. Figures appearing in parentheses (*n* = 43) exclude Voix Express.

Le Monde study showed that a thematic, multigenre approach to the news had only strengthened over the past twenty years: her analysis of *Le Monde*'s stylebook found thirty-six distinct genres of articles.

As with narrative, the "topic of the day" approach should be understood as a particular hybrid of commercial and civic logics inside the French journalistic field. In the same way that the U.S. narrative format can vary, *événement* can likewise be more or less saturated with dramatic images and large headlines, more or less pluralist and pedagogical. Its precise form can vary across media outlets and over time.

Événement's demand for something to fill up three to five pages regardless of the day's events surely increases the pressures for sensationalism. As *Le Monde* immigration reporter Philippe Bernard commented on the format: "Sometimes it means that you have to pump up the news, overdo it."[48] Normatively, however, passion and "procedural" reason are not necessarily opposed (Hallin 1994, 9). It is important to distinguish between sensationalism that is a- or antipolitical (Freiberg 1981), as in the celebrity- or crime-driven scandal coverage of tabloids such as the *New York Post* or the (London) *Sun*, and a sensationalism that is politically driven and motivated. A certain amount of *political* sensationalism

---

[48] "Il faut quelque fois être obligé de gonfler ses sujets, d'en rajouter": from Philippe Bernard interview with Philippe Juhem, 1996, Paris (transcript shared with the author). Other French journalists and scholars have criticized the headline-heavy *événement* format for its "theatrical staging" of the news (Poulet 2003, 134–137; Saïtta 2005, 220).

may be necessary to make people care enough to get involved and to engage in reasoned debate; this is the argument in favor of a "participatory liberal" model of democracy (see Ferree et al. 2002).

Moreover, with its multiple points of entry, the French multigenre format ensures a certain level of in-depth analysis and reflection. Political communication scholar Regina Lawrence (2000) has shown how breaking "events" provide potential openings to more wide-ranging discussions of social issues. The French *événement* format seems uniquely equipped to develop this potential. It provides a way to transform *fait divers* (literally, diverse facts, but also a label that connotes sensationalistic crime and disaster news) into *faits de société* (literally, social facts, connoting a more thematic, contextual orientation) (M'Sili 2000). For example, in the wake of a recent party polemic about the "problem" of the replacement of traditional French butchers with Islamic halal butchers in the Paris region, *Le Monde*'s Elise Vincent sought to bring the debate down to earth with a feature about a local butcher shop that had recently made such a transition. The 731-word profile, substantially shorter than most page-one U.S. articles, made a few references to larger trends but was mostly a colorful, highly localized portrait. To provide thematic contextualization, Vincent conducted and published in full an interview with demographer Patrick Simon that ran alongside the feature article.[49]

As will become evident in the next chapter, U.S. narrative journalism also often aspires to integrate the thematic (historical/structural context) with the episodic (accounts of particular actions by individuals, prominent and not-so-prominent), to use the terminology developed by political scientist Shanto Iyengar (1991, 14). French-American differences thus seem in part to be about the location of episodic-thematic mixing: in the United States, it mostly occurs within articles; in France, it mostly occurs across articles on the same or adjacent pages.[50] As I will show, however, the formal demands of narrative often

[49] See Elise Vincent, "Yves Béguin et Lahcen Hakki, un passage de témoin en douceur dans la boucherie: A Pantin, le dernier boucher 'traditionnel' a cédé son pas de porte à un artisan 'halal'"; Transcript of interview with Patrick Simon by Elise Vincent ("Une forme d'intégration locale assez réussie"), March 6, 2012, p. 12. An English-language translation of Vincent's article appeared online in the London *Guardian* on March 13, 2012: http://www.guardian.co.uk/world/2012/mar/06/le-medi-bospolder-housing-multiculturalism. In line with the typical French journalistic understanding of balance as occurring among articles, Vincent lamented the fact that the interview with Simon did not appear alongside the profile in this or other online appearances (Elise Vincent interview 2012).

[50] On the other hand, the mixing of information with overt interpretation (assessments of significance or motives) and opinion (judgments of factual accuracy or optimal policy) inside news articles is more common in French newspapers (Benson and Hallin 2007). The lack of commentary within news articles may even be seen as an ethical lapse, especially in regard to news about political organizations viewed as extreme. Explaining why he found a certain article about the far right National Front "monstrous," veteran *Libération* political journalist Gilles Bresson said: "There was practically no commentary! One can always include at least a little irony ..." (interview 1998).

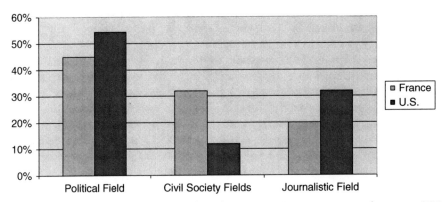

FIGURE 2.5. Field generation of French and U.S. news. Percentages are of page-one/TV evening news immigration news packages from 1973–2006 core sample of newspaper and TV outlets (France *n* = 735; U.S. *n* = 765).

privilege the episodic over the thematic, agency over structure. In a trenchant essay on the epistemology of journalism, Elihu Katz (1989) observed that journalists tend to operate according to implicit theories of action and causality – a "voluntaristic theory of action" and an emphasis on singular "events" over long-term process – sharply at odds with the dominant structural/historical thrust of the social sciences. This characterization seems to fit American journalism. However, the French newspaper format – precisely because it is more generous in ceding the stage, so to speak, to nonjournalists – at least has the potential to present fully developed structural epistemologies, not just passing asides.

A final distinction between the French and U.S. journalistic fields lies in how most news is generated (Molotch and Lester 1974), whether from the political field (government and political party actions), civil society fields (protests, conferences, reports by nongovernmental actors), or the journalistic field (journalistic-initiated investigations, features, profiles, and polls). Previous research has shown that the U.S. public sphere is poised between the political field and the journalistic field, with civil society a generally weak driver of discourse and debate (Hallin and Mancini 1984; Ferree et al. 2002). French journalism, in contrast, is much more attuned to civil society–generated news (Benson and Hallin 2007). Figure 2.5 shows that these patterns of news generation hold for French and U.S. immigration coverage as well.

FIELD STRUCTURE

To conclude this mapping of the French and U.S. journalistic fields, I consider elements of field structure in the two countries, specifically, the habitus of the journalists working for and audiences of the major media outlets, as well as the spatial organizational ecology of competition in the field.

Relative to their respective national populations and thus to many of the nonelite sources of information they may come into contact with, U.S. and French journalists are drawn from increasingly elite social and cultural backgrounds – at least as indicated by level of education. Ultimately, "interactions between journalists and their interlocutors are meetings between different habitus and different positions in the field" (Marchetti 2005, 76). Between 1970 and the early 2000s, the college-educated proportion of the total U.S. population rose from 10 percent to 27 percent; during the same period (1971–2002), the proportion of U.S. journalists with a four-year college degree or higher rose from 58 percent to 89 percent (U.S. Census Bureau 2003; Weaver, Beam, Brownlee, Voakes, and Wilhoit 2007, 36–37). Thus, the U.S. percentage point gap between journalists and public rose from 48 points to 62 points. At leading national newspapers, degrees from prestigious private universities are especially common: a study of national reporters based in Washington, D.C. found that more than one-third had degrees from Ivy League or other highly selective universities (Hess 1981; see also Gans 1979 and Diamond 1994). In France, the percentage of journalists with a post-bac[51] university degree increased from 46 percent in 1973 to 69 percent in 1990 (Devillard, Lafosse, Leteinturier, Marhuenda, and Rieffel 1992, 27); a separate study found that the proportion of journalists new to the profession with a post-bac degree increased from 74 percent in 1990 to 82 percent in 1998 (Marchetti and Ruellan 2001, 24). As in the United States, this level of education is far superior to the national average: in 2006, only 32 percent of the national adult population in France had any degree beyond the bac (TNS-SOFRES surveys: see Appendix B). Likewise, journalists working at the major national media based in Paris are far more likely than other French journalists to have degrees from Paris-based universities, highly selective *grandes écoles* such as the Paris Institute for Political Studies (Institut d'Etudes Politiques, "Sciences Po"), or the most prestigious graduate journalism schools such as CFJ-Paris (Center for Journalism Studies) and ESJ-Lille (Graduate School of Journalism) (Rieffel 1984; Devillard et al. 2001; Marchetti and Ruellan 2001, 12).

Analysis of audience demographic composition for comparable national media outlets indicates the social "breadth" of the journalistic field in relation to the larger society of which it is a part. As Table 2.2 shows, using standardized index scores,[52]

---

[51] The "bac" (*baccalauréat*) is a national exam taken upon completion of high school which many French students do not pass and thus represents, on average, a higher level of education than a U.S. high school diploma.

[52] For example, 16 percent of the national adult population in the U.S. and 14 percent in France, respectively, are low income according to their national measurements (see Appendix B). Using these numbers, we can construct comparable indexes of low-income readership for the *Wall Street Journal* (4 percent; 4/16 = 25 percent or 25 index score) and its French equivalent *Les Echos* (7 percent; 7/14 = 50 percent or 50 index score). Thus, index scores below 100 indicate underrepresentation of a demographic subset and scores above 100 indicate overrepresentation.

both the French and U.S. national newspaper journalistic subfields tend to be produced for audiences that have higher than average education and income levels. Occupational data refer to the percentage of readers who are "professionals" (lawyers, doctors, architects, clergy, professors and teachers, etc.) as a rough indicator of the proportion of cultural versus economic capital. Generally higher index scores for U.S. newspapers may, in part, be due to differences in national construction of census categories (see Appendix B: Sources and Methods). Compared to U.S. national newspapers, the audience composition of French national newspapers is more concentrated at both the top (320 vs. 240 average index scores for high-income readers, respectively) and bottom of the income spectrum (64 vs. 37 index scores for low-income readers). On the other hand, American newspapers have higher concentrations of well-educated, professional audiences than their French counterparts. On average, both French and U.S. newspaper readers are more likely to be older and male than the general population. Hispanics tend to be underrepresented in U.S. newspaper audiences (not shown in table)[53]; ethnic-racial data on audiences are not available for French newspapers, but it is probably safe to assume that a similar pattern holds for North African-origin immigrants in France.

Overall, per capita newspaper sales (not shown in tables) are higher in the United States than in France (264 vs. 190 per thousand, respectively), although this difference should not be exaggerated. Both France and the United States occupy the middle of an international "Western" range, between a high of 720 per thousand for Norway and a low of 78 per thousand for Greece (Hallin and Mancini 2004, 23). When the relative reach of only these leading national newspapers is compared, France and the United States are about the same. Although the 2006 circulations of the leading U.S. national newspapers included in this study are generally much higher than their French counterparts, their average circulation as a percentage of the national population is roughly equal to that of the French newspapers included in this study (both about 0.4 percent, based on census figures of 63 million total French population and 300 million total U.S. population for 2006).

The demographic breadth across these leading newspapers in each country is comparable, with the within-country income gap being greater for the French newspapers and the within-country education and professional status gap greater for American newspapers. Taken in the context of their respective national fields, demographic profiles for each of the newspapers will be helpful

---

[53] Although black and Asian-Pacific Islander audiences were at rough parity with their proportion of the newspaper's adult market population (regional for the *Los Angeles Times* and *Washington Post*, national for the *New York Times*), Hispanics tend to be underrepresented: 21 percent for the LA *Times* (39 percent in the market), 9 percent for the *New York Times* (vs. 13 percent), and 4 percent for the *Washington Post* (vs. 11 percent). Statistics are from 2006 Audit Bureau of Circulation-Scarborough reports (see Appendix B).

TABLE 2.2. *Audience Size and Composition of French and U.S. Newspapers*

Newspapers	Circulation (1,000)	Advertising (% of Revenues)	High Income and Low Income Indexes of Parity (Ratio)	High Income and Low Income Indexes of Parity (CSP+/CSP−)* (Ratio)	Higher Education Index of Parity	Professional Occupation Index of Parity	Age 60+ Index of Parity	Female Index of Parity
L'Humanité	52	11	92:78 (1.2)	129:60 (2.2)	120	126	139	61
La Croix	97	8	321:98 (3.3)	100:22 (4.5)	169	81	216	104
Libération	132	20	328:52 (6.3)	248:47 (5.3)	219	171	50	74
Le Monde	321	45	379:49 (7.7)	204:38 (5.4)	223	130	93	84
Le Figaro	332	70	413:42 (9.8)	140:41 (3.4)	176	95	169	85
Les Echos	117	70 (est.)	590:51 (11.6)	253:44 (5.8)	235	130 (est.)	33	65
Le Parisien	517	28	118:77 (1.5)	117:113 (1.0)	85	105	84	86
France Average	224	36	320:64 (5.0)	170:52 (3.3)	175	120	112	80
High-Low Gap	465	62	498:56	143:91	150	90	183	43
C.S. Monitor	59	12	310:14 (22.1)	–	346	250	176	115
L.A. Times	776	80	206:50 (4.1)	–	179	150	135	88
N.Y. Times	1,087	65	253:38 (6.7)	–	250	193	88	87
Wash. Post	656	61	276:25 (11.0)	–	213	186	106	94
W.S. Journal	2,043	69	290:26 (11.2)	–	261	134	100	67
USA Today	2,270	75	193:41 (4.7)	–	154	113	71	65
Daily News	693	53	149:68 (2.2)	–	95	95	112	87
U.S. Average	1,083	59	240:37 (6.5)	–	214	160	113	86
High-Low-Gap	2,211	68	161:54	–	251	155	105	50
New York Post	704	50 (est.)	184:57 (3.2)	–	128	109	91	80

Index Scores: 100 = national population mean

* CSP⁺ refers roughly to white-collar or white-collar professions whereas CSP⁻ refers to blue-collar or service occupations. These data are presented to facilitate French newspaper comparisons with French television. *Sources:* See Appendix B.

to situate them in the field and to make cross-national comparisons of types of newspapers according to capital composition.

Over the past several decades, audience composition of the leading national newspapers in both countries has become increasingly composed of upper-income groups and decreasingly composed of low-income groups (see Appendix B for information sources). Between 1980 and 1996, the New York metropolitan area audience of the *New York Times* has been increasingly likely to include the relatively wealthy (high-income index rising from 199 to 365) and less likely to reach poor readers (low-income index falling from 52 to 38) (figures not shown in tables). Across this period, the education level of the *Times'* readers remained high (higher education index of 219 in 1980 and 227 in 1996).[54] As the *New York Times* shifted its marketing efforts beginning in the early 1990s to attract a national audience (over half of its print audience today, substantially more of its online audience), this targeting of the wealthy and highly educated has only intensified (Diamond 1994) and is reflected in the audience statistics shown in Table 2.2. Similar trends are evident in France. For instance, working class readers (laborers/craftsmen) of *Le Monde* fell from 14 percent of its total audience in 1973 to 7 percent in 2006. Shortly after its reformulation from a Maoist activist newspaper to a more mainstream media outlet in 1981, *Libération* began to attract more and more high-income executives and managers (*cadres*) (Bourdieu 2000). To be clear, however, the tendency of the leading national newspapers to appeal to relatively high-income, highly educated readers was strong in the 1970s as well as in the 2000s (Freiberg 1981, 242). The change is one of degree rather than fundamental type.

Table 2.3 shows that television news in both countries is, not surprisingly, much more of an omnibus medium than are newspapers. In both France and the United States, low-income audiences are disproportionately likely to watch television news, whereas high-income audiences are less likely than average to watch. As with newspapers, television audiences tend to be older. In both countries, public television (France 2, Arte, PBS) audiences tend to be more elite than audiences for commercial television (TF1, ABC, CBS, NBC). The main differences are that French national television as a whole reaches a broader proportion of the population (about 29 percent of the total national audience versus 20 percent in the United States) and that French television news audiences, both public and private, have a higher proportion of low-income viewers. In terms of education, PBS has by far the most elite audience, with its viewers more than twice as likely as the general population to have a college degree (roughly comparable to the *Washington Post*, the metropolitan newspaper for the nation's capital and its wealthy suburbs). At the same time, PBS's total audience, as a proportion of national population, is

---

[54] For 1980, high income is defined as $50,000 or more and low income is less than $8,000; for 1996, high income is $250,000 or more and low income is less than $15,000. Source: U.S. Audit Bureau of Circulation Reader Profiles.

TABLE 2.3. *Audience Size and Composition of French and U.S. Television News*

Television Channels	High Income and Low Income Indexes of Parity (Ratio)	High Income and Low Income (CSP$^+$/CSP$^-$) Indexes of Parity (Ratio)	Higher Education Index of Parity	Age (60+) Index of Parity	Size of Audience (million)	% of Total Potential Audience
France						
TF1 20 heures (8 p.m. news)	49:138 (0.4)	65:83 (0.8)	88	149	8.2	17.1
France 2 20 heures (8 p.m. news)	88:113 (0.8)	86:60 (1.4)	113	181	5.0	10.4
Arte Info	113:163 (0.7)	67:47 (1.4)	138	218	0.6	1.2
U.S.						
Network evening news: ABC, CBS, NBC	93:103 (0.9)	–	85	146	26.0	18.2
PBS NewsHour	106:95 (1.1)	–	204	232	2.4	1.7

Index Scores: 100 = national population mean
For sources, see Appendix B: Sources and Methods.

more closely comparable to France's tiny Arte channel than to the main French public news channel France 2.

Competition within the Field: Concentration and Distribution

In addition to a hierarchical class space, journalism also exists in geographical space. The French national journalistic field is highly concentrated and centralized. In France, more than 60 percent of all journalists live in the Paris metropolitan region (Ile-de-France) (Devillard et al. 2001, 67). French television is among the most centralized television systems in the world (Paracuellos 1993, 142). France's TF1 evening news alone captures 40 percent of the actual (not potential, as shown in Table 2.3) television audience on any given night, and most of the rest of the news audience is split among the two public channels, France 2 and 3, and, to a lesser extent, the commercial channel M6 (with only news shorts) and Arte (CSA 2000). There are only four local broadcast television channels in all of France (although the France 3 public television channel tailors its local news broadcasts by region); only 15 percent of the French public subscribes to cable television (Benson 2005).

Although there is some market class segmentation, as documented in Table 2.2, many of the French national newspapers compete directly for the same readers and advertisers, particularly in the Paris region. In France, 72 percent of sales are made at kiosks on a daily or weekly basis rather than through subscriptions (and sales can vary significantly from one issue to the next), so newspapers and magazines have a strong incentive to create headlines and to frame the news in ways that will entice readers to buy (Devillard et al. 2001, 28). In contrast, in the United States, the exact opposite situation holds: 81 percent of sales are due to subscriptions, which conceivably lessens incentives to dramatize the news (Newspaper Association of America 2001), although, of course, a different dynamic increasingly prevails on the Internet (Boczkowski 2010).

French and American national journalists tend to perceive their respective competitive environments differently, although there is significant variation within each national field depending on one's position in that field. French journalists at the leading national newspapers and newsmagazines are intensely aware of their cross-town competitors, whose news decisions in turn may have immediate effects on sales or audiences. In the United States, the major national newspapers, particularly the *Washington Post*, the *Los Angeles Times* and the *New York Times* are aware of each other and compete as a "matter of professional pride," but this competition often has "little to do with business."[55] This process is changing as more media move online and are thus better able to compete directly, although it is still the case that most newspapers and television gain the vast majority of their revenues from "offline" distribution.

CONCLUSION

The influence of market logics on journalism has increased in both the United States and France since the early 1980s but, abetted by laissez-faire state policies to a greater extent in the United States, substantially more so for the American news media. French media policies help strengthen civic logics over market logics in shaping journalistic practices. However, the French journalistic field is more highly concentrated – socially, professionally, and economically – thus potentially increasing competitive pressures. For newspapers, narrative is the dominant logic of journalistic practice in the United States, whereas the debate ensemble format dominates in France, but some qualitative characteristics of these formats have varied over time and across types of media outlets. In both

---

[55] Leo Wolinsky interview (1998). Julia Preston (interview 2008), the chief national immigration reporter for the *New York Times*, said she occasionally reads the *Los Angeles Times*, since they have some "terrific" immigration reporters, but that she sees her chief competition as the *Washington Post* (against which the *Times* competes more heavily for readers in the D.C. metropolitan area).

national fields, these symbolically dominant forms are counterbalanced by their opposites: in the United States, narrative is counterbalanced by a debate orientation at outlets such as PBS, and in France, debate is opposed to narrative story-telling on evening television news. Finally, the class composition of audiences of the two national fields is roughly comparable, with both relatively elitist and becoming more so over time. This structural similarity provides some assurance that any national differences in news coverage will *not* be because journalism is being produced for totally different kinds of audiences in the two countries. With this background in mind, I now turn, in Chapters 3 through 5, to a closer look at how and why immigration coverage changed and stayed the same in the United States and France between the 1970s and 2000s.

3

Narrating the Immigrant Experience in the U.S. Media

From Jobs Threat to Humanitarian Suffering

It's self-evident – if you have a large pool of poor workers, that's bound to have a demeaning effect on worker wages.
> – Harry Bernstein, *Los Angeles Times* labor reporter

It's like having these thirsty people fighting among themselves for the little bit of wetness from this petty little plant, and the media come in and cover the people who are thirsting . . . when the guy who stole the water source of the entire oasis took off without even being questioned.
> – Roberto Lovato, director of the Central American Resource Center

Newspapers maybe aren't as good with stories that are very, very high concept . . . To some extent I think we try to tell stories.
> – Patrick McDonnell, *Los Angeles Times* immigration reporter[1]

Between the mid-1970s and mid-2000s, U.S. immigration news coverage decreasingly focused on jobs and the global economy and increasingly focused on racism, the threat to public order, and humanitarian concerns about immigrant suffering. Media attention to fiscal costs of immigration rose in the early 1990s. Across the four decades, the dominant sources or "speakers" cited in the news were government officials and unaffiliated individuals[2] (the proverbial man or woman on the street), with the latter speaker increasing over time. Patterns of coverage were similar for newspapers and television news, with a couple of exceptions: threat frames (especially public order) and unaffiliated

---

[1] All three quotes are from interviews conducted by the author. Positions listed are those relevant to the study and are not current. See Appendix B.
[2] Specific individuals and poll categories (opinions attributed to categories of surveyed individuals) are combined to capture "populist" elements of news coverage. Individuals dominate this combined category and account for the increase over time: across the four decades, mentions of polls are fairly constant (about 3 percent, and during the 1990s and 2000s equally likely to appear in newspapers or television news).

68

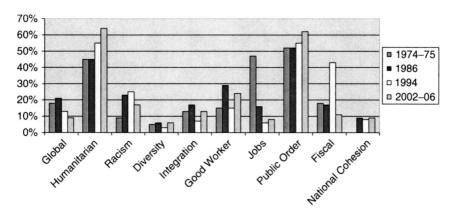

FIGURE 3.1. United States: Immigration frames, 1970s–2000s. Percentages are of news packages mentioning each frame (1974/75 *n* = 75; 1986 *n* = 118; 1994 *n* = 161; 2002–2006 *n* = 411), with core newspaper and television news samples equally weighted. Given that most packages mention multiple frames, the sum of percentages exceeds 100.

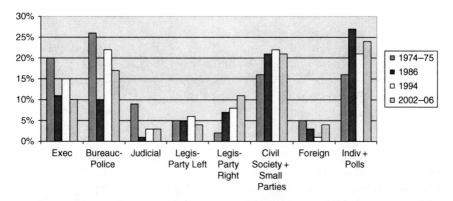

FIGURE 3.2. United States: Types of speakers, 1970s–2000s. Percentages are of total speakers cited (1974/75 *n* = 494; 1986 *n* = 1,070; 1994 *n* = 1,725; 2002–06 *n* = 4,319), with core newspaper and television news samples equally weighted. Because not all speaker types are shown, sum of percentages does not equal 100.

individuals were even more prominent on television. These conclusions are based on a content analysis of news packages starting on page one of the *New York Times, Washington Post,* and *Los Angeles Times* and on the national network evening news programs (ABC, CBS, and NBC) during peak media attention years since immigration (re-)emerged as a central issue of public debate: 1974–1975, 1986, 1994, and 2002–2006 (see Figures 3.1 and 3.2).

These changes in immigration coverage coincided with an increasing neo-liberal restructuring and hypercommercialization of the global and American economies, including the news media. Regulations were relaxed in every sector, encouraging competition and innovation while also reducing most individuals' employment, health, and retirement security (Harvey 2005). During the same period, total immigration (legal and especially illegal) also increased dramatically and the national origins of immigrants also changed, from largely European to mostly central/south American and Asian. The immigration issue became increasingly politicized, at first pitting border patrol officials against Chicano activists; subsequently, membership and funding of both pro- and anti-immigration groups ballooned beginning in the 1980s. Over time, Republicans became more associated with anti-immigration politics than Democrats, although both parties remained divided on the issue (the former split between laissez-faire neo-liberals and social conservatives; the latter divided between civil libertarians and trade union members). These broad societal and political changes surely shaped the public discourse but, as French media sociologists Patrick Champagne and Dominique Marchetti (2005, 121) remind us, such external changes are always "translated" by the journalistic field "into its own terms."

This chapter is about these terms, that is, the concrete ways in which journalists at leading media outlets shaped the news about immigration. In the pages that follow, I argue that three shifting aspects of American journalism – specific forms of the general field features and changes described in the previous chapter – played a crucial role in shaping U.S. immigration coverage. First, the decline of labor reporting and the limited rise of a diversity orientation toward immigration reporting contributed to the decline of the jobs frame and the rise of the racism frame. Second, a substantial habitus gap between elite journalists and immigration restrictionists contributed to lesser and more negative, denigrating coverage of restrictionist groups than to their pro-immigration activist counterparts. However, because of the tendency of news media to index policy coverage to elite political debate, threat frames have been prominent when strategically promoted by centrist political parties or the government. Third, the rise of narrative journalism has contributed to the increasing prominence of the humanitarian frame over global economy and other structural frames.

CLASS VERSUS RACE? LABOR AND LATINO JOURNALISTS FACE OFF

"The reason people [immigrants] come is big business. It's because of the economy, there are work opportunities." This analysis by *Los Angeles Times* assistant metropolitan editor Paul Feldman[3] closely echoes that of one of the leading sociologists of immigration, Princeton's Alejandro Portes. As Portes (1999, 388) emphasizes, immigration's raison d'être is economic, driven by the

---

[3] Paul Feldman interview (1998).

"needs and interests of employers, their bearing on native workers, and the investment plans and consumption patterns of the immigrants themselves." Yet U.S. news coverage of the economics of immigration is sporadic and often superficial or one-sided. The neo-liberal good worker frame is decreasingly counterbalanced by the labor-left jobs frame.

Observing California news media during the late 1970s, British media scholar Jeremy Tunstall and journalist David Walker (1981, 91) were struck by the virtual absence of reporting on the agricultural industry and of farm workers' union activist Cesar Chavez. After Chavez's boycott of the grape growers, they noted, "he and the UFW [United Farm Workers union] have retreated into the shadows, lit only occasionally." Tunstall and Walker also observed that "corporate power is as invisible as the Hispanics." Journalists covering immigration today confirm the ongoing difficulty of gaining access to major employers of immigrants.[4]

Businesses are more often referred to in general than quoted by name; there are occasional references, as a 1986 *Los Angeles Times* article puts it, to "western growers" who "rely heavily on illegal labor at harvest time" and "maintain that domestic labor supplies for the work are inadequate."[5] Shortly after passage of the 1986 Immigration Reform and Control Act (IRCA) legislation providing "sanctions" for employers of undocumented workers, another *Los Angeles Times* article adopted a curious angle on the new legislation. Rather than critically examining the widespread practice of illegal hiring, the article focused on the problems businesses would face because of the new penalties (while incorporating the complementary strange bedfellows frame of racism/xenophobia): "Housecleaners and nannies may be harder to find and more expensive to hire. Building contractors may find themselves overwhelmed with new record-keeping responsibilities. And restaurateurs and others who fear the civil and criminal penalties associated with hiring illegal aliens may decide to stay clear of anyone who looks foreign or speaks with an accent."[6] Only late in the article, and briefly, sandwiched in between the dominant business and immigrant rights perspectives, is another way of looking at the problem presented. Against the common sense view that "there aren't enough Americans willing to do these jobs," an AFL-CIO representative argued: "Bring up the wages and the working conditions – then you'll be able to find people to do the work."

---

[4] At a May 7, 2010, Miami conference on immigration reporting sponsored by the French-American Foundation, Susan Ferriss of the *Sacramento Bee* spoke to me about the difficulty of writing "economic stories": "These are enterprise, not press release stories. Businesses aren't beating down your door to talk to you." Ferriss said that she did have contacts at the Western Growers Association, but "they try to work behind the scene." Similar observations were made to me by *Los Angeles Times* reporters.

[5] Bob Secter, "House Votes Not to Evict Aliens; Approves Ban on Ouster at Federally Run Units," *Los Angeles Times*, June 12, 1986, p. 1.

[6] Maura Dolan and Henry Weinstein, "Labor Shortages, Higher Costs Seen; Business Ponders Effects of New Immigration Law," *Los Angeles Times*, October 18, 1986, p. 1.

New York Times columnist and Nobel Prize-winning economist Paul Krugman made a similar point in a March 2006 column, in the midst of the immigrant protest marches held that spring: "I'm instinctively, emotionally pro-immigration. But a review of serious, nonpartisan research reveals some uncomfortable facts about the economics of modern immigration, and immigration from Mexico in particular." Krugman notes that the aggregate economic benefits of immigration are small, while the costs are disproportionately borne by the "worst-off native-born Americans" whose wages would be higher if not for the immigration-induced increased supply of less-skilled laborers from Mexico. "That's why it's intellectually dishonest to say, as President Bush does, that immigrants 'do jobs that Americans will not do.' The willingness of Americans to do a job depends on how much that job pays – and the reason some jobs pay too little to attract native-born Americans is competition from poorly paid immigrants."[7] However well-reasoned Krugman's argument may be, it is rarely heard in the mainstream U.S. media.

It has not always been this way. In the early 1970s, the jobs frame appeared in 47 percent of news packages. By the 2000s, however, this proportion had fallen to just 8 percent. There has also been a related shift in the kinds of sources cited by journalists. During the early 1970s, among nongovernmental speakers, labor unions and immigrant rights groups shared a small portion of the media spotlight. By the 2000s, labor unions had all but disappeared (less than 1 percent of all speakers cited), replaced by a veritable social movements industry of immigrant rights associations (such as the Mexican-American Legal Defense and Educational Fund [MALDEF] and the National Council of La Raza), which constituted almost 10 percent of speaker citations and far outnumbered anti-immigration or restrictionist groups.[8] (See Figure 3.3.) By the 1990s and 2000s, when the jobs frame was mentioned at all, it was usually either by academics (called upon by reporters to debate the pros and cons of immigration's effects on employment and wages) or restrictionist groups (such as the Federation for American Immigration Reform [FAIR]), with the latter's promotion of the jobs frame further serving to marginalize (as discussed below) the frame in mainstream public discourse.[9]

---

[7] Paul Krugman, "North of the Border," *New York Times*, March 27, 2006, p. 19.

[8] This finding accords with a study of immigration coverage in nine English-language California newspapers during 2008 and 2009 by the Tides Center–funded, pro-immigration group Opportunity Agenda (2010), although the gap it found between citations of immigrant advocacy groups (155) and restrictionists (122) was not so wide. Because my research focuses on national newspaper front pages and network evening news, it provides a better measure of relative prominence.

[9] Frames (presence/absence) and speakers (raw number of distinct individuals or groups in a category) were coded separately. In 1974–75, trade union speaker mentions had a .321 ($p < .01$) correlation with the presence of the jobs frame in the core media sample (newspapers and TV combined); by 1994, this correlation had fallen to .186 ($p < .05$), less than that of restrictionist associations, with .209 ($p < .01$). Correlations are not definitive proof (e.g., even if the speaker mentioned the frame, it might have been to refute rather than promote it). When making claims about frame promotion activities, I thus rely not only on frame–speaker correlations but also on qualitative analysis and secondary historical sources.

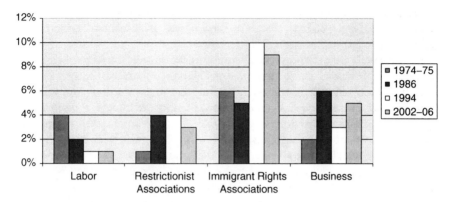

FIGURE 3.3. United States: Nongovernmental speakers, 1970s–2000s. Percentages are of total speakers cited (same as for Figure 3.2), with core newspaper and television news samples equally weighted.

In this shift in news coverage, we can see that a neo-liberal reconfiguration of the economic and political fields had its counterpart in the journalistic field. At the moment when the contemporary immigration debate emerged in the 1970s, labor unions and a Republican administration made common cause against rising illegal immigration. During the early 1970s, Cesar Chavez's UFW held a number of protests against illegal immigration, including setting up picket lines on the border to try to stop Mexican workers from crossing the border to break farmworker strikes.[10]

Around the same time, top officials of the Immigration and Naturalization Service (INS, an agency that, starting in 2003, has been distributed among three agencies inside the massive Department of Homeland Security) began sounding the alarm against illegal immigration. Leonard F. Chapman, the former Marine who was appointed INS Commissioner in 1973 by President Nixon, penned articles for *Reader's Digest* and other publications warning about the dangers of illegal immigration (Gutiérrez 1995, 268, fn21); a year later, Attorney General William Saxbe gave a speech to police officers in Brownsville, Texas, in which he termed illegal immigration a "national crisis." Around this time, a young Frank del Olmo was getting his start covering immigration at the *Los Angeles Times*. Del Olmo recalled to me the aura of power that allowed Chapman, in particular, to set the media agenda[11]: "He was the one that first started using these

[10] In 1974, UFW founder Cesar Chavez often publicly criticized the government immigration agencies for their lax enforcement and argued that "illegal workers from Mexico are a severe problem ... these illegal workers will accept 30 percent to 50 percent less than the Chicanos." See Richard Severo, "The Flight of the Wetbacks," *The New York Times Magazine*, March 10, 1974, p. 80.

[11] Frank del Olmo interview (1998). Susan Jacoby makes a similar argument about Chapman's "public relations campaign" in "Immigration and the News Media: A Journalistic Failure," a 1975 report prepared for the Alicia Patterson Foundation and the Rockefeller Foundation.

metaphors of 'invasion' on our southern border, and when a former comman-
dant of the Marine Corps talks, the media tend to listen and take it rather
literally."

By the mid-1980s, left and right in immigration politics were beginning to
reconfigure. Whereas in the early 1970s, labor unions had opposed illegal
immigration, by the end of the decade ethnic group pressure (including against
Chavez) and the need to find new members led many unions to rethink their
opposition to illegal immigration (Rodríguez 1977, 109; Delgado 1993; Watts
2002). This new pro-immigration "left" – pro-immigrant unions and ethnic
advocacy organizations (La Raza, MALDEF) funded by major foundations,[12]
allied with western farming, restaurant, hotel, and construction industries, and
immigration attorneys – sought to emphasize the positive economic contributions of immigrants (good worker frame) and the dangers of racial discrimination (racism/xenophobia) against Latinos or Asians that would likely result from
any attempted crackdown on illegal immigrants (O'Connor and Epstein 1988;
Skerry 1993).

The new restrictionist right actually emerged out of what was previously
thought of as the left, that is, the population-control wing of the environmental movement, along with some labor unions, African Americans, and
prominent Democratic party leaders, such as former U.S. senators Eugene
McCarthy and Gaylord Nelson and former Colorado governor Richard
Lamm. It eventually allied itself to former border control officials, conservative Protestant denominations and other cultural conservatives, and a variety
of local neighborhood groups. The central organization in this movement,
then as now, was FAIR, which was founded by environmentalists and
population control advocates William C. Paddock (a founder of the
Environmental Fund) and John Tanton (a board member of Zero Population
Growth). From its founding, FAIR's primary goal was to convert illegal
immigration and ultimately immigration itself into a "debatable" issue.[13]
FAIR picked up the jobs frame formerly emphasized by labor unions, while
at the same time supporting local restrictionist efforts mostly concerned with
national cohesion (such as the English-only Proposition 63 in California),
fiscal costs, and public order.

In its news coverage, the journalistic field has not simply and transparently
relayed these events and trends in the political and civil society fields. It helped to
amplify and legitimate them. For instance, the drop in media mentions of the
jobs frame preceded the AFL-CIO's shift in position in 2000 to no longer support

---

[12] MALDEF grew out of 1967 meetings between the long-established League of United Latin-
American Citizens (LULAC), the National Association for the Advancement of Colored People
Legal Defense and Educational Fund (NAACP-LDF), and the Ford Foundation. In 1968, MALDEF
received a $2.2 million start-up grant from Ford (O'Connor and Epstein 1988, 258–259), and it
continues to receive funding from Ford and other major foundations.

[13] Interview with Ira Mehlman, FAIR media outreach director (1995). For histories of FAIR's
origins, see Cooper (1986) and Conniff (1993); see also Tanton (1986).

sanctions against employers of undocumented workers.[14] Even in 1986, when employer sanctions were written into national immigration legislation and many unions continued to raise concerns about undocumented immigrants taking jobs or lowering wages, the jobs frame had already dropped precipitously in U.S. media coverage of immigration. Why? At least two factors specific to the U.S. journalistic field seem relevant. First, inside newsrooms, the journalists most likely to emphasize the jobs frame – labor reporters – became increasingly rare. Second, an organized diversity journalism movement partially shifted coverage to emphasizing problems of racism and discrimination.

Why did the labor beat decline? To begin with, as maximizing profitability became the chief concern of publicly traded news organizations, keeping down labor costs within the industry became a major obsession (Squires 1993), including, in many cases, active efforts to suppress union organizing within newsrooms (Hart 1981). In this climate, labor reporting is obviously in a precarious position, despite the fact that most readers are workers, not employers. William Serrin (1992, 11), the *New York Times'* chief labor reporter during the 1980s, recalls that the *Times* had just two reporters covering labor compared to forty reporters in the business section. Profitability came to be seen as linked to attracting a more targeted, high-income and high-spending audience (Turow 1997; Klinenberg 2005), less likely to be members of or supportive of labor unions. Likewise, as documented in Chapter 2, journalists have been increasingly drawn from elite socioeconomic and educational backgrounds, making them less likely to feel they have anything in common with manual and service workers, and thus increasingly less interested in taking on such a low-prestige assignment.[15] Thus, increasingly, editors are not asking journalists to cover labor, nor are most journalists clamoring for the assignment. The result, predictably, is diminishing labor reporting, except (to a limited extent) in the context of "workplace" reporting, which tends to adopt an implicit pro-management perspective (Tasini 1990; Serrin 1992).

During this period of labor's decline, aided and abetted by the news media, the civil rights movement was in ascendance and gradually extended its influence into newsrooms. Prominent journalists, otherwise apolitical, even today romanticize their involvement with the "Race Beat," as one well-known memoir of reporting on the Civil Rights movement was titled (Roberts and Klibanoff 2006). By the late-1980s, the influence of an increasingly united and visible "diversity journalism" movement was being felt in newsrooms. In 1988,

---

[14] More recently, the AFL-CIO and the break-away "Change to Win" labor federation agreed in 2009 to both support comprehensive immigration reform (including a "path to citizenship" for illegal immigrants) sponsored by leading Democrats. Of course, not all rank-and-file union members support the AFL-CIO's pro-immigration positions.

[15] As Serrin (1992, 15–16) writes: "It used to be, too, that reporters and editors often came from working class backgrounds. Some brought working class concerns to their journalism. No more. Today, many reporters and editors regard unions and the working classes as beneath them ... I know another journalist who was asked if he would like to cover labor. He immediately assumed his career at his newspaper was at an end and quickly found another job at a newsmagazine."

UNITY: Journalists of Color, Inc. brought together associations of black, Hispanic, Asian-American, and Native-American journalists to form one of the largest and fastest-growing professional journalistic groups in the United States (see unityjournalists.org). By the late 1990s, internal diversity committees were being established at national and local newspapers and television channels across the country, specifically to monitor immigration coverage and ensure that adequate attention was being paid to various ethnic "communities."[16]

At least in part for these reasons, immigration, once considered an essential part of the labor beat, was progressively reconceived as a story of race and culture. The case of the *Los Angeles Times* is instructive. The *Los Angeles Times* has had a long tradition of antilabor union politics and, for most of its history, provided only occasional, and usually derogatory, coverage of labor unions (Gottlieb and Wolt 1977; Hart 1981). However, in the wake of the newspaper's early 1960s "professionalization," led by publisher Otis Chandler, the newspaper hired its first full-time labor reporter who was *not* openly hostile to labor unions, Harry Bernstein, who had previously been the labor editor at the *Los Angeles Herald-Examiner*. As INS raids on immigrants increased during the early 1970s, Bernstein wrote many articles emphasizing the negative effects of illegal immigration on American jobs and wages. One article's blunt subhead would seem almost unimaginable today: "Employers Prefer Workers Who Can Be Exploited, Paid Miniscule Wages, U.S., State Officials Say."[17]

Almost from the very beginning, this jobs framing of immigration was contested by an alternative racism framing. At the same time that Harry Bernstein was writing about immigration's negative effects on domestic jobs and wages, Frank del Olmo began paying greater attention to Chicano groups and thus emphasizing the ethnic-racial aspects of immigration.[18] Bernstein and del Olmo clashed. Del Olmo recalls Bernstein as a "knee-jerk" propagandist of the "AFL-CIO line" on immigration who would corner him in the newsroom and "make a fuss" about del Olmo's stories.[19] In 1980, del Olmo began writing an occasional

---

[16] For overviews of the diversity movement inside U.S. newsrooms, see Glasser (1992), Robertson (2000), and Benson (2010a).

[17] Harry Bernstein and Mike Castro, "Bid to Give Illegal Aliens' Jobs to Americans Failing," *Los Angeles Times*, July 3, 1975, p. A1.

[18] According to Fernández and Pedroza's (1981, 13) study of news coverage of Mexican immigration by the *New York Times, Los Angeles Times, Washington Post,* and *Arizona Daily Star* from 1972 to 1978, del Olmo alone wrote more than half of the stories with bylines by reporters with Spanish surnames and about one-fifth of all stories. In many ways, del Olmo was carrying on the tradition established by the L.A. *Times'* legendary first Mexican-American reporter, Rubén Salazar (García 1995).

[19] Frank del Olmo interview (1998). Bernstein's recollections basically line up with those of del Olmo (1998 interview): "[Frank] really was sympathetic to the people coming into this country because they needed jobs, they were hungry. And I agreed with him that they needed jobs, but they were taking jobs away from people not from Mexico [and] other people who were born in this country. He felt that I was too negative about it, that I was immigrant bashing ... I mean we just disagreed fundamentally. I did not think it was immigrant bashing ..."

column on immigration, often focusing on Latino/Hispanic opposition to employer sanctions and other proposed immigration legislation. In 1984, as congressional debate on immigration policy was heating up, Bernstein was provided space on the op-ed page to present an opposing view, yet del Olmo's five columns that year outnumbered Bernstein's two.

Over the past four decades, similar developments have occurred at newsrooms across the United States. In a 2008 interview with *Daily News* columnist Juan Gonzalez on the radio show Democracy Now!, *New York Times* labor reporter Steven Greenhouse suggests that, other than he and Gonzalez, who sometimes writes about labor issues for the *Daily News*, only the *Chicago Tribune* and *Wall Street Journal*, among the largest U.S. newspapers, still have labor reporters.[20] Greenhouse's reporting on labor issues has occasionally touched on immigration, but his immigration-related labor articles rarely make page one. Greenhouse's book about growing inequality in America, *The Big Squeeze*, seems at various points to acknowledge the validity of the jobs frame. He writes in the book that "illegal immigrants have quietly undermined the nation's workplace standards not only because they are often willing to work for less but because they tolerate conditions Americans wouldn't" (Greenhouse 2008, 225). Elsewhere, he quotes an African-American worker at a North Carolina slaughterhouse: "They're dragging down the pay ... It's pure economics. They say Americans don't want to do the job. That ain't exactly true. We don't want to do it for eight dollars. Pay fifteen dollars and we'll do it" (Greenhouse 2008, 233). Yet Greenhouse, who offers policy prescriptions throughout the book, never issues any recommendations based on such linkages between low wages and high levels of illegal immigration.

At the same time, the ultimate "success" of diversity journalism inside American newsrooms and its capacity to frame immigration solely as a problem of racism should not be overstated. Although most immigrants are of Latin-American background, most immigration reporters are not, and this pattern has changed little over the years.[21] After rising sharply from the 1970s to 1990s (from appearing in 9 percent to 25 percent of all media coverage), the racism/xenophobia frame fell slightly to 17 percent in the 2000s. Although it may have played a role in sidelining the jobs frame, the racism frame has not been able to establish itself as *the* dominant immigration frame. The U.S. journalistic field

[20] Democracy Now! Transcript, "The Big Squeeze: Steven Greenhouse on Tough Times for the American Worker," July 29, 2008, interview by Juan Gonzalez.

[21] At the *New York Times*, *Washington Post*, and *Los Angeles Times*, immigration reporters with Spanish-language surnames were 7 percent of the total in 1974–75, 4 percent in 1986, 8 percent in 1994, and 9 percent in 2002–2006. As Mercedes Lynn de Uriarte, University of Texas-Austin journalism professor and former assistant editor of the Opinion Section at the *Los Angeles Times*, cautioned me (personal communication, Palo Alto, March 2010), it is certainly possible that because of mixed (Latino, non-Latino) marriages or the adoption of their husbands' names by some female reporters, surnames could either under- or overestimate the actual number of Latino reporters.

logic of personalized narrative refracts, and potentially counteracts, any ideo-logical tendencies arising from the structural position of the media outlet or the habitus of its reporters and editors. Responding to political scientist Peter Skerry's charge that reporters have adopted a "civil rights mindset" in their immigration coverage,[22] *Los Angeles Times* assistant editor Frank Sotomayor (who was in charge of the newspaper's Pulitzer Prize-winning 1982 series on southern California Latinos) told me: "I don't think anyone thinks in the civil rights context . . . there are certain groups, the ACLU [American Civil Liberties Union], immigrant rights groups [that have such views] and we cover a signifi-cant amount of them . . . [but] that mindset concept seems vague and not applicable to our daily newsroom. . . . We think of individuals, of individual stories."[23]

Market demands inside the journalistic field also manifest themselves in the ongoing search for novelty. Over time, absent any new angle or event, the racism frame loses its capacity to generate journalistic interest. Roberto Lovato, at that time executive director of the Central American Resource Center, recalls the reactions he often received from *Los Angeles Times* reporters during the elec-toral campaign for Proposition 187 (a 1994 California ballet measure to pro-hibit education and other social services for illegal immigrants): "[We'd] say this stuff about [Proposition 187] being immoral, racist and what not, and they'd shut their ears and . . . they'd even say literally do you have anything new? Do you have anything new to say? God, this sounds like the same stuff we always hear from you guys."[24]

IMMIGRANTS AS THREAT

In the 1970s, when the immigration issue first emerged as a politically conten-tious topic, threat frames appeared slightly more often than victim/hero frames. In subsequent decades, the balance see-sawed between the two broad perspec-tives, with victim/hero frames strongly predominating in 1986 and 2002–06 and threat frames drawing even in 1994. On average, across the four decades, combined victim/hero frames made up 55 percent of all frames mentioned versus 45 percent for threat frames. At the same time, it is fair to say that most of the

---

[22] Skerry (1993, 320) writes that media are "willing and largely uncritical conduits for [a racialized framing of immigration] because they are, like generals, fighting the last war: the struggle for black civil rights. Sustained by the moral capital accumulated during the civil rights years . . . journalists, particularly those in the national media, are keen to play this role again. This predisposition, in addition to the time constraints under which they work, means that journalists tend to accept uncritically the racial minority interpretation of the Mexican-American experience offered by advocates and activists."

[23] Frank Sotomayor interview (1998).

[24] Roberto Lovato interview (1998).

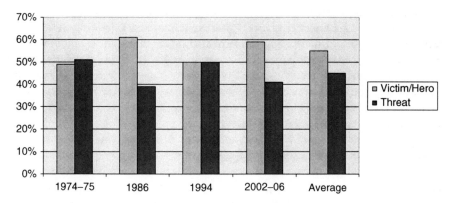

FIGURE 3.4. United States: Victim/hero versus threat frames, 1970s–2000s. Percentages are of total frames mentioned (each coded as presence/absence in a news package; 1974/75 n = 179; 1986 n = 302; 1994 n = 399; 2002–2006 n = 948), with core newspaper and television news samples equally weighted.

news was negative: hero frames alone made up just 17 percent of frames.[25] (See Figure 3.4.)

Much of the critical commentary about anti-immigration discourses in the media refers to "extremist" restrictionist activists. Yet there is a large gap between the media's high attention to threat frames (appearing in almost three-fourths of newspaper and TV news coverage) and the low visibility accorded to restrictionist groups (appearing in less than one-sixth of coverage).[26] Thus, I now want to explore two related puzzles. Why are immigration restrictionist voices not all that prominent in immigration news coverage? And if restrictionist groups cannot account for the appearance of threat frames in immigration coverage, who, or what, can?

Let us first address the question of treatment of the far right and restrictionist associations, such as FAIR, Numbers USA, or more extremist grassroots groups like the Minuteman Patrol. When restrictionist groups do appear in the U.S. media coverage, they are more likely than immigrant rights groups to be

[25] Percentages of victim and hero frames for combined newspaper and television coverage are as follows: 1974–75 (victim 33 percent, hero 16 percent); 1986 (victim 40 percent, hero 21 percent); 1994 (victim 40 percent, hero 10 percent); and 2002–06 (victim 39 percent, hero 20 percent). When a frame appears in a news package, it is coded 1 for presence; no count is made of the number of times the frame reappears (if at all) in the package. Thus, total frames refer to all instances in which a news package mentions a particular frame, summed for all ten frames.

[26] These statistics refer to the presence, respectively, of any threat frame (as opposed to specific frames, shown in Figure 3.1) or any mention of a restrictionist association or activist (as opposed to percentages of all cited speakers, shown in Figure 3.2) in the core sample averaged across the four decades. Restrictionist associations appear in 14 percent of news packages whereas immigrant rights groups appear in 33 percent of packages (statistics not shown in tables or figures).

demonized and discredited, treated as occupants of what Daniel Hallin (1986) has termed the "sphere of deviance." My point is not to defend the restrictionists, any more than I defend the immigrant rights activists. It is simply to note that, despite the fact that opinion surveys consistently show the public genuinely divided over the immigration issue, with many surveys showing a plurality support for restrictionist views,[27] the media attention provided to restrictionist advocates and think tank researchers is lower and generally less positive than that accorded the immigrant advocates.

The most patronizing or alarmist treatment is generally accorded to local, grassroots organizations, such as the sponsors of Proposition 187 (in 1994) in California and Proposition 200 (in 2004) in Arizona, or the Minuteman Project, with its branches in Arizona, Chicago, and elsewhere. Descriptions of the Proposition 187 sponsors were sometimes especially harsh, as in this passage from the *Los Angeles Times*[28]:

When they all met last October 5 [1993] at the members-only Center Club in Costa Mesa, the future leadership of the campaign knew little about each other except that they shared the same contempt for illegal immigrants, a group some scorned in their newsletters for the "stench of urination, defecation, narcotics, savagery and death."

Likewise, this passage from a *New York Times* article about the Minuteman Project expresses a sort of exoticizing disdain. The article begins with a profile of Walter McCarty, an 82-year-old retired Marine sergeant and new Minuteman Project volunteer[29]:

"I hope to go out on patrols at night, find some illegals," said Mr. McCarty, who had his .38-caliber pistol strapped to his leg as he stood outside the citizen patrol's makeshift headquarters here in Tombstone, the town where Wyatt Earp and Doc Holliday engaged

[27] For historical reviews of survey data, see Espenshade and Hempstead (1995), Lapinski et al. (1997), and Fetzer (2000a). As Dionne (2008, 79) summarizes the data, "roughly speaking, a third of the country is broadly pro-immigration; a third is strongly inclined to favor restrictionist measures; and the middle third is ambivalent." A 2004 survey by the Chicago Council on Foreign Relations (cited by Teitelbaum 2006) showed a major gap between elite opinion (drawn from a subsample of political, business, university, and other leaders) and broad public opinion: whereas 33 percent of the elites favored increased legal immigration, only 11 percent of the public did; and whereas only 10 percent of the elites wanted to decrease legal immigration, 54 percent of the public favored such action.

[28] See Gebe Martinez and Doreen Carvajal, "Prop. 187 Creators Come under Closer Scrutiny: From Secret Location, Veterans and Novices Lead the Campaign against Illegal Immigration," *Los Angeles Times*, September 4, 1994, p. 1.

[29] Timothy Egan, "Wanted: Border Hoppers. And Some Excitement, Too," *New York Times*, April 1, 2005, p. A12. The lead paragraphs of a *Los Angeles Times* article eight years earlier (J. Michael Kennedy, "Vigilantes or Helpful Volunteers?," July 11, 1986, p. 1) adopt a similar tone: "J. R. Hagan, repo man and paramilitary buff, is basking in the excitement he has caused – the talk shows, the constantly ringing telephone . . . Never mind that the U.S. Border Patrol has called him and his pals a bunch of vigilantes . . . He thinks he and his group did right . . .."

in a shootout with the Clanton gang in 1881. "I need some excitement. And this is better than sitting at home all day watching rattlesnakes crawl out of the den."

This amusing quote may indeed capture the colorful character and extreme politics of Mr. McCarty. But is he representative of all of the Minutemen or, for that matter, restrictionist activists? Even if such coverage is appropriate in its criticism, it is worth noting that a similar type of critical tone is rarely if ever used to describe immigration rights advocates. Recalling the *Los Angeles Times'* coverage of the Proposition 187 campaign, one *Times* journalist told me that he felt that the newspaper had erred seriously in treating "proponents of 187 as nuts." Referring to the *Los Angeles Times* article quoted above, this journalist added: "If you check the clips, you'll see there was a story on page one that dealt with one of the 187 authors like he was all but armed. But if you went to one of those meetings with people supporting 187, these were just your neighbors and sure, racism and xenophobia existed, but not everyone who supported it [was] a nut."[30] When I asked reporters and editors who had been responsible for coverage of immigration during the early 1990s which aspects of the issue they thought had not been treated adequately, several pointed to their not taking seriously enough the "grassroots" restrictionist activists. As *Los Angeles Times* chief immigration reporter Patrick McDonnell recalled[31]:

I think that one of the things that was not covered sufficiently [was the] shock, disbelief, unhappiness that a lot of white, non-Latino people, around here particularly, had about this really incredible historic influx of immigrants. So it kind of burst out ... we were caught totally by surprise by the vehemence of the reaction.

Subsequently, in his conversations with his desk editor, McDonnell said the two agreed "that it was important to air out this anger as much as possible." Here, we see the American journalistic "professional" habitus of dispassionate, balanced coverage at work, partially tempering social distance. The failure to see this discontent in advance, however, may have been due in part to the social distance that separated the well-educated and cosmopolitan *Los Angeles Times* journalists from immigration restriction activists. As former *Los Angeles Times* reporter Jill Stewart remarked, L.A. *Times* journalists pride themselves on living in "diverse" urban neighborhoods, such as Silverlake or Hollywood. Most of them, she said, would "sooner live in Kansas" than in the vast suburbs of the San Fernando Valley and Orange County, where most of the immigration restriction activists resided.[32] This tension between professional aspirations of neutrality

---

[30] Interview with *Los Angeles Times* journalist (who requested that this quote not be attributed), 1998. The article of September 4, 1994, does indeed begin with intimations of violent militancy: "Like other political neophytes who banded together last autumn for an all-out war against illegal immigration, Ronald Stephen Prince had a story to tell."

[31] Patrick McDonnell interview (1998). See also McDonnell's (2011) recent reflection on this and other aspects of his immigration reporting, elaborating on many of the issues he raised in his interview with me.

[32] Jill Stewart interview (1998).

and a worldview rooted in social milieu was also noted by *New York Times* immigration reporter Nina Bernstein. When I asked Bernstein how she had come to write an article about anti-immigration activism in a Long Island suburb of New York City, she responded thoughtfully[33]:

I had felt for some time that we weren't giving enough attention to that [restrictionist] perspective. And one of the problems of covering immigration from New York is that . . . well, New York is really different. Most people who ride the subway in Manhattan just can't have the perspective of someone who, let's say, is living in a southeastern town where there was virtually no immigration until a decade ago. In general, in New York, there is this lack of understanding of the perspective of people [who oppose immigration]. It's like, gee, you can see that immigrants are great for, you know, look at these great restaurants and take-out food options. I mean, you understand what I mean.

The cultural gap between some of the leading immigration restrictionist activists and the journalists who cover them (or, rather, mostly fail to cover them, despite aspirations to the contrary) is in fact striking. To use just one admittedly imperfect indicator of cultural capital, universities attended by some of the most prominent national immigration reporters over the past several decades include Yale (Julia Preston, *New York Times*; Roberto Suro, *Washington Post*), Harvard (Nina Bernstein, *New York Times*), Stanford (Frank Sotomayor, *Los Angeles Times*), University of California-Berkeley (Sonia Nazario and Doreen Carvajal, *Los Angeles Times*), and Dartmouth (Deborah Sontag, *New York Times*); in addition, Suro and Sontag, as well as Patrick McDonnell and Nicole Gaouette of the *Los Angeles Times*, earned master's degrees at the prestigious Columbia University School of Journalism. In contrast, although most restrictionist leaders have college degrees, these tend to be from somewhat less prestigious universities and in more applied, technical fields.[34] To be fair, a few of the best-known restrictionists have resumés just as impressive as their immigrant rights counterparts, especially those scholars associated with the Center for Immigration Studies (CIS), a research institute founded by FAIR. Executive director Mark Krikorian has a B.A. from Georgetown and an M.A. from Tufts' Fletcher School of Law and Diplomacy; director of research Steven Camarota has an M.A. in political science from the University of Pennsylvania and a Ph.D. in public policy analysis from Virginia; and recently hired senior research fellow Jerry Kammer is a former Pulitzer Prize-winning journalist for the *Arizona Republic* and was a Harvard Nieman fellow. FAIR and CIS are the "respectable" and most-cited representatives of the restrictionist

---

[33] Nina Bernstein interview (2008).

[34] FAIR founder John Tanton is an ophthalmologist; California Proposition 187 sponsor Ron Prince is an accountant; Rick Biesada of the Chicago Minuteman Project owned a trucking business; Fred Elbel of Defend Colorado Now is a computer and website consultant; and Glenn Spencer, founder of the southern California Voice of Citizens Together and the Arizona American Border Patrol, has degrees in mathematics and economics and worked as a computer systems engineer.

movement,[35] although some immigrant rights advocates do not accord them such respect: for example, both FAIR and CIS have been labeled "hate groups" by the Southern Poverty Law Center.[36]

It is not just the leadership that counts, however, but rather who the group represents. It is in this way that journalistic perceptions, conscious or unconscious, and ultimately, discursive representations are linked to class distinctions largely within the middle class: a pro-immigration, relatively young, cosmopolitan, highly educated, culturally liberal, urban, middle- to upper-middle-class versus a restrictionist, older, male, suburban small business and technical professional lower-middle to middle class.[37] In the American case, some political analysts might subsume this particular opposition to conservative "red states" versus liberal "blue states," but, in truth, it emerges within as well as across regions and is not entirely synonymous with "liberalism" or "conservatism." As a result, the immigration debate is not just about immigration: immigrants are just one of the stakes, at this historical moment, in an ongoing struggle over social and cultural hierarchies.

One major consequence of this habitus gap is that the political actors who have most consistently identified immigration as a threat have not by themselves been the drivers of negative news coverage of immigration. In the mid-1980s, FAIR executive director Roger Connor (1986) urged a new emphasis on "acculturation or citizenship training, encouraging the new immigrants to become Americans instead of forming into separate political and social groups." The 1986 passage of Proposition 63 (Crawford 1992) to declare English the official language of California would seem to confirm the success of this strategy, but, in

---

[35] This conclusion is based on my own content analysis, as well as the findings of content analysis studies by the pro-immigration Opportunity Agenda, "Media Content Analysis: California Public Discourse on Immigration [2008–2009], 2009," www.opportunityagenda.org, and by CIS (national coverage, Lexis-Nexis search of media references discussing immigration, 2003–2008; see www.cis.org).

[36] Heidi Beirich, "The Teflon Nativists," *SPLC Intelligence Report* (winter 2007, no. 128). In response to this report, Jerry Kammer wrote a CIS Backgrounder (March 2010) entitled, "Immigration and the SPLC: How the Southern Poverty Law Center Invented a Smear, Served La Raza, Manipulated the Press, and Duped Its Donors." This labeling of CIS as a "hate group" was still a live issue at a May 8, 2010 conference on immigration reporting sponsored by the French-American Foundation. As a speaker on one of the panels, Kammer remarked: "CIS is a restrictionist group. What I don't accept are attempts by La Raza and the Southern Poverty Law Center to smear CIS and FAIR as hate groups ... I don't see how this advances democracy" (author notes).

[37] Berg's (2009) analysis of white public opinion toward undocumented immigrants in 1996 and 2004 finds higher agreement with the proposition that "America Should Take Greater Measures to Exclude Illegal Immigrants" among older, male, Republican, lesser-educated individuals (or those connected to social networks of lesser-educated individuals), and those living in less ethnically mixed neighborhoods with fewer Latinos. Pettigrew et al. (2007, 19) show that "opposition to immigration is routinely found strongest among the older and less-educated segments of the population who live in areas with anti-immigration norms and little contact with immigrants."

contrast to other threat frames, national cohesion has never gained consistent media attention or public traction. For the most part, it has remained the pet project of the most marginal restrictictionist groups. For example, newsletters produced by the southern California immigration restrictionist group Voice of Citizens Together (VCT) during 1992 and 1993 dramatized alleged problems of cultural warfare and elite betrayal.[38] According to a VCT-produced video entitled "The Invasion of the United States: A Historic Betrayal," Mexicans in Mexico and America, along with their white liberal allies, have been working to recreate a Mexican nation in the southwest United States, using the Aztec name "Aztlan."[39] National cohesion has also been a major frame for the Arizona-based Minutemen border control group. As Minutemen founder Jim Gilchrist writes in his book, *Minutemen: The Battle to Secure America's Borders* (Gilchrist and Corsi 2006, xxii), "Look at the disunity the millions of illegal immigrants are creating in this country: the balkanization, the language problems, the resentment."

Frames promoted by restrictionist groups have attained significant media attention only when they have also been promoted by mainstream political actors. Neither Republicans nor Democrats have been consistent promoters of the national cohesion frame: as a result, this frame is negatively correlated with news generated by the political field.[40] In contrast, the fiscal frame, which had also been long promoted by restrictionists, became more visible in the United States beginning in the early 1990s. This is because it was promoted vigorously by government officials, especially at the state and local levels, and became an important marker of political identity in state-level elections, but it subsequently dropped sharply in media prominence.[41] Such patterns of media coverage support the indexing hypothesis that elite mainstream political actors will be the primary definers of the media agenda.

[38] This conclusion is based on a quantitative and qualitative analysis I conducted of a sample of the newsletters, which were mailed to me by VCT founder Glenn Spencer.

[39] Voice of Citizens Together video (1994), mailed to the author by Glenn Spencer, May 1995. In a telephone interview (May 1995), Spencer emphasized, unprompted, the national cohesion frame. For the more mainstream articulation of the national cohesion frame during this period, see FAIR (1993).

[40] For correlations between news generation (political field, civil society, or journalistic fields) and frames, see Appendix Table A.1.

[41] In 1994, when the fiscal frame appeared in 43 percent of the core media sample, it was strongly correlated with citations of local government, primarily California's governor ($.238$, $p < .01$); restrictionist groups ($.246$, $p < .01$); and national Republicans ($.188$, $p < .05$). In 2002–06, when the fiscal frame dropped to just 11 percent of news coverage, it continued to be strongly promoted by restrictionist groups ($.292$, $p < .01$), but the frame's links to more mainstream actors had either weakened considerably (local government, $.138$, $p < .01$) or disappeared. These findings counter sociologist Kitty Calavita's (1996) sweeping claims of a long-term ideological realignment around "balanced budget conservatism," including the dominance of a fiscal frame for the immigration issue.

In fact, the predominant threat frame since the 1970s has been public order, which has appeared in 52 to 62 percent of news coverage during peak media attention periods over the past four decades. After immigration reemerged as a public issue in the early 1970s, top government officials consistently emphasized border control and security, the problem of illegal immigration, and the control of crime. Across the decades, public order is most likely to be mentioned in political field–generated news (see Appendix Table A.1). Public order is thus a prominent frame because it has been emphasized by political officials, because the majority of immigration news is political news, and because elite mainstream journalists tend to index their political coverage to the debate among political elites. As elite political attention varies so will media attention, to a certain extent. Thus, in 2002, as U.S. political elites emphasized the public order frame in the wake of the 9/11 attacks, media attention to the frame increased (rising from 55 percent of coverage in 1994 to 64 percent). In 2004, the public order frame then fell back to 53 percent, before rising again in 2006 to 62 percent in the wake of passage of a Republican-sponsored House of Representatives' bill (HR 4437) to "criminalize" illegal immigration.

The public order frame (similarly to the humanitarian frame, as I will argue shortly) also has a fundamental formal advantage in gaining media attention over more complex frames. Conceptual frames, whether they are "right" (fiscal, jobs, national cohesion) or "left" (racism, global economy), are always at risk of seeming stale and boring according to journalistic standards of novelty and narrative.[42] For example, when *New York Times* immigration reporter Julia Preston expressed some hesitations about quoting certain restrictionist sources, it was less because of their credibility or ideology than because of their lack of novelty. They had fallen into the "category of the usual suspects," offering predictable responses to any given situation.[43]

Indeed, as Todd Gitlin (1980, 28) once noted, "the archetypal news story is a crime story." Whether or not reporters themselves think of immigrants as criminals – and clearly, mostly they do not – reporting conventions encourage criminal framing. The problem of public order does not need to be explained; it speaks for itself. And, more than that, it shows itself in vivid pictures and word images of border stations, police, guns, chases, and arrests. Although the theme

[42] Dan Hallin (1994, 78) offered a similar explanation of why the human rights frame, operationalized in his study to include historical and structural elements, lagged behind the Cold War frame in U.S. television news coverage of El Salvador during the early 1980s: it "lacked the simplicity" of the latter frame and "required journalists to go into considerable detail about unfamiliar societies," something difficult to do in a two-minute news report.

[43] Julia Preston interview (2008). Preston also emphasized that, for this reason, she made an effort to seek out a broad variety of restrictionist viewpoints. My point is simply that considerations of novelty played an important role in shaping her decisions on what events or topics to cover and which sources to include. However, not all sources are equal: the president and other high-level government officials generally gain coverage even if they repeat the same clichéd arguments over and over.

may be the same, the particulars always change. Public order is the frame that literally shows the first order of immigration's "problematic" status, the immediate presence of "strangers" (who have broken the law), who constitute a problem by their very presence.

The drama inherent in the public order frame is evident in this excerpt from a lengthy 1974 *Los Angeles Times* feature article about a border patrol station at the U.S.-Mexico border[44]:

> A change of point men. A half hour at a time up front, that's the policy. . . . The second point man is in position only a few minutes when a dark green, late-model Ford approaches. It rolls in a little fast, and the point man spreads his hands, palms down, to stop. At 30 feet and closing, the driver stabs his foot down and the front of the car rises under heavy acceleration. As he flashes by, 18 inches from the point man, he raises a single middle finger in salute. The thrown flashlight misses and 100 yards down the road the Ford's lights disappear. The driver has turned them off. He knows what he's doing. "Get that son-of-a-bitch," screams the point man.

Three decades later, the dramatic appeal of the border patrol profile has not diminished, as this 2006 segment from NBC Nightly News[45] illustrates:

> BRIAN WILLIAMS, ANCHOR: NBC News In-Depth tonight, the battle over illegal immigration in this country. . . . Right now there are 12,000 border patrol agents, with another 6,000 to be added over the next two years' time. NBC's Don Teague has a rare behind-the-scenes look at their training tonight.
> TEAGUE: Border patrol agents work in remote areas with little backup. That's why new agents spend so much time here . . . learning to deal with life and death situations . . . in the field with armed role players. To make this training as realistic as possible, the border patrol uses nonlethal ammunition. It allows agents to make a mistake and live to tell about it.
> UNIDENTIFIED MAN: Put your head back.
> TEAGUE: These agents have stopped an armed robber who carjacked a motorist. The scenario unfolds in seconds.
> OFFSCREEN VOICE: Drop the weapon.
> ANOTHER OFFSCREEN VOICE: Drop the weapon.
> TEAGUE: It ended with a dead suspect and a freed victim. Just the reason student Dominic Boswell joined the border patrol.

Public order-focused coverage does, of course, sometimes make room for other frames. For example, while the passage from the 1974 *Los Angeles Times* article may suggest a mean-spirited attitude toward the undocumented immigrants, a border patrol agent is also quoted in the same article expressing a humanitarian understanding of the problem and a degree of personal empathy toward the immigrants:

---

[44] From Evan Maxwell, "Second Frontier: the Final Hurdle for Illegal Aliens in U.S.; It's Door to the Promised Land – and They Keep It Hopping," *Los Angeles Times*, August 19, 1974, II-1.

[45] NBC Nightly News, "Border Patrol Agents Undergo Rigorous Training," June 22, 2006, Lexis-Nexis transcript.

"I don't blame them, not at all," remarked one patrol agent. "They keep coming this way because they want to work. They are good people for the most part, but they can't make it in Mexico. There is no work. If I were in their shoes, I'd be doing the same thing. But they set themselves up for the rottenest kind of exploitation – smugglers, bad employers, cheap whores to take their money."[46]

In most cases, however, and especially in television news, such explanatory complexities and caveats are generally overwhelmed by the overriding audience-attracting imperative for conflict and drama.

In sum, even if many journalists are uncomfortable with restrictionist activists, when similar arguments are made by political elites they are quite likely to grant them news status. This is especially true in the case of the public order frame, which consistently meets commercially driven journalistic criteria for conflict and dramatic action. But in the right mix of circumstances, controversial proposals to cut off social benefits (fiscal) may also be seen as much more compelling news than the complex policies of "comprehensive reform" against which they are usually juxtaposed. The rhetorical strategies and intensity of motivation of political elites on both sides (backed by their armies of less news-worthy activists) surely make a difference and, in recent years in the United States, many of the policy battles (even if only to prevent another "amnesty") have been won by the restrictionists. In their political coverage, at least, journalists have not resisted this tendency: political field–generated news gives more space to threat frames than other types of news.[47]

NARRATIVE AND THE HUMANITARIAN FRAME

Increasingly, the humanitarian frame has been a dominant frame in public discourse about immigration. Of course, immigrants do suffer, and their political or basic human rights have often been violated (as documented in Appendix C). But the reason these problems are picked up by the media is not solely due to their objective merit. It matters who is promoting the problem and how well the problem fits with the dominant form of news.

Clearly, the "social problems industry" (Hilgartner and Bosk 1988) of immigrant rights advocacy – much better funded than its restrictionist counterpart – has been a key driver of the humanitarian frame. Once established, these organizations, with their growing payrolls of professional advocates (lawyers, public policy experts, organizers, etc.), have strong incentives to keep

---

[46] Maxwell, "Second Frontier...," 1974.

[47] Only in political field–generated coverage does the public order frame appear more often than the humanitarian frame (72 vs. 63 percent of packages) over the four decades (see Appendix Table A.1). Overall, combined victim and hero frames outnumber threat frames in all types of coverage, but the relative emphasis on threat frames is highest in political field–generated news (46 percent vs. 41 percent in civil society–generated news and 37 percent in journalistic field–generated news, as proportions of all frames); statistics are not shown in tables.

humanitarian concerns on the public agenda. Professional, media-savvy organizations able to provide journalists with "information subsidies" (Gandy 1992) – background information, the latest statistical research, quotable quotes, etc. – are the most likely to get and maintain the attention of a shrinking journalistic workforce laboring longer hours with increasingly severe time pressures to produce news across multiple platforms (Klinenberg 2005; Deuze 2007; Waldman 2011). In addition, there is a close habitus fit between elite journalists and immigrant rights advocates, facilitating a "natural" mutual sympathy and communication between journalists and groups promoting the humanitarian frame. In the United States, prominent immigrant advocates tend to have educational profiles quite similar to elite journalists.[48] This is not to say that journalists and pro-immigration advocates do not sometimes clash, especially when the activists are socially marginal or openly espouse strong leftist positions. Yet there is clearly an affinity of interests and outlook between elite journalists and the professional immigration advocates (many of them attorneys) that reflects both educational and broader cultural milieu affinities rooted in the affluent neighborhoods of Manhattan, Washington, D.C., or Los Angeles. Lawyers and legal scholars also are useful sources in that they can suggest policy-relevant stories based on individual "cases" that offer strong human interest appeal.

For all of these reasons, the humanitarian frame has become a dominant U.S. media frame. When and if journalists cover civil society activism – which is not all that often compared to France – the humanitarian frame is likely to be mentioned (see Appendix Table A.1). However, the frame's prominence extends beyond news events created by activists. When journalists generate news with their investigations and in-depth features, the humanitarian frame is also a dominant frame: in fact, by the 2000s, it was more likely to be associated with journalistic field–generated news than with civil society–generated news.[49] An increasing emphasis on the humanitarian frame correlates with an increasing use of personalized narrative. Comparing immigration news in the 1970s/1980s with that of the 2000s, the proportion of page-one articles with "anecdotal leads" in the U.S. core newspaper sample increased from 22 percent to 33

---

[48] Frank Sharry, executive director of the National Immigration Forum and America's Voice, earned his B.A. at Princeton; Tamar Jacoby, a senior fellow at the Manhattan Institute and subsequently director of ImmigrationWorks, has a B.A. from Yale and was a former staffer at the *New York Review of Books* and deputy editor of the op-ed page of the *New York Times*; Lucas Gutentag of the ACLU Immigrant Rights Project has a B.A. from Berkeley and a J.D. from Harvard; Chrystal Williams, executive director of the American Immigration Lawyers Association has a J.D. from Georgetown; Cecelia Muñoz of the National Council of La Raza earned a B.A. from Michigan and an M.A. from Berkeley; Chong-Wha Hong, executive director of the New York Immigration Coalition is a B.A. graduate of the University of Pennsylvania; and the long-time organizer and vice president of Unite (the former International Ladies Garment Workers Union), May Chen, has a B.A. from Radcliffe and an M.A. from UCLA.

[49] In the 2002–2006 core U.S. newspaper sample, there is a .139 ($p < .01$) correlation between journalistic field–generated news and the humanitarian frame versus .111 (NS) for civil society generated news and –.202 ($p < .005$) for political field–generated news. Data not shown in tables.

percent, with all three newspapers exhibiting almost an identical upward trend. Moreover, articles with anecdotal leads are more strongly associated with the humanitarian frame (0.169, p < .000) than with any other frame (figures not shown in tables).[50]

American news is narrative driven, and the humanitarian frame is tailor-made for this format. Narrative "dramatization with a focus on individuals" is an important means for both newspapers and television news to attract audiences in an increasingly competitive media marketplace (Jackall and Hirota 2000, 132). In field terms, strong external commercial pressures on journalism are refracted inside the U.S. journalistic field in the form of personalized, emotional story-telling. Former *Times* immigration reporter Mirta Ojito remarked that she believes it to be "hugely important" for immigration articles to "weave in the narrative of one or several persons."[51] Nina Bernstein, the *New York Times*' chief metropolitan immigration reporter, told me that for a complex issue such as immigration, "showing the human-ness [of the immigrant] becomes very important ... this human narrative becomes the way to connect with the reader."[52] In subsequent public remarks, Bernstein made a point of emphasizing that narratives need not preclude taking seriously broader structures of power[53]:

I know that some people criticize immigration coverage as too episodic ... and distorted by individual narratives that exaggerate the migrant's agency and ignore the push and pull of larger economic forces. I don't disagree entirely but I want to argue for the centrality of human narratives and human voices. I want to argue that with proper attention to the telling detail, individual stories are a powerful way to convey larger forces.

Bernstein illustrated her remarks with examples of her investigative reports, persuasive and moving coverage of mistreatment and abuse of immigrants trapped in the nightmare of the immigration detention system. Such reporting, as she notes, plays an important role in confronting the "dehumanization" of illegal immigrants and assuring that, even if they have violated the law, their human and legal rights are respected. In fact, such an affinity between narrative techniques and investigative journalism has been well-documented (Ettema and Glasser 1998) and will be explored further in Chapter 7 on critical news. Moreover, the capacity of narrative to "humanize" immigrants and their personal difficulties has been demonstrated not just by the reporting of Nina Bernstein but also by her colleagues at other national newspapers.

---

[50] Only the page-one article was coded for type of lead paragraph in cases in which the package also included related inside articles.

[51] Remarks by Mirta Ojito delivered February 6, 2008, Barnard College Migration Series, New York.

[52] Nina Bernstein interview (2008).

[53] Nina Bernstein, remarks to French-American Foundation conference, "Covering Immigration," November 2009, Paris.

For instance, in "Two Jobs and a Sense of Hope; A Young Man from Mali Discovers a Tough Life on a Time Clock,"[54] a *Washington Post* article by Anne Hull captures the ironies of being an African immigrant in the American South. Presented as an example of a wave of sub-Saharan African immigration to the United States, this profile of Malian Adama Camara also provides a rare glimpse of the day-to-day experiences, feelings, and viewpoints of a janitorial worker, not the kind of individual who usually gets much opportunity to speak and be heard in the public sphere. Another example of an in-depth individual profile is a Pulitzer Prize-winning *Los Angeles Times* six-part series by Sonia Nazario entitled "Enrique's Journey." Drawing on dozens of interviews with the seventeen-year-old Enrique, as well as his relatives, eye witnesses, officials, and other migrants met while researching the story, Nazario sought to retrace the journey taken by this illegal immigrant boy from Honduras to rejoin his mother in North Carolina.[55] Often, these personalized narratives incorporate social structure through a third or fourth "nut" (para-)graph explaining, in so many words, that "she is not alone."[56] But how often do such narratives fully "convey larger forces," including the "push and pull of economic forces," in Nina Bernstein's words, or the conflicts between powerful organizations shaping immigration policy, or the social and economic impacts of immigration on the host society?[57] A close reading of U.S. news coverage suggests that a trade-off is often made between human interest narrative and structural analysis.

For example, a personalizing narrative logic is evident in the particular way that *New York Times* reporter Julia Preston describes her extensive coverage of a mass government arrest of immigrant workers at a meat-processing plant in Iowa (e.g., "270 Illegal Immigrants Sent to Prison in Federal Push," May 24, 2008). Although her perspective reflects her background as a foreign correspondent in central America and Mexico, what is central to Preston's account[58] are not the macro-structural forces or corporate and governmental policies at work but rather the suffering and tragedies of the immigrants themselves.

[T]his [government] raid was particularly terrifying for [the immigrant workers] because the agents came in with ... semi-automatic weapons ... and they were wearing vests and there were helicopters overhead. And so, for these immigrants, this immediately brought back the imagery of the 1980s when there was a genocidal violence in their communities.

---

[54] Anne Hull, *The Washington Post*, December 11, 2002, p. A-1.

[55] See, for example, Sonia Nazario, "Enrique's Journey/Chapter 5; A Milky Green River Between Him and His Dream," *Los Angeles Times*, October 6, 2002, p. A-1. The series was later published in book form as *Enrique's Journey* (New York: Random House, 2007).

[56] I am grateful to Gary Younge, New York correspondent for *The* (London) *Guardian*, for providing this apt description of the anecdotal lead.

[57] As former *Los Angeles Times* labor reporter Harry Bernstein (interview 1998) put it, if you have a "very warm touching story about a family of five children or ten children, no bread winner, that focus is more readable than a big corporation breaking the union. I don't agree with that but I understand [why the editors might make that choice]."

[58] Julia Preston interview (2008).

And, I covered that. So I know they're not making that up. Perhaps some of them were small children at the time, to judge from their ages, but still it's not an inconsequential backdrop to the attitudes that they bring to a very oppressive workplace in Iowa.

Preston continued:

And then … an even more heartbreaking thing was … when they … were hit with very severe criminal charges as a sort of prosecutorial strategy by the U.S. attorney in the northern district of Iowa. Instead of just deporting them on the immigration charges, they also brought these quite severe … criminal charges. But, then … one of the … extra-ordinary ironies of that situation was that this court in Iowa [treated] the immigrants like normal, like regular defendants in the court system … One of the judges apologized to them and said, I understand that you just came here to help your families and I respect what you did but unfortunately you violated federal law. These immigrants got up and thanked this judge [laughs], and said, you know, we're so grateful to you sir that you treated us with respect. [So, these immigrants go] from this village in Guatemala where the military was shooting at them in the '80s, and then … peace [comes to] Guatemala but the economy doesn't recover, so they end up in Postville, Iowa. And then they end going to this court room where [when] finally someone's treating them like a human being is the day when a judge sentences them to five months in federal prison.

In similar fashion, Nina Bernstein's profile of a Long Island restrictionist activist ultimately privileges story-telling over structural analysis ("On Lucille Avenue, the Immigration Debate," June 26, 2006). In this article, the structural is doubly disadvantaged, both by the demands of narrative and the empathetic gap of two distinct types of habitus. From its opening paragraph, there is no doubt about the social distance between the reporter (and her likely audience) and the union member/local restrictionist activist at the center of the story.

ELMONT, N.Y. – The streets where Patrick Nicolosi sees America unraveling still have the look of the 1950's. Single-family homes sit side by side, their lawns weed-whacked into submission to the same suburban dream that Mr. Nicolosi's Italian-American parents embraced 40 years ago when they moved to this working-class community on Long Island.

Commenting on the article a few years later, Bernstein said, "Certainly, the working class perspective, the white working class perspective can be quite different. … I like the fact that I have the freedom as a reporter to lay out those contradictions and give voice to someone like this who in fact was coming from a union perspective, from a, at least in some ways, a progressive perspective." In the article, Bernstein gives Nicolosi his say, but always couched in relation to personal, even irrational emotions ("resentment," "worries," "working himself into a speech"), not to the kind of hard data that could either confirm or refute his arguments. The article continues:

It is the economics of class, not the politics of culture or race, that fires Mr. Nicolosi's resentment about what he sees in Elmont, which is probably as diverse a suburb as exists in the United States. Like many working-class Americans who live close to illegal immigrants, he worries that they are yet another force undermining the way of life and the social contract that generations of workers strived so hard to achieve ... "They're telling us Americans don't want to do these jobs," Mr. Nicolosi said. "That's a lie. The business owners don't want to pay. I know what my grandparents fought for: fair wages and days off. Now we're doing it in reverse."... "'It's either a country of law and order and what my parents fought for, or we just turn it over to big business," he went on, working himself into a speech that connected many dots.

Instead of opening up a discussion about the validity of these "progressive" critiques, the article's underlying narrative thrust is humanitarian. The story's ultimate punch line is intensely personal, a melodramatic "parable about being careful what you wish for." Nicolosi's campaign to stop homeowners from leasing unregulated basement apartments to illegal immigrants ultimately results in the eviction of the Mexican family with two children, one disabled, living across the street. Nicolosi is isolated, even by Republicans who share his view on immigration. The reason (echoing Bernstein's reporting creed): "People forget the human dimension." Given the inevitable human costs of enforcing or trying to enact any change to immigration policy, the article's closing sentence effectively endorses the status quo. As Nicolosi's next-door neighbor laments: "For every problem, there's a solution. For every solution, there's another problem."

Over and above policy solutions, personal dramas are paramount. But whose personal dramas? As both Bernstein and *Los Angeles Times* reporter Patrick McDonnell noted, the "anger" of native workers and residents tends to be systematically undercovered. The article about Nicolosi, a balanced but hardly sympathetic profile, was not followed by many others emphasizing the economic or social struggles of other native workers impacted by immigration. Narrative journalism encourages reporting to focus on personal trials and tribulations; habitus empathies place the object of upper-middle-class *noblesse oblige* (the immigrant) rather than the object of upper-middle-class cultural disdain (the "Archie Bunker" white working class male) at the sympathetic center of the narrative arc. The aspiration of American-style narrative journalism is to "draw on the personal experience of a particular individual caught up in a story to dramatize a broader social issue" (Wahl-Jorgensen 2012, 7). This seems like a noble goal, but dramatization is not the same as understanding. In the Lucille Avenue article, narrative serves not to supplement structural analysis but effectively to silence it: there is no grand synthesis of the two.[59] I turn now to a closer consideration of how and why critical, especially global, economic analyses are submerged in immigration coverage.

---

[59] See Nina Bernstein (2011, 31–34) for a different reading of this article. See also Schuck (2011, 82–88), in the same volume, for a listing of the "structural" problems and "invisible victims" generally ignored by U.S. immigration journalists, driven by a "passion for narrating the drama of individual lives."

SHUNNING THE GLOBAL ANGLE

Columbia University sociologist Saskia Sassen (1999, 40) shows that, in addition to overpopulation, poverty, or unemployment, a crucial cause of increasing immigration to the United States has been "a common pattern of expanding U.S. political and economic involvement with emigrant-sending countries" (see also Massey 1998; Gonzalez 2001; Bacon 2008). In particular, U.S. trade and foreign investment policies seeking to promote export-oriented agriculture and manufacturing have undermined rural subsistence economies and created a new migrant worker class. Although these uprooted farmers and laborers may initially find employment in manufacturing or service employment in their own countries, they will almost inevitably become ripe recruits for emigration to the United States or other Western developed countries. As Sassen writes: "People uprooted from their traditional ways of life, then left unemployed and unemployable as export firms hire younger workers or move production to other countries, may see few options but emigration, especially if an export-led growth strategy has weakened the country's domestic market oriented economy." At the same time, high levels of immigration are driven by the changing structure of labor demand, specifically "the rapid expansion of the supply of low-wage jobs in the United States and the casualization of the labor market associated with the new growth industries" (Sassen 1999, 43).

In other words, the same neo-liberal economic globalization that is restructuring the Mexican and other immigrant-sending countries is also transforming the U.S. economy in ways that make it easier for displaced Mexicans to find off-the-books employment in "flexible" manufacturing and service jobs in hotels, restaurants, construction, and similar fields. The immigration issue should not "divide Americans into legals and illegals or immigrants versus native-born," writes immigration scholar Peter Kwong (1997, 16–17), when in fact global laissez-faire economics are producing a "downward slide in working conditions that will eventually affect us all."[60]

Foreign governments and international organizations have sometimes promoted this frame (at least in a watered down form that stresses the need for development aid), but these sources rarely appear in U.S. immigration news (see Figure 3.2). Except for the 1970s, when the global economy frame was part and parcel of the postcolonialist critique of many U.S. radical Chicano activist groups (Rodríguez 1977; Skerry 1993, 256–257), few immigration advocacy organizations or immigration scholars have actively promoted the frame.

Compounding the dearth of frame promoters, most journalists have not been receptive to this complex and ideologically marginal framing of the immigration "story." The supposed threat, after all, is nothing less than the global neo-liberal

[60] This does not preclude short-term rises in living standards for the countries providing the low-wage labor, either through increases in domestic wages or from remittances sent home from migrant workers. For further analysis of how a reliance on low-skill immigration is helping fuel increasing inequality in the United States, see Noah (2012).

order; although agency is dispersed, villainy could reasonably be attributed to the U.S. and other Western governments and transnational corporations. What journalist under deadline pressure working in a corporate-owned newspaper would want to venture into that thicket? In my interviews with American journalists, few contested the validity of such a frame when it was suggested to them, but none volunteered it as one of the important angles that they themselves were pursuing.[61]

Roberto Lovato, during the mid-1990s the executive director of the Central American Resource Center immigrant rights group, recalls his group's attempt to get publicity for a university-sponsored conference on immigration and globalization[62]:

[W]e held a [press] conference called "Proposition 187 and immigration: an international perspective" because the way it was framed [by the media], it was framed very simplistically ... it was framed within the borders of the United States ... There's no look whatsoever at the push factors, what's going on in Mexico, what's going on in Central America, what's going on in Asia, why people migrate from these countries. ... So the value of a white worker in California was reduced in the past 20 years because of the changes in the economy [and] politicians are playing to those fears. Globalization is what was really driving Prop. 187 ... we tried to draw those elements out ... [And] the L.A. *Times* pushed it into the back section.[63]

Rather than focusing on the difficulties of individual immigrants, as legitimately important as these or any other individual injustices are, a deeper form of investigative journalism would raise questions about the structuring of the global economic order and the ways in which the foreign, trade, and labor policies of powerful nations such as the United States foster the conditions that make emigration from the developing world to the developed world all but inevitable. In 1974, a lengthy *Washington Post* editorial ("Illegal Immigration: A Global Problem," November 13, 1974) insisted on the primacy of the global economy frame: "And so this problem gets stood on its head. [Attorney General] Saxbe chooses to focus, as does the AFL-CIO, on the problem of the illegal alien;

[61] One notable exception to this journalistic silence on the global angle is Susan Ferriss of the *Sacramento Bee*. In an online article for the Society of Professional Journalists website, "Immigration Reporting: How to Advance It and Make It Original," (May 30, 2007, accessed July 9, 2008), Ferriss writes: "Look for why immigrants end up in a particular place .... Why did they leave? What's happened to their home area economically? ... When I was a correspondent in Mexico, I wanted to explore the dynamic behind Mexican migration. I reported on the ways in which economic policies pushed by the United States had, in fact, undermined some communities' own business options and prompted more migration."

[62] Roberto Lovato interview (1998). Lovato is now a writer for New America Media, *The Nation*, and other publications.

[63] In fact, I was unable to find any coverage about the conference in the *Los Angeles Times*, with the exception of a short announcement (taken almost verbatim from the university press release) that only appeared in the Valley local edition. See David E. Brady, "Northridge; Conference to Address Legacy of Prop. 187," *Los Angeles Times* (Valley Edition), October 9, 1995.

but the real problem is how the countries of the world are going to work out the problem of redistributing the wealth in general and of stabilizing the food supply in particular." Ironically, as the global and U.S. economies have become more liberalized and the gap between wealthy and poor has dramatically widened, the U.S. news media have been increasingly less likely to even mention the global economy frame. Between the 1970s and 2000s, mentions of the global economy frame dropped from 18 percent of immigration news packages to 9 percent.

Why this lack of interest in issues of economic justice that affect immigrant and domestic workers alike? For the *Los Angeles Times*, former reporter Nancy Cleeland lists the following causes: the *Times'* increasingly "antiunion" editorial policy (resuming, under Tribune Company management, an old tradition); the fact that senior editors, with their "six-figure incomes," simply "may not see the inequities in their own backyard"; and the belief, probably well-founded, that celebrity reporting will attract more affluent readers than developing an "economic justice" beat. In an impassioned essay for the *Huffington Post*, "Why I'm Leaving the L.A. Times,"[64] Cleeland clearly articulated a global economy frame, placing immigrants' problems alongside those of other low-income workers:

> The Los Angeles region is defined by gaping income disparities and an enormous pool of low-wage immigrant workers, many of whom are pulled north by lousy, unstable jobs ... I was a seasoned journalist with lots of experience in Third World countries. Still, the level of exploitation shocked me. ... In a range of industries, [illegal immigrants] were routinely underpaid and fired after any attempt to assert rights or ask for higher wages. That disregard for workers spread up the chain of regional jobs. ... The same is happening to various degrees across the country. Rather than reverse those troubling trends, recent political leaders have done just the opposite. Enabled by a Milton Friedman-inspired belief in free markets and the idea that poverty is proof of personal failure, not systemic failure, federal trade and regulatory policies have consistently undermined workers. ... In the easy vernacular of modern journalism, the [Los Angeles] *Times* and other newspapers routinely cast business and labor as powerful competitors whose rivalries occasionally flare up in strikes and organizing campaigns. What I saw was that workers almost always lose.

Cleeland left the *Los Angeles Times* to join an economic research institute that she hoped would "tap into the wealth of economic research being generated by academic institutions, business groups, labor unions, and others, as well as the vast experience of ordinary Angelinos." Yet, in this remark, Cleeland sidesteps another possible factor underlying the press's failure to adequately explain the "systemic failures" she identifies, this fundamental tension between the demands of systemic analysis and personalized story-telling. Although, in principle, journalism could do both, in practice, American journalism puts the emphasis heavily on the latter. *Los Angeles Times* immigration reporter Patrick McDonnell admitted to me that he would "like to do some more" stories on

---

[64] Nancy Cleeland, "Why I'm Leaving the L.A. Times," *The Huffington Post*, May 28, 2007.

immigration "in the whole context of economic globalization." But McDonnell conceded, "newspapers maybe aren't as good with stories that are very, very high concept." *High concept,* in other words, refers to stories in which agency is obscured and obscures itself from view, yet it is precisely here, in the realm of corporate decision making and global economics, that a crucial aspect of the immigration story is to be found. McDonnell continued, "To some extent I think we try to tell stories."[65] But what happens when story-telling journalism, that is, "narrative" journalism, encounters a structurally complex issue like immigration? Can immigration's relationship to the global economy be captured in a story?

It is not as if American immigration reporters lack international experience. Many of them have, in fact, spent ample time reporting outside of the United States. McDonnell, a native New Yorker, had previously covered the Mexico-U.S. border and, as of 2010, was the *Los Angeles Times'* bureau chief in Buenos Aires. *New York Times* immigration reporter Julia Preston also boasts an impressive international resumé. After having received her B.A. in Latin American studies from Yale, Preston worked for the *Boston Globe,* National Public Radio, and the *Washington Post,* covering Central America and the United Nations. In 1995, she joined the *New York Times* as a foreign correspondent covering Mexico City for six years. It was while promoting her book on the Mexican pro-democracy movement, *Opening Mexico* (Preston and Dillon 2004) at various public venues across the American southwest that Preston came to realize the intensity of the American public's concern with the immigration issue. "Every time I was on any form of talk radio in the southwest, I realized that no one wanted to know anything about Mexican politics, they only wanted to talk about immigration."[66] Preston then effectively lobbied for the "immigration" beat and wrote a lengthy memo to then managing editor Jill Abramson, laying out how she viewed the immigration "story." Preston recounted the content of the memo, which laid out the unique features of the current wave of immigration:

I just pointed out the things that have become commonplace, by this time, which is that the United States underwent a huge surge of immigration starting in the early 1990s that had some characteristics that made it quite different than anything the country had experienced before. One was the predominance of one nationality, i.e., Mexican immigration. The other was the predominance of one language group, i.e., Spanish speakers . . . the pattern has been in the past that people came from many places. The third factor is that we've never had immigration in which so many people were out of [legal] status . . . And a fourth one, which is that these new immigrants were spreading out across the country to places that had not experienced immigration in generations, in some cases. So all of this was creating a vast new social experience for people across the country . . . [in] some places people were reacting positively, and then many places some people were

[65] Patrick McDonnell interview (1998).
[66] Julia Preston interview (2008).

reacting very negatively. And I made a list of stories which I think, I'm pleased to say, that in one way or the other, virtually all of them have been in our paper.

Preston's reporting (along with those of other *New York Times'* immigration reporters) over the years has indeed covered a wide range of frames.[67] What is strangely missing from her reporting wish list, however, especially given her background as a foreign correspondent, is a critical analysis of the links among the local, the national, and the global. Preston's reporting, like most U.S. immigration reporting, emphasizes the human dimension, the lived experience of individual immigrants. In contrast, the global economy frame is mostly a conceptual frame – it is more about "immigration" than about "immigrants," as demographer Michael Teitelbaum puts it.[68]

Global economy, as noted, is also a frame that directly challenges the neo-liberal order. It suggests that there might be something unjust or misguided about an economic system that most U.S. political elites – and journalists – take for granted as normal, as simply the way things are. This ideological marginalizing occurs, in part, through the division of news and opinion in American newspapers. The fact is that some U.S. journalists *have* offered a broad, critical economic analysis; for the most part, however, their views have been restricted to the "opinion" pages, thus sharply distinguishing and margin-alizing the global economy frame from those frames that appear as "factual" news. One example of this tendency is the 1974 *Washington Post* editorial cited earlier. By the 1990s, however, the "ghettoization" of the frame was even more extreme. For example, Robert Scheer, author of the now discontinued "Column Left" column in the *Los Angeles Times*, wrote in 1994 about the U.S. Labor Department's lack of inspection staff to enforce labor wage and safety laws: "What this means is that the only program with any real promise of cutting down the incessant demand for cheap immigrant labor barely exists. Jobs are the magnet that pull people to this country, and if employers continue to get away with violating our labor standards, then the migrants will keep coming, no

---

[67] Two of the more substantial special series on immigration published by the *New York Times* include "Three Sisters" (December 2006) and "Remade in America" (March–April 2009). In the "Three Sisters" series, *Times* reporters "spent a week ... following three sisters who immigrated to the United States [from Mexico]." The "Remade" series was explicitly oriented to making links between the "newest immigrants and their impact on American institutions" (the family, social services, businesses, politics, hospitals, workplaces, and schools). See also Roger Lowenstein's July 9, 2006, *New York Times Sunday Magazine* article, "The Immigration Equation," a comprehensive sorting through of the immigration policy debate, as well as the "Border Crossings" occasional series of in-depth global investigative reports on immigration by Jason DeParle (June 2007 to March 2008).

[68] Remarks at French-American Foundation, Miami, May 2010 (author notes). Teitelbaum is program director for research and technology at the Alfred P. Sloan Foundation and served as a commissioner of the U.S. Commission on Immigration Reform (1996–97).

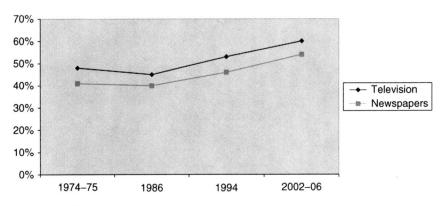

FIGURE 3.5. United States: Dominance of combined public order and humanitarian frames, 1970s–2000s. Percentages are of total frames mentioned in each medium.

matter how many propositions the voters pass."[69] In comments made to me, *Los Angeles Times* city editor Bill Boyarsky was dismissive of Scheer's analyses: "Scheer thinks in terms of classic Marxist economics, he thinks economics is at the root of everything."[70] But, except for Scheer, the *Los Angeles Times* coverage of immigration, especially after the 1970s, has often left the impression that economics is at the root of nothing. Likewise, at the *New York Times*, as noted earlier, only Paul Krugman's column very occasionally discusses immigration in the context of economic justice for immigrant and nonimmigrant workers alike. It makes a difference that fiscal, racial, public order, and humanitarian aspects of immigration can be raised in "news" stories, naturalized as information, whereas critical economic frames (jobs, global economy) have been marginalized by being largely presented only as opinion – and, indeed, as a "left" and thus, in advance, discredited opinion – in the context of the dominant neo-liberal economic worldview of the American political field.

So, the global economy frame – in the United States – is doubly disadvantaged. It is ideologically out of step with the mainstream (this is rarely openly acknowledged); it is also too complex and too structural to be easily turned into a "story" (this is easily admitted). What is left? A mediated debate that increasingly condenses and collapses the diverse aspects of immigration into two dramatic, conflict-laden and emotional frames: public order and humanitarianism. (See Figure 3.5.)

[69] Robert Scheer, "Column Left: Instead of 187, Enforcement of Labor Laws," *Los Angeles Times*, November 20, 1994, p. 5.
[70] Bill Boyarsky interview (1998).

CONCLUSION

If U.S. immigration news were a simple reflection of economic changes, one might have expected the global economy or jobs frames to have predominated. If it were purely an expression of neo-liberal ideology, the good worker frame should always have been dominant. And if any one of the many interest groups vying to shape the public debate had prevailed, the national cohesion, racism, or fiscal frames would have consistently risen to the top of media attention. But patterns of U.S. news coverage have not played out according to any of these scenarios. And the reason why is that all of these social forces and social actors have been taken up, processed, and refracted in various ways by the journalistic field, which itself is riven by complex, competing, and sometimes contradictory, imperatives.

As American society has become increasingly commercialized, newsrooms have responded with changes that have directly or indirectly helped journalism adapt to the new economic order – generally not in ways that constitute a form of resistance, but at the same time also not in ways that would consistently accord with favorable treatment of either pro- or anti-immigration advocates. Labor reporting has been downsized or eliminated, reducing attention to the jobs frame. Journalists are increasingly encouraged to write their immigration reports as personalized narratives, which effectively favors the humanitarian frame over more conceptual frames like racism and global economy.

If new practices and new hierarchies of reporting have emerged, other structural influences are more long-standing. Social class hierarchies contribute to journalists covering restrictionist groups less often and less sympathetically than their more elite immigrant rights counterparts. This does not mean that threat frames are ignored. The public order frame holds special appeal for journalists because it embodies the central news values of drama, conflict, and emotion. And when any threat frame is also promoted by top government officials, bringing into play the power of the political field, it is virtually assured media attention.

4

Organizing the Immigration Debate in the French Media

Giving Voice to Civil Society and Strategizing against Le Pen

'*Événement*' is about putting the emphasis on what we judge to be the day's most important news. . . . All the newspaper's desks contribute, and the topic is approached and problematized from as many angles as possible: whether through investigation or analysis, news reports or interviews, the point is to show, decode, explain, confront, give sense to the news . . . giving rise to the newspaper's own editorial position.

– Serge July, *Libération* director[1]

Libération shifted its position on integration in line with SOS-Racisme. We did it together. It was a parallel reflection . . . around the question of what would provide a solid base to fight the National Front and to convince public opinion, to show how the defense of immigrants was linked to the French republican tradition. We concluded that "equality of rights" (*égalité des droits*) was stronger than the discourse of "the right to be different" (*le droit à la différence*).

– Laurent Joffrin, *Libération* managing editor[2]

Between 1973 and 2006, the French journalistic construction of the immigration debate went through several phases. An analysis of news coverage by leading national newspapers *Le Monde*, *Le Figaro*, and *Libération* and national television evening newscasts of TF1 and France 2 reveals the following: During the 1970s and early 1980s, French news coverage of immigration was dominated by the racism and humanitarian frames; the latter remained dominant through the 2000s. In the early 1980s, cultural diversity emerged as an important frame. By the 1990s and 2000s, however, the discourse shifted toward cultural unity, either celebrating successful cases of immigrant integration or expressing fears of a lack of national cohesion. Public order was also a major frame throughout the four decades and was highest in the early 1990s. In contrast to the United States, attention to the global economy frame held steady or increased during the 1990s and 2000s. Civil society

---

[1] Serge July, "*Libération* encore plus Libé," *Libération*, October 11–12, 2003.
[2] Laurent Joffrin interview (1997).

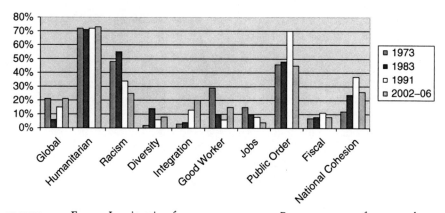

FIGURE 4.1. France: Immigration frames, 1970s–2000s. Percentages are of news packages mentioning each frame (1973 *n* = 63; 1983 *n* = 116; 1991 *n* = 220; 2002–2006 *n* = 336), with core newspaper and television news samples equally weighted. Given that most packages mention multiple frames, the sum of percentages exceeds 100.

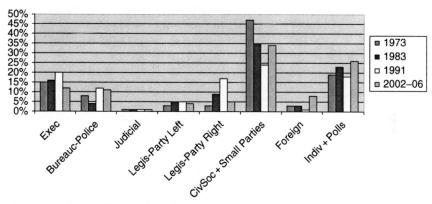

FIGURE 4.2. France: Types of speakers, 1970s–2000s. Percentages are of total speakers cited (1973 *n* = 461; 1983 *n* = 1,084; 1991 *n* = 2,073; 2002–2006 *n* = 3,869), with core newspaper and television news samples equally weighted. Because not all speaker types are shown, the sum of percentages is less than 100.

associations, as well as far left and far right political parties, tended to be strong drivers of news coverage, with the exception of 1991, when the immigration issue moved to the center of government and major political party struggle. Unaffiliated individuals increased gradually in prominence over time. (See Figures 4.1 and 4.2.)

The main cross-medium difference in France is that the humanitarian frame tends to be more prominent on television news than in newspapers (as a proportion of all frame mentions; see Online Table 5.3). By the 2000s, television tends to emphasize integration over national cohesion, the opposite of the tendency in newspapers. Quotes or paraphrases from unaffiliated individuals or survey results are much more common on television news (30 percent of all speakers cited across the four decades vs. 13 percent in newspapers). Poll mentions make up only a small percentage of this total – just 1 percent for newspapers and less than 1 percent for television news (not shown separately in Figure 4.2).

Shifts in television news frames generally accord with those of newspapers, but newspapers tend to lead television coverage, rather than vice versa as Bourdieu (1998) argued in *On Television*.[3] Newspapers highlighted cultural diversity and national cohesion in the early 1980s far more than did television; only in the 1990s did television follow suit, with a substantial rise in national cohesion frames and a slight increase in cultural diversity frames. Likewise, in the 1980s and 1990s, newspapers began focusing attention on integration before television did (appearing in 8 vs. 0 percent of coverage in 1983, and 16 vs. 9 percent in the 1990s, respectively); only in the 2000s did television news surpass newspapers in attention to this frame (22 percent vs. 17 percent of newspaper packages). Television seems to have been more tightly attuned than newspapers to shifts in the political climate. Whereas both the humanitarian and public order frames remained relatively steady for newspapers, French television coverage shifted sharply as political elite discourse and policy took a strong restrictionist turn: between 1983 and 1991, humanitarian frames fell from being mentioned in 62 percent to 53 percent of news packages, while public order frames increased their presence from 26 to 58 percent of news packages (see Online Table 5.2.)

In contrast to the United States, however, the French mediated immigration debate does not become increasingly simplified as a binary opposition between the humanitarian and public order frames. Between the 1970s and 2000s, these two frames increased very slightly for French newspapers (from 43 to 45 percent of all frames) and declined for television news (from 61 to 57 percent; see Online Table 5.3.). Thus, French newspapers remained less concentrated around these two frames than their U.S. counterparts, while French television was steady at the highest level of frame concentration achieved in the United States (compare to Figure 3.5).

These discursive shifts were linked, as in the United States, to a host of political and economic transformations and contingent events. France was caught up in the same wave of neo-liberal globalization, although its national health, retirement, tax, and unemployment insurance policies tended to mitigate against the kind of widening wealth gap experienced in the United States. Immigration flows approached historic levels in the 1970s and then leveled off, with the foreign-born percentage of the population remaining high. After the protests of May 1968, France experienced its own rise of "new" social movements, including human rights, feminist, gay rights, and environmentalist groups (Noiriel 2007). France's well-known nationalist anti-immigration backlash, led by Jean-Marie Le Pen's National Front party, began in earnest in the

---

[3] Siracusa (2001, 25) documents a general tendency for *Le Monde* and *Libération*, in particular, to set the agenda for French television news.

early 1980s and contributed to a realignment of the French political field away from classic economic left-right oppositions toward an increasing emphasis on cultural identity (Juhem 2001).

French media coverage tracked these changes in the market and political fields, even as it was the product of the journalistic field's own distinctive logics. Between the 1980s and 2000s, there was a marked commercialization of television in France, with the launching of private channels, increases in advertising, and introduction of Nielsen-style audience tracking (Balle 2001). At the same time, especially as compared to the U.S. journalistic field, government policies and journalistic professional logics in France have continued to promote civic and partisan conceptions of journalistic excellence against market criteria.

My aim, as in the preceding chapter on the United States, is to show how the French journalistic field refracted political and economic trends and events through a particular set of professional practices. In France, these practices include the rise of a multidesk, comprehensive "social" approach to reporting immigration, self-conscious positioning of news form or content in relation to those of competing news outlets, and a tendency to discredit the far right while indexing news coverage to political elites, whether right or left. I now turn to a closer look at these specific elements in news framing and journalistic field dynamics, in each case situated in relation to immigration social processes and political trends and events.

HUMANITARIAN AND GLOBAL ECONOMY FRAMES: CONTEXTUALIZING NEWS FORMATS

Since the 1970s, the humanitarian frame has consistently been the dominant frame in French media coverage of immigration, appearing in at least 70 percent of the coverage. Only in 1991 did any other frame – public order – rival the humanitarian frame for dominance. The global economy frame has been an important secondary frame, especially in newspapers, where it appeared in about one-third of coverage most years (see Online Table 5.2).

Certainly, French immigrants and the so-called second generation have suffered socially and economically, all in the context of an increasingly brutal global capitalist economy, and there have been many cases of human rights violations concerning *sans papiers* (undocumented immigrants) and *banlieue* "second-generation" immigrant youths (Siméant 1998; Hargreaves 2007; Schain 2008). The social suffering of immigrants has been a long-standing cause of the far left, chiefly the Revolutionary Communist League (LCR, founded in 1969) and the Workers' Struggle group (LO, founded in 1968). In more recent years, the immigrants' cause has also been taken up by the Green Party (Les Verts, founded in 1984) and the French Communist Party (PCF, founded in 1920, and during the 1970s and early 1980s quite hostile toward immigrants). Historically, immigrant associations were organized by the migrant-sending countries, such as Algeria or

Morocco, or by French citizens on behalf of or in "solidarity" with immigrants, such as the Protestant humanitarian organization Cimade and antiracism groups such as Movement Against Racism and for Friendship Between Peoples (MRAP). After the law was changed in 1981 to permit immigrants to form their own associations, many new immigrant-led associations emerged.

Immigrant rights associations played a major role in getting immigration on the public agenda in the late 1960s and early 1970s by framing it as a problem of human rights and racism. During the 1980s and 1990s, the socialist government in turn became the strongest promoter of the humanitarian frame. With the right returned to power for most of the 2000s, it fell back upon immigrant rights groups, especially those advocating for *sans papiers*, to keep the focus on humanitarian problems.[4]

Helping assure attention to humanitarian concerns has been a close fit between the habitus of journalists covering immigration and their counterparts in the associations. French reporters at the leading national media outlets tend to have degrees in the social sciences and humanities from the most prestigious universities, *grandes écoles* (especially the Paris Institute of Politics [IEP], commonly known as "Sciences Po"), and journalism schools (CFJ Paris or Lille).[5] For the most part, their French homologues at the leading antiracism and immigrant rights advocacy groups exhibit similar elite educational profiles: many of the leaders are lawyers or law professors.[6] Thus, socially and culturally, French elite journalists and immigrant rights advocates share a common world – although this does not mean that tensions do not sometimes exist between the two groups.[7]

---

[4] For histories of immigrant rights activism around these issues, see Feldblum (1993), Blatt (1997), Wihtol de Wenden and Leveau (2001), Iskander (2007), and Monforte (2009).

[5] Just to cite a few examples, editors and reporters who have frequently written about immigration include Xavier Ternisien (IEP, CFJ-Paris), Philippe Bernard (M.A. in law, M.A. in journalism at CFJ-Paris), and Robert Solé (CFJ-Lille) of *Le Monde*; Laurent Joffrin (IEP and CFJ-Paris), Eric Favereau (economics degree from a grande école), and Jean Quatremer (legal degree) of *Libération*; and Nicolas Beau (IEP), who worked for both *Le Monde* and *Libération*. (Some immigration reporters also have backgrounds in student, labor, or humanitarian activism, such as *Le Monde*'s Sylvia Zappi and Alain Lebaube.)

[6] For example, Danièle Lochak, the long-time president of the legal rights advocacy group GISTI, was a professor of law (now emeritus) at the University of Paris-Nanterre; Jean-Pierre Dubois, also a law professor, and Michel Tubiana, a practicing attorney, are the current and former presidents, respectively, of the French Human Rights League (LDH). Malek Boutih, president of SOS-Racisme, has graduate degrees in law and journalism (CFJ-Paris), and Mouloud Aounit of MRAP received multiple graduate degrees in economics.

[7] Most French journalists do not see themselves as simply allies of the pro-immigrant associations. "You have to be careful with the associations. You can't assume that the information they give you is true," *Libération* immigration reporter Dominique Simonnot told me (interview 1997). "You have to verify what they say with the appropriate government sources." Similarly, Elise Vincent of *Le Monde* (interview 2012) told me that the newspaper in recent years was trying to move away from being overly dependent on immigrant rights associations for ideas about newsworthy topics.

As the last chapter showed, in the United States, journalist-initiated coverage and feature articles were associated with the humanitarian frame – demonstrating the affinity between the American narrative form and this kind of personalized, human interest frame. No such special affinity exists in French coverage, although French reporters do from time to time write in-depth features detailing the difficulties of the migrant experience. But the narrative approach is usually not as focused, or formulaic, as is typical in American articles. A frequently used alternative to narrative is an approach that might be called a "collection of voices." A range of individuals, organizationally affiliated or not, speak in series. There is generally no clear storyline, just a cinema verité of impressions, observations, snippets of conversations, often incorporating the journalistic questioning voice. For example, on the eve of a pan-European immigration policy meeting, *Libération* examined migrant smuggling from Turkey into Greece and Italy: the article quoted several migrants and smugglers but did not construct a strong storyline around any of them.[8] On another occasion, a *Libération* article provided short profiles of four *sans papiers* waiting in a city hall line to "regularize" their residency status.[9]

Nevertheless, there is an indirect relationship between French journalistic practice and the consistent strength of the humanitarian frame in French news coverage. Civil society actions, such as demonstrations and protests, make up a substantial proportion of immigration news coverage in France (see Figure 2.5). Thus, it is both because French associations are likely to promote the humanitarian frame *and* because French journalists are likely to cover events sponsored by such associations that the humanitarian frame is so prominent in French mediated immigration discourse.[10]

The global economy frame, in contrast, first emerged in French media discourse as one promoted by government (concerned with development issues

---

[8] Marc Semo, "Événement: Istanbul, porte d'entrée du 'paradis,'" *Libération*, June 21, 2002, p. 4.

[9] Emmanuelle Philippart, "Dans la foule, quatre trajectoires," *Libération*, September 3, 2002, p. 3. Similarly, Florence Aubenas's "investigation [enquête]" of the reasons behind anti-Semitic attacks in North African immigrant-dominated *banlieues* ("Un soir, la meuf du JT nous a chauffés," *Libération*, April 2, 2002) mostly consists of a string of quotes of *banlieue* residents identified only by first name or pseudonym. In another *Libération* article, unnamed reporters survey the range of opinion on the street after Le Pen won second place behind incumbent Jacques Chirac in the first round of presidential voting in 2002 ("Votez escroc, pas facho!" [Vote for the crook, not the fascist!], *Libération*, April 23, 2002). French articles with a stronger narrative structure do exist (e.g., Cécile Chambraud, "Emigration: le long chemin de Mady et Yaouba vers l'Espagne," *Le Monde*, May 25, 2006, p. 1), but they are rare and in almost all cases are part of multigenre ensembles including interviews, analyses, and commentaries.

[10] Some might argue that the French are simply more "contentious" (Tilly 1986) and that civil society demonstrations, strikes, and public policy conferences are more common in France than in the United States. This may be true, although on any given day there are likely many such events in both countries, providing plenty of opportunities to cover civil society if media chose to do so. The key difference likely lies in political cultural attitudes about the importance and legitimacy of civil society protest, attitudes which the media both draw on and help sustain.

in its former colonies) and the far right, in a more critical, anticapitalist vein. An editor of the far right journal *Faire face pour l'Occident* (Stand Up for the West) offered a succinct expression of the global economy frame in a 1973 commentary published in *Le Monde*: "For uncontrolled capitalism ... uncontrolled immigration."[11] During the early 1980s, the global economy frame dipped in prominence as the far right dropped its anticapitalist stance at the same time that immigrant rights advocates focused mainly on racism and cultural diversity. During the 1990s and especially 2000s, global economic links to immigration were once again stressed by migrant-sending countries, international bodies such as the European Union, immigrant rights associations, and far left parties. For example, as part of its comprehensive *événement* coverage of Interior Minister Sarkozy's proposal to suppress "endured immigration" (*immigration subie*, i.e., migration from poor countries) in favor of economically strategic "selected immigration" (*immigration choisie*), a *Libération* reporter interviewed African officials and activists attending a World Forum on Human Rights in Nantes. Offering a sharply critical explanation of why Sarkozy's plan was bound to fail, a Togolese researcher for Amnesty International articulated well the global economy frame: "Africa's profound malaise accentuates the massive exodus, which cannot be stopped by any wall, even if it touches the sky. The scheming of the multinational corporations, the arms sales, the control of resources, the authoritarian governments supported by France, all of these push people to flee at the peril of their lives, forced out by hunger and war."[12]

In contrast to the United States, where the global economy frame has become less prominent over time, in France, it has continued to be highlighted in newspaper immigration coverage. This divergence may be linked to broader U.S.-French differences: as a member of the European Union and as a former colonial power in close touch with its many former colonies, arguably France looks outward more than the United States. The organization and presentation of news, however, shapes the degree to which journalists are able to convey such an outward-looking perspective on immigration. Because of the lesser reliance on narrative conventions, French journalism has been able to make more room for the global economy frame, as well as for other more conceptual frames. French journalists are less likely to think of their job as one of finding a human interest story to tell, but rather as one of decoding official pronouncements, offering historical and other background context, and giving voice to a range of perspectives.

---

[11] Jack Marchal, "Libres opinions: A capitalisme sauvage ... immigration sauvage," *Le Monde*, September 26, 1973, p. 18. Buzzi (1994, 22) characterizes the National Front during this period as a "revolutionary-nationalist" party, offering, among other things, a "virulent condemnation of capitalism and communism [and] an interventionist conception [of the state] in economic matters."

[12] Nicolas de la Casiniere, "A Nantes, les carences de la France décriées," *Libération*, July 12, 2006, p. 3.

Beginning in the late 1970s at several leading French newspapers, immigration reporting came to be organized under a thematic "social problems" (*société*) desk grouping together education, housing, immigration, and crime reporting. For example, *La Croix*'s *société* webpage defines its purview as "poverty, associations, and immigration."[13] This *société* desk was set up in explicit contrast to both the "general information" beat that focused on crimes, disasters, and light "human interest" news, and the "political" beat that covered the daily pronouncements and policy actions of government and the political parties (Hubé and Kaciaf 2006; see also Saïtta 2005). In their study of *Le Monde* editorial conferences, Hubé and Kaciaf (2006, 192–204) found that the *société* desk editor consistently opposed the political desk editor: "For her, the duty of journalists is to '*resist* the problem definitions' being imposed by powerful actors in the political space" (my emphasis). According to Hubé and Kaciaf, *société* reporters see their jobs as "emphasizing the background questions" and "helping civil society speak." And, in contrast to political reporters focused on the day's events, *société* beat editors and reporters have "a more magazine-like conception of information ... understanding events as illustration of broader problems." Thus, the *société* desk pages consist of "thematic dossiers, mixing analyses, reportages and testimonies, less strictly tied to breaking news."

Even beyond the in-depth, multiperspectival coverage encouraged by the *société* desk, which by the 2000s included immigration reporting at most French national newspapers, the immigration beat itself came to be seen as demanding additional cross-desk coordination. *Le Monde*'s former chief editor in charge of immigration coverage, Philippe Bernard, described to me how immigration came to be coordinated across multiple beats (*rubriques*) and desks (*services*): "I had constructed it as a transversal beat ... [bringing together] several desks – politics, international, and others ... this horizontal mode of functioning is [more and more] considered at *Le Monde* as the best way to work."[14]

As explained in Chapter 2, this kind of multidesk approach to news coverage has also been progressively institutionalized in French journalism since the 1980s through the *événement* page-one format pioneered by *Libération* and progressively adopted by other French newspapers. *Événement* requires a high level of teamwork and coordination. For better or worse, French journalists are acutely aware of how this format provides a ready-made framework to break down any topic into multiple genres: editorial, event chronology, historical context, photo, interview, etc. (Blin 2002, 183; Hubé and Kaciaf 2006, 197; Hubé 2008). Integration – within desks, across desks, and on the page – is especially important when attempting to articulate a frame, such as global economy, that only a handful of civil society or governmental actors are actively

---

[13] See *La Croix* website, Editorial positions (rédaction), http://www.la-croix.com/Services/La-Croix/La-Redaction/L-equipe-_NG_-2011-04-29-565338, accessed September 3, 2011.
[14] Philippe Bernard interviews (1997, 2004).

promoting and that runs against the grain of much of the popular public discourse.[15] In this debate ensemble format, commentaries and news articles often appear together on the same page, making it easier for alternative viewpoints expressed in commentaries to be picked up in news articles (often focused explicitly on documenting the range of opinion on a given issue) and vice versa. This format thus breaks down any sharp "wall" between news and commentary and any attendant privileging of the former over the latter, which can serve to narrow the range of discourse (as in the U.S. press, where critical economic frames are relegated to the opinion pages).

In addition, the *événement* formula helps ensure the presentation of multiple frames (and speakers) regardless of whether the news concerns ordinary individuals or political elites. For example, the January 21, 2004 edition of *Libération* features a page-one *événement* entitled "The New Chinese of Paris," which elaborates five distinct frames, including global economy. The news package is pegged to the Chinese New Year, the French government's official designation of 2004 as "The Year of China," and the trend of rapid growth in Chinese immigration to France. The main article on page two provides a "Tableau" of the Chinese in France, with subheads such as "Who are the Chinese migrants in France?", "How do they emigrate?", and "Why do they leave [China]?" At the bottom of page three are interviews with Chinese immigrants (Nicole, thirty-three, store clerk, and Veronique, thirty-four, restaurant owner) about their successes in adapting to French culture and impressions of "their community and their host country." Along the far right side of page three is *Libération*'s official editorial, which discusses the problems as well as opportunities posed by the Chinese "diaspora" in relation to both Chinese and French domestic politics and economics and French-Chinese governmental relations.

The use of a thematic-oriented format does not mean that French journalists are indifferent to the "new" in news. During the early 1980s, the antiracism organization SOS-Racisme was initially popular with French reporters because of its "fresh" approach. As one French journalist recalls, "[until the rise of SOS-Racisme], antiracism was done by these bloody pains, these bores in the journalistic sense, I mean, these guys who always had the same line, always the same ideas" (Juhem 1999, 134). However, as argued throughout this book, French newspaper journalism – both because of its closer relation to civil society through the social problems desk and its use of the debate ensemble format – is able to push beyond the easy search for novelty, or at least has the luxury of digging deeper for something new.

---

15 *Le Monde*'s more conceptual orientation toward news coverage is also related to its long-standing status as the only major afternoon newspaper in France. Although it sometimes does scoop its competitors, often it finds itself in the position of searching for some way to "go a little beyond the morning newspapers ... to advance the story" (Bernard Brigouleix interview 1998). Often, *Le Monde*'s "extra" contribution is its analysis and reflection, placing breaking news in broader perspective.

French media writer Amaury de Rochegonde insisted to me that even former *Le Monde* executive editor Edwy Plenel, known for his investigative journalism, nevertheless also wanted *Le Monde* during his tenure in the early 2000s to "be a crossroads of opinion, to offer the entire palette, to give the right to speak to everyone."[16] Likewise, *Le Figaro* immigration reporter Jean-Michel Decujis described his vocation in the following terms: "I'm a journalist, so above all [I'm committed] to giving people the ability to speak."[17]

This primary concern with ideas and ideological diversity, rather than the "reporting" of information or the crafting of stories – as in the United States – helps make more room for the exploration and interrogation of not simply more marginal or complex frames like global economy, but, in general, for a broader range of frames, as shown in Chapter 6 on multiperspectival news.

RACISM AND CULTURAL IDENTITY: LIBÉRATION AND LE MONDE STRUGGLE FOR DISTINCTION

France is sometimes presented as having a long-standing aversion to multiculturalism and an indifference to problems of racism and xenophobia (Horowitz and Noiriel 1992). Yet, during the 1970s and 1980s, racism was one of the dominant media frames of immigration, before declining in the 1990s and 2000s. Moreover, during the early 1980s, cultural diversity was widely debated and often celebrated in some quarters of the French media.

If French news media framing were a simple reflection of social conditions, one would expect actual immigrant diversity and anti-immigrant xenophobia to have been highest in the early 1980s and to have subsequently dropped, but this is not the case (see Appendix C). The non-European–origin population in France has continued to increase into the 2000s, and artists, musicians, and writers from these communities have become increasingly visible and respected. And although anti-immigrant prejudice as measured by opinion surveys seems to have decreased since the 1960s, racial/ethnic discrimination in housing and employment, as well as hate crimes – especially against North African-origin individuals – have increased.

On the other hand, the trajectory of antiracism and diversity activism, both governmental and nongovernmental, maps relatively closely to patterns of media coverage. During the late 1960s and early 1970s, a series of violent racist attacks on North African immigrants prompted high-profile public protests supported by such intellectuals as Michel Foucault, Jean-Paul Sartre, and Jean Genet, and provided additional momentum to the 1972 passage of antiracism legislation. In 1981, President Mitterrand officially recognized and provided government funding for immigrant-led associations; subsequently, combating

---

[16] Amaury de Rochegonde interview (2002).
[17] Jean-Michel Decujis interview (1997).

racism and discrimination became a central cause of these groups.[18] The association SOS-Racisme was self-consciously groomed by the new socialist administration to attack racist aspects of anti-immigration rhetoric and policies advocated by the National Front and some mainstream right politicians (Juhem 1999).

Pro–cultural diversity claims first began to be raised during the early 1970s by immigrant worker associations, influenced by anticolonial critiques, who insisted that their particular problems and identities could not be subsumed entirely within French universalistic religious, humanitarian, or labor projects. Sending countries, often via associations they funded inside France (such as the Algerian government-sponsored *Amicale des Algériens*/Association of Algerians), also sought to maintain the cultural traditions of immigrant communities as a way to assure the continued allegiance (and remittances) of immigrant workers living in France (Weil 1991, 145). French state policies during the 1970s that promoted immigrants' "right to be different" (*le droit à la différence*) likewise reflected less of a desire to create a "pluricultural" France than to ensure the eventual return of immigrants to their homelands. After 1977, however, President Giscard d'Estaing's "rhetoric of choice and pluralism was largely dropped from the official language of immigration" (Wihtol de Wenden 1988, 243–244). Partly to distinguish himself from Giscard d'Estaing and from the communist left, socialist François Mitterrand explicitly endorsed *le droit à la différence* during his 1981 presidential campaign (Hargreaves 1995, 194) and continued to do so for the first two years he was in office (Hollifield 1994, 159). Not all immigrant rights organizations embraced the cause of cultural diversity, but many did. MRAP (via its magazine *Différences*), the Federation of Associations in Solidarity with Immigrant Workers (FASTI), and the trade union French Democratic Confederation of Labor (CFDT) actively promoted immigrants' right to preserve their own cultures in order to create a new "*pluriculturelle*" and "*multiraciale*" France.[19] From October to December of 1983, the nascent *beur*[20] movement launched its first "march for equality": included in the demonstrators' many demands was the "right to expression of minority cultures."[21] SOS-Racisme also initially supported multiculturalism and, for a time, was among its most prominent and "mediagenic" proponents

---

[18] Mogniss Abdallah interview (1997). For histories of racism and antiracism activism and policy in France, see Hargreaves (1995, 2007), Bleich (2003), Chapman and Frader (2004), and Noiriel (2007).

[19] See, e.g., "Les Français plus," *Différences*, no. 1, April 1981 and Michel Lefranc and Manuel Vaz Dias (respectively, president and member of the national bureau of FASTI), "Vers une société inter-culturelle," *Sans Frontière*, May 9, 1981.

[20] *Beur* is a French slang term that refers to second-generation North African immigrant youths, most of them French citizens.

[21] See, e.g., *Témoignage Chrétien*, November 7–13, 1983.

(Blatt 1997; Juhem 1999). Pro-diversity claims continued to be made by some prominent intellectuals and activist groups as late as 1985.[22]

During the mid- and late-1980s, however, the public discourse changed completely. By the late 1980s, pro-diversity claims had been effectively excommunicated from the realm of "legitimate controversy" (Hallin 1986). The turning point came in September 1983, when the far right National Front party used anti-immigration rhetoric to win a municipal election in Dreux, a small village near Paris. French news media not only conveyed this broader political shift, they also played an active role in making it happen. Prior to 1983, *Libération* had celebrated cultural diversity in its news choices as well as official editorials; after 1983, it led the fight to refocus the public debate around integration.

Libération, formerly a small Maoist newspaper, had closed in the months leading up to the 1981 election. After Mitterrand was elected, it relaunched itself with a dramatic new visual format and a more tempered politics. Immigration, which had long been a major focus for the newspaper, now became a means by which it would forge its new distinctive "cultural" image, both ideologically and stylistically: such differentiation helped ensure its commercial success in a national newspaper field largely reliant on daily street sales.[23] In 1983, half of *Libération*'s news packages mentioned – and often embraced – the cultural diversity frame.[24] One of its editorials proclaimed: "In France [today], it will be necessary to learn how to live in a multicultural [*pluriculturelle*] society."[25] Former *Libération* reporter Eric Dupin interpreted the newspaper's militant pro-immigrant stance as a kind of "compensation" for its neo-liberal right turn on economics in the early 1980s.[26] Confirming this impression, this study finds that *Libération* has been consistently more likely to emphasize the neo-liberal good worker frame than either *Le Monde* or *Le Figaro* (even as it has also featured many left-leaning viewpoints and voices). Because *Libération* was read attentively both by its direct competitors at *Le Monde* and by television journalists[27] who were impressed with its graphic, emotional style, *Libération*'s framing of

---

[22] The important immigrant-edited newspaper *Sans Frontière*, which, since its founding during the late 1970s, had equally stressed social and cultural issues, began emphasizing more forcefully the case for a multicultural France in 1985, when it transformed itself into the (short-lived) weekly *Baraka* (Driss El Yazami interviews 1996 and 1997). See, e.g., "La culture sans filet," *Baraka*, No. 0, December 1985.

[23] Between 1975 and 1983, *Libération* published more news items about immigration than *Le Monde*, *Le Figaro*, and national television news combined. Its annual number of immigration articles ranged from 241 in 1976 to 576 in 1983 (Bonnafous 1991, 33). See also Battegay and Boubeker (1993, 62).

[24] See Online Table 6.2., Immigration Frames in French Core Newspapers by Decade, 1970s–2000s.

[25] François Paul-Boncour, "Une implosion statistique, une bombe dans l'imaginaire," *Libération*, September 9, 1983.

[26] Philippe Juhem interview with Eric Dupin, 1995, Paris, transcript shared with author.

[27] Author interviews with Michel Trillat (France 2), Pierre Allain (France 2), Guilaine Chenu (France 2, former TF1), and Antoine Lefèvre (TF1).

immigration in cultural terms was also influential, at least in terms of setting up one of the intellectual poles against which other actors were forced to contend.

At *Le Monde*, whose readership composition most closely matched that of *Libération*, a struggle inside the newspaper pitted three factions against one another: those who continued to view immigration in purely economic terms, those who wanted to get on the multicultural bandwagon, and those who wanted a new emphasis on integration. *Le Monde*'s long-time immigration reporter, Jean Benoît, focused on wages, working conditions, and slum housing (*bidonvilles*). More than any other journalist during the 1970s, according to historian Patrick Weil, Benoît helped put the humanitarian suffering of immigrants on the political agenda.[28] By the early 1980s, however, this focus on immigrant workers was quickly being displaced by a concern with the "second generation" and their relationship to French culture. Benoît, who would shortly retire, had a hard time "switching to this new reality."[29]

Opposed to Benoît were two factions inside the newspaper. The first was represented by reporters like Nicolas Beau, relatively sympathetic to the politics of cultural identity (as was the socialist party and *Libération* at the time; Beau himself would move on to *Libération* in 1985). The second, which ultimately prevailed, was made up of many of *Le Monde*'s senior editors, practicing Catholics, who aligned themselves with the anti-multicultural "Jacobin" left, thus consciously or unconsciously marking the newspaper's independence both vis-à-vis the government and *Libération*. After unabashedly campaigning against the Giscard d'Estaing administration and achieving its avowed goal of electing the socialists, *Le Monde* had struggled to stop a steady decline in readership. To revive itself commercially, it also needed to demonstrate that it had not lost its independent voice.[30]

Differences in *Libération*'s and *Le Monde*'s coverage of the "*beur* march for equality and against racism" from Marseille to Paris illustrate the widening gap between the two leading newspapers of the French left. The event was extensively and prominently covered in *Libération*, from its first steps on October 15 through its triumphant arrival in Paris in December. *Libération* heralded the march's arrival in December as the beginning of a new "multicultural" France.

---

[28] Patrick Weil interview (1997). Benoît was a former foreign correspondent in Africa for several French magazines before joining *Le Monde* in 1968. His position on immigration was made clear in the opening lines of his 1980 book *Dossier E ... comme esclaves* (File S ... as in Slave): "My thesis is that immigrant workers are a new sort of slave."

[29] Interviews with Nicolas Beau (1997) and Philippe Bernard (1997). Bernard, who joined *Le Monde* in 1983 and became the chief immigration reporter during the late 1980s, remarked that, until the mid-1980s, immigration was not perceived as a problem of "integration ... because there was a perception [among journalists and politicians] that immigrants were not here permanently ... there was a refusal to see that they would stay."

[30] See Benson (2004) for a detailed account of *Le Monde*'s successive editorial and commercial regimes from its founding after World War II through the mid-2000s.

Le Monde, which initially ignored the event, eventually embraced it but reinterpreted the march's message to fit with Catholic universalism. This task was made somewhat easier by the fact that the march was unofficially sponsored by the Catholic priest Christian Delorme, who had drawn parallels between the *beurs'* struggle and the universalist messages of Mahatma Gandhi and Martin Luther King, Jr. When *Le Monde* finally featured the march on its front page, it was no accident that the editors headlined the article "Forty apostles of anti-racism."[31]

Throughout the 1980s, Robert Solé, *Le Monde's société* editor, wrote numerous page-one analyses/commentaries in favor of integration and assimilation. Solé described his position in no uncertain terms: "I was never, instinctively, favorable towards the emphasis being put on anti-racism [in terms of the right to be different]. I was always favorable, by contrast, toward a certain right of resemblance."[32] In fact, *Le Monde* was less likely than *Libération* to include the cultural diversity frame during the 1980s, 1990s, and 2000s, and also less likely to mention the racism frame during the 1980s and 1990s.

The National Front's breakthrough in the 1983 Dreux election created a new configuration of positions in the political field, which were soon amplified and extended in the intellectual and journalistic fields. In its campaigning leading up to this election, the National Front turned multicultural antiracism on its head: on behalf of "the French," Le Pen insisted that "it is our duty to affirm our national personality and, us too, our right to be different."[33] A number of leading intellectuals, most notably the philosopher Pierre-André Taguieff (1988), interpreted Le Pen's use of the differentialist logic as proof of an inherent weakness in multicultural politics, even accusing SOS-Racisme and other antiracist groups of sharing the same "racist" logic as the National Front, and called for reframing antiracist discourses in terms of integration. When the Socialist Party lost control of the legislative branch in 1986, Taguieff and other Jacobin left intellectuals, journalists, and politicians – including President Mitterrand – saw the need, and the opportunity, to put distance between the left and SOS-Racisme's soft multicultural brand of antiracist activism. Although immediately occasioned by the rise of both SOS-Racisme and the National Front, this intellectual and political revival of republicanism via the notion of integration was also necessitated by a number of national and international forces challenging the supremacy of the French centralized state: the threat from "above" posed by the European Union, the threat from below of regionalist movements in Corsica and Brittany, and growing financial difficulties

---

[31] See "Paris-Marseille: ça marche pour les immigrés" (October 15–16, 1983), "Marche pour l'egalité: beur is beautiful" (December 1, 1983), "Paris sur 'Beur'" (December 3–4, 1983) and "Paris grande finale des beurs" (December 5, 1983), all multigenre debate ensembles in *Libération*; and Nicolas Beau, "Quarante apôtres de l'antiracisme," *Le Monde*, November 23, 1983.

[32] Philippe Juhem interview with Robert Solé (transcript provided to author), September 9, 1995, Paris. See also Solé (1988).

[33] Le Pen in *Le Monde*, September 21, 1982, cited in Guiraudon (2000, 185).

in maintaining the social welfare state, linked to chronic long-term unemployment and stagnant economic growth.[34]

Libération managing editor Laurent Joffrin, who had actively promoted SOS-Racisme and even served as an informal advisor to the group, was one of the first leading journalists to reverse course. Only a few years after the Marche des Beurs, *Libération*, which had been so openly multiculturalist in 1983, joined the integrationist bandwagon.[35] Although *Libération*'s coverage continued to acknowledge the cultural diversity frame, by 1991, it was more likely to mention the integration frame than was *Le Monde* (29 percent vs. 12 percent, respectively), a pattern that continued, if a bit tempered, into the 2000s.[36]

How did this turn-around happen? As the quote from my interview with Laurent Joffrin at the beginning of this chapter indicates, a sense of political necessity and urgency drove the shift: an engaged press allied itself with the leading antiracist organizations to combat the rise of the far right National Front. (*Le Monde*'s current immigration reporter, Elise Vincent, stressed to me that this concern not to cover issues in a way that might help, directly or indirectly, the electoral prospects of the National Front has continued to be a major factor shaping many French journalists' news judgments.[37])

When the political winds turned against diversity politics and antiracism, there was also no internal professional counterforce constraining (even slightly) the journalists from likewise shifting position. The number of Arab-origin or Asian-origin French journalists is extremely small: at many of the major national news organizations, their number probably could be counted on one hand.[38] Efforts to organize French journalists of color on behalf of "diversity" have not yet made major headway. Compared to the multimillion dollar–funded UNITY,

---

[34] Denis Lacorne personal communication (1997). See also Favell (1998) and Guiraudon (2000). A French "consensus" on how to treat cultural difference continued to be negotiated during the 1990s and 2000s. The so-called headscarves affairs (*affaires des foulards*), which began in 1989 and then reemerged in 2003 and 2004, are probably the best known events prompting public debate about integration and national identity (Thomas 2006; Bowen 2007).

[35] Laurent Joffrin interview (1997). See also Joffrin (1992, 143).

[36] Even so, the racism frame, although shedding its connection to identity politics and receiving less journalistic attention today than it received in the 1970s and early 1980s, has not disappeared from the French mediated debate. In large part, this is due to the continuing salience of racism as a charge regularly leveled at far right politicians such as Le Pen or more mainstream politicians who copy his discourse. Other sources of continued attention to racism are the occasional policy initiatives to combat racism undertaken by both parties. In recent years, discrimination or "access" racism has finally begun to be taken seriously at the highest levels, although the shift has been more rhetorical than substantive (Hargreaves 2004, 229).

[37] Elise Vincent interview (2012).

[38] My analysis of immigration news journalistic bylines (see previously noted methodological caveats in Chapter 3 footnote 21) finds less than 3 percent of *Le Monde* and *Libération* bylines with North African/Arab names; *Le Figaro* had none. See Online Table 1.6., Gender and National Origin of French and U.S. Immigration Reporters.

the only comparable organization in France is Diversity Club (Club Diversité), a small informal, unfunded association of journalists and other professionals of North African, sub-Saharan African, and Asian background. As the president of the association told me, "the right [in government] more than the left has been more willing to make extra efforts for diversity. The socialists say 'we are the diversity.' But it's clear if we leave it up to the good will of the media, nothing will happen – ever."[39]

DEFINING THE THREAT: IMMIGRANTS OR LE PEN?

If the early 1970s news coverage of immigration primarily portrayed immigrants as victims or heroes, by the 1980s and especially the 1990s, threat frames had become increasingly prominent – almost achieving parity with combined victim and hero frames[40] in 1991. During the 2000s, this tendency was reversed, as coverage again became more positive or at least more sympathetic to the plight of immigrants. (See Figure 4.3.)

Despite the heavy media attention accorded occasional riots and other crimes involving the "second generation" of immigrants (along with other residents of low-income *banlieues*), there has been no dramatic increase in the amount of criminal activity related to immigration in France. Nor is there substantial evidence

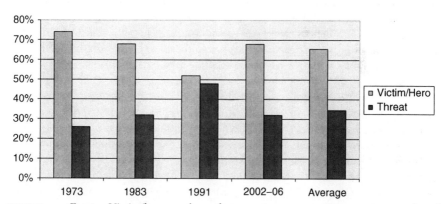

FIGURE 4.3. France: Victim/hero vs. threat frames, 1970s–2000s. Percentages are of total frames mentioned (each coded as presence/absence in a news package; 1973 *n* = 169; 1983 *n* = 301; 1991 *n* = 621; 2002–2006 *n* = 811), with core newspaper and television news samples equally weighted.

---

[39] Abou Diarra interview (2009). Information about the organization is available at: http://www.club-diversite.org/edito.html. See also Rigoni (2007).

[40] During all periods, victim frames vastly exceeded hero frames: 1973 (victim 59 percent, hero 15 percent); 1983 (victim 58 percent, hero 10 percent); 1991 (victim 43 percent, hero 9 percent); 2002–06 (victim 50 percent, hero 18 percent).

to support claims that immigrants to France are taking jobs or lowering wages, adding substantially to government fiscal costs, or failing to integrate (and thus threatening national cultural cohesion) (see Appendix C). If the mediated public debate about immigration were simply a reflection of actual social conditions, one would expect threat frames to remain steady or to even decline in prominence between the 1970s and 2000s. Instead, we see a slight rise in threat frames from 1973 to 1983, a sharp spike upward in 1991, followed by an equally dramatic drop in the 2000s. In part, this pattern of coverage is due to the decline, from the 1970s to 1990s, in the role played by civil society associations in generating immigration news coverage (from 36 to 18 percent of total cited speakers) followed by a revival of civil society in the 2000s (rising back to 30 percent of cited speakers). In France, civil society groups have tended to promote more victim-oriented coverage; conversely, when the government and major political parties drive news coverage, they tend to highlight threat frames (see Appendix Table A.1).

To be sure, the far right National Front party led by Jean-Marie Le Pen (and more recently by his daughter Marine) has been a consistent promoter of threat frames. As with issues of racism and cultural diversity, news outlets have tended to differentiate themselves from one another in their treatment of Le Pen. Among mainstream French media outlets, *Le Monde* has most consistently covered the far right. During the early 1970s, *Le Monde* political desk reporter Bernard Brigouleix wrote about Ordre Nouveau (New Order), the National Front, monarchists, and other far right organizations not because they were politically powerful but because the newspaper, as "a point of principle," aspired to "comprehensiveness"; Brigouleix considered his task to be like that of "an entomologist . . . I treated them like an insect to be dissected."[41] For Alain Rollat, Brigouleix's successor at *Le Monde* beginning around 1978, it was likewise "a point of honor to give Le Pen the right to speak, like all political opponents [to the government]."[42] *Le Figaro* executive editor Franz-Olivier Giesbert expressed a similar argument, that while he "personally was very hostile" to Le Pen's politics, it was *Le Figaro*'s policy to treat him in a "journalistically honest" manner, which meant that the newspaper would not be opposed in principle to publishing a commentary by him or an interview transcript.[43] During 1983, the year in which the National Front first emerged as a potential political power broker, *Le Monde* made good on its honor. While the newspaper founded by journalistic legend Hubert Beuve-Méry was no friend of the far right, the National Front and other far right groups made up nearly 10 percent of all speaker mentions in *Le Monde*'s immigration coverage (vs. 3 percent at *Libération*, and less than 1 percent at *Le Figaro*).

---

[41] Bernard Brigouleix interview (1998). See also Brigouleix (1977).
[42] Alain Rollat interview (1998). Rollat has published two books about the National Front (see Rollat 1985; Rollat and Plenel 1992).
[43] Franz-Olivier Giesbert interview (1997).

In contrast, as political reporter Gilles Bresson saw it, *Libération*'s own point of honor was never to allow Le Pen to use the newspaper as a mouthpiece for his "extreme racist, anti-Semitic" views. Thus, while the paper covered Le Pen, unlike *Le Monde* or *Le Figaro*, it never accorded him an interview or allowed him to publish a commentary.[44] This is not to say that *Libération* entirely ignored Le Pen. Former *Libération* reporter Eric Dupin recalls that, despite its principled opposition to Le Pen, the newspaper published "a certain number of cover articles [*unes*] about the National Front," with "the motivation being sometimes rather commercial, at least unconsciously, because the cover articles on Le Pen always sell very, very well."[45] In similar fashion, when Le Pen appeared on the prominent television news magazine Hour of Truth (*L'Heure de vérité*) in 1985, he helped the show achieve its highest audience share ever for a politically oriented show. The interview of Le Pen attracted 32 percent of the French audience, well above François Mitterrand's high score of 23 percent (Nel 1988, 170).

Even so, the rise in threat frames cannot be clearly linked directly to any increase in the prominence of immigration restrictionist voices. As in the United States, the media in France have tended to give minimal attention to anti-immigration or restrictionist groups. Far right parties, chiefly the National Front and its predecessors (such as New Order in 1973) and fellow travelers (the National Republican Movement or MNR, founded by former National Front lieutenant Bruno Megret in 1998), make up only a small proportion of all speakers cited, and the percentage has decreased over time (see Figure 4.4). This is not to say, however, that the National Front and other far right parties have not been able to exert influence by pushing the mainstream right – and left – to

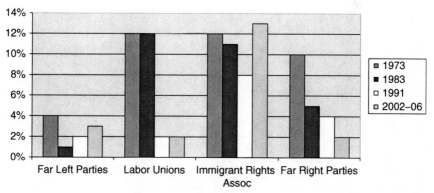

FIGURE 4.4. France: Nongovernmental and peripheral party speakers, 1970s–2000s. Percentages are of total speakers cited (same as for Figure 4.2), with core newspaper and television news samples equally weighted.

---

[44] Gilles Bresson interview (1997).
[45] Philippe Juhem interview with Eric Dupin (1995), transcript shared with the author.

adopt harsher immigration positions and policies. As will become evident, this is precisely what has happened.

From its beginnings, the National Front has been the object of the blatant derision, even disgust, of French journalists.[46] Most French reporters and editors do not hesitate to express their hostility toward Le Pen and his ideas. For example, *Libération* reporter Gilles Bresson admitted that even when he was covering the far right, during the early 1990s, he found it "impossible to buy the [National Front-leaning newspaper] *Présent*. I'd be ashamed to go to the newspaper stall and ask for it. Compared to that, I'd rather buy a pornographic magazine."[47]

As in the United States, a habitus gap structures relations between the French journalistic field and far right, anti-immigration political groupings. The reporters who cover the far right for the leading national newspapers tend to have degrees in the social sciences and humanities from the most prestigious universities, *grandes écoles*, and journalism schools – perhaps even more than their "*société*" colleagues – given that anti-immigration activism is mostly party-based in France and thus comes under the surveillance of the high-prestige "politics" desk (Marchetti 2005). Among top editors and political reporters who have written about the far right, *Le Monde*'s Bernard Brigouleix and Eric Dupin, and *Le Figaro*'s Eric Zemmour are graduates of Sciences Po; *Le Monde*'s Christiane Chombeau and Alain Rollat are graduates of one of the Paris-based elite journalism schools; and *Libération*'s Laurent Joffrin has both Sciences Po and graduate journalism degrees.

By contrast, National Front leader Jean-Marie Le Pen is of modest, provincial social origins. His father, who died when Jean-Marie was a teenager, had a small fishing business. Le Pen went on to earn graduate degrees in law and political science at the University of Paris. Since 1977, when a wealthy monarchist left Le Pen his fortune (and castle), the National Front party leader has not lacked for means. But this has only more clearly marked Le Pen's status in relation to the ongoing status tension between economic and cultural capital. Even if Le Pen has money, according to the standard view, he still lacks class; he is nouveau-riche, uncouth, "vulgar" as *Libération*'s editor once labeled him in an editorial.[48]

---

[46] See especially the excellent, comprehensive research on this question by French sociologist Jacques Le Bohec (2004a; 2004b).

[47] Gilles Bresson interview (1998).

[48] Serge July, "Un politicien de faits divers," *Libération*, October 16, 1985, cited in Le Bohec (2004b, 86–87). In private, views of Le Pen as a person can be more nuanced, even positive. During his student days, Le Pen was a friend of filmmaker Claude Chabrol, who remembers him with fondness: "Le Pen was really funny, he was a magnificent hell-raiser!" ("C'est un marrant Le Pen, c'était un fout-la-merde magnifique!" from "Bouillon de culture," France 2, January 8, 1999, cited in Le Bohec 2004a, 297, fn 50). Bernard Brigouleix, the *Le Monde* journalist who covered Le Pen during the early 1970s, volunteered to me that he had enjoyed Le Pen's company, finding him "very cultivated" and "amusing" (*drole*) (interview 1998); Le Bohec (2004a,b) reports other examples of French journalists taking quiet pleasure in Le Pen's humor, intelligence, and candor.

Coming from mostly upper-middle-class backgrounds, prominent French national television journalists likewise perceive Le Pen "as a sparring partner, indeed a punching bag, ideal for this purpose because of his [perceived] low social and intellectual level, thus easy to manipulate and ridicule" (Le Bohec 2004b, 70–71). Of course, not all of the far right leaders can be so easily dismissed because of their social or educational backgrounds (including, notably, Le Pen's daughter Marine, now leading the party).[49] But, just as in the United States, what counts are the social characteristics of the group's adherents and their proximity/ distance to those of journalists and their audiences. Juxtaposed to the younger, secular, and highly educated national journalists, National Front supporters are composed disproportionately of older, Catholic individuals with nonprofessional/ nonmanagerial occupations who lack university or even high school (baccalaur- eate) degrees (Fetzer 2000b, 15; Lubbers and Scheepers 2002, 138). This social chasm is then translated, and in the process partially mystified, by an upper- middle-class dominated journalistic field into a purely ideological or even moral dispute. Much of the news coverage about the National Front has been more about the threat to democracy posed by the party than any supposed threat posed by immigration. In France, as in the United States, the fiscal and jobs frames have been most strongly promoted by the restrictionist right, and this has contributed to the relative marginalization of these frames.

Only two threat frames have taken hold in the French media coverage of immigration: the public order and national cohesion frames. Some French media scholars have argued that the media's focus on public order is largely attributable to commercial factors (Battegay and Boubeker 1993; Collovald 2001; Berthaut, Darras, and Laurens 2009; Sedel 2009). If one looks at the pattern of news coverage over time, the public order frame rises sharply in prominence between the 1970s and 1990s, a period when television news espe- cially became more commercialized. In 1991, when the public order frame is highest in this study, the recently privatized TF1 placed much more emphasis on public order than did the public France 2 (appearing in 67 percent vs. 48 percent of coverage, respectively). In addition, *Le Figaro*, the most commercialized of the three leading national newspapers, is consistently more likely than *Le Monde* or *Libération* to emphasize the public order frame (averaging 83 percent vs. 69 percent at *Le Monde* and 62 percent at *Libération* between the 1980s and 2000s).

Ultimately, however, commercialization is not an adequate explanation for the prominence accorded to public order. Mentions of the public order frame dropped sharply across the French journalistic field between the early 1990s and the 2000s (even more at the private TF1 than at the public France 2, with the result that they became virtually the same). On the other hand, *Le Figaro*'s

---

[49] Marine Le Pen has two law degrees from the University of Paris II (Panthéon-Assas). In addition, Le Pen lieutenant Bruno Gollnisch has a graduate degree from Sciences Po and a Ph.D. in public law, and Bruno Megret, who left the National Front to found a rival far right party, has degrees from two French grandes écoles and an M.A. from the University of California-Berkeley.

greater tendency to highlight public order and other threat frames compared to all other French media outlets is consistent across the four decades. This suggests political as much or more than commercial influences. *Le Figaro*'s emphasis on public order was highest in the early 1980s, when its owner at the time, conservative media mogul Robert Hersant, openly used the immigration issue as a polemical weapon against the socialist government (Bonnafous 1991; Gastaut 2000). Rather than a gradual increase in the public order frame according with a steady rise in commercialization, the rise and fall of the frame fits more closely to policy shifts by the government, which promoted an increasingly tougher line on immigration during the 1980s and 1990s, but drew back from this stance to some extent in the 2000s (with periodic exceptions; see Marthaler 2008). This pattern suggests that although commercial factors may have contributed to an increasing focus on public order, political field power – and the ongoing professional journalistic imperative to index coverage to events and stances in the political field – offers a better explanation.

National cohesion is the other major threat frame emphasized by the French media. During the late 1960s, Gaullist government ministers voiced their increasing concern with the non-European origins of most of the new immigrants and worried that there would be an increase in "tensions between communities" (Wihtol de Wenden 1988, 148). It was during this period that the notion of a "threshold of tolerance" (*seuil de tolérance*) guided French immigration policy.[50] At the same time, political elite concerns about national cohesion were not paramount because the government continued to believe that most immigrant "guest-workers" would eventually return to their original homelands.

The presidential victory of socialist François Mitterrand in 1981 forced a rearrangement of power and discourse in the political, media, and intellectual fields. In the exuberance of the first two years, immigrants and their children benefited from the left's extension of legal rights and the general spirit of generosity toward economically and culturally marginalized groups. By 1983, however, Mitterrand's economic socialist program was in full-scale retreat toward "realism." The ensuing austerity policies hit immigrant workers the hardest. In the face of increasing layoffs, workers at the nationalized Renault factory went on strike, and, as the television cameras showed, most of the workers were North African immigrants who spoke Arabic and claimed their rights to pray and observe Muslim dietary practices at the factories. Even though these religious practices had long been quietly accommodated by factory officials,[51] socialist prime minister Pierre Mauroy now accused Muslim

---

[50] On the anthropological and sociological origins (including from the United States) of *seuil de tolerance*, see Freeman (1979, 156–161) and Horowitz (1992, 25). Michel Massenet, the minister in charge of the Office of Population and Migration during the 1960s and early 1970s, played a key role in promoting and legitimating the term (Silverman 1992, 75).

[51] Hargreaves (1992, 167, fn 5) notes that the first Islamic prayer room had been established at Renault's Billancourt factory in 1976.

immigrants of being manipulated by foreign religious influences and of representing a threat to French national security. Mauroy was reacting in part to the increasing and often successful politicization of the immigration issue by the right and far right during the months leading up to the 1983 municipal elections. At the same time, the French communist party, ostensibly part of the ruling government, played the "immigration card" in its local competition with the National Front for working-class voters (Schain 2008). From this point forward, the government and the leading political parties – both left and right – tended to be the main proponents of the national cohesion frame, in an attempt to woo the National Front's voters even as they attacked the party for being too extreme.

Just as it has done with the public order frame, *Le Figaro* has led the way in emphasizing national cohesion. In 1983, the national cohesion threat frame appeared in 82 percent of *Le Figaro*'s coverage, compared to 23 percent at *Le Monde*, 22 percent at *Libération*, and just 5 percent on French television news (at that time, TF1 and France 2 were both still part of the public television system). During this period, the tone of *Le Figaro*'s coverage was often aggressively hostile to immigrants, closely amalgamating national cohesion and public order. In a 1983 "investigative" article (*enquête*) headlined, "Marseille: the limit of intolerance," a *Le Figaro* reporter related her observations of several immigrant youths stealing a car and laughing sarcastically, while making obscene gestures at her and her official government escorts.[52] She then quotes "ordinary French" who have had enough of immigrant crime and delinquency, including one who concludes: "One day ... one day, I'll kill one of them." A "French Algerian" who dines with the reporter is portrayed as offering the view of a seemingly reasonable, older immigrant who acknowledges the problems that North Africans have largely brought upon themselves:

A little bit later, in a decent enough Arab restaurant, near the Reformist Church, I dine with a French Algerian. Serge sadly shakes his head. He is neither deaf nor blind. Conscious of the danger, he sees two communities that regard each other with hostility. Explosive. But softly Serge tries to explain, to justify perhaps. He recounts experiences of humiliation, insults because of the way he looks, the stubborn refusal of a police officer to admit that "Mohammed" could have a [French] passport, the ostracism of the landlord who refuses to rent his apartment to an Arab. Serge shrugs his shoulders. "I know how to defend myself," he says, "but the younger ones? Everyone speaks in generalizations about immigrants, but it's really about the second generation, those who are now between 15 and 20 years old. How did all this start? Who is responsible?" Serge wonders if it's not too late, if all his questions aren't beside the point now. He recognizes that the cohabitation with North Africans was never easy. Too many differences: culture, religion, values, lifestyle. But it's essentially the explosion of violence that has crystallized the rejection.

By the 1990s and 2000s, the national cohesion frame – balanced somewhat by the relatively positive integration frame – had become a staple of the French mediated immigration debate. Newspapers could still be distinguished by their

---

[52] Irina de Chikoff, "A Marseille, la haine ouverte," *Le Figaro*, March 28, 1983, pp. 1 and 2F.

political allegiances, but not as clearly as before. *Le Figaro* was the least likely to emphasize integration, but in 1991, national cohesion showed up just as or even more often in *Le Monde* and *Libération*. Likewise, during the 1990s and 2000s, TF1 was slightly more likely to emphasize national cohesion than was the public France 2 (21 vs. 16 percent of frames, respectively), with the inverse being true for integration (13 vs. 19 percent of frames).

CONCLUSION

Patterns of French media coverage accord in some ways with the changing "reality" of immigration in France. Many immigrants and their offspring have endured a variety of humanitarian problems; at the same time, many immigrants are successfully integrating. Yet the phenomenological fit with the mediated immigration debate is far from tight. As media attention to racism has declined, "real-world" discrimination and hate crime have remained steady or increased. In contrast to patterns of media attention to national cohesion and public order, there is little evidence that the actual problems of national cohesion (either in behaviors or attitudes) grew dramatically worse between the 1980s and 2000s, nor that public order problems spiked in the early 1990s and then dropped dramatically thereafter.

As in the United States, political elite strategies and maneuvering tend to set the agenda for news media coverage. Thus, the French media emphasis on racism and cultural diversity can be linked to the dominant political rhetoric of the leading parties of the left and right. Likewise, the sharp rise in the national cohesion and public order frames in the early 1990s can be attributed to the intensifying run-up to the 1995 presidential election, as the major competing parties sought to compete over who could be toughest on immigration.

At the same time, factors specific to the French journalistic field have shaped news coverage. Due to ideological and social habitus disaffinities, journalists have tended to write about the French far right in more disparaging and dismissive ways than about other parties and organizations. At various moments, field-level relational dynamics of distinction have shaped coverage, most clearly in the early 1980s as the three leading French national newspapers followed different strategies to come to terms with the election of a socialist president. As in the United States, the humanitarian frame has been a major frame, but for a different reason: in France, it has been linked less to the demands of narrative story telling than to practices and formats that prioritize the representation of diverse civil society voices and viewpoints. The importance of the form of news is also evident in medium differences in coverage of the complex global economy frame. With the exception of 1983, when the national immigration debate turned inward toward domestic questions of cultural diversity, racism, and national cohesion, the global economy frame was a major frame in French national newspapers – even at the conservative *Le Figaro*. In contrast, at no time was it a major frame on French television news.

This suggests that the presence of the global economy frame is not simply a reflection of a slightly left-leaning French political culture. French newspapers, through their use of the multigenre *événement* news format and the *société* (social problems) desk, have been better attuned and organized to cover this kind of complex frame than have French television, or for that matter, U.S. newspapers and television news.

5

Explaining Continuity and Change in French and U.S. Immigration News

We have a tendency to only speak about immigrants either from the angle of crime or the angle of human misery, to see them only as aggressors or as victims.
– Robert Solé, *Le Monde* social problems editor[1]

My editor told me: Bernstein, ya know, mix it up! Can't you find some immigrants who aren't being detained or deported? Where are the more upbeat immigration stories?
– Nina Bernstein, *New York Times* immigration reporter[2]

In both French and U.S. news coverage of immigration, the humanitarian and public order frames have been dominant. In both countries, victim and threat frames far outnumber hero frames. Likewise, there have been similar tendencies over time to increasingly marginalize restrictionist voices and highlight unaffiliated individuals.

Yet there have also been many cross-national differences in news coverage. Economic frames, such as the good worker, jobs, and fiscal frames, are mentioned more often in the U.S. media. Although the French media continue to put a greater emphasis on racism, over time, this frame drops in France while rising in the United States. Cultural unity frames (integration, national cohesion) increase more in France than in the United States. The global economy frame becomes less prominent in the United States as it becomes more so in France. U.S. immigration news is dominated more by government and other political elites. Civil society speakers appear substantially more often in French news, although they have also increased over time in U.S. news, narrowing the gap somewhat.

Newspapers and television news generally follow the same patterns, with a few exceptions: French mainstream television news does not follow newspapers in emphasizing the global economy frame and is even more likely to give voice to

---

[1] Solé (1988, 160–161), in an interview with French immigration scholar Jacqueline Costa-Lascoux.
[2] Nina Bernstein interview (2008).

unaffiliated individuals than are U.S. television news and newspapers (these and other characteristics of television news coverage, including for PBS and Arte, will be analyzed further in Chapter 8.)

As the previous chapters showed, journalistic fields are dynamic spaces of contestation. Whether or not a particular speaker or frame dominates at a given moment depends in part on historically contingent events and strategies of communication. In the early 1970s, French industrial policy placed heavy emphasis on the recruitment of foreign guest workers: this helps explain why the good worker frame was more visible in France than in the United States during this period (appearing in 28 vs. 15 percent of coverage, respectively). There were also differences in how the immigration issue first came to be politicized in the contemporary period: in France, human rights associations, labor unions, and small leftist and far right parties played a leading role; in the United States, the process was more top-down, with the first move taken by an Attorney General and Immigration Service chief anxious to make their marks by creating a moral panic over illegal immigration. These differences in early "authorship" are evident in media sourcing patterns during the 1970s. In France, civil society and small parties make up nearly half of all speakers (47 percent vs. just 16 percent in the U.S.); in the United States, the early mediated immigration debate is overwhelmingly dominated by government officials and other political elites (63 percent vs. just 29 percent in France). (See Online Tables 5.2–5.5.) Across the four decades, other contingencies are evident. In the early 1990s struggle of the Socialist Party to hold on to its parliamentary majority (ultimately won by the right in 1993), immigration was at the heart of the partisan struggle for power: this temporarily heightened French media attention to the political field at the expense of civil society. The unevenness of patterns of news coverage is partly a by-product of this study's focus on peak media attention years. Almost by definition, those years in which media attention to an issue spikes are not typical. Each of these periods will involve a unique configuration of events, actors, and social structural conditions.

At first glance, this complexity of news coverage seems to accord with many journalists' self-perception of their practice as random or unplanned. And yet, as the previous chapters demonstrated, if there is dynamism in fields, there also seem to be regularities. I thus now explore potentially generalizable linkages between patterns of social structural and discursive continuity and change.

EXPLAINING CONSISTENT SIMILARITIES

Why are the public order and humanitarian frames the two consistently dominant frames in both France and the United States? Public order is a basic frame of police and governmental agencies and addresses the substantively important questions of safety and security. In both the United States and France, the public order frame was most likely to be generated by the political field. Similarly, the humanitarian frame raises vital and enduring questions of basic human rights; it is also promoted by a large nonprofit organizational sector in both the United States and France. Yet these "objective" explanations are not sufficient. They beg the question: why did the media in both countries highlight these two frames over all other frames (which also are grounded in social and political realities)? Despite differences in their precise relation to the state and the market, the French and U.S. journalistic fields – as with all professional fields in liberal, capitalist democracies – are shaped to some extent by both. This tug of war, what Patrick Champagne (2005) has aptly called the journalistic field's "double dependency," manifests itself as two distinct news imperatives (Ryan 1991; Cook 1998). The most highly valued news will combine elements of both governmentally defined "importance" and commercially defined "interest," and this is precisely what humanitarian and public order frames are likely to do better than other immigration frames. Both frames concern significant issues of societal concern; both bring together drama, emotion, and conflict in heightened form.

News coverage of immigration in both countries has become increasingly populist, emphasizing the voices of ordinary individuals not connected to government, business, or organized civil society. Most of this increase is due to reporters interviewing particular individuals. References to polls do not increase substantially, hovering around 3 percent for U.S. media and just 1 percent for French media. At least for the news coverage of immigration during these peak media attention years, claims that polling is increasingly dominating public discourse seem overstated.[3] This populist element of news coverage may, in fact, be one way that increasing commercialization of the journalistic fields in the two countries is reshaping news coverage. This French-U.S. convergence, however, is limited. During all periods, institutional civil society and political parties, large and small, continued to be a much more visible presence in the French media. Moreover, even as there has been a concurrent quantitative rise in references to individuals, in Chapter 6, I show that French and U.S. media continue to present both individuals and civil society actors in qualitatively different ways.

Class structuring of the field in terms of the habitus of journalists and sources helps account for other cross-national similarities. A significant "habitus gap" between elite journalists and immigration restrictionist groups (their typical members or sympathizers as much or more than their leaders) contributes to more negative, denigrating coverage of restrictionist groups (including far right parties in France) and lesser media visibility of these groups than for their humanitarian activist counterparts. Such habitus disaffinities serve as a brake on the presentation of threat frames. It is only when threat frames are also taken up by the government or the leading political parties that they are prominently covered. Positive habitus affinities between journalists and well-educated, socially connected humanitarian activists, conversely, help assure that the latter will be taken seriously and thus help account for the high standing of the

---

[3] See, e.g., Champagne (1990) and Herbst (1995).

humanitarian frame. It must be emphasized, however, that habitus affinities (or disaffinities) are not simply between individual journalists and their sources but rather express a structural relation. Although it is important for a reporter to reflect on potential habitus biases, any attempt he or she might make to adjust coverage would have to overcome an institutional habitus bias rooted in the homologous circuit of production/reception in which both the reporter and his or her media outlet is structurally situated.

Despite such positive journalistic affinities with immigrant advocates, in both France and the United States, hero frames – good worker, cultural diversity, and integration – are much less likely to be mentioned than victim or threat frames. In this common emphasis on real or potential disruption and problems, there does seem to be a universality in journalistic practice – at least for the front (or home) page or evening news broadcasts of mainstream print and television news (other news criteria may be at work in arts, entertainment, or other softer, more "lifestyle"-oriented news departments). Of course, there may be disagreements around this issue inside newsrooms, as indicated by this chapter's opening quotation from *New York Times* reporter Nina Bernstein. Aspirations for journalistic excellence and peer recognition may ultimately tip the balance. Whether or not dramatic conflict trumps the light-hearted touch in attracting audiences, it certainly is the case that civically oriented professional awards (of which Bernstein has received many) tend to go to more serious, inevitably downbeat reporting.

EXPLAINING CONSISTENT DIFFERENCES

Field relations extend to the global as well as the national level. Bourdieu (1998, 41) has insisted that for a media field analysis to be complete, "the position of the national media field within the global media field would have to be taken into account," for example, "the economic-technical, and especially, symbolic dominance of American television, which serves a good many journalists as both a model and a source of ideas, formulas and tactics." In this passage, Bourdieu assumes the symbolic dominance of the United States, similar to classic theorists of American cultural imperialism (Schiller 1991). Yet my research shows that global inequalities of power can produce indifference or backlash as much as imitation, and there is little evidence that similarities in immigration news coverage are due to American influence (at least since the 1970s). In fact, it is American news that becomes increasingly focused on the humanitarian and public order frames over time, not French news, which remains relatively constant across the four decades.

Differences in within-nation positioning of the journalistic field help explain why France has not followed America's lead in economic and cultural framing of the immigration issue. In France, state power is used in part as a cultural/civic bulwark against purely market-based criteria; in contrast, U.S. media policies tend to be more market-driven. As a result, U.S. political culture tends to be dominated by "market-based arguments" (in which questions of economic competition, utility, and costs and benefits are central) whereas French political culture is dominated by "civic solidarity arguments" (which stress egalitarian and nonmaterialist values) (Lamont and Thévenot 2000, 14). To the extent that these cultural understandings are shared by most journalists and their sources alike in each country, one would expect to see more market-oriented immigration frames in U.S. immigration coverage and more civic solidarity-oriented frames in French coverage, and that is indeed the case.

Within-nation relations of autonomy and heteronomy shape what cultural producers are able or likely to see or not to see, and thus to pass on to their audiences. Critical perspectives are produced from positions of relative autonomy; blind spots are produced from positions of proximity or heteronomy. France's greater focus on the critical global economy frame is enabled by its journalistic field's relative autonomy from the market field. Conversely, dependence on a social solidarity-oriented civic field subtly encourages an emphasis on cultural unity frames (integration, national cohesion). In contrast, in the United States, a journalistic field increasingly dominated by market-based criteria emphasizes the positive good worker frame and de-emphasizes the critical jobs and global economy frames.

Field position thus supplements a micro-orientation to practice by seeking the sources of resonance (Schudson 1989) of particular claims. The fiscal frame succeeded in the United States for a time because it could be linked to a larger conservative reframing of poverty and marginality as problems of "welfare abuse" (Gans 1995; Calavita 1996).[4] It resonated with an increasingly powerful neo-liberal *doxa* in a way that other threat frames did not. Conversely, the jobs frame risks bringing up inconvenient questions of economic equality and worker rights; likewise, the national cohesion frame does not fit well with an increasingly segmented market economy or a reconfigured left's politics of identity. In France, widespread public support for a universal welfare state has made it difficult for the fiscal frame to resonate. The existence of a strong welfare state also helps maintain the sense of the nation as a "community," thus providing legitimacy to the national cohesion frame. Cultural resonance may thus override "objective" factors in shaping public discourse. Because European countries have "more extensive welfare states," Zolberg (2006, 15) assumes that public debate about immigration's fiscal costs will be "understandably much hotter" than in the United States. In fact, at least in France, the opposite is true.

Of course, other factors also come into play – the need for novelty, favoritism of mainstream political elites over more marginal actors, and a bias against complicated, conceptual frames (especially in the United States) – to influence whether a given frame, culturally resonant in a given national context, will

---

[4] As Gamson (1992, 11) notes, "media-amplified images" from one issue may be "generalized and transferred to other issues", that is, used as a resource for understanding and action by political actors and citizens.

actually rise to the top. Thus, even if the fiscal frame is predisposed to succeed in the U.S. public discourse, over the course of the past four decades all the necessary stars were aligned only once – during the first half of the 1990s. Likewise, while far right groups, as well as influential conservative media like *Le Figaro* and especially *Le Figaro Magazine*, were promoting the national cohesion frame in the early 1980s, it was not until the 1990s that it became one of the dominant frames in the French immigration debate. In the balance, however, mainstream news media in each country will tend to reinforce rather than challenge widespread doxic assumptions.

In addition, field position helps determine a field's relative vulnerability to external pressures for change. Cultural analysts sometimes speak of the "inertia" of fields and how, once formed, they tend to continue on in a path-dependent fashion (Schneider 2001). With comparative research, however, one can explore the question of how different types of fields vary in their tendencies toward cultural inertia. Fields dominated to a greater extent by civic-cultural capital might be expected to better resist both external economic pressures and foreign cultural influences. For this reason, one might expect that French coverage of immigration will change less over time than U.S. coverage. There is some support for this claim. Looking at the average percentage change of the ten immigration frames between the 1970s and 2000s, change is less for both French national newspapers and television news compared to their U.S. counterparts. Commercial pressures are higher for television news than newspapers and have increased relatively more for television during the past four-decade period: in fact, over-time change in immigration framing is slightly greater for television news than for newspapers in both countries.[5] Most pointedly, the tendency to emphasize the most commercially appealing frames – such as the humanitarian and public order frames – has increased over time in the U.S. media while remaining steady in France. Between the 1970s and 2000s, as a proportion of all frames, the humanitarian and public order frames (combined) increased from 45 percent to 57 percent in the U.S. media while only shifting from 52 to 51 percent for French media (press and TV combined).[6]

In sum, French and American framing of immigration exhibit both similarities and differences. What they do not demonstrate, with a few exceptions, is convergence. Distinct paths of immigration news coverage can be explained, at least in part, through a close analysis of field position, logic, and structure. Although both the French and U.S. journalistic fields are poised between market

---

[5] Between the 1970s and 2000s, the average percentage point change (as a proportion of all frames) across the ten frames was 3.4 and 5.5 for French newspapers and television news, respectively, and 4.9 and 6.2 for U.S. newspapers and television news, respectively. See Online Table 5.3.

[6] The same over-time tendencies hold for both television news and newspapers; however, in both countries and in both periods, TV news is more concentrated on these two frames than are newspapers.

and civic demands, the particular positions they occupy in the larger field of power and the path by which they arrived there differ substantially. Where there is a less than perfect structural homology, there will also be a less than complete discursive affinity. In the chapters that follow, I further explore these questions in relation to democratic normative ideals of multiperspectival and critical journalism. I do so first by expanding my analysis to incorporate a broader range of newspapers in both countries and subsequently by focusing on television news, both commercial and public.

6

What Makes News More Multiperspectival?

The ideal goes by many names – the marketplace of ideas, pluralism, inclusion – but the basic goal is the same: providing space for a wide-ranging debate among diverse voices and viewpoints. With deep roots in political philosophy, the ideal continues to be articulated in scholarship, civic activism, and legal codes.[1] Journalists around the world, to differing extents and in distinctive ways, articulate this aspiration with words like *balance, fairness,* or *comprehensiveness*.[2] There are also civic benefits to what Herbert Gans (2003) has labeled "multiperspectival news." Audience research has shown that "when people are exposed to several competing interpretations [or frames] they are able to think about the political situation in more complex and original ways" and are thus better able to "perform their civic duties" (Porto 2007, 312–318; see also Chong and Druckman 2007, 110). Yet, despite increasing interest in how the news media frame issues and how framing processes shape audience cognition (Scheufele 1999; Reese, Gandy, and Grant 2003; Snow, Vliegenthart, and Corrigall-Brown 2007), there has been little empirical research that systematically measures or explains variation in frame (or speaker) diversity.

What are the concrete elements of multiperspectival news? For some democratic theorists, such as Jürgen Habermas (1996), the most important criterion is that the media give voice to civil society associations and other groups from the "lifeworld" periphery. If this is true, one should pay particular attention to how

---

[1] See Baker (2002), Ferree et al. (2002), and Christians et al. (2009).

[2] Lemieux and Schmalzbauer (2000) emphasize the similarities between the U.S. journalistic ideal of "balance" and a French ideal of "polyphony" (their term). Hanitzsch (2011), reporting the results of an eighteen-country study, finds widespread journalistic affirmation across the subsample of Western democracies of two ideals linked to multiperspectival news: providing "citizens with information they need to make political decisions" and motivating "people to participate in civic activity and political discussion" (although, with the latter ideal, in agreement with this study, finding the least support in the United States).

often – and how fully – the perspectives of such civil society groups are represented in the media. Other definitions of pluralism (Ferree et al. 2002) go beyond civil society to stress the need to give voice to a broad range of speakers (organizationally and ideologically) inside and outside of government and stress the primacy of diverse viewpoints (regardless of who is expressing them).

It has sometimes been suggested that the chief difference between the U.S. and French (or other European) journalistic fields is that the former is more internally pluralist whereas the latter is more externally pluralist. Internal pluralism means that each individual media outlet expresses a diversity of viewpoints; external pluralism is present when the media system as a whole expresses a wide range of viewpoints (Hallin and Mancini 2004, 29). In this chapter, I put this claim to the test by analyzing seven U.S. and French newspapers encompassing a range of types of funding, ownership, and audience demographics.[3] In the United States, in addition to the *New York Times, Los Angeles Times*, and the *Washington Post* examined in the previous chapters, I also include the *Wall Street Journal, USA Today*, the (New York) *Daily News*, and the *Christian Science Monitor* (as well as the *New York Post* for selected purposes). In France, in addition to *Le Monde, Le Figaro*, and *Libération*, I also consider the financial newspaper *Les Echos*, the popular *Le Parisien/Aujourd'hui en France*, as well as the communist/leftist *L'Humanité* and Catholic *La Croix*. I focus mostly on the period 2002–06, but, as necessary, supplement this sample with the three-newspaper data for each country from the 1970s through 1990s.

How do structural factors promote or inhibit a diversity of voices and viewpoints? From a liberal "First Amendment" anti-state perspective, state intervention compromises journalistic autonomy and thus censors free and open speech (Christians, Glasser, McQuail, Nordenstreng, and White 2009, 226). Thus, because of greater state media policy intervention in France, both restrictive and enabling, French news might be expected to be less multiperspectival. Following from Bennett's (1990) hypothesis that news media tend to index their news coverage to political elites, liberal theorists might expect this indexing effect to be stronger in France than in the United States. Likewise, newspapers such as *La Croix* or *L'Humanité*, which during the 2000s received extra subsidies from the French state, would be expected to index their coverage to political elites more than other newspapers.

Conversely, from a political economy perspective, advertising-supported news would be expected to be less multiperspectival because corporate advertisers generally support the status quo and thus discourage, directly or indirectly, journalistic attention to marginal speakers or viewpoints (Baker 1994). In contrast, audience-supported media would be expected to offer a more wide-ranging discourse (Bagdikian 2004). Because American newspapers are more dependent on advertising, they should be less multiperspectival than

---

[3] For other notable multioutlet studies of news content, see Page (1996), Rohlinger (2007), and Anderson (2013), although these are U.S.-focused.

French newspapers. However, American newspapers that rely relatively less on advertising (such as the *Christian Science Monitor*) and French newspapers that rely relatively more on advertising (such as *Le Figaro*) might tend not to follow their respective national patterns.

With these competing hypotheses in mind, let us now turn to a closer examination of immigration news in the two countries. I begin by considering both quantitative and qualitative aspects of media representations of civil society activism, and then present findings on internal and external pluralism for U.S. and French national newspapers. My content analysis challenges assumptions of both the standard liberal and political economy models. As I will show, analysis of field factors – position, logic, and structure – helps provide a more satisfying account of what makes for mutiperspectival news.

GIVING VOICE TO CIVIL SOCIETY

Countering assumptions of negative effects of state intervention, French national newspapers during the 2000s are *not* dominated to a greater extent than the U.S. press by political elite voices and, conversely, are more likely to emphasize civil society voices. In fact, national U.S. newspapers are simultaneously more government-focused and more populist than their French counterparts. Governmental and dominant political institutions (including the judiciary and the leading political parties) make up, on average, 41 percent of speakers cited in the full range of U.S. newspapers versus 34 percent in French newspapers. Likewise, unaffiliated individuals and polls make up 23 percent of speakers cited in U.S. newspapers versus 16 percent in the French press.[4] French newspapers, by contrast, come closer to the Habermasian ideal by giving greater voice to organized civil society viewpoints (31 percent of all citations vs. 26 percent in the U.S. press). To the extent that many peripheral parties (such as the environmentalist Greens and the anti-immigration National Front) serve political functions taken up by social movement organizations in the United States, these parties also ought to be included as part of French "civil society" – in which case, the French-U.S. gap increases to 10 points (36 percent vs. 26 percent). (See Appendix Table A.3.) These findings echo over-time tendencies for both French and U.S. newspapers and television news, with one exception (discussed further in Chapter 8): French television news has been more likely than U.S. TV news to highlight individual voices.

In addition, academics and other representatives of civil society make up a majority or strong plurality of all individuals featured in interview transcripts

---

[4] Unaffiliated individuals are also more likely to be a part of any given news package. At least one unaffiliated individual is quoted or paraphrased in 58 percent of all U.S. packages, compared to 44 percent of French packages. News packages citing no one except for unaffiliated individuals are rare in French newspapers but are published at least occasionally in most U.S. newspapers. For example, whereas 2 percent of packages in *Le Parisien* only cite unaffiliated individuals, almost 12 percent do in its closest U.S. counterpart, the *Daily News*. (Data not shown in tables.)

published in most French newspapers (see Table 2.1). Publication of these transcripts ensures that civil society speakers are able to express their ideas in some depth. When these transcripts are included in a word-length subsample, speakers in French news are quoted an average of 81 words compared to 37 words in U.S. news; the subgroup of academic experts are quoted an average of 315 words in the French press versus just 44 words in the U.S. press.[5] This French emphasis on providing room for the elaboration and development of diverse viewpoints is exemplified by *Libération*'s coverage of the May 1, 2006 U.S. immigrant rights protests. Whereas spokespersons for the League of United Latin American Citizens (LULAC) were only mentioned or quoted briefly in U.S. news coverage, *Libération* published a 680-word transcribed interview with LULAC organizer Angel Luevano.[6] Even when interview transcripts are excluded from this word-length subsample, a French-U.S. gap remains of 57 versus 37 words per quoted speaker.

It could be argued that these findings represent a difference in the function of the front page. Whereas French newspapers routinely provide opinion forums for civil society speakers on the front page and related inside news coverage, U.S. newspapers might provide that space solely on their opinion or "op-ed" (opposite the editorial) pages. There is some truth in this claim, although, at least since the 1990s, most French newspapers also have had separate op-ed pages. A comparison of all non–page one op-ed articles from 2002, 2004, and the first half of 2006 related to immigration in leading newspapers in each country (*New York Times, Washington Post, Los Angeles Times* in the United States; *Le Monde, Libération, Le Figaro* in France) actually finds many similarities.

Newspapers in the United States are virtually the equal of French newspapers in providing a forum for civil society voices on op-ed pages: in both countries, civil society speakers make up around 80 percent of all immigration-related op-ed article authors. This does not compensate for the relative lack of civil society voices in U.S. *news* pages, but it does show that civil society is able to "speak" at least somewhere in the U.S. newspaper. Looking more closely at particular voices, there are some cross-national differences. Most noticeably, humanitarian association activists (11 vs. 7 percent) and academics (35 vs. 30 percent) are more likely to author op-ed articles in France, whereas think tank researchers and other experts write more op-eds in the United States (15 vs. 5 percent) (see Figure 6.1). In both countries, however, op-ed authors associated with restrictionist or anti-immigration associations or political parties make up 1 percent or less of all articles (not shown

---

[5] These findings are based on word counts of the first five speakers quoted in a given day's page-one news coverage (including all words attributed to these speakers throughout the article). Interviews – ranging from 50-word extended quotes to 1,000-word (or more) lengthy transcripts – are very common in French newspapers. However, they tend to appear after the lead news article, as parts of larger news packages and thus the interviewees are only occasionally among the first five speakers cited. If all speaker citations rather than just the "first five" were included, French-U.S. differences in quotation length would likely be even greater. See Online Table 6.1.

[6] Richard Emmanuelle interview with Angel Luevano, "Les clandestins sont exploités," *Libération*, May 2, 2006, p. 9.

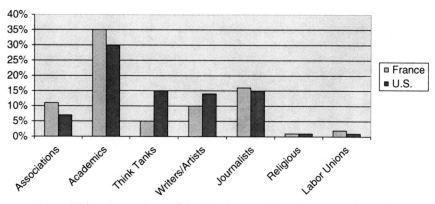

FIGURE 6.1. Civil society authors of immigration op-ed articles in French and U.S. core newspapers, 2002–2006. Percentages are of total op-ed authors; U.S. *n* = 332; France *n* = 288.

in figure). Also scarcely represented are articles by writers associated with trade unions and religious groups.

Individuals unaffiliated with any organization rarely author op-ed articles in either the United States or France (2 vs. 1 percent, respectively). However, letters to the editor are much more common in U.S. newspapers than in French newspapers, which typically publish only a scattering of letters and not in every edition. In contrast, during the sampled years, the aforementioned three leading U.S. newspapers published more than 800 letters to the editor related to immigration and more than 80 percent of these were authored by unaffiliated individuals.

In their study of abortion discourse in U.S. and German newspapers, Myra Marx Ferree and colleagues (2002, 94) included unaffiliated individuals (whom they term "individuals speaking only for themselves") in their broader category of civil society "periphery." Using this broad definition, they found that American newspapers were more democratically "inclusive" (Ferree et al. 2002, 235) than were German newspapers. This is an idiosyncratic use of the term "civil society," which is typically understood as the organized reflection and activism of a range of nonstate collective actors (Taylor 1990; Sobieraj 2011) rather than the atomized, ad hoc observations of individuals as encountered or summoned by journalists. Putting so much of the spotlight on individuals who speak "only for themselves" arguably does more democratic harm than good. When journalists systematically privilege unaffiliated over affiliated voices, they help perpetuate a society devoid of the intermediary associations essential to democratic self-renewal. (See Figure 6.2.)

In the United States, journalists also often misrepresent the character of organized activism by denuding individual activists of their (actual) organizational affiliations or by seeking out and highlighting colorful activists evidently without such affiliations. French coverage of activism, in contrast, emphasizes and acknowledges the particular organized collective character of civil society.

CLAUDE PIÉPLU : la dérision faite art
Les Shadoks restent sans voix. L'acteur est mort à l'âge de 83 ans. PAGE 20

« *En fait,
je n'apprends rien, c'est
un métier qu'on ne peut
apprendre que quand
on le connaît déjà.* »
CLAUDE PIÉPLU

l'Humanité

Ils parrainent des SANS-PAPIERS
Ils protègent leurs enfants nés en France

Ils défient Sarkozy !

La résistance s'organise contre les menaces d'expulsion
de parents d'élèves et de jeunes scolarisés. PAGE 2

CANNES

FILMER LA CLASSE OUVRIÈRE
Avec *la Raison du plus faible*, Lucas Belvaux a présenté l'un des films les plus poignants de la compétition. PAGE 21

SOGERMA
EADS sous pression. PAGE 5

ALGÉRIE
Un nouveau premier ministre. PAGE 11

ÉCONOMIE
Conjoncture en berne. PAGE 14

TRANSPORTS
NOUVELLE BATAILLE DU RAIL
Avant les 2es Rencontres de Tours, débat contradictoire entre cinq responsables du secteur. PAGE 6

PARIS, 20ᵉ ARRONDISSEMENT. Nazha El Khouly, avec sa fille, rencontre sa marraine, Brigitte Duchène. Leurs enfants sont scolarisés à l'école Olivier-Métra. Le mari de la première saura aujourd'hui s'il est expulsé.

L'HUMANITE . VENDREDI 26 MAI 2006 . N° 19203 . 1,20 EURO

FIGURE 6.2. Mobilizing civil society in the French press. *L'Humanité*'s *événement* of May 26, 2006, "They defy Sarkozy!", interviews the leader of a French association coordinating efforts to prevent deportations of undocumented immigrant children and provides readers with times and dates of future protest events. Reproduced with permission of *L'Humanité*.

ÉVÉNEMENT 3

*** Cette année, les élus aussi s'en sont mêlés (lire ci-dessous). Le 1er février, la municipalité du 20e arrondissement de Paris a organisé une cérémonie de parrainage de familles sans papiers, les plaçant symboliquement sous sa protection. Rebelote mercredi prochain pour sept familles et deux lycéens.

UN RÉSEAU DE VIGILANCE POUR L'ÉTÉ

L'inquiétude, désormais, ce sont les vacances d'été. La circulaire Sarkozy prend fin le 30 juin. Et après ? Parents, enseignants et élus se préparent à une « veille républicaine et citoyenne ». Mercredi 31 mai, la mairie du 20e organise le parrainage une cérémonie de parrainage. L'occasion de mettre en place un réseau de vigilance pour l'été.

Dans le préau de l'école maternelle Olivier-Métra, ce mardi soir, les futurs parrains rencontrent leur filleul. Délissoir Destrat, le Haïtien, est « ému ». « Cette mobilisation, ça me rassure », dit-il. Dominique Grattepanche, de RESF, est inquiète : « Va-t-on retrouver tous nos enfants à la rentrée ? »

Vincent Defait

« Ils ont grandi ici, ils sont d'ici »

Entretien avec l'un des responsables nationaux du Réseau éducation sans frontières, Jean-Michel Delabre.

Q *u'en est-il, aujourd'hui, de la mobilisation pour protéger les enfants d'ici à la fin de l'année scolaire, puisqu'ils risquent d'être expulsés sans ménagement ?*

Jean-Michel Delabre. Notre impression est relativement favorable, même si nous pensons que nous pouvons faire encore mieux. La pétition atteint les 30 000 signataires, mais si nous voulons vraiment créer un rapport de forces favorable pour sauver les jeunes qui risquent l'expulsion de masse en juillet et en août, il faut faire encore plus important, encore plus massif, il faut créer un mouvement de solidarité qui soit général. Nous devons redoubler d'efforts, mais nous constatons que les collectifs, les citoyens dans leur ensemble, beaucoup de personnalités, de tous les domaines de la société civile, commencent à se mobiliser, jusqu'aux médias qui font de plus en plus de place à cette urgence citoyenne, solidaire.

Comment expliquez-vous cette réactivité ?

Jean-Michel Delabre. Je crois qu'il y a réellement un problème de société, avec des milliers, voire des dizaines de milliers de jeunes, qui sont bien insérés dans la société française, qui sont normalement scolarisés, qui sont soit seuls, soit en famille, mais qui sont des nôtres. Ils ont grandi

ici, ils sont d'ici. Ils sont vécus comme des jeunes qui font partie de notre société telle qu'elle est aujourd'hui, diverse, multiculturelle, riche de ses diversités. Beaucoup de citoyens, quelles que soient leurs opinions, leur tendance philosophique ou religieuse, ont envie que ces jeunes puissent vivre normalement et poursuivent leur insertion dans notre société.

Peut-on vraiment parler de mouvement de résistance ?

Jean-Michel Delabre. Je crois. Nous organisons en ce moment, pour étendre la solidarité et très nombreux parrainages, en province, dans certains arrondissements de Paris. Le 1er juin, en Seine-Saint-Denis, nous parrainons, sous l'égide d'Hervé Brami, le président du conseil général, plus de cent cinquante jeunes dans la même soirée. Nous constatons un afflux de demandes pour participer à ces initiatives et apporter la protection, comme le dit notre pétition sur notre site, educationsansfrontiere.org. Il nous faut construire un rapport de forces, avant juillet, pour imposer des solutions avant qu'on arrive à l'échéance, mais, s'il le faut, il y aura beaucoup de citoyens en France, et pas seulement des militants, qui iront jusqu'à accepter la perspective d'accueillir ces jeunes, de les cacher, de les emmener en vacances, de leur faire connaître autre chose. Nous avons eu l'exemple de Rachel et Jonathan au début de l'année, nous venons d'en avoir un autre exemple sur Lyon et nous avons, d'ores et déjà, des propositions de gens qui sont prêts à le faire, s'il le faut. C'est un mouvement d'ensemble qui se dessine.

Comment réagissez-vous au vote de la loi sur l'immigration dite « choisie » ?

Jean-Michel Delabre. Il y a une véritable distorsion, une fois de plus, entre le pays réel et le pays légal. On peut craindre que les discussions du Sénat ne changent pas grand-chose à ce qui a été voté à l'Assemblée nationale et que nous soyons en présence, en début d'été, avec un dispositif législatif encore plus répressif que celui qui existe actuellement. Ce sera une difficulté de plus qui nous incite encore davantage à développer la solidarité et la mobilisation.

Entretien réalisé par Émilie Rive

Saint-Nazaire. Manifestation pour soutenir une lycéenne camerounaise.

De nombreux élus bravent les lois

En organisant des parrainages de parents ou de jeunes sans papiers, les élus deviennent le relais institutionnel des associations et organisations politiques.

«C'est un acte de résistance. » Assis au milieu des enseignants et des parents d'élèves de l'école Olivier-Métra (Paris 20e), Pierre Mansat s'explique. « La cérémonie de parrainage (des familles sans papiers) se déroule à la mairie, le lieu de représentation locale de la démocratie dans notre pays », dit l'adjoint communiste au maire de Paris.

Depuis des mois, les associations de défense des jeunes et des parents d'élèves sans papiers ont trouvé un relais institutionnel auprès de certains élus. De gauche, tous. Le 14 janvier, Danielle Simonnet, adjointe (PS) au maire du 20e arrondissement de Paris, parraine deux lycéens menacés d'expulsion. L'expulsion signifie à ces jeunes que la société les rejette. Le parrainage, avec les élus, les enseignants, les parents, restaure une recon-

naissance sociale », justifie l'élue, chargée de la jeunesse, de l'accès à la citoyenneté et des résidents étrangers non communautaires. Pierre Mansat lui fait écho : « Symboliquement, des élus de la République contestent des lois de la République qu'ils jugent iniques. Et aux familles, ils disent : vous faites partie de la communauté des citoyens. » « Il s'agit d'accueillir ces personnes au sein de notre République », selon Mireille Elmalan, maire de Pierre-Bénite (Rhône), citée dans le journal municipal.

Depuis, l'initiative fait florès. Plusieurs arrondissements de la capitale ont consacré leurs parrainages, ainsi que plusieurs villes de province. « Nous ouvrons ainsi la maison commune qu'est la mairie, aux associations et aux organisations politiques », explique Michel Charzat, maire (PS) du 20e

arrondissement de Paris. Le 15 mai dernier, lors du Conseil de Paris, les élus communistes ont déposé le vœu d'un « que les mairies d'arrondissement soient des lieux de veille contre l'expulsion (des jeunes étrangers et de leurs parents sans papiers) à partir du 30 juin ». Les élus parisiens font ainsi leur le slogan du Réseau éducation sans frontières : « Nous prenons sous notre protection. »

V. D.

LES PROCHAINS PARRAINAGES EN RÉGION PARISIENNE

▶ Celui du 31 mai, à la mairie du 20e arrondissement, à 18 h 30, sera suivi par une réunion publique.
▶ Le 1er juin : 150 personnes seront parrainées en Seine-Saint-Denis. Deux autres cérémonies auront lieu dans les mairies du 14e (à 16 heures)

et 18e (le matin) à Paris.
▶ Le 9 juin, à 17 heures, à la mairie du 4e, d'où une délégation se rendra à la préfecture.
▶ Le 17 juin : parrainages dans les mairies du 2e, du 18e et du 14e de la capitale.
▶ Le 24 juin, à 15 heures, rendez-vous est pris à la mairie du 11e.

Éditorial

Frères humains !
PAR JEAN-EMMANUEL DUCOIN

Face à l'injustice et l'inhumanité, faut-il savoir désobéir ? Certains Français découvrent que l'engagement civique emprunte parfois des routes inattendues. Beaucoup n'étaient pas prédisposés ni préparés à vivre semblable expérience. Mais parce qu'ils connaissent leur entourage proche des enfants de sans-papiers dont un parent est menacé d'expulsion, parce que leurs gamins sont des compagnons de scolarité de bambins pas moins citoyens de France qu'eux, ils ont décidé de s'organiser et d'entrer en résistance. Mêlant le geste symbolique à l'acte concret, beaucoup sont devenus parrains et marraines de sans-papiers. D'autres, fiers de la légitimité de leur combat, appellent même à la « désobéissance civile » pour honorer une « certaine idée de la République » et des droits de l'homme.

Partout en France, souvent anonymement comme aux pires heures, des êtres humains aident d'autres êtres humains en défiant les décisions préfectorales mêmes, en contestant l'autoritarisme du ministre de l'Intérieur. On le sait, la dernière loi Sarkozy sur l'immigration bafoue non seulement les droits fondamentaux des étrangers mais s'inspire ouvertement d'idées xénophobes qui nous font penser, hélas, que la vieille France réac, loin d'être sur le recul, tente régulièrement de prendre sa revanche. Nicolas Sarkozy, dont le récent voyage en Afrique fut marqué par des manifestations, revendique sa « relecture » d'une société française dont le modèle craque de toutes parts, et pose causer à la loi Sarkozy.

Des milliers de citoyens ont décidé de protéger des sans-papiers pour éviter leur expulsion. Pour dire non à la loi Sarkozy.

Le calcul du patron de l'UMP est simple : le « cycle » des sondages lui donnant raison, le retour à l'ivresse de la nation repliée et conservatrice est plus que jamais d'actualité. D'ailleurs, pense-t-il, le 21 avril 2002 a accrédité sa philosophie droitière. N'affirme-t-il pas : « Si le FN a progressé, c'est que nous n'avons pas fait à droite notre boulot... en refusant de parler d'un certain nombre de sujets dont Le Pen s'est emparé, nous avons désespéré une partie de notre électoral... » ? C'est signé. Depuis, le petit boss de Neuilly n'a qu'une obsession : suivre à sa manière le sillon tracé par Le Pen, à la fois pour récupérer les électeurs frontistes en 2007 et, dans le même mouvement, installer la précarisation générale de la société au service du néolibéralisme (celle dont rêve le MEDEF) tout en jouant sur la peur et l'étranger bouc émissaire.

Des jeunes qu'on voulait transformer en Kleenex aux immigrés jetables, la dérive de nos gouvernants pourrait prendre un relief pré-totalitaire si le peuple n'en contestait la logique même, comme ce fut le cas avec le CPE. Or, la loi Sarkozy est une trace supplémentaire de l'indignité de la France UMP, étriquée et faiblissante. Loin de s'attaquer à l'immigration illégale, elle renforce ajoute, en effet, l'injustice au désordre. On le publions jamais : les périodes où la société française a fait porter aux étrangers le poids de ses problèmes correspondent aux pages les plus sombres de notre histoire. L'idée qu'on puisse « choisir » les immigrés est une double spoliation, intellectuelle et concrète, car favoriser l'arrivée de travailleurs qualifiés pour les besoins du patronat aboutira à saigner les pays concernés, sans régler la question de l'immigration. L'Espagne et l'Italie, dont le nouveau gouvernement vient d'annoncer de nouvelles régularisations, ont, elles, montré le chemin en réussissant à intégrer économiquement et socialement plus d'un million d'étrangers depuis l'an 2000.

Alors ? La protestation ne s'arrêtera plus ! Des Églises aux associations, des élus contestataires aux anonymes agissants, un mouvement éthique se solidifie. Tous ces gens, qui savent ce que signifie le sens des responsabilités devant la détresse humaine, refusent le sacrifice du vivre-ensemble. N'en déplaise à Sarkozy : tenter de nous faire croire que les frustrations exprimées par les enfants de parents immigrés sont la conséquence d'une immigration mal maîtrisée et non des discriminations dont ils font l'objet est plus qu'un mensonge. C'est est renier l'idée une nous faisons de la République.

Les sans-papiers sont nos frères. Donnons-leur notre protection !

FIGURE 6.2. (cont.)

A TALE OF TWO PROTESTS

A close comparison of news coverage of two comparable immigration-related protests in France and the United States during the early 1990s demonstrates this tendency of the U.S. press to strip activism of its organizational underpinnings.[7] On January 25, 1992, upwards of eighty French trade unions, political parties, and antiracism associations organized a protest through the streets of Paris, drawing between 50,000 and 100,000 demonstrators. The protest sponsors and participants opposed not only the National Front, but also a broader tendency to scapegoat immigrants in the governing Socialist Party, as reflected in a number of incendiary statements over the previous year (e.g., Socialist Prime Minister Edith Cresson's call for more "charter [airplanes]" to deport immigrants, and President François Mitterrand's off-hand remark that France had surpassed its "limit of tolerance" toward immigrants). The antiracist coalition called for dramatic changes in immigration policy, such as greater access to political asylum and additional protections against discrimination in lodging, employment, and social benefits for immigrants. At the same time, the Socialist Party announced that it would join the demonstration and would seek to reframe the march's primary purpose as opposition to the extreme right rather than advocacy for immigrant rights.

On October 16, 1994, a similar type of demonstration was organized in the United States against California's Proposition 187 by some eighty civil rights, ethnic advocacy, religious, and labor organizations. An estimated 70,000 people marched across Los Angeles from the Eastside to City Hall for a rally. The largest anti-Prop. 187 umbrella organization, Taxpayers Against 187, took a position similar to that of the leading state Democratic politicians: that illegal immigration indeed was a problem but that Proposition 187's exclusion of basic social services, including medical care, was a far too draconian solution. Latino rights associations disagreed with this strategy and sought to reframe the problem as one of "racism" rather than "illegal immigration"; they and other civil rights groups were the chief organizers of the march.

These brief vignettes show that although the particular circumstances of the French and American protests were different, in broad substantive and structural terms they were quite similar. In addition, the numbers of sponsoring organizations and actual marchers were almost identical in the two cases. Yet we see clear and consistent differences in U.S. and French coverage of their respective demonstrations. In U.S. news stories, activist leaders are often portrayed as free agents ("a Pomona-based activist," "Proposition 187's

---

[7] This separate sample includes all newspaper articles and television news items related to the respective protest events from two weeks prior to two weeks after the event. In this capsule description, which typifies tendencies across the two national fields, I focus on news coverage in French newspapers *Le Monde*, *Le Figaro*, and *Libération* and U.S. newspapers the *Los Angeles Times*, the *New York Times*, and *USA Today*.

co-author"), freed of any link to a specific constituency or organizational base, as in these lead paragraphs of a *Los Angeles Times* article[8]:

A day after the largest demonstration in recent Los Angeles history, enthusiastic organizers and participants exuded optimism Monday about a new political activism that would energize an increasingly diverse Latino community. "This is the beginning of a new era of civil rights struggle – headed by Latino immigrants," said Fabian Nunez, a Pomona-based activist and one of the march coordinators. But to proponents of Proposition 187, the hotly debated immigration measure on the November ballot, the march was an outrageous display of Mexican nationalism that bolsters the case for reducing immigration. "Any time they're flying Mexican flags, it helps us," concluded Alan C. Nelson, Proposition 187 co-author.

As noted, at least eighty organizations were involved in organizing the protests in both countries. Yet only a handful of these organizations were specifically named in any of the American news coverage the day after the event. At one extreme was the wire service article in *The New York Times* (October 17, 1994, p. B8), which simply reported that "about 80 groups, among them labor unions and religious and human rights organizations, were represented," or the *USA Today* short article (October 17, p. 3A) by its own correspondents, which portrayed the march as a "spontaneous" gathering of 70,000 people with no mention at all of organizational involvement. But even the extensive *Los Angeles Times* article the day after the demonstration named only four specific organizations among the eighty involved: the Mexican-American Legal Defense Fund, Taxpayers Against [Prop.] 187, the Southern Christian Leadership Conference, and the umbrella group that organized the march, the National Coordinating Committee for Citizen and Civic Participation.[9]

In contrast, French articles tended to identify in detail the range of organizations involved. For instance, pre-march news coverage in *Le Figaro* mentioned thirty associations and political parties by name, ranging from the Human Rights League (LDH) to the Green and Communist Parties, and further left, the Communist Revolutionary League (LCR). Post-demonstration coverage in *Le Monde* and *Libération* listed, respectively, thirty-seven and twenty-three distinct associations, trade unions, and political parties supporting the protest.[10]

Moreover, the French national press provided "mobilizing" information (Lemert 1984) about the protest march whereas the American newspapers did

---

[8] Patrick McDonnell and Robert J. Lopez, "Some See New Activism in Huge March," *Los Angeles Times*, October 18, 1994, p. B1.

[9] Patrick McDonnell and Robert J. Lopez, "L.A. March Against Prop. 187 draws 70,000," *Los Angeles Times*, October 17, 1994, A-1.

[10] See *Le Figaro*, "Après la plainte d'Edith Cresson; L'offensive du PS contre Le Pen; 95 associations et parties de gauche descendront dans la rue samedi," January 21, 1992, p. 1 [summary of inside coverage]; *Le Monde*, "La Manifestation antiraciste à Paris," [articles by Philippe Bernard and Robert Solé], January 28, 1992, p. 12; *Libération* [L'Événement], "Le PS rate la marche Le Pen," January 27, 1992, p. 1. *Le Monde* is an afternoon newspaper dated the following day, so its coverage actually appeared on the same day as that of *Libération*.

not. With the exception of a tiny notice in the *Los Angeles Times* the day before the protest (October 15, 1994, p. B-2), which primarily served to notify drivers of which streets would be closed, the U.S. press failed to alert readers in advance about the anti-Proposition 187 march. In contrast, the French newspapers began substantive coverage of the Paris demonstration several weeks before it was held. Although the right-leaning *Le Figaro* presumably did not share the ideals of most of the demonstrators, its short article two weeks before the march gave detailed information about the associations involved and their reasons for protesting.[11]

In contrast, U.S. news tends to define civil society activism primarily in terms of crimes (real or potential). These opening paragraphs of *USA Today*'s October 17, 1994 article offer an illustration:[12]

A *peaceful* march of a few thousand protestors spontaneously swelled to an estimated crowd of 70,000 people Sunday opposing California's controversial "Save Our State" measure, a ballot proposal that would cut off most public services to illegal immigrants. The day-long march in mainly Hispanic East Los Angeles consisted mostly of Hispanic demonstrators chanting slogans and waving signs as they proceeded *peacefully* to City Hall. Police equipped with riot gear stood by and a number of streets were cordoned off from traffic, but authorities said there were *no signs of trouble.* "For such a large crowd, it was incredibly quiet," said Officer Arthur Holmes, a spokesman for the Los Angeles Police Department. The protest was large even for Los Angeles, said officer Sandra Costella, a police spokeswoman. She did not know whether more demonstrations would follow in the final three weeks before the Nov. 8 election. [my emphasis]

Other than for estimates of crowd size in *Le Monde* (January 28, 1992, p. 12) and *Le Figaro* (January 27, 1992, p. 5), no police officers were cited, let alone directly quoted, in any of the French news coverage of the equally peaceful Paris march. Contrasting sharply with *USA Today*'s opening paragraph is *Le Monde*'s institutionally and politically oriented extended subhead in its January 28, 1992 coverage:[13]

The demonstration against racism and the government's anti-immigration policies brought together 50,000 people, according to police sources, and 100,000, according to the collective of five associations organizing the march. The Federation of Associations in Solidarity with Immigrant Workers (FASTI), The Human Rights League (LDH), The Movement against Racism and for Friendship among Peoples (MRAP), SOS-Racisme and the International League against Racism and anti-Semitism (LICRA) were in the front row of the march, along with a group of refugees whose asylum requests had been turned down. The four leading associations, as well as the French Communist Party, the Greens, the Communist Revolutionary League and labor unions including the CGT, the CFDT, the FEN and the UNEF-ID, constituted a "unitary permanent collective" calling for a week of action at the beginning of April and a mobilization "for equality and fraternity"

---

[11] *Le Figaro*, "Avant leur manifestation: Le PS appuie les 'antiracistes,'" January 9, 1992, p. 6.
[12] Leo Mullen and Maria Puente, "70,000 in L.A. denounce immigration ballot measure," *USA Today*, October 17, 1994, p. 3A.
[13] *Le Monde*, "La Manifestation antiraciste à Paris," op cit.

on May 1. The Socialist Party, criticized by a majority of the participants, gathered its activists at the Place de la Bastille, but did not join in the march.

Le Figaro, not surprisingly, given its right-leaning political orientation, emphasized the divisions within the left and the Socialist Party's embarrassment, but still put the emphasis on the political message and organizations (January 27, 1992, p. 5).

Although there are, of course, exceptions[14], a tendency has continued in U.S. news coverage to portray activists as anonymous masses (or colorful personalities) rather than as members of particular organizations with particular agendas, which is most often the case. The *New York Times'* coverage of the national immigrant rights protests of April and May 2006 followed the same template as coverage of the 1994 Proposition 187 protests. The lead article on April 11 failed to say anything about the organizational impetus of the marches until the tenth paragraph and then only very briefly; the May 2 lead article referred to the organizers simply as a "small group of grass-roots immigration advocates" and provided cursory descriptions of the protestors' demands.[15] Subsequent social scientific research (Bloemraad, Voss, and Lee 2011, 22–28), however, has clearly established the crucial organizing role played by a network of local organizations, including local union affiliates (SEIU and UNITE-HERE), Roman Catholic parishes, schools, immigrant "hometown" associations (organizations designed to raise funds for projects in immigrants' "communities of origin"), and Spanish-language media. The latter, indeed, played precisely the kind of civic mobilizing role that English-language mainstream media consistently decline to play.

It may be that U.S. narrative-driven articles often meet the "constructionist" democratic ideal of recovering the experiences of nonpowerful individuals (Ferree et al. 2002, 268–272). However, in relation to coverage of civil society, this focus on individuals not only means less attention accorded to citizens' groups, but also a personalization and depoliticization of activism. In contrast, French news media (including television, as we will see in Chapter 8) celebrate and promote the democratic self-renewal of organized civil society. To say the least, this is a sad and ironic reversal of Alexis de Tocqueville's admiring portrait

---

[14] See, e.g., N.C. Aizenman, "Immigration Debate Wakes a 'Sleeping Latino Giant,'" *Washington Post*, April 6, 2006, p. A-1. Although typical of the U.S. journalistic tendency to not identify very many groups by name, Aizenman's article at least puts organizational activity front and center.

[15] See Rachel L. Swarns, "Immigrants Rally in Scores of Cities for Legal Status," *New York Times*, April 11, 2006, p. A-1; Randal Archibold, "Immigrants Take to U.S. Streets in Show of Strength," *New York Times*, May 2, 2006, p. A-1. Is it possible that the United States simply has more activists unaffiliated or loosely affiliated with organizations than does France? Courtroom-based activism by charismatic individual lawyers acting on behalf of their clients is arguably a more prominent political strategy in the United States than in France. U.S. immigration reporters also see immigration attorneys and legal scholars (more than other academics) as highly useful sources. However, the phenomenon I point to here involves ignoring or downplaying the many other kinds of immigration activist organizations that are in fact active in the U.S. public sphere.

of American democracy – although it must be emphasized, it is not associational life per se but the media's support for it that is at issue here.

INTERNAL PLURALISM

Turning to quantitative measures of multiperspectival news, I define a news package as more *ideologically* pluralist when it contains more distinct frames and more *institutionally* pluralist when it mentions more types of speakers. These measures supplement Habermas's (1996) new public sphere model, with its singular emphasis on "center" and "periphery": my approach focuses on the diversity of institutional logics rooted in distinct fields. In other words, the "system" is not of a piece. There is democratically significant structural variation within the center – or better, field of power – and paying attention to these distinct types of (relatively) powerful speakers is just as important as searching for voices at the outer margins of society. (See Tables 1.1 and 1.2 for complete lists of the ten frames and sixteen speaker types.) At the level of the individual news package (page one and all related articles in a given day's news coverage), frame diversity can range from 0 (in rare cases when no substantive frame appears) to 10; institutional diversity can range from 0 to 16.

Immediately, we find strong evidence against the stereotype that French newspapers are not as internally pluralist as their American counterparts. As shown in Table 6.1, during the 2000s, a range of French newspapers provide greater frame diversity than American newspapers. In France, frame diversity (unique frames per news package) ranges from 2.7 at *Le Parisien* and *Les Echos* to 3.4 at *Libération*; in the United States, the spread is from the *Daily News*' 1.7 frames per news package to the *Christian Science Monitor*'s 3.1. Overall, French newspapers offer 3.0 frames compared to 2.6 frames per news package in U.S. newspapers ($p < .000$). French newspapers also offer greater institutional (speaker) diversity than U.S. newspapers, ranging from *Les Echos*'s 3.0 unique types of speakers per news package to *Libération*'s average of 6.2; in the United States, speaker diversity ranges from 2.8 speakers at the *Daily News* to 4.8 at the *New York Times*. As a whole, French newspapers average 4.5 speakers per news package versus 4.2 in U.S. newspapers ($p < .01$).

The extent to which individual news packages "balance" opposing perspectives provides another indicator of internal pluralism (see Table 6.2). If a given news package includes at least one hero, victim, and threat frame, it is defined as providing "broad balance"; if it includes either one hero or victim frame on the one hand, and at least one threat frame on the other hand, it is defined as providing "some balance." Over the four decades of this study, French newspapers, on average, are slightly more likely than U.S. newspapers to provide broad balance (26 vs. 22 percent, respectively, although the difference is not statistically significant) and substantially more likely to provide some balance (68 vs. 60 percent). French newspapers possibly tilt slightly more to the pro-immigration side, with 24 percent of coverage offering *only* victim or hero

TABLE 6.1. *Frame and Speaker Diversity of Individual French and U.S. Newspapers, 2002–2006*

Newspapers (N News Packages)	Average Word Length per Package/ (% Mixed Genre)	Speaker Diversity: Average Institutional Speakers per Package (0–16)	Speaker Diversity: Institutional Concentration Index (600–10,000)	Frame Diversity: Average Frames per Package (0–10)	Frame Diversity: Frame Concentration Index (1,000–10,000)
L'Humanité (63)	1,731 (41)	4.43	1,010	3.05	1,930
La Croix (56)	2,209 (46)	4.75	1,225	2.82	1,807
Libération (60)	3,195 (80)	6.22	987	3.38	1,524
Le Monde (60)	2,498 (27)	4.32	1,048	3.08	1,647
Le Figaro (48)	2,868 (44)	4.15	1,243	3.04	1,441
Les Echos (45)	1,237 (13)	3.00	1,786	2.67	1,709
Le Parisien (47)	1,784 (53)	4.62	1,393	2.68	1,790
France Average (43)	2,217	4.50	1,242	2.96	1,693
C.S. Monitor (56)	1,352 (7)	4.55	1,250	3.13	1,476
L.A. Times (87)	2,091 (8)	4.46	1,205	2.79	1,791
N.Y. Times (68)	1,963 (10)	4.79	1,301	2.74	1,693
Wash. Post (81)	1,468 (6)	4.05	1,469	2.73	1,914
W.S. Journal (62)	1,616 (2)	3.97	1,291	2.40	1,837
USA Today (48)	1,379 (6)	4.73	1,291	2.79	1,653
Daily News (69)	573 (10)	2.81	1,564	1.70	2,847
U.S. Average (7)	1,492	4.19	1,339	2.61	1,887
N.Y. Post (71)	509 (6)	2.15	1,831	1.42	2,509

For each country, the most multiperspectival scores are highlighted (lower concentration index scores are more multiperspectival). Averages (means) refer to presence or absence of a given frame or speaker category in a news package. Institutional Concentration Index is based on raw speaker mentions (distinct speakers by category cited in each news package, summed for all packages); Frame Concentration Index is based on news package presence of frames (only coded for presence/absence) summed for all frames. So that newspapers with larger sample sizes do not dominate the analyses, national averages equally weight all of the media outlets. Data for *New York Post* are presented for supplemental analysis.

TABLE 6.2. *Balancing of Hero, Victim, and Threat Frames by French and U.S. Newspapers, 1970s–2000s*

Nation-State (N News Packages)	Hero Only (%)	Hero-Victim Only (%)	Victim Only (%)	Some Balance (%)	Broad Balance (%)	Threat Only (%)
France (620)	1	9	14	68	26	8
United States (721)	3	8	10	60	22	16
Percentage point difference	−2*	1	4	8**	4	−8**

Some Balance indicates simultaneous presence within a given day's news package of Threat with Hero or Victim frames; Broad Balance indicates simultaneous presence of at least one Threat, Hero, and Victim frame. Sample includes core newspapers 1970s–2000s and extended newspaper sample, 2002–2006. U.S.-French Difference: * $p \leq .05$; ** $p \leq .005$.

frames versus 21 percent in the United States (sum of first three columns in Table 6.2). In contrast, there is a more robust U.S. tilt toward immigration as threat, with 16 percent of news packages only including threat frames versus 8 percent in France.

Again, countering claims that immigration coverage is "too positive" (McGowan 2002), very few newspaper packages *only* present immigrants as heroes (either good worker, integration, or cultural diversity frames): just 3 percent in the U.S. media and 1 percent in the French media. Given business's need for cheap immigrant labor, however, it should probably not be surprising that two of the newspapers that stand out from the pack in presenting only hero frames are the financial newspapers in the two countries: the *Wall Street Journal* (frames appearing in 11 percent of packages) and *Les Echos* (4 percent) (figures not shown in tables).[16]

To supplement these indicators of daily news coverage, I also measure frame and speaker diversity across total news coverage for each media outlet (see Table 6.1). I adapt the Herfindahl index,[17] a measure of market concentration, to assess the extent to which news coverage is concentrated or dispersed evenly across the sixteen institutional speaker categories (*institutional concentration index* or ICI) and ten immigration-related ideological frames (*frame concentration index* or FCI). In each case, the index is calculated by squaring the percentage that each speaker type or frame appears in a given

---

[16] The *Washington Post* (over the four decades) and the French *Le Parisien* also had 4 percent. All other French and U.S. newspapers ranged from 0 to 2 percent.

[17] For other cultural sociology and media studies' uses of the Herfindahl index, see DiMaggio and Stenberg (1985), Dowd et al. (2002, 51–52), Entman (2006), and Hindman (2008).

newspaper's total coverage (relative to all speaker types or frames appearing in its news coverage) and then summing the total. The highest possible score is 10,000 (indicating a discursive monopoly held by a single frame or speaker; i.e., 100 x 100). How low the score goes depends on the number of categories in the model, but the lower the score, the more even the dispersion of coverage across the range of possible institutional speakers or frames (hence, the more multiperspectival). For example, the ICI score for the *Daily News* is calculated by squaring each speaker type's percentage of all citations (e.g., a squared 6 percent for business equals 36) and then summing the 16 squared percentages, for a total of 1,564.

As Table 6.1 shows, using these frame and speaker concentration indexes, French newspaper coverage of immigration is also more multiperspectival. Against a standard of 1,000, representing a perfectly evenly balanced presentation of all possible immigration frames (10 frames of 10 percent each), French newspapers have an average FCI score of 1,693 compared to the U.S. average FCI score of 1,887, which is more than 11 percent higher. Against a standard of 624 representing perfectly evenly balanced presentation of all possible speaker viewpoints (16 institutional fields of 6.25 percent each), French newspapers have an average ICI score of 1,242 versus a U.S. average of 1,339, an 8 percent difference.

This tendency of French newspapers to be more multiperspectival is generally consistent over time, as shown by the content analysis of the leading agenda-setting national newspapers (*The New York Times, Washington Post,* and *Los Angeles Times* vs. *Le Monde, Le Figaro,* and *Libération*) over the past four decades (see Table 6.3). At the news package level, French speaker diversity is higher to a statistically significant extent during the 1970s, 1980s, and 2000s. Likewise, French average ICI scores are lower (more multiperspectival) than U.S. average scores during all four periods. French frame diversity is also higher at the news package level during all four periods. There is some evidence of cross-national convergence over the four decades. Between the 1970s and 2000s, speaker diversity rose in the leading French newspapers from 4.5 to 4.9, while U.S. speaker diversity increased from 2.8 to 4.4, closing the cross-national gap from 1.7 to 0.5. Likewise, French newspaper frame diversity fell from 3.8 to 3.2 frames per news package, while U.S. frame diversity rose from 2.5 to 2.8 frames per news package, thus narrowing the gap from 1.3 to 0.4.

Cross-national differences in balancing within news packages also decline somewhat over time (data not shown in tables). In my core sample of three leading newspapers in each country, twice as many French news packages as U.S. packages were broadly balanced (32 vs. 16 percent) during the 1970s. By the 2000s, French news packages were still more broadly balanced, but the gap had fallen to just 7 percentage points (31 vs. 24 percent). For the entire seven newspaper sample, the French-U.S. gap in the 2000s was only 3 percentage points (27 vs. 24 percent). Thus, by the 2000s, cross-national differences were

TABLE 6.3. *Speaker and Frame Diversity by Time Period*[a] *and News Generation*[b]: *French and U.S. Newspapers, 1970s–2000s*

	1970s	1980s	1990s	2000s	Political Field–Generated	Journalistic Field–Generated	Civil Society Fields–Generated
France (N)	(37)	(72)	(132)	(168)	(328)	(127)	(167)
Average Institutional Speakers Per Package	4.50	4.79	4.31	4.90	4.30	3.94	5.23
Average ICI	1,228	1,409	1,587	1,093			
U.S. (N)	(63)	(81)	(106)	(236)	(396)	(245)	(83)
Average Institutional Speakers Per Package	2.83	3.61	4.06	4.43	3.69	4.26	4.71
Average ICI	2,379	1,725	2,184	1,325			
French-U.S. Differences	1.67** 1,151[c]	1.18** 316	0.25 597	0.47* 232	0.61**	−0.32	0.52
France (N)	(37)	(72)	(132)	(168)	(328)	(127)	(167)
Average Frames Per Package	3.75	3.43	3.45	3.17	3.17	3.21	3.05
Average FCI	1,673	1,801	1,744	1,537			
U.S. (N)	(63)	(81)	(106)	(236)	(396)	(245)	(83)
Average Frames Per Package	2.50	2.85	2.80	2.75	2.37	2.87	3.43
Average FCI	1,607	1,447	1,675	1,799			
French-U.S. Differences	1.25** −66	0.58 −354	0.65* −69	0.42* 262	0.80**	0.34*	−.0.38

ICI, Institutional Concentration Index; FCI, Frame Concentration Index

The most multiperspectival scores are highlighted; N's are news packages. Averages are means.

[a] Means of *New York Times, Washington Post,* and *Los Angeles Times* for U.S.; means of *Libération* (only 1980s–2000s), *Le Monde,* and *Le Figaro* for France

[b] Over-time core sample (1970s–1990s) plus total sample (2000s)

[c] Because lower ICI and FCI scores are more multiperspectival, negative French-U.S. differences are represented as a positive amount.

* French-U.S. Difference, $p \leq .05$; ** French-U.S. Difference, $p \leq .005$

less substantial with the exception of emphasis on the threat frames, which appeared uncontested in nearly one out of six U.S. news packages versus one out of twelve French packages.

Even if the two countries have converged somewhat over time, these are important and surprising results because they go against the usual expectation – at least in the United States – that individual U.S. newspapers will offer substantially more balanced coverage than French (or other European "partisan") newspapers. In fact, that is far from the case. For the most part, the French national newspapers are at least as broadly balanced and internally pluralist as their American counterparts – and usually more so. If anything, U.S. newspapers are moving toward the French level of internal pluralism rather than vice versa.

EXTERNAL PLURALISM

In general, the framing and sourcing differences across the major national newspapers in France are greater than in the United States, although the gap is not dramatic. External pluralism is measured as the average gap between the extremes in the prominence accorded to all frames and speakers by all newspapers.[18] During the early 1970s, differences in percentages of frame and speaker mentions between *Le Monde* and *Le Figaro* in France were actually less than the average differences between the *Washington Post, Los Angeles Times*, and *New York Times* (compared in pairs, with the binary differences averaged). This suggests that external pluralism among mainstream media, at least, was not higher in France than in the United States at this time. (Of course, France's external pluralism "score" would have been considerably higher if the many small partisan papers of the early 1970s were included.) Subsequently, with the inclusion of *Libération* as a mainstream national newspaper from the 1980s onward, external pluralism is greater in France than in the United States, although over time the degree of external pluralism declines in both countries (see Table 6.4). Taking into account the wider spectrum of seven roughly comparable national newspapers in each country, during the 2000s the average gap for frames is about 25 percentage points in France and 21 points in the United States (see also Appendix Table A.2). Replacing the *Daily News* with the avowedly conservative *New York Post* in the U.S. seven-newspaper sample changes some of the individual frame percentage spreads but leaves the average gap unchanged.

---

[18] For example, among French newspapers, *Le Figaro* mentioned the humanitarian frame least often (65 percent of coverage) and *L'Humanité* mentioned it most often (97 percent), creating a high-low gap for this frame of 32 percentage points (see Appendix Table A.2). To calculate external pluralism, gaps for each frame or speaker category are derived, summed, and then averaged across the ten frames or sixteen speaker types.

TABLE 6.4. *External Pluralism*[a] *of Frames and Speakers: French and U.S. Newspapers, 1970s–2000s*

	1970s (Core)[b]	1980s (Core)	1990s (Core)	2000s (Core)	2000s (Expanded Seven Newspaper Samples)
Frame Diversity	Avg. % point gap	Avg. % point gap	Avg. % point gap	Avg. % point gap	Avg. % point gap
France	10.4	24.9	13.7	9.6	25.3
U.S.	12.0	14.6	13.3	8.8	20.9
Difference	−1.6	10.3	0.4	0.8	4.4
Speaker Diversity					
France	2.0	5.6	4.1	3.1	8.7
U.S.	4.1	4.1	5.1	2.8	6.4
Difference	−2.1	1.5	−1.0	0.3	2.3

[a] External pluralism is indicated by average high-low percentage point gaps for ten frames and sixteen speaker types (see Tables 1.1 and 1.2) across the sampled newspapers in each country.

[b] The 1970s French data only include *Le Monde* and *Le Figaro*; to facilitate comparison, the 1970s U.S. figure is the average of the binary differences between the three U.S. core newspapers.

An analysis of specific frames shows that neither multicultural/identity politics frames (racism, cultural diversity) nor threat frames such as national cohesion (through the 1980s) separate U.S. newspapers one from the other to the degree they do for French newspapers. The high point of French external pluralism is 1983, due in part to the political realignment of the French journalistic field in the wake of the election of a socialist president along with *Libération*'s bold (and successful) bid to reposition itself as a mainstream rather than alternative media outlet. In that year, *Libération* was 50 percentage points more likely to mention the cultural diversity frame in its daily coverage than *Le Figaro*; conversely, *Le Figaro* was about 60 percentage points more likely to mention the national cohesion frame than either *Libération* or *Le Monde*.[19]

In the United States, differences across media outlets can be mostly attributed to conjunctural, "place"-based political and cultural factors. For example, during 1994, a year in which California media coverage of immigration was dominated by Proposition 187, it should not be surprising that the fiscal frame was far more prominent in the *Los Angeles Times* (67 percent) than in the *New York Times* (40 percent) or *Washington Post* (37 percent). Based largely on an analysis of this 1994 coverage, sociologist Kevin Keogan (2002) argues

[19] French and U.S. individual newspaper over-time data are shown in Online Tables 6.2 and 6.3.

that the political culture of southern California is more anti-immigrant than that of New York. Although making a compelling case for the role of symbolically laden public places (Ellis Island for New York, the U.S.-Mexican border for southern California) in shaping local political cultures, Keogan's conclusions do not hold up as well when news coverage is examined over a four-decade period. For instance, in 1986, the *Los Angeles Times* placed less emphasis on any of the threat frames than did the *New York Times*. During the 2000s, the *Los Angeles Times* was slightly more likely to publish news packages only emphasizing threat frames (15 percent of its total compared to 10 percent at the *New York Times* and *Washington Post*). At the same time, it equaled or led its competitors in the proportion of packages that only featured hero or victim frames (21 percent vs. 22 percent at the *New York Times* and 16 percent at the *Washington Post*).

Over time, in both France and the United States, differences among the three leading national newspapers narrow considerably, although probably for different reasons. In the United States, during the 1970s, these "national" newspapers in reality had mostly regional audiences and interests, and such decentralization seems to have produced, as Paul Starr's (2004) analysis would suggest, a relatively high degree of ideological and topical pluralism of news coverage. Subsequently, through technological means (satellite-aided printing across the nation, and later, the Internet), as well as journalistic ambition (a Washington "edition" of the *Los Angeles Times*, flown from Los Angeles to the nation's capital from 1992 to 2004; a "national" weekly edition of the *Washington Post*, published from 1983 to 2009[20]), the *New York Times*, *Los Angeles Times*, and *Washington Post* became, at least partially, economic as well as professional competitors. The gradual convergence in their respective approaches to covering immigration counters Barnhurst and Nerone's (2001, 294) prediction that a technologically "recentralized" journalistic field will necessarily lead to greater ideological differentiation. In the French case, the newspapers were, from the start, part of an intensely competitive, centralized national journalistic field. Thus, any within-nation French journalistic convergence may be due to the ideological convergence in the political field that occurred during the mid-1980s, as well as to a convergence, particularly between *Le Monde* and *Libération*, in the class profiles of their national newspaper audiences.

Focusing on 2002–2006 coverage across a wider range of newspapers (see Appendix Tables A.2 and A.3), there are a number of similarities and

---

[20] See Frank Ahrens, "L.A. Times to End National Edition," *Washington Post*, December 3, 2004, p. E02; Andy Alexander, "Post's National Weekly Edition to Close," Omblog, washingtonpost. com, August 10, 2009, http://voices.washingtonpost.com/ombudsman-blog/2009/08/posts_natio nal_weekly_edition.html.

differences. For example, in both France and the United States, financial newspapers (*Wall Street Journal, Les Echos*) are the most likely to emphasize the good worker frame. The *Daily News* is generally the least likely to emphasize various threat frames and among the most likely to emphasize the humanitarian frame. In France, the communist *L'Humanité* is the most likely among national newspapers to emphasize the humanitarian and racism frames and the least likely to emphasize the public order frame. The left-leaning *Libération*, likewise, is the most likely to emphasize global economy and is close behind *L'Humanité* in its focus on the humanitarian frame. *Le Figaro* is the least likely to mention the humanitarian and racism frames and the most likely to mention all of the threat frames. (See Appendix Table A.2.)

External pluralism in voices (speakers) is also clearly bolstered when a journalistic field has a variety of types of media outlets (see Appendix Table A.3). Within their respective national journalistic fields, the financial papers the *Wall Street Journal* (16 percent) and *Les Echos* (4 percent) make the most room for business voices. Popular or "down-market" mass newspapers like the *Daily News* (38 percent), the *New York Post* (31 percent), and *Le Parisien* (31 percent) accord about one-third or more of their source citations to unaffiliated individuals and polls. In the case of the *New York Post* (33 percent) and *Le Parisien* (30 percent), these popular papers also are the most likely to amplify the voices of executive branch and government bureaucratic officials. International or foreign speakers are highlighted in France's financial daily *Les Echos* (26 percent) and the conservative paper *Le Figaro* (18 percent), more so, surprisingly, than in *Le Monde* (15 percent), with its long-standing reputation for international coverage. No U.S. newspaper stands clearly above the rest in bringing global speakers into the public debate; the most international among them offer just 4 to 6 percent of their citations to foreign and international organizations. Finally, civil society perspectives are emphasized in smaller, political party or religious-sponsored newspapers like *L'Humanité* (39 percent), *La Croix* (35 percent), and the *Christian Science Monitor* (40 percent). In the case of the communist *L'Humanité*, not surprisingly, minor political parties (11 percent) also receive a substantial boost in visibility.

External pluralism in the French national press is also evident in the institutional affiliations of individuals chosen for published interview transcripts (see Table 2.1). Nine out of the ten political officials interviewed by *L'Humanité* were affiliated with the French communist party. At *La Croix*, eleven of the twenty-four civil society interviews (46 percent) were conducted with either Catholic priests or Catholic-affiliated laypersons. Although this does represent a certain "bias," it also shows that these two newspapers are fulfilling their state-funded mandate for "ideological pluralism," giving voice to perspectives (communist, Catholic) that are heard far less often in the other national newspapers.

The degree and type of balancing within news packages provides additional insight into differences among media outlets. Appendix Table A.4 shows the proportion of packages for each news outlet that present "only hero and/or victim frames," "only threat frames," "some balance" (defined as inclusion of a threat frame with either a hero or victim frame), and "broad balance" (defined as simultaneous inclusion of threat, hero, and victim frames). Of all the newspapers in the sample, the *Christian Science Monitor* offers in many respects the most balanced coverage: 71 percent of its coverage offers some balance, 32 percent is broadly balanced, and a nearly identical proportion of the remaining coverage tilts toward only hero/victim frames (13 percent) or threat frames (14 percent). According to the *Monitor*'s lead editorial writer Clay Jones, this balanced approach – in both editorials and news – is due to a conscious effort to take seriously the views of restrictionists as well as pro-immigration advocates:[21]

We try to make important distinctions between legal immigration, which we support and want to expand, and illegal immigration, which we come from the premise that it is fundamentally law breaking but should be handled compassionately. The Bush-type raids were maybe badly done but there still has to be some type of enforcement. In our editorials, we say enforcement has to be effective and long-term, while we also deal with the compassionate side of things. I mean, what are you going to do with 11 million people? ... It's so easy to get labeled racist, but it's clear we approach it from the point of view [that there has to be enforcement]. It's an illegal act, it's happening on a massive scale and it's corroding our society and we have to deal with it on that basis.

What sets apart both the *Daily News* and *New York Post* from other U.S. newspapers is their low degree of balancing within news packages. Their news coverage is more likely to provide a solely one-sided portrait of immigrants as either heroes or victims (in both the *Daily News* and *New York Post*) or as a threat (in the *New York Post*). In France, although slightly more than half of *L'Humanité*'s news coverage offers some balance, the remainder presents only hero or victim frames. Most of the remaining U.S. and French prestige, financial, and mass market newspapers offer some balance in a majority of their news packages. When they are not balanced, however, they tilt toward only hero or victim frames. Other than the aforementioned *New York Post*, only *Le Figaro* and *USA Today* are more likely to solely present threat frames (25 percent in both cases) than victim/hero frames (12 percent in *Le Figaro* and 14 percent in *USA Today*).

CONCLUSION: EXPLAINING MULTIPERSPECTIVAL NEWS

How does a consideration of field factors – position, logic, and structure – help us understand what makes news more (or less) multiperspectival? First, the

---

[21] Clay Jones interview (2011).

liberal assumption that the state can never play a positive role in promoting press freedom meets a powerful counterexample in the French case. French government media policy is explicitly oriented toward promoting multiperspectival news. The extra subsidies that *L'Humanité* and *La Croix* receive are encouragements, not hindrances, to adding their own distinct voices to French public debate. Civil society perspectives are much more prominent in the French press than in the U.S. press. It is not in spite of the state but because of the state, at least in part, that the French press is more pluralist than the U.S. press.

Second, commercial pressures are clearly mediated both by field structure and logic. If lack of advertising or profit pressures were the only relevant factor, *L'Humanité*, *La Croix*, and the *Christian Science Monitor* would be in all cases the most multiperspectival newspapers. Although the news coverage of these three outlets is indeed quite pluralist (especially the *Monitor*), in France, *Libération* and *Le Figaro* (by one measure) were among the most multiperspectival, and in the United States, the *New York Times* and *Los Angeles Times* had greater speaker diversity than the *Monitor*. Class position of media outlet helps account in part for these findings. As Table 2.2 shows, what *Libération*, the *Christian Science Monitor*, and the *New York Times* have in common are audiences especially high in cultural capital (as indicated by overrepresentation of professional and creative occupations and high levels of education). Cultural capital potentially provides some degree of distance from the dominant worldviews (Bourdieu 1984). Research has also shown that persons with more cultural capital have more "omnivorous" cultural tastes (Peterson and Kern 1996): conceivably, this omnivorousness could also include a taste for diversity in news. The *Daily News* and the *New York Post*, newspapers with popular (down-market) readerships, are the least multiperspectival in the sample (however, the equally popular *Le Parisien* is much more multiperspectival, closer to slightly more elite newspapers such as *La Croix* and *L'Humanité*, suggesting in this case the power of field-level "form" effects).

Over-time changes are also mediated by structural and contingent field-level factors. To the extent that there is convergence, it is *not* simply a case of ever-downward frame and speaker diversity due to increasing commercialization. Internal pluralism of voices (types of speakers cited) actually increases in both countries. The trend in frame diversity is more mixed: up slightly for U.S. newspapers at the level of the individual news package but down at the level of frame concentration across total news coverage, with the portrait reversed for French newspapers. External pluralism has decreased in both countries. In France, any decline in pluralism, internal or external, may be due to political as well as commercial factors – in particular, a chilling effect induced by fear of the National Front. As Lemieux and Schmalzbauer (2000, 167) argue, "widespread concern about the rise of the extreme Right in France has made French journalists less open to reporting 'all sides' of the debate than they otherwise might have been." In the United States, the nationalization of a previously regionally oriented newspaper system has produced contradictory effects, increasing pluralism in some ways and reducing it in others. In both countries, trends in overall pluralism – and the predominance of certain speakers and frames over others – may be linked to increasing class homogenization of the leading newspapers.

Whereas market and audience composition effects vary depending on the newspaper, all newspapers within a given national field are affected to a similar degree by both political field influences and by the internal logic of the journalistic field as expressed in the dominant form of news. How can the relative impact of these influences be sorted out? One answer is provided by the second part of Table 6.3, which categorizes the total sample (1970s–2000s) according to how the news coverage was generated, whether by the political field, the civil society field(s), or the journalistic field itself. Table 6.3 shows that the largest French-U.S. difference in speaker and frame diversity is for political field–generated news, suggesting that cross-national differences in political fields are a strong influence. Political field news generation has no statistical effect on French speaker or frame diversity but, in the United States, actually reduces types of speakers per news package by 0.198 and frames per package by 0.227 (2002–2006 data, not shown in tables). Perhaps this is due to an ideologically narrow two-party system, as well as to the strategic focus of so much U.S. political reporting.

In contrast, in both France and the United States, civil society–generated news tends to be more multiperspectival (2002–2006 data, not shown in tables), increasing speakers by 0.181 and frames by 0.183 per news package in the United States, and speakers by 0.187 per package in France (with no statistically significant effect on frame diversity). In this regard as well, differences in political systems are crucial. Although civil society–generated news is quite multiperspectival in both countries, the French political system seems to do more to encourage civil society activity than does the U.S. system (Veugelers and Lamont 1991). Thus, part of the reason for more multiperspectival immigration news in France than in the United States is due to a much greater tendency for immigration news to be civil society generated in France (about 26 percent of news packages vs. 11 percent in the U.S. for the broad 2002–06 sample of newspapers; see also Figure 2.5).

Finally, there is clear evidence that a multiarticle, multigenre "debate ensemble" format helps make news more multiperspectival. As the newspaper that pioneered the *événement* debate ensemble formula, *Libération* is also the most consistently multiperspectival of all the newspapers in the sample. Widespread French adoption of the debate ensemble format also helps explain how

Shaping Immigration News

TABLE 6.5. *Effect of News Genre on Speaker and Frame Diversity: French and U.S. Newspapers, 2002–2006*

	France Speaker Diversity	U.S. Speaker Diversity	France Frame Diversity	U.S. Frame Diversity
Multigenre (News and any other)	0.601** (0.358**)	0.255** (0.124**)	0.361** (0.148**)	0.211** (0.107*)
News only (Event and/or feature/background)	-0.462** (-0.201**)	-0.203** (-0.107*)	-0.354** (-0.163**)	-0.188** (-0.112*)
Other Only (Commentary, analysis and/or interview transcript)	-0.247** (-0.187**)	0.008 (0.033)	-0.009 (0.036)	0.033 (0.053)

$p \le .05$; ** $p \le .005$. Figures in parentheses hold constant for word length.

even admittedly partisan newspapers, such as the communist *L'Humanité*, as well as the popular audience-oriented *Le Parisien*, are nevertheless quite multiperspectival. Admittedly, not all French newspapers are more multiperspectival than their U.S. counterparts in every way, and the *Christian Science Monitor* exhibits a high degree of frame and institutional diversity even though it does not frequently use the debate ensemble format.

Nevertheless, as Table 6.5 shows, there are strong and statistically positive multiperspectival effects in both France and the United States from multigenre news, that is, coverage that mixes (1) event news or feature/background articles with (2) any of the following: journalist-authored analyses or commentaries (including editorials), non-journalist-authored commentaries, or interview transcripts. Even when controlling for word length, multigenre coverage increases French speaker and frame diversity news package means by 0.358 and 0.148, respectively, and U.S. speaker and frame diversity means by 0.124 and 0.107, respectively (2002–06 period; effects across entire four decades are very similar).

The higher French scores may be interpreted as reflecting, at least in part, the more closely coordinated interplay of genres in news coverage with the avowed purpose of making news coverage more multiperspectival, as expressed in the remarks by *Libération* editor Serge July at the beginning of Chapter 4. Conversely, use of only news genres correlates with less multiperspectival news in both France and the United States. This might be interpreted as confirmation of Hartmut Wessler's (2008, 8) observation that narrative-driven formats focusing on "persons" and "personal attributes" ultimately "restrict the room for deliberative exchange of ideas."[22] Over the course of several weeks, an American newspaper might cover a topic from as many angles as a French newspaper, but the multiperspectival approach in a single day's edition of a French newspaper offers the civic advantage of seeing the world whole, in all its complexity, rather than as a succession of seemingly unrelated fragments.[23]

[22] In France, coverage limited to analysis, commentary, or interview transcripts also has a negative effect on speaker diversity, probably due to the tendency of these genres to limit citations of social actors other than the author or person being interviewed; effects on U.S. news coverage are difficult to determine because of the small number of "other only" articles in the U.S. sample.

[23] See Bennett (2011) for a similar analysis of a "fragmentation bias" in the U.S. news media.

7

What Makes for a Critical Press?

On both sides of the Atlantic, the press is often accused of being inadequately critical of political and economic power.[1] But what exactly is meant by "critical" news coverage? How can one go beyond the anecdotal to measure the systematic presence or absence of this discursive quality in news stories? And what are the structural forces that lead the press to be more or less critical in its coverage of immigration in France and the United States? In this chapter, I expand both how critical journalism is defined and how it is explained.

FACTORS SHAPING DEGREE AND TYPE OF CRITICISM

The liberal diagnosis is that any state intervention – whether restricting or enabling – will inhibit press criticism of government and the ruling political parties. The French state is more likely than the U.S. government to intervene in an overtly restraining manner and also offers more generous financial support of newspapers, which some observers see as a form of "soft" control.[2] Conversely, business advertising funding – the dominant form of funding of U.S. newspapers – is seen as enabling press "independence" from the state (Eveno 2003; Picard 2005, 341) and thus as a factor likely to *increase* journalistic criticism of government and the party in power.

From a liberal perspective, then, it is obvious that the French press should be less critical than the American press, especially of government and the political party in power. Moreover, those newspapers that are most reliant on state subsidies (such as *La Croix* and *L'Humanité*) should be the least critical of government, whereas those newspapers that are most financially independent

---

[1] See, e.g., De Tarlé (1980), Sparrow (1999), Halimi (2005), and Bennett et al. (2007).
[2] The term is from De Tarlé (1980, 146), arguing that press subsidies make French newspapers "feel indebted to a government that has been so generous to them." See also Charon (1991, 118–122), Murschetz (1998), and Dennis (2004) for similar arguments.

(as indicated, roughly, by greater advertising funding) should be the most critical. This means that, in France, *Le Figaro* and *Les Echos* should be the most critical, whereas in the United States, there should be little difference among newspapers except for the *Christian Science Monitor* (which receives very little advertising and is not profitable), which should be less critical than the others.

From a political economy perspective, it has also been argued that advertising discourages partisan position-taking or criticisms that might risk alienating some audiences (Baker 1994, 70). Thus, for self-interested reasons, one would expect the heavily advertising-dependent U.S. press to be the more balanced in its criticisms. At the same time, commercialization might also reduce the overall amount of criticism, as coverage becomes more focused on personalities than on substantive issue debates (Frank 2002; Bagdikian 2004). Finally, for-profit ownership and reliance on advertising should reduce the amount of critical reporting or commentary about business (Collins 1992). From this perspective, one would expect the French press – especially newspapers with fewer ties to business investors as well as advertisers, such as *L'Humanité* and *La Croix* – to be more critical of business than the American press. In the United States, the nonprofit *Christian Science Monitor* should be *more* critical of business than other newspapers; in France, business-oriented and advertising-reliant *Le Figaro* and *Les Echos* should be *less* critical of business than other newspapers.

In fact, what do we discover? Again, I find patterns of news coverage that do not fit entirely within either the standard critiques of the state or market. Despite greater state intervention in France than in the United States, French press coverage contains more critical statements – even when controlling for article length – than the U.S. press. French newspapers in general are *not* less critical of government and the party in power than the U.S. press; in fact, the opposite is generally true. The individual newspapers that receive the highest direct subsidies are *not* substantially less critical of the government or dominant party than other French newspapers or than U.S. newspapers. In fact, one of the most critical newspapers in the study is the state-subsidized *L'Humanité*. Conversely, newspapers whose "independence" is secured via advertising are not substantially more critical of government and dominant parties than non–advertising funded newspapers. U.S. newspapers are, in fact, slightly more balanced in their criticisms, indicating lesser political polarization, although the difference with France is small. This difference cannot be solely attributed to advertising: the most advertising-dependent French newspaper, *Le Figaro*, is also one of the most partisan. Despite their lack of reliance on advertising, French newspapers are no more likely than U.S. newspapers to criticize business. Finally, investigative reporting is somewhat higher in U.S. newspapers than in their French counterparts, although quite low in general in both countries, and I suggest a rethinking of what truly constitutes critical investigative journalism.

MEASURING CRITICISM

In this chapter, I focus on immigration news coverage in French and U.S. national newspapers during the 1990s (1991 in France, 1994 in the U.S.) and 2000s (2002, 2004, and the first half of 2006), two periods of heavy media coverage of immigration in both countries, and, crucially, also two periods that differ in terms of whether the right or left was in power.

Many analyses of critical journalism focus on "investigative reporting,"[3] and I, too, examine in qualitative detail immigration-related investigative coverage in France and the United States. Yet this is not the only significant form of journalistic criticism. The press performs another important critical role by publishing substantive critical statements about government, political parties, businesses, and other powerful organizations. Critical statements, uttered by either journalists or their sources (spokespersons for various organizations or unaffiliated individuals), are sometimes dismissed as evidence of excessive negativity in the press, yet assuming that they remain within the bounds of "civility" (Wessler 2008, 8), such statements are also clearly an important part of what Habermas (1989) means by "*rational-critical*" debate. Although they may or may not be linked to investigative reporting per se, such critical statements perform an important "signaling" function of their own by calling attention to incoherent policy planning, ideological mystification, ineffective administration, or misleading information, thus raising questions and concerns that may prompt further private or public inquiries.

Thus, in this chapter, criticism is first measured by the frequency of various types of "critical statements" in news packages. To be coded, critical statements had to have a clear target in the form of an organization or an individual linked to an organization. Criticisms of unaffiliated individuals or categories of individuals (immigrants, Latinos, etc.) are not measured, nor are broad criticisms of the society or culture. My purpose in this instance is not to assess the overall negativity of the press, but rather to document the prevalence of specific criticisms of the dominant governing (and challenging) political and economic institutional actors. Critical statements are classified according to their *target* (government in general; the dominant "left" political parties, i.e., U.S. Democrats and French Socialists, in or out of government office; the dominant "right" parties, i.e. U.S. Republicans and French UMP leaders in or out of government; minor political parties or civil society organizations; business; and foreign or international organizations) as well as by their *substantive focus* (administrative, character, truth, ideology, policy, and strategy).

---

[3] See Ettema and Glasser (1998), Marchetti (2000), Waisbord (2000), Chalaby (2004), and Schudson (2008, 14–16).

Administrative criticism refers to failure (whether through corruption, incompetence, or mismanagement) in the execution of legal or administrative responsibilities. *Truth criticism* attempts to "set the record straight," usually offering evidence to demonstrate the falsity of claims. *Character criticisms* are ad hominem attacks on the personal characteristics of powerful individuals in public life (e.g., that they are arrogant, insensitive, hypocritical, etc.). *Policy criticism* concerns the logical coherence, feasibility, or empirical justification or evidence supporting any proposed policy; it might also call attention to a past or ongoing policy's failure to achieve its stated aims (in contrast to administrative criticism, which would focus on improper implementation or deviation from legally mandated procedures). *Ideology criticism* focuses more on ultimate ends rather than the best means to a given end and is conceptually broader than policy criticism. It would encompass criticisms of fascism, racism, sexism, or other worldviews portrayed as objectionable in and of themselves. *Strategy criticisms* are negative assessments of the effectiveness of a particular idea or action for the attainment of desired political (partisan) ends; they may also encompass normative criticisms of overt or covert political strategies as being "too negative," "dirty," or in some other way morally objectionable.

Finally, in addition to critical statements, I searched for investigative journalism news packages (usually individual articles) that specifically focus on the malfeasance of political or business elites, either personal or professional. These articles may or may not contain explicitly critical statements, but they clearly offer an important form of criticism through the accumulation of damning facts.

CRITICAL STATEMENTS

Amount and Types of Criticism

French page-one news packages tend to include a greater number of critical statements about organized political actors than do U.S. packages (4.7 vs. 2.0, respectively, for the combined 1990s–2000s sample).[4] One might at first suspect that the difference is purely due to the greater "size" of French page-one news coverage, which averages 2,100 words versus 1,500 words for U.S. coverage. However, even when total word length is controlled for, the French press is still

---

[4] At $p < .001$, t-test for equality of means. See Benson (2010b) for complete details of statistical significance tests. To preserve a rough symmetry in the national samples, seven U.S. newspapers are compared to the seven French newspapers for the 2002–2006 period; *New York Post* data are shown but are not included in the national averages. So that newspapers with larger sample sizes do not dominate the results, reported national averages equally weight all of the media outlets. Statistical significance tests are based on raw totals of all articles in each country or media outlet.

TABLE 7.1. *Types of Criticism: French and U.S. Newspapers, Combined 1990s and 2000s (Critical Statements per 1,000 words)*

Country (N 1,000 word units)	Administrative	Character	Truth	Ideology	Policy	Strategy	Total
France (1,147)	0.22	0.07	0.08	0.40	1.05	0.36	2.17
% of Total	10	3	4	18	48	17	
U.S. (917)	0.28	0.06	0.06	0.10	0.70	0.18	1.37
% of Total	20	4	4	7	51	13	

Due to rounding, frequencies or percentages may not add up exactly to totals.

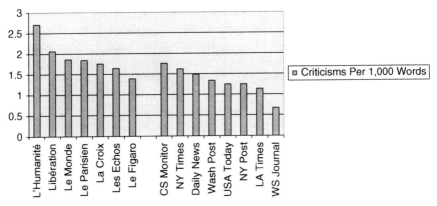

FIGURE 7.1. Critical statements in individual French and U.S. Newspapers, 2002–2006. Numbers are for critical statements per 1,000 words.

substantially more critical – thus offering greater "critical density" as well as raw numbers of criticisms. French immigration coverage averaged 2.2 criticisms per 1,000 words versus 1.4 criticisms per 1,000 words in the U.S. coverage – in other words, nearly 60 percent more criticisms. In the remainder of this chapter, only word length-adjusted criticisms are reported and analyzed. As Figure 7.1 shows, from 2002 to 2006, virtually all French newspapers tended to be more critical than their U.S. counterparts. *L'Humanité* was the most critical of the French newspapers, and the *Christian Science Monitor* was the most critical U.S. newspaper.

Given the debate of ideas orientation of the French press and the personalized narrative thrust of the U.S. press, one might also expect that substantive issue criticisms – such as truth, ideology, and policy criticisms – would be more common in the French press while character and administrative criticisms would appear more frequently in the U.S. press. In fact, as Table 7.1 demonstrates, every form of criticism but one (administrative) appeared more often in the French press than in the U.S. press.

Criticism of Government and the Party in Power

Because of greater state media intervention in France, liberal theory predicts that the French press will be less critical of the party in power and of government in general than will the U.S. press. Tables 7.2 and 7.3 demonstrate that this clearly is not the case. During the 2002–2006 period, when the right was in power in both the United States and France (except for a short period of "co-habitation" in France during the spring of 2002), the French press averaged 0.8 anti-right criticisms per 1,000 words versus 0.5 anti-right criticisms in the U.S. press (see Table 7.2). The U.S. press tended to present slightly more critical statements about government in general (meaning criticisms aimed at non–politically appointed civil service officials, sub-Cabinet level agencies, legislative committees, or initiatives involving both dominant left and right parties): 0.6 criticisms per 1,000 words versus less than 0.5 in the French coverage ($p < .01$). However, when criticisms of government and the dominant right are combined, French coverage was still more critical: 1.3 versus 1.1 in the U.S. press ($p < .05$; combined total not shown in table).

When only the core sample newspapers are compared (Table 7.3), the two countries are about the same for the 2000s, with 1.11 combined criticisms of government and the party in power in the French press and 1.16 criticisms in the U.S. press (difference not statistically significant). During the 1990s, when the left was in power in both countries, the leading French newspapers were much more critical than their U.S. counterparts of the party in power (1.5 vs. 0.2 criticisms per 1,000 words), whereas the leading U.S. newspapers were more critical of government in general (1.1 vs. 0.4 criticisms). However, when left and general government criticisms are combined, the leading French newspapers

TABLE 7.2. *Targets of Criticism: French and U.S. Newspapers, 2002–2006 (Critical Statements per 1,000 words)*

Country (N 1,000-word units)	Government	Dominant Left	Dominant Right	Minor Parties/ Civil Society	Business	Foreign	Total
France (853)	0.47	0.13	0.81	0.23	0.04	0.23	1.89
% of Total	25	7	43	12	2	12	
U.S. (716)	0.61	0.05	0.50	0.05	0.07	0.04	1.33
% of Total	46	4	38	4	5	3	

Due to rounding, frequencies or percentages may not add up exactly to totals.

TABLE 7.3. *Targets of Criticism: Core French and U.S. Newspapers,*
1990s vs. 2000s

Target	France Critical Statements per 1,000 Words	U.S. Critical Statements per 1,000 Words
	1991 (*n* = 296)	1994 (*n* = 95)
Government	0.40	1.14
Dominant Left (Party in Power)	1.45	0.23
Dominant Right	1.18	0.22
Government + Party in Power	1.85	1.37
All Other	0.38	0.17
Total	3.41	1.76
	2002–2006 (*n* = 480)	2002–2006 (*n* = 434)
Government	0.33	0.60
Dominant Left	0.18	0.08
Dominant Right (Party in Power)	0.78	0.56
Government + Party in Power	1.11	1.16
All Other	0.48	0.15
Total	1.77	1.37

N is for 1,000-word units. Due to rounding, frequencies or percentages may not add up exactly to totals. Core newspapers are *Los Angeles Times, New York Times, Washington Post, Libération, Le Monde,* and *Le Figaro.*

were overall more critical (1.9 criticisms vs. 1.4 in the U.S., $p < .05$). Thus, the assumption that the French press would be *less* critical of the government and the party in power (whether "right" or "left") is clearly refuted. During both the 1990s and 2000s, the French press is more critical of the party in power, and even when government and the party in power are combined, the French press is at least as critical as or even more critical than the U.S. press.

Liberal press theory also predicts that those newspapers that receive the most direct subsidies – specifically *L'Humanité* and *La Croix* – will be the least critical of the party in power and government in general. In fact, for the period 2002 to 2006, *L'Humanité* (with 2.2 critical statements per 1,000 words; not shown in tables) is substantially more critical of the government and the (right) party in power than all French or U.S. newspapers in the study. *La Croix* is not more critical, but neither is it substantially less critical than other newspapers (with the exception of *L'Humanité*).

Finally, liberal theory predicts that the most advertising-dependent French newspapers – *Le Figaro* and *Les Echos* – will be more critical than average of government and the party in power. During the 2002–2006 period, when the right was in power, *Le Figaro* was actually *less* critical than all other French newspapers, especially the much less advertising-dependent *L'Humanité* and

Libération. Similarly, *Les Echos* is no more critical of government and the right than other newspapers (figures not shown in tables). Conversely, during 1991, when the left was in power, *Le Figaro* was more critical than either *Le Monde* or *Libération*. Rather than a case of advertising ensuring independence, *Le Figaro*'s pattern of criticism indicates the workings of a partisan logic.

Criticism by "Partisan" Media Outlets

In France, between 2002 and 2006, leftist *L'Humanité* was much more critical of the right than all other French newspapers. *Libération*, for its part, was more critical of the right than *Le Figaro* and *La Croix*, but differences with other French newspapers were not statistically significant. Conversely, as noted, during the 1990s, when the left was in power, the conservative *Le Figaro* was the most critical French newspaper.

However, the political parallelism of the French press should not be overstated. From 2002–2006, when the right was in power, all of the French newspapers, including *Le Figaro*, offered more criticisms of the right than of the left. During the 1990s, when the left was in power, *Le Figaro* was substantially more critical of the left than of the right (1.9 vs. 1.2 criticisms per 1,000 words, respectively), whereas *Libération* (1.1 vs. 1.0) and *Le Monde* (1.3 vs. 1.3) were even-handed (data not shown in tables). Thus, there are partisan distinctions among French newspapers, but these do not extend to the point of completely one-sided coverage, regardless of which party is in power.

Among the U.S. newspapers, the *New York Post*, owned by the conservative News Corporation, was the most likely during the 2000s to present criticisms of the left (0.22 vs. 0.06 average at other newspapers). Otherwise, there were no substantial (statistically significant) differences in the partisan direction of criticism among U.S. newspapers. Similar to the French press, all U.S. newspapers (including the *New York Post*) tended to be more critical of the party in power than of the party out of power. This U.S. pattern also largely held for the 1990s sample, which only included the *Washington Post*, *Los Angeles Times*, and *New York Times* (separate data not shown in tables).

Finally, is there any evidence that more advertising-dependent newspapers are less partisan than less advertising-dependent newspapers? In the French case, in fact, one newspaper highly dependent on advertising, *Le Figaro*, was among the most partisan, whereas another strongly advertising-dependent newspaper, *Les Echos*, was indistinguishable from the remaining French newspapers. In the United States, the only national newspaper that does not rely substantially on advertising – the *Christian Science Monitor* – was *not* more partisan than its peers, sharing the general U.S. tendency to criticize the government and the party in power.

In sum, although at least some French newspapers could be distinguished from their counterparts according to the partisan "tilt" of their criticisms (especially *L'Humanité*, *Le Figaro*, and *Libération*), this was not the case in the United States, with the partial exception of the *New York Post*. However, this French partisan fragmentation was not so prominent that it overcame the general tendency of all newspapers in both countries to aim greater criticism toward the party in power, whichever that might be, rather than the party out of power.

Rather than simply portraying the French as "partisan" and the U.S. as "nonpartisan," it would be more accurate to say that the French press was more "engaged" with partisan politics than was the U.S. press and more likely to hold one or the other of the dominant parties accountable for their words and actions. In contrast, U.S. journalists were primarily critical of government as a bureaucratic institution, both reflecting and perhaps helping to reproduce anti-statist attitudes.

Criticism of Business

A political economy critique suggests that dependence on advertising should be inversely related to the amount of business criticism. Providing some support to this thesis, the most advertising-dependent French newspapers had lower than average levels of business criticisms – at *Le Figaro*, in fact, there were none at all – but the difference between these newspapers and other French newspapers was not statistically significant, with the exception of the communist *L'Humanité* (0.14 criticisms per 1,000 words), which, of course, criticized business for ideological as much as for funding reasons. Supporting the political economists, the least advertising-dependent U.S. newspaper – the *Christian Science Monitor* – was slightly above average in its criticisms of business (0.08 criticisms per 1,000 words) but differed little from the heavily advertising-funded *New York Times* (0.07 criticisms) and was less critical of business than the mass market, half advertising-funded New York *Daily News* (0.16 criticisms). Overall, the amount of business criticism in both the U.S. and French press is miniscule – just 0.07 criticisms per 1,000 words in the United States and 0.04 in France. The general pattern, regardless of amount of advertising, is a *lack* of criticism of business.

INVESTIGATIVE JOURNALISM

Investigative journalism concerning immigration is relatively rare in both countries, but as expected, is slightly more common in the United States than in France. This section focuses on the high-prestige core national newspapers in each country – *Le Monde*, *Libération*, and *Le Figaro* in France, and the *New York Times*, the *Washington Post*, and the *Los Angeles Times* in the United States. In the 2002–2006 sample, none of the other French newspapers conducted any investigative reporting related to immigration. Likewise, with the exception of one article in the *New York Post* in 2006, none of the other U.S. newspapers offered investigative reporting in their page-one coverage. Overall, the *New York Times* offered the most investigative reporting among the U.S. newspapers, but this finding is almost entirely due to its publication of eight in-depth articles about corruption and mismanagement inside the Immigration and Naturalization Service (INS) during 1994. In France, *Le Figaro* offered the most investigative reporting.

Quantitatively, the three U.S. papers offered more investigative reporting than their French counterparts. Combining the 1990s and 2000s samples, an average of 8 percent of immigration news packages in the "big three" U.S. newspapers could be classified as investigative; in France, in contrast, an average of 3 percent of news packages in the three leading newspapers is investigative. Without the *New York Times*' 1994 special series, the U.S. core average is just over 3 percent. Newspapers in the two countries differed in the quality as well as quantity of investigative reporting, and I now turn to a closer consideration of these qualitative differences.

French investigative coverage seems to have involved very little enterprise reporting. In 1991, *Le Figaro* published two investigative articles. The first, on August 5, revealed a 1986 administrative report documenting how funds allo-cated by the socialist government of that time to help *"harkis"* (Algerians who had fought during the Algerian war on the side of the French) had actually been paid to associations close to the Socialist Party (*"Le Figaro* reveals the conclu-sion of an administrative investigation; *Harki* subsidies went to socialist-linked associations").[5] Why was this 1986 report only revealed, and by *Le Figaro*, in 1991? This might seem curious until one realizes that the summer of 1991 marked extensive protests by *harki* youths against the socialist government. On the heels of these protests, this report was a further embarrassment for the socialists. Partisan motives also seem evident in *Le Figaro*'s second immigration-related investigative article of that year, on the very next day, which reported that North African immigrants sentenced to deportation and ostensibly held at Paris-Orly airport were instead being quietly released, allowed to go free in Paris and its environs ("Turned back by their countries; Deported North Africans let free").[6] Any information that the socialist government was failing to carry out deportations would be highly embarrassing to Prime Minister Edith Cresson, given that, only a month earlier, she had insisted on prime-time television on her commitment to carrying out all scheduled deportations ("if there are 10 that need to be deported, that doesn't mean 3 or 5 that need to be deported, that means 10," she had said at the time; see, e.g., *Le Monde*, July 9, 1991, p. 7).

---

[5] Michel Demelin, "'Le Figaro' révèle les conclusions d'une enquête administrative; Les subventions des harkis allaient à des associations proches du PS," *Le Figaro*, August 5, 1991, pp. 1, 6.
[6] Benoît Charpentier, "Refoulés par leurs pays; Des Maghrébins expulsés remis en liberté" and on the p. 6 "jump," the even more damning headlines, "Les curieux 'clients' d'Aéroport de Paris; Orly: l'affaire des faux expulsés" [The curious 'clients' of the Paris Airport; Orly: Affair of the Phony Deportees], *Le Figaro*, August 6, 1991, pp. 1, 6.

Between the 1990s and 2000s, French investigative reports on immigration became less frequent and less obviously partisan. One 2002 *Le Figaro* report is essentially a collection of complaints from provincial mayors, both right and left, about immigration policy – such as lack of adequate funding, inadequate clarification of regulations, and the need for new policies to crack down on immigrant smugglers ("Immigration – Mayors say 'enough is enough'").[7] Another article purports to "reveal" a secret administrative report critiquing the efficiency and effectiveness of the right-led government's policies to deport rejected political asylum candidates.[8] For their part, *Le Monde* and *Libération* do not attempt to dig up any dirt about the right government in power. Instead, their investigative fire is aimed at extremists. *Libération* reveals that National Front party leader Jean-Marie Le Pen has misreported his residency, thus forfeiting his candidature for a regional elected office ("Le Pen, a candidate on the streets").[9] And *Le Monde*'s only (arguably) investigative article relies heavily on an "inside" police report to paint a menacing portrait of Salafist Islamic fundamentalists attempting to spread their influence among French immigrant populations ("Investigation into the Salafists").[10]

In contrast, investigative reporting in the United States seems to involve more independent initiative, to be better funded and more extensive, and to be less clearly partisan. If anything, it is stubbornly antipartisan. In 1994, the *Los Angeles Times* published two major investigative reports. The first report revealed the gap between publicity and reality regarding legislation sponsored by incumbent Democratic Senator Barbara Boxer to deploy National Guard troops on the Mexican border to keep illegal immigrants out.[11] The newspaper discovered that the law had been blocked by the Defense Department and was never implemented. The lessons of this case for the *Times* had little to do with the Democrats per se, but with any and all over-reaching politicians, as the following passage shows:

At a time when California's politicians are rushing to offer solutions to the problems . . . of illegal immigration, this is an account of one major initiative that generated tremendous publicity, yet has accomplished little or nothing. The failure of the Boxer plan reveals the difficulties of finding answers to the vexing problem of unlawful immigration as well as the risks of proposing quick fixes.

Later that year, the *Los Angeles Times* had far more devastating news to report about a leading Republican politician. Only days after announcing his support

---

[7] Christine Clerc, "Immigration – le ras-le-bol des maires," *Le Figaro*, November 4, 2002.
[8] Marie-Christine Tabet, "Droit d'asile: les chiffres qui dérangent," *Le Figaro*, September 15, 2004, pp. 1, 8.
[9] "Paca: Le Pen refoulé," *Libération*, February 19, 2004, pp. 1, 2–3.
[10] "Enquête sur les salafistes," *Le Monde*, January 25, 2002, pp. 1, 10–11.
[11] Glenn F. Bunting, "Boxer's Bid to Put National Guard at Border is Stymied; Immigration: Pentagon Refuses to Implement Senator's Plan, Which It Says Lacks Legal Authority," *Los Angeles Times*, p. A-1.

for the restrictionist Proposition 187, the newspaper reported that U.S. Senate candidate Michael Huffington had employed an illegal immigrant nanny without paying any taxes on her income, a federal crime, as well as an obvious case of hypocrisy.[12]

While both of these *Los Angeles Times* articles concerned elected officials (with Huffington losing the close election, at least in part due to the newspaper's revelation), the *New York Times'* investigative focus in 1994 was on the vast unelected INS bureaucracy.[13] This multipart series, entitled "Chaos at the Gates," documented widespread corruption, sexism, racism, and gross incompetence across the immigration agency's national and regional bureaus. Problems were shown to have long predated the administration of President Bill Clinton, who had been elected only two years earlier. Nevertheless, it is worth noting that the series offered not a single criticism directed at either Clinton nor at the Republican administrations preceding him. All of the blame is directed at the civil service bureaucracy, which is portrayed as virtually beyond reform.

Between 2002 and 2006, both the *New York Times* and the *Los Angeles Times* published daring "under cover" articles about immigrant smuggling operations, with the *New York Times* going so far as to employ an Ecuadorian reporter pretending to be a migrant worker.[14] The *Washington Post* also published a powerful inside account of abuses inside the Mexican prison system.[15] For its part, the *New York Post* deployed a reporter to investigate the illegal market in forged immigration papers or Social Security cards: "The well-organized underground market that churns out these fraudulent documents is surprisingly easy to penetrate – The [New York] *Post* was able to find a man who deals in the bogus cards and buy one in just under three hours."[16] However, in contrast to the 1990s, there were no probing investigative reports about U.S. government bureaucracies or elected politicians. (To be fair, in recent years, some ambitious investigative reporting on immigration has reappeared, as, for instance, in the case of the previously noted 2008 series by *New York Times* reporter Nina Bernstein about immigrant detainee mistreatment.)

In sum, investigative journalism makes up only a small minority of total immigration coverage in both France and the United States but is slightly more common in the latter. Even at its best, however, this investigative journalism as

---

[12] Dave Lesher and Greg Krikorian, "Huffington Admits Fault in Hiring Illegal Immigrant," *Los Angeles Times*, October 28, 1994, p. 1.

[13] See, e.g., Joel Brinkley, "At Immigration, Disarray and Defeat: Chaos at the Gates – First of five articles," *New York Times*, September 11, 1994, p. 1. In addition to this series, the *New York Times* published additional "special reports" about the INS during 1994.

[14] Ginger Thompson and Sandra Ochoa, "[Series] Dangerous Passage...," June 13, 2004, op cit.

[15] Mary Jordan, "In Mexico, Justice at a Price; Inmate Couldn't Buy What He Needed – His Name," *Washington Post*, March 25, 2002, p. A01.

[16] Douglas Montero, "3 Hours on Qns. Street All It Takes to Get Forged Papers in Security Shocker – I Bought a 'Green Card' for $110 from I.D. Ring," *New York Post*, July 5, 2006, p. 4

generally practiced has its limitations. A powerful critique is offered by David Simon, former *Baltimore Sun* reporter and creator of the HBO series *The Wire* (Lanahan 2008, 26–28). Simon criticizes the standard formula for winning Pulitzer Prizes: "Surround a simple outrage, over-report it, claim credit for breaking it, make sure you find a villain, then claim you effected change as a result of your coverage. Do it [all] in a five-part series." In contrast to narrative-driven stories with "good guys and bad guys," Simon calls for in-depth reporting that emphasizes the systemic complexity of social problems. Unfortunately, Simon argues, journalists tend to focus on the symptoms rather than the causes:

You can carve off a symptom and talk about how bad drugs are, and you can blame the police department for fucking up the drug war, but that's kind of like coming up to a house hit by a hurricane and making a lot of voluminous notes about the fact that some of the roof tiles are off.

In the case of immigration, perhaps the hypocritical politicians and the corrupt bureaucrats are "roof tiles." They deserve to be exposed and criticized, but doing so will do nothing about the "hurricanes." One hurricane is neo-liberal globalization (with a leading but by no means sole role played by the U.S. government), which has created the economic and social conditions for circuits of low-wage labor (as described by Saskia Sassen in Chapter 3). As shown in Chapters 3 and 4, critical explanatory journalism that examines these kinds of underlying conditions, often through in-depth interviews with academic experts, has tended to be more common in France than in the United States.

Another hurricane is the "strange bedfellows" character of immigration policy alliances: who are the business and foundation backers of immigrant rights groups, and what is their stake in maintaining a supply of cheap and compliant foreign workers?[17] Here, what is needed, as Michael Teitelbaum has argued, is journalism that "follows the money."[18] Unfortunately, neither French nor American journalists have seriously taken up this quest.

Although not engaging in "gotcha"-style investigative journalism, the *Christian Science Monitor* offers the closest American approximation of structural investigation, consistently examining the complex realities of immigration, even when these go against political fashion or conventional wisdom. In the midst of the generally celebratory coverage of immigration in the *New York Times* and *Washington Post* during the spring of 2006, the *Monitor* balanced its coverage of pro-immigrant protests with other articles pointing to an array of inconvenient truths: ongoing conflicts between poor African-American and

---

[17] There have been a number of investigations of the funding of restrictionist groups such as the Federation for American Immigration Reform, including its disgraceful link to the eugenicist Pioneer Fund. However, I am not aware of similar investigative reports about the links between business groups, immigration attorneys, major philanthropies, neo-liberal think tanks, and the various pro-immigration advocacy associations.

[18] Remarks at French-American Foundation conference, Miami, May 2010 (author notes). See also Teitelbaum (2006).

illegal immigrant Latino workers, the game played by both the government and businesses not to seriously enforce "employer sanctions" against hiring of illegal immigrants, and an examination of the ongoing links between and tensions within the environmental and immigration restriction movements.[19] Perhaps most significantly, the *Monitor* made a rare, noncondescending link between the pro-immigrant protests in the United States and the pro-job security protests taking place in France at the same time. The two protests, wrote the *Monitor's* Mark Trumbull, highlighted different national approaches to job market flexibility. Although most of his quoted experts proclaim the superior dynamism of the American model, Trumbull at least provides space for more critical views, as in these passages:[20]

But for all the challenges Europe faces, the U.S. has its own troubles with labor and immigration policies. The typical American worker isn't necessarily marching in the streets, but millions feel anxiety about job security, global competition, and stagnating wages. The fruits of America's recent prosperity have gone disproportionately to the wealthiest in society – a trend that could eventually fray the social fabric. "It does seem as though the U.S. economy is more dynamic than the European economy," says James Parrott, an economist at the Fiscal Policy Institute, a liberal research organization in New York. "But dynamism that is also characterized by greater extent of layoffs, real wage declines, and dramatically greater income inequality is not necessarily a good thing."

EXPLAINING CRITICAL JOURNALISM

Proximity to the commercial pole of the field of power provides U.S. journalism with potentially greater material resources for investigative reporting. Conversely, with smaller newsrooms and budgets, French journalism's forays into investigative journalism are more limited. Smaller reporting staffs and lesser resources in France may also explain, in part, the greater tendency to structure news reports around arguments and counterarguments of competing political groups (similar to U.S. cable news). It is simply cheaper and easier to construct news as a debate of prepackaged ideas, however critical, than as a dramatic narrative painstakingly constructed by journalists. Strong French defamation laws and weak information access laws also no doubt have a chilling effect on aggressive investigative reporting.

And yet the findings do not provide a ringing endorsement of the liberal diagnosis. One cannot say that commercialism per se is what drives critical investigative journalism. In the United States, it is not the most profitable or pro-market newspapers that conduct the most investigative reporting on

[19] See Daniel B. Wood, "Rising Black-Latino Clash on Jobs," May 25, 2006, p. 1; Faye Bowers, "Employers Risk Little in Hiring Illegal Labor," April 18, 2006, p. 1; and Brad Knickerbocker, "For Environmentalists, a Growing Split over Immigration," May 12, 2006.

[20] Mark Trumbull, "For Workers in Europe, U.S., Distinct Aims," *Christian Science Monitor*, April 3, 2006, p. 1.

immigration. Rather it is newspapers like the *New York Times* and the *Washington Post*, those with ownership structures that provide them with some insulation from profit pressures. The fact that the chain-owned *Los Angeles Times* also continues to invest in substantial investigative and in-depth reporting demonstrates the enduring power of professional traditions to shape practice (in this case, the proud tradition of a Pulitzer Prize-winning newsroom first established under publisher Otis Chandler).

In France, *Le Figaro* is simultaneously the most commercial and the most conservative national newspaper, as well as the paper most likely to engage in investigative reporting. Its choice of investigative targets – generally, the left in power – suggests, however, that partisan political considerations, rather than commercially enabled "independence," are the driving factor. The high volume of critical statements in the communist *L'Humanité*, likewise, is driven by a partisan logic.

At the same time, proximity to the civic pole of the field bolsters, both symbolically and materially, the critical clash of ideas in French journalism. This form of critical journalism is not simply what is left over when there is no money or motivation for investigative journalism; it represents its own distinct form of critical political and intellectual engagement that often goes beyond easily identifiable heroes and villains to explain and expose hidden forms of institutional power. It is made possible by a long-standing critical political culture, institutionally anchored in the public universities, political parties, trade unions, and other civil society organizations (Clark 1987; Chaplin 2007). The *Christian Science Monitor*'s brand of intellectually critical journalism is similarly strengthened by its nonprofit ownership structure.

As with multiperspectival news, various types of criticism correlate with different types of news formats. The U.S. narrative format provides a strong fit with morally charged investigative reporting. Conversely, U.S. personalized narrative is not a good fit for the critical clash of ideas easily facilitated by the French debate ensemble format. Not only do U.S. news packages, as a whole, have fewer criticisms than French packages, but those articles most fully dominated by a story-telling logic – such as articles with anecdotal leads – also have the strongest dampening effect on amount of criticism. Focusing on U.S. core newspaper coverage during the 2000s, I found that, even when holding constant for word length, use of anecdotal leads lessened the amount of criticism per news package by 0.340 ($p < .000$) (data not shown in tables). As for structural investigation, what Herbert Gans has termed "explanatory journalism" (2003, 99), this form of critical practice seems to have a weaker affinity with personalized narrative and a stronger affinity with the debate ensemble format, especially given the latter's emphasis on incorporating academic expert analyses.

Although I have so far been emphasizing cross-national differences, it is important to acknowledge French-U.S. journalistic similarities as well. Investigative reporting may occur more often in the United States, but it is not common in either country. In both France and the United States, criticisms of business are especially rare. Newspapers in both countries tend to direct more criticism at the party in power than at the party out of power. Although the U.S. press is more likely to offer administrative criticisms and the French press is more likely to emphasize ideology criticisms, a rough majority of all criticisms presented in each country's press are policy criticisms.

Why such similarities? Although state policies and commercialism differ in France and the United States, these differences are more of degree rather than fundamental type: both countries are democracies (thus reining in state abuses of power) and are deeply integrated into the world capitalist economy. Mainstream journalism in both countries occupies a central position in the field of power. Although less dependent on business advertising, many French newspapers are owned by consortiums of business investors. Moreover, given the state's many business partnerships, the distinction between business and government in France is not always easy to make (Chalaby 2005). Due to the obvious downside of public exposure of employment of illegal immigrants, both French and U.S. businesses have tended to adopt an especially low profile on the immigration issue. In France, the low public acceptance of "market-oriented" values (Lamont and Thévenot 2000) provides a further incentive for French business to avoid the public limelight.

However, other cross-national similarities can be understood to derive from the ongoing aspiration for journalistic professional autonomy in both countries. The perceived need to maintain a certain credibility with audiences and sources alike (e.g., focusing on policy over character or tempering partisan impulses) may serve to unite the most prominent "mainstream" newspapers across all democratic societies. Even at newspapers admittedly of the "right" or "left" – labels that French journalists are far more likely to use than their American counterparts – there is a concern with "credibility" and "honesty." As Dominique Simonnot, a *Libération* reporter, told me, "Because *Libération* is a newspaper of the left, when the left is in power we can't let anything get by, meaning we have to have the same critical approach toward the left as toward the right. In spite of our sympathy for the left, I think we have to be honest in this way ..."[21]

---

[21] Author interview with Dominique Simonnot (1997). Similar arguments were voiced by many other journalists I interviewed, including Philippe Bernard at *Le Monde* (1998, 2004) and Jean-Jacques Rouche of *La Dépêche du Midi* (2008).

8

Does the Medium Matter?

Television News about Immigration

> Television News is the only global media product that is the same everywhere . . .
> it's a bit like the big chain hotels that are the same whether you're in Paris, Hong
> Kong, or New York.
>
> – Hervé Brusini, France 2 Evening News director[1]

> Compared to the other media we've done a good job covering immigration. And
> that's probably because of the nature of the program which allows us to do more
> in-depth stories and provide more of a context to the immigration issue. . . . My
> stories are eight, nine, ten minutes in length, sometimes more. . . . No one ever says,
> keep it to six minutes.
>
> – Jeffrey Kaye, PBS NewsHour immigration correspondent[2]

Are French and U.S. television news, in fact, the same? Are public and commercial television news really that different? And how is television news similar to or
different from newspaper coverage? Answering these questions will help sort out
the discursive effects of field position, logic, and structure, as well as fill out this
book's portraits of the French and American journalistic fields. In this chapter,
I focus on immigration news coverage from 2002 to 2006 in the leading
national, non–cable television channels in the two countries: the commercial
ABC, CBS, and NBC networks and the Public Broadcasting Service (PBS) network in the United States and the commercial TF1 channel and public France 2
and Arte channels in France.

As with the press, state intervention is greater for television news in France
than in the United States. French and U.S. television journalists are subject to the
same laws and regulations applicable to the press in their countries, with, in

---

[1] Hervé Brusini interview (1997). Brusini is the co-author (with Francis James) of a well-regarded
theoretical text on television news, *Voir la verité* (Paris: PUF, 1985) and has held a number of
high-level positions at France 2 over a long career.

[2] Jeffrey Kaye interview (1998).

some cases, additional obligations (for instance, the requirement of French television news to assure proportional airtime to the political parties during electoral campaigns).

As with newspapers in the two countries, market pressures on television news tend to be more mitigated in France than in the United States. In France, although TF1 is mostly advertising funded, France 2 currently receives about one-third of its funding from advertising (Palmeri and Rowland, Jr. 2011, 1101) and the French-German Arte channel receives virtually no advertising funding. In the United States, all three national networks rely on advertising funding, and the public channel PBS receives just over one-third of its funding from corporate business underwriting, a "soft" form of advertising.

Liberal theory suggests that, due to greater state intervention, French television news will tend to index its news coverage more closely to the government and dominant political parties and that French TV news will tend to be less critical of government and the party in power than would be the case with U.S. TV news. Conversely, political economy predicts that the most commercialized channels in each country (the U.S. Big-Three networks and TF1) will be the least multiperspectival, least civic-oriented, and most sensationalistic in their coverage of immigration.

As with newspapers, however, to fully understand French and U.S. television news we need to go beyond the classic liberal and political economy models and take into account field-level factors.

FIELD POSITION AND CLASS STRUCTURE OF AUDIENCES

State intervention can enable as well as restrict, and, as with newspapers, French state involvement in the television sector (especially since the 1980s) has been oriented toward promoting civically oriented news coverage. Thus, in comparison to the United States, the French journalistic field as a whole – including both commercial and public television news – is closer to the civic pole than market pole. The privatization of TF1 in 1987 also must be understood in light of its previous historical trajectory: the market model was built on top of a long-standing public service foundation.

Compared to national newspapers, television news is an omnibus medium. Its goal is to reach the largest possible mass audience. When there is a strong mixed private-public system, as in France, competition to reach this same mass audience may lessen differences in news coverage. It also seems noteworthy that, compared to their U.S. network counterparts, both TF1 and France 2 lean "downmarket": high-income audiences are underrepresented, whereas low-income audiences are overrepresented (see Table 2.3). Low-income audiences are also overrepresented in Arte's audience. By contrast, the public channels in both countries – France 2, Arte, and especially PBS – have audiences with above-average levels of education.

FORMS OF TV NEWS

Because of the medium's visual characteristics, one might expect U.S. and French television to be substantially the same. Medium theory (Postman 2005) would predict that both French and U.S. television news will focus on image over substance, emotion over sustained argument.

Yet, just as with newspapers, previous comparative research indicates that there is no "inherent" logic of the medium. Hallin and Mancini (1984) found substantial differences between Italian public television and U.S. commercial networks: whereas the former focused on presenting political party viewpoints, the latter emphasized dramatic narrative. Comparing British BBC and ITV-Anglia to U.S. network and PBS-affiliated channels, Raymond Williams (2003) likewise discovered numerous differences in form and content linked to national system, funding, and audience. Tamara Chaplin's (2007) fascinating history of philosophy programs on French television provides additional evidence against claims that the medium is inherently anti-intellectual.

During the early 1980s, French public television, inspired by *Libération*, attempted to adopt a similar multigenre, multisegment approach to the news. Claude Carré, who was evening news director for the French public television channel Antenne 2 (now France 2) in 1981, recalls how *Libération*'s multiple "dossiers" approach led him to revise the television channel's evening newscast so that each news topic was constructed "around a system of multiple entryways, with several items on the same subject, so that we were sure to cover it from every angle" (cited in Asline 1990, 149). Within a few years, this commitment to a new format had evidently faded. In my 1983 sample of immigration news, I find little evidence of such a multigenre approach.

In fact, news package formats are roughly similar for TF1, France 2, Arte, and the U.S. commercial networks, although overall program lengths vary. Arte Info broadcasts for just 15 minutes (Utard 2008). The evening news programs of TF1 and France 2 average around 35 minutes, compared to 30 minutes for the U.S. commercial networks. These numbers are somewhat misleading, however, unless advertising is taken into account. The 30-minute U.S. news programs include on average about 19:30 minutes of news programming, or only 18 minutes when the short announcements of "upcoming stories" before each of three commercial breaks are subtracted from the total. In contrast, none of the French evening news programs, including TF1, is interrupted by advertisements.

Each night, the two main French channels show about seventeen to eighteen news items, not counting short "news briefs." In contrast, the U.S. network evening news programs generally include about seven to eight news items.

U.S. individual news items average about 2 minutes 20 seconds compared to 1 minutes 50 seconds for French items.[3] In my sample of immigration news packages, which on some evenings included multiple related items, U.S. TV news coverage tended to be about 30 seconds longer than French coverage (2 minutes 55 seconds vs. 2 minutes 27 seconds, respectively). Arte immigration news packages, however, were about the same duration as the American commercial average.

Working within this same basic 2- to 3-minute format, most French and U.S. television news items use a narrative approach. When I asked France 2 (and former TF1) journalist Guilaine Chenu how she defined good journalism, she first mentioned "story-telling ... You have to tell a story."[4] Inside the binational Arte newsroom, shortly after its founding in 1992, German journalists favored the "exhaustive exposé of facts in relation to any particular event," whereas French journalists (whose approach ultimately won out) sought to cover events "with a closed angle" in order to "reduce complexity to a single dimension considered to be the most important and interesting." Non–government-centered, narrative stories fit well with Arte's mission to produce news potentially interesting to both French and German audiences (Utard 2008, 270–271).

Although less exclusively focused on an individual personality, as is typical of the U.S. approach, a narrative logic is evident in this France 2 report on *emigration clandestine* from Senegal (May 24, 2006):

[Journalist voice-over, images of people on beach getting into boats]: A final "au revoir," a final smile. With their life jackets strapped on, these clandestine emigrants are ready to take to the sea. Most of them have never been in a boat, many don't even know how to swim. These images were taken on Sunday at a Senegalese beach somewhere between Dakar and St. Louis. There were nearly a hundred emigrants, from all parts of the country, each with only a thin bundle for baggage. ... If everything goes well, if the weather is good, if they don't get lost, after five days voyage, they should reach their goal: the Canary Islands, the Spanish archipelago, the door to Europe, 1,400 kilometers from here. [Switch to image of back of man walking] This guy is the smuggler. He prefers to be called developer [*promoteur*] – that sounds better ... [shift to interview with smuggler]

PBS is the outlier in a number of ways. Like the French news programs, it is not interrupted by commercials. However, its nightly hour of programming is nearly twice as long as either TF1 or France 2 evening news. PBS's video reports on immigration (not including in-studio interviews or debates) are almost three times as long as those on any other news program. PBS video reports averaged over 8 minutes; when segments with in-studio interviews and discussions are included, PBS

---

[3] These statistics are based on a randomly selected constructed week of 2009 evening news broadcasts. Examining two weeks' worth of TF1 and France 2 evening news in May 1994, Siracusa (2001, 201–203) similarly found an average of eighteen segments with the majority (59 percent) lasting between 1 minute 15 seconds and 2 minutes 20 seconds.

[4] Guislaine Chenu interview (1997). The importance of narrative approaches for French television news is noted by French media scholars, notably Soulages (1999), Terral (2004), and Lochard (2005).

immigration news packages averaged over 11 minutes. TV news on the other U.S. and French channels consists almost entirely of either a breaking news item or a short background feature item. PBS, alone among the television channels examined in this study, regularly uses the mixed-genre debate ensemble format. More than 60 percent of its immigration segments include some combination of breaking news or in-depth background news reports, "reactions" from leading legislators to new policy proposals, in-studio debates, and journalistic commentary (usually a closing debate between *New York Times* columnist David Brooks and syndicated columnist Mark Shields).

With this context about television funding, audiences, and formats in mind, let us now examine television news content. In addition to using indicators of pluralism and criticism previously deployed to analyze newspapers, I also analyze television news images for types of activities depicted, dramatic and emotional images, and tempo (see Appendix B for data sources and methods).

MULTIPERSPECTIVAL NEWS

U.S. core television news (ABC, CBS, NBC) is more political elite-centered than its French counterpart (TF1 and France 2), citing or interviewing to a far greater extent executive branch officials, government bureaucrats, judges, and legislative officials: altogether, 44 percent of all speakers interviewed or cited versus 26 percent in France. (See Appendix Table A.5., TV core, combined first three speaker categories.) Within the category of "Executive/Bureaucratic," immigration enforcement officials and other police or military agents are more prominent in U.S. television news, making up 9 percent of speakers on the network evening news and 6 percent on PBS versus a range of 1 percent (Arte) to 4 percent (TF1) on French television news (figures not shown in table).

French and U.S. television news, however, do not always imitate their national cohort newspapers. Although political parties are much more likely to be cited in French newspapers than in U.S. newspapers, they are scarcely heard from on television news in both countries. Whereas U.S. newspapers were more likely to highlight individual voices than were their French counterparts, the inverse is true for television news. Unaffiliated individuals and references to polls make up 37 percent of speakers cited in French core television newscasts versus 27 percent in U.S. core newscasts. There is no clear-cut nonmarket versus market divide: Whereas unaffiliated individuals and poll references make up just 13 percent of speakers on PBS, France 2 (39 percent) and Arte (36 percent) are highest in this category. For all TV news programs, immigrants are the overwhelming majority of unaffiliated individuals interviewed (not shown in tables). Immigrants are thus often accorded the right to speak, pictured at talking distance, and treated as "subjects" rather than "objects" (Tuchman 1978, 114), which does not preclude these "simple citizens" (or noncitizens) from being deployed for a variety of strategic purposes by television journalists (Siracusa 2001, 76–81). (See Figure 8.1.)

FIGURE 8.1. Images of immigrants. Unaffiliated individuals, mostly immigrants, are often interviewed on television news in both countries. In France, problems identified by immigrants are more likely to be linked to collective action. In the United States, journalists tend to get in the picture, too. TF1 image provided by INA; CBS image reproduced with permission. (A) TF1 20 heures (8 o'clock news), April 29, 2006 (B) CBS Evening News, April 11, 2006.

Despite the predominance of so many "private" persons on French TV news, coverage is less purely personal and private than it is in the United States. In her analysis of U.S. Pulitzer Prize-winning journalism, Karin Wahl-Jorgensen (2012, 7) finds narrative personalization generally begins with a lead anecdotal paragraph and that it is relatively rare to find "stories which have other types of leads but feature stories of individuals." In fact, what may be rare in the United States is common on French television news: news items will often start with a government policy or debate and then move to illustrations of effects on various individuals. These differences are related to a greater French tendency to peg news coverage to events, generated either by the political or civil society fields; American journalism, in contrast, is more likely to present news simply on its own authority, in reference to a broad social phenomenon. These cross-national differences hold for television as well as for newspapers.[5] Thus, for example, there is no breaking news justification for this ABC profile of Mexican migrants (July 8, 2006): "Tonight, we go to a small village in Mexico to view immigration from the other side of the border. It's estimated that there are more than 6 million undocumented Mexican workers in the United States – [this] mass migration is a source of anger and debate in this country." In contrast, an Arte profile of North African migrants is pegged to a twenty-seven-nation European-African summit on migration (July 10, 2006): "North African refugees are surging in increasing numbers toward the Canary Islands in the hope of joining, often at the risk of their lives, the promised land: Europe. In Rabat, Europe and Africa are assembling for the first time in order to reflect together about this migratory flow." A lengthy profile of a Moroccan "candidate for illegal emigration" [*emigration clandestine*] is only presented after the report on the conference.

Moreover, in contrast to U.S.-style populism, French television populism is joined to an almost equally strong tendency to highlight civil society voices. Civil society groups make up 30 percent of all speakers cited or interviewed on French core television news versus just 20 percent on U.S. core television. The French proportion rises an additional three points when peripheral political parties (as noted in Chapter 6, the functional equivalents of many U.S. social movement groups) are added to the mix. In both France and the United States, the channels most reliant on state funding are the most civil society–oriented: Arte (41 percent) and PBS (28 percent). (See Appendix Table A.5.)

Civil society speakers are more prominent in France partly because civil society–generated events are covered more heavily by French TV; but even in political field–generated coverage, civil society speakers are more frequently cited in France than in the United States. As with newspapers, immigrant rights groups far outnumber restrictionist voices on television news in both countries.

---

[5] Across the four decades, journalistic field–generated news makes up 22 percent of French TV news versus 32 percent of U.S. TV news, compared to 18 percent of French newspapers and 33 percent for U.S. newspapers. See Online Table 2.3.

Immigrant rights activists make up 18 percent of speakers at TF1, 14 percent at France 2, and 31 percent at Arte; this compares to a range of 7 to 9 percent on the three U.S. commercial networks and PBS. Restrictionist voices range from 0 to 2 percent of all speakers on French TV news and from 2 to 4 percent on U.S. TV news.[6]

At the same time, just as with newspapers, U.S. television news personalizes and depoliticizes collective action. The specific organizational affiliations of civil society activists are less likely to be mentioned – and emphasized – on U.S. television than on French television. For example, in an NBC report (May 28, 2002), David Ray, a spokesperson for the Federation for American Immigration Reform, is simply identified as an "immigration reform advocate." In similar fashion, a CBS report on the massive immigrant protests during the spring of 2006 (March 24) does not mention a single civil society organization: Angelica Salas, director of the Coalition for Humane Immigrant Rights in Los Angeles, is identified only as an "immigrant rights activist."[7] As with newspapers, U.S. television news coverage of activism often seems to be following the script of the movie "Erin Brokovich," in which Julia Roberts plays a crusading, lone do-gooder. Activism is misleadingly portrayed as typically an individual rather than a collective pursuit.

Conversely, even French television news reports ostensibly focused on individual experiences usually make a connection to one or more projects of collective action. This individual-civil society linkage is strongest at Arte, but also distinguishes French core channels from their U.S. counterparts.[8] The following excerpt from a 3 ½ minute portrait of two families of *sans papiers* on TF1 is a good example of this tendency. Starting with a cinema verité glimpse of immigrant daily life, it quickly makes connections to organized political activism[9]:

[6] See Online Tables 8.4 and 8.5.

[7] For other examples of such individualizing of civil society spokespersons, see NBC Nightly News, James Hattori report on illegal immigration (April 30, 2004) and Gustavo Mariel report on President Bush's proposed guest worker program (February 15, 2004); and ABC News "Closer Look" on President Bush's proposed immigration reforms (January 7, 2004).

[8] In Arte Info coverage during the 2000s, citations/interviews with immigrants and associations are highly likely to appear in the same news package ($.305, p < .05$). For French mainstream TV news, the news package correlation between all unaffiliated individuals and associations is weaker but also statistically significant for the 1990s and 2000s combined ($.135, p < .05$). There is no statistically significant relation between citations of unaffiliated individuals and civil society associations within U.S. TV news packages, including PBS.

[9] TF1, "Portraits de familles sans papiers," April 27, 2006. Likewise, on France 2, a feature on Malian illegal immigrants profiles Ibrahim, a former boatman ferrying illegal immigrants, who now works for a humanitarian association – the Association for the Development of Peoples – and tries to dissuade other would-be *clandestins* from making the dangerous cross-sea voyage (France 2, "Forum Bamako passeur," January 21, 2006); an Arte Info profile of "Khalid," an illegal immigrant who started his own restaurant and is now threatened with deportation, emphasizes his effort to enlist the help of the immigrant legal rights association Cimade (Arte, "Projet de loi sur l'immigration," May 1, 2006).

[Reporter voice-over] After school, Rabiah and her two little girls go to the park. In another Parisian neighborhood, another mother, Maya, prepares dinner for her family. At Rabiah's home, it's now snack time. And at Maya's, the father leaves work and comes home. Just like every night. What could be more ordinary?

We come across people like this every day. And yet, they lack something essential: French papers … [Maya's family] is eligible to be deported at the end of the month.

What follows next is an account of Maya's son's campaign to obtain signatures from his teachers and local businesses to support his application for a resident visa.

[Voiceover]: The teachers and students did not hesitate a second to mobilize themselves.

[Jacqueline Campagne, teacher at Lycée Jules Ferry]: Because this student has been in France for more than 5 years and has a junior high certificate, because he is doing well in his courses, I don't see why we should send him back to his country and prevent him from taking his bac [high school baccalaureate examination].

[Voiceover] And there's not much time. Likewise, [Rabiah's] Algerian family fights alongside an association as the moment of deportation arrives.

FIGURE 8.2. Representing civil society. On French TV news, activists are linked to their sponsoring groups, no matter how small. On U.S. TV news, activists are presented as lone rangers. TF1 and France 2 images provided by INA; CBS and NBC images reproduced with permission. (A) Mouloud Aounit, President of MRAP (Movement Against Racism and for Friendship Between Peoples), France 2 20 heures, March 8, 2006.

FIGURE 8.2. (B) Saddok Guitoune, Leader of the National Undocumented Immigrant Collective, France 2 20 heures, May 3, 2006.

FIGURE 8.2. (C) Wei Zihang, Third Collective of Undocumented Immigrants of Paris, TF1 20 heures, April 29, 2006.

FIGURE 8.2. (D) NBC World News Tonight, May 28, 2002.

FIGURE 8.2. (E) CBS Evening News, March 24, 2006.

[Saddok Guitoune, Collective Against Disposable Immigration]: We're trying to knock on all the doors. Eighty percent of undocumented immigrants [*sans papiers*] work. They participate in the construction of our country and its development.

Televised immigration news in both France and the United States encompasses a broad range of immigration frames, yet, as with newspapers, the humanitarian and public order frames are most prevalent. At the same time, the relative emphasis on these two frames differs sharply on French and U.S. television news. On French core television, humanitarian frames, often promoted by

FIGURE 8.3. Visually powerful frames. In France, the humanitarian frame dominates; in the U.S., the public order frame appears most often. France 2 image provided by INA; NBC image reproduced with permission. (A) Senegalese emigrants beginning the dangerous crossing to the "promised land" of Europe, France 2 20 heures, May 24, 2006. (B) Border Patrol agents in training, NBC World News Tonight, June 22, 2006.

immigrant rights associations, are mentioned in nearly two-thirds of news items (65 percent) whereas the public order frame is mentioned in less than one-third of coverage (29 percent). Arte places even more emphasis on the humanitarian frame, which appears in 84 percent of its news packages. On U.S. core TV news programs, it is the public order frame that dominates but in not so lopsided a manner: 55 percent of news packages mention the public order frame (often promoted by border patrol and other immigration enforcement sources) whereas 48 percent mention the humanitarian frame. In this case, the U.S. commercial networks diverge somewhat: NBC heavily highlights public order over the humanitarian frame (62 vs. 35 percent, respectively), ABC gives slightly more prominence to the humanitarian frame (58 vs. 52 percent for public order), and CBS mentions the two frames equally (both appearing in 52 percent of news packages). (See Appendix Table A.6.)

Why the much greater focus on public order in the United States than in France? The visual and dramatic appeal of the public order frame would seem to be equally operative for television news in both countries. In both countries, the public order frame is strongly associated with political field–generated news; the difference is that, in the French case, during the 2000s, the political field generated a smaller proportion of news and, as noted, enforcement officials were less likely to be quoted in news items. When the political parties have competed with one another to show how "tough" they could be on immigration, as in the early 1990s, French television news followed suit and likewise emphasized the public order frame. In addition, France's multiparty system and the perceived threat to democracy posed by the far right National Front party may play a role in suppressing coverage of public order and other threat frames. French television journalists, like their newspaper colleagues, are wary of portraying immigrants as a threat lest they inadvertently "play the National Front's game."[10] Of course, French television journalists will not ignore mainstream political leaders who emphasize the threat frame, but they will not go out of their way to cover the issue. In the United States, despite the complaints of immigrant rights activists, news coverage emphasizing threat frames does not carry the same ideological stigma or perceived danger for democracy.

Television news packages, with the exception of those at PBS, are much less multiperspectival than newspapers, failing to provide on average even two distinct frames or three types of speakers. Unlike their newspaper counterparts, French television news programs do *not* provide more multiperspectival coverage than U.S. television news. In both countries, the core channels average about 1.7 frames per news segment. U.S. news networks offer broader speaker diversity at the level of the news package (3.1 types of speakers vs. 2.6 on French news), but there is little difference at the level of total coverage

---

[10] Interviews with Jean-Luc Mano (1998) and Elise Vincent (2012). See also Lemieux and Schmalzbauer (2000).

TABLE 8.1. *Frame/Speaker Diversity and Critical Statements: French and U.S. Television News, 2002–2006*

Media Outlet (N News Packages)	Average Length of News Packages in Minutes / Words	Average Frames per News Package (Frame Concentration Index)	Average Institutional Speakers per News Package (Institutional Concentration Index)	Average Criticisms per News Package	Standardized Criticisms (per 1,000 words)
France					
TF1 (85)	2:20 / 443	1.65 (2,163)	2.49 (1,748)	0.86	1.94
France 2 (83)	2:33 / 507	1.65 (2,268)	2.69 (1,826)	1.19	2.35
Core Average	2:27 / 475	1.65 (2,216)	2.59 (1,787)	1.03	2.15
Arte (58)	2:56 / 542	1.81 (2,827)	2.59 (2,085)	1.41	2.60
U.S.					
ABC (50)[a]	2:58 / 544	1.84 (2,058)	2.92 (1,687)	1.00	1.84
CBS (54)	2:46 / 522	1.67 (2,199)	3.28 (1,624)	1.09	2.09
NBC (71)	3:00 / 546	1.63 (2,214)	3.07 (1,855)	1.07	1.96
Core Average	2:55 / 537	1.71 (2,157)	3.09 (1,722)	1.05	1.96
PBS (56)	11:25 / 1,965	2.50 (1,462)	3.41 (1,421)	2.93	1.49

[a] Because of missing data, Ns for U.S. time length are somewhat smaller: ABC (46), CBS (45), NBC (68), and PBS (43).

(institutional concentration indexes [ICI]).[11] The public France 2 is slightly more critical than the commercial TF1, but otherwise the differences are minor, continuing a tendency also observed for the 1991 news coverage (see Chapter 4).[12] Only comparing the public channels, PBS's NewsHour (2.5 frames and 3.4 speakers) is more multiperspectival than France 2 (1.7 frames and 2.7 speakers) and Arte (1.8 frames and 2.6 speakers). (See Table 8.1.)

Whereas French newspapers tend to give speakers more room to express their views than do American papers, the French-American difference in television news is not so clear-cut. Speakers (any nonjournalists interviewed who directly express their views) average 37 words on the two main French channels

[11] Arte demonstrates well the differences in what is measured by news package-level indicators and total coverage concentration indexes. Per news package, Arte offers as many or more distinct frames and speakers as the other French news programs. As Appendix Tables A.5 and A.6 show, however, Arte's coverage is strongly focused on the humanitarian frame and unaffiliated individual and civil society speakers (especially immigrant rights activists [see Online Tables 8.3 and 8.4]). In other words, Arte tends to present multiple frames and speakers but often these are the same frames and speakers (rather than drawing from the full range of ten frames and sixteen speaker types). As a result, Arte has higher than average frame and institutional concentration index scores.

[12] In the 1991 television news sample (n = 88), frames per news package were 1.91 for TF1 and 1.95 for France 2; types of speakers cited per news package were 2.13 for TF1 and 2.12 for France 2.

(no substantial difference between TF1 and France 2) versus 29 words for the three major U.S. networks. Arte is slightly higher, with 49 words per speaker, and PBS is substantially higher with 188 words per speaker (including its frequent use of in-studio panels of politicians, activists, and experts). Even when speaker discourses of 300 words or more are excluded from the sample, PBS is highest with 89 words per speaker. (See Online Table 8.6.)

Within each country, there are some differences between public and commercial television news. However, the differences between PBS and the rest of U.S. television are much greater than those between Arte or France 2 versus TF1. Unlike all the other evening news programs, PBS frequently includes in-studio interviews with experts, civil society association leaders, and government officials, as well as extended analyses or commentaries by journalists, thus extending the scope as well as the time devoted to a topic. In the spring of 2006, NewsHour interviews included lengthy and lively exchanges between Xiomara Corpeno, director of the Los Angeles Coalition for Humane Immigrant Rights, and Ira Mehlman of the Federation for American Immigration Reform (March 27); Rafael Fernández de Castro, a political scientist at the Autonomous Technical Institute in Mexico, and Jose Carreno, Washington correspondent for the Mexican newspaper *El Universal* (March 30); and Reverend Luis Cortis, president of Esperanza USA, a national network of Hispanic churches, Yanira Merino, national immigration coordinator for Laborers International Union of North America, and Victor Cerda, a former U.S. immigration enforcement official (April 10).

PBS studio interviews – moderated in a calm, neutral style, especially compared to most U.S. cable news talk shows (Jacobs and Townsley 2011) – facilitated in-depth discussion of a range of frames. For instance, the March 31, 2006 program pitted progressive economist Dean Baker of the Center for Economic and Policy Research against libertarian Cato Institute researcher Daniel Griswold in a debate about the jobs and good worker frames. PBS moderator Ray Suarez started the discussion by directly calling into question the conventional wisdom:

SUAREZ: Dean Baker, it's a commonplace in President Bush's speeches that illegal immigrants take jobs Americans will not do. Is it true?

BAKER: Well, you have to add one more clause to that: At the wages that are being offered. If you look at the situation of less-skilled workers, workers with just a high school education, particularly those who are high school dropouts, their wages have gone nowhere over the last quarter century, and part of that story is because they have to compete with immigrants coming in who are willing to accept those jobs at much, much lower wages. ... So, yes, native-born workers aren't willing to take those jobs anymore, but we have to get wages up, that's the key.

SUAREZ: Daniel Griswold, is the president right that illegal immigrants are taking jobs that Americans will not do?

GRISWOLD: The president is right. And companies just can't raise wages willy-nilly. They're restrained ultimately by what customers are willing to pay on the other end. If wages go up, customers will turn away from the higher prices and those industries will shrink.

The debate continued for some time, with no ultimate meeting of the minds, but it did offer an all-too-rare elaborated presentation and justification of non-mainstream restrictionist[13] and open borders positions. As noted, PBS news reporting segments are also three to four times longer than news segments on all other evening news programs, French or American. For example, in 2006, immigration correspondent Jeffrey Kaye and other PBS journalists offered special reports on the "fortified frontier" with Mexico (February 15), the visit of Mexican president Vicente Fox to Oregon (May 26), and immigrant rights protests in Los Angeles, Chicago, and Washington, D.C. (May 1). In sum, PBS NewsHour is different from other U.S. and French television news programs in its depth of reporting and its use of a multigenre format: both of these come together to foster multiperspectival news coverage.[14]

TELEVISION IMAGES

Building on Krauss's (2000) research on television news in Japan, as well as Tuchman's (1978) and Gans's (1979) classic U.S. studies, I now analyze various properties of images on French and U.S. television news. To constitute the sample, I selected one-third of all television news packages (only field reports, not in-studio news briefs or interviews). Research assistants watching videos of the reports (on-site in Paris at the Institut national d'audiovisuel, on DVDs provided by the Vanderbilt Television News Archive, or available on the PBS online archives) used software packages that allowed them to freeze all distinct images (unique camera angles) in order to code them along multiple dimensions.

TV news reports were coded first for the types of individuals or activities depicted (see Figure 8.4). On the core French and U.S. TV newscasts, approximately one-third of the images are of immigrants or other individuals in their ordinary day-to-day existence. Another one-fourth to one-fifth are of "official" life, that is, law enforcement or other government bureaucracies. Images of collective action (demonstrations, strikes, etc.) constitute 11 percent of French core TV images and 9 percent of U.S. core TV images. In all of these depictions, the

---

[13] For instance, Baker distinguished his position from public order–focused restrictionists ("Let me just say at the outset, sending them [undocumented immigrants] home is barbaric . . . You can't send these people home. They work; they contribute to the economy. So you can't send people that have been working here home") and advocated increased immigration of highly skilled workers but tougher restrictions on low-skilled immigration ("Let's start with the competition at the top, rather than making those who are most disadvantaged already in society have to compete.")

[14] Multigenre television news in the U.S. correlates positively with total critical statements (.522, $p < .001$), frame diversity (.179, $p < .01$), and speaker diversity (.177, $p < .01$). In contrast, "news only" segments correlate negatively with total criticisms (-.412, $p < .001$) and frame diversity (-.189, $p < .001$), with no statistically significant relationship with speaker diversity. In contrast to the press, however, multigenre news is highly correlated with word length (.801, $p < .001$), and PBS news coverage is much lengthier and more likely to include multiple genres than all other television news outlets, so it is difficult to sort out clearly what amount of PBS's greater level of frame and speaker diversity is due to the multigenre format and what is due to other aspects of PBS journalism.

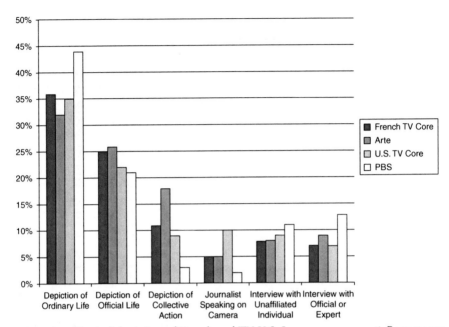

FIGURE 8.4. Topical depiction of French and TV U.S. Images, 2002–2006. Percentages are of total images (French TV Core *n*=4,369; Arte *n*=1,757; U.S. TV Core *n*=3,666; PBS *n*=1,722).

image is foregrounded as we hear the journalistic voice "off-camera." U.S. core television journalists are twice as likely to put themselves at the center of the screen speaking on camera as are French core television journalists (10 percent vs. 5 percent of images, respectively). On-camera interviews with unaffiliated individuals make up 8 percent of images on French core TV news and 9 percent on U.S. core TV news; officials or experts make up 7 percent in both countries. (The remaining small misc. categories are not shown.)

Arte is distinctive in that it accords far more images to collective action (18 percent) than do the other channels. At PBS, a substantially higher proportion of its images are of interviews (24 percent total unaffiliated individuals and officials/experts) than at the other channels. PBS also is least likely to focus its camera on its own journalists (less than 2 percent) and to depict collective action (under 3 percent), but presents more images of ordinary life (44 percent) than any other channel. These findings generally support the textual analysis, highlighting similarities among the major omnibus TV news programs and some differences provided by the smaller public channels (Arte, PBS).

Image analysis can also be useful for measuring dramatic or sensationalistic aspects of news programs that inhere in the images rather than scripts. Using the typology developed by Krauss (2000, 35–36), I classified all images according to five categories of action: nonmoving visuals (depictions of buildings

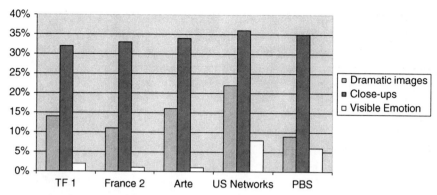

FIGURE 8.5. Dramatic, close-up, and emotional images on French and U.S. TV news. Percentages are of total images (TF1 n = 2,360; France 2 n = 2,009; Arte n = 1,757; U.S. networks n = 3,666; PBS n = 1,722).

or landscapes), moving visuals-staged action (such as press conferences or speeches), moving visuals-limited action (scenes of ordinary life), moving visuals with nonviolent drama (such as protest marches, strikes, parliamentary shouting matches, etc.), and violent drama (crime depictions, etc.).

Images of violent drama are rare on all of the channels, French or American, constituting less than 2 percent of all images (statistics not shown). Overall, U.S. core television news tends to have more dramatic images (nonviolent and violent dramatic images combined) than French core television news: 22 percent versus 12 percent, respectively (see Figure 8.5). PBS was lowest again with just 9 percent dramatic images. At the other end of the spectrum, non-dramatic staged images of press conferences and other official events were more prevalent on Arte (49 percent of all images) and PBS (55 percent) than on French core channels (37 percent) or U.S. core channels (36 percent).

U.S. television news is the most likely to use close-up and extreme close-up shots (Tuchman 1978, 116–124) of people and to show visible emotion (generally more positive than negative) on the faces of individuals. Thirty-six percent of U.S. core television images are close-ups or extreme close-ups versus less than 33 percent for French core TV. Visible emotions are shown in almost 8 percent of U.S. core television images whereas they are shown in just 1 percent of French core TV news images. In this case, national conventions seem to be more important than commercial versus noncommercial distinctions: PBS is close to the Big-Three U.S. networks in its use of close-ups and visible emotion, whereas Arte is quite similar to TF1 and France 2.

Newscasts also differ in their temporal rhythm or "flow" (Williams 2003). Lacking the need to constantly bring viewers back after each commercial break, one might expect French TV news to have a more leisurely flow. In fact, there is very little difference in the tempo of French and U.S. TV news. The

French tempo was even slightly quicker: 15 images per minute versus 13 images per minute on U.S. network TV news (data not shown). Even lacking advertisements, TF1 and France 2 compete for audiences: maintaining similar tempos may help minimize the level of channel switching. PBS news segments move at the slowest pace, at less than 10 images per minute.

CRITICAL NEWS

As Table 8.1 shows, critical statements about government and other major institutions appear with about the same frequency in U.S. and French core television news (1.05 criticisms per U.S. news package, 1.03 per French news package), a tendency that remains largely the same even when one controls for word length. Although this seems a low amount of criticism, television news' "critical density" (criticisms per 1,000 words) is actually higher than most newspapers: all TV news programs have higher critical density than U.S. newspapers on average, and most TV news programs are higher than the French newspaper average (compare Table 8.1 to Figure 7.1).

Similar to the patterns identified for the press in each country, administrative criticisms tend to be higher in the United States, whereas ideology criticism is higher in France. Likewise, similar to newspapers, U.S. television news tends to aim criticism at the government in general, whereas French television news is slightly more likely to aim criticism at the leading parties, minor parties such as the National Front, and foreign/international organizations (primarily the European Union, which plays an increasingly important role in shaping immigration policy for all member nations).

Both France 2 and Arte present more critical statements about the government and conservative majority party leaders than does TF1, and, overall, present both a higher raw number and higher density of criticisms. PBS offers the highest number of critical statements of U.S. television news programs, which is partly due to the much longer duration of its reports. However, even when controlling for transcript word length, PBS offers as much criticism of the political party in power as do the other channels.[15]

During the 1990s and 2000s, television investigative reports were not common in either country: 4 percent of U.S. news packages versus 2 percent for France. In the United States, the reports tended to focus on the failures or excesses of government enforcement efforts, with disgruntled immigration control officers and immigration attorneys, respectively, serving as the main sources. CBS reported that the immigration service was failing in its mission to deport illegal immigrants (May 28, 2002) and warned about the "gaping holes" in the "security net's capacity to effectively detect fake identification cards" (February 26, 2002). Border patrol agents told NBC journalists that a budget

---

[15] For complete data on types and targets of criticisms on television news, see Online Tables 8.10 and 8.11.

crisis was forcing "them to release most illegal immigrants back on to American streets within hours of catching them, even some who are criminals or from countries known to produce terrorists" (July 13, 2004). Focusing on excesses, ABC took a "closer look" at "some very vulnerable children" who were being kept in detention centers with criminals, sometimes for months, "because they came into the country illegally" (July 18, 2002).

Both CBS and TF1 presented reports on businesses employing undocumented workers. The CBS report offered up the irony of illegal immigrants being employed by federal government construction contractors, many of them operating "near highly sensitive military bases" (April 12, 2006). In a rare presentation of the labor union perspective, the CBS reporter noted that the undocumented workers receive "pay that is less than half what a union member makes," with no health and retirement benefits, and concluded that the 1986 law prohibiting employment of illegal immigrants has "enough loopholes ... to drive a couple of those concrete construction trucks right through them." TF1's report on a "Chinese workshop" employing illegal aliens (January 26, 2006) is likewise pegged to inadequate enforcement of illegal employment, which in France is of special concern because it often involves nonpayment or underpayment of government taxes (which is less the case in the United States, where illegal immigrant workers submit false Social Security cards and pay taxes). In contrast to a typical U.S. report, however, there is no follow-up on what became of the specific workshop featured in the report and no indication of whether or not it was ultimately subject to government enforcement.

In 1991, in a different kind of "investigation," France 2 (then Antenne 2) presented several reports that tested – and ultimately found lacking – the specific and general claims of then mayor and conservative party leader Jacques Chirac that there was a widespread problem of polygamous immigrant families, with 20 children or more, receiving exorbitant welfare payments (June 20 and 21, 1991).

In sum, critical investigative reports of government performance – either as lax or abusive – appeared only occasionally on U.S. television news coverage of immigration. French immigration investigative reports were even more rare and, when they did occur, they were linked either to helping illustrate (in highly dramatic fashion) a general societal trend (such as illegal work) or to adjudicate the facts in a political polemic.

CONCLUSION

Hervé Brusini's claim at the beginning of this chapter is not far from the truth: French and U.S. mainstream television news are not dramatically different. Certainly, distinctions in form and content among the core television channels appear to be less than those for newspapers. As shown, similarities across television outlets, in both France and the United States, are also facilitated by similar narrative approaches.

TF1 and France 2 both share the ambition to assemble a large heterogeneous public (Terral 2004, 113), and the same applies to the U.S. commercial networks. Omnibus media, by definition, cannot afford to stake out strong or controversial ideological positions, lest they alienate large segments of viewers.

Although France 2 may not be commercially owned or profit-driven, both the government that sets its license fee and the businesses that pay for advertisements expect it to seriously compete for audience share with TF1. As Jean-Luc Mano, a well-regarded television news director who has worked for both TF1 and France 2, told me:[16]

There are differences between TF1 and France 2, but they aren't major. The two channels have a common history. TF1 may be the major private channel, but at its origin it was part of the public system. And France 2 is a "false" public channel. It earns almost half of its revenues from advertising [a percentage that has since declined]. ... It's true that France 2 still has protected spaces for culture and debates. But in their approach to news, [France 2 and TF1] are not fundamentally different. Their journalists have the same professional training, they have the same culture.

Thus, despite their labels of "public" and "private," France 2 and TF1 occupy, in many ways, quite close structural positions in the French journalistic field. Historical formation and trajectory matter. Contra Bourdieu, the commercial TF1, carved out from this public system thirty years after its founding, retains much of its origins. By contrast, U.S. television was from the beginning a commercial venture, and news programming was gradually expanded in the 1960s. Given that PBS was a late add-on to an already commercialized system, it might also be expected to be commercial in style or orientation. But its origins lie outside the commercial system, in a decentralized network of university and other educational television stations. It continues to be small and decentralized in many ways, with every incentive to distinguish itself from rather than imitate the major commercial networks. Founded in opposition to the "American [commercial] broadcasting model," Arte is both more populist and more politically engaged than the U.S. PBS. At the moment of its creation, it was committed to values like "permeable boundaries" and "tolerance" (Berning 2010, 2–4). This founding ideological commitment helps account for Arte's strong emphasis on the humanitarian and good worker frames and weak emphasis on national cohesion.

---

[16] Jean-Luc Mano interview (1997). Antoine Lefèvre of TF1 (interview 1998) told me much the same thing: "It's not where the funding comes from, it's how big of a budget you have and how much resources you put into covering a story. And France 2 and TF1 have very comparable budgets ... If you look at evening news on channels 1, 2, and 3, you'll see they often take the same extract – we all have the same reflexes and the same ways of working ... Information is treated in an almost identical manner at all the TV and radio channels. With the written press, it's a little different." Competition between TF1 and France 2, Lefèvre continued, is mostly over who can get a live interview [*plateau*] with "the political newsmaker with a [big] announcement to make."

Less commercialized television channels tend to offer more critical state-ments: PBS (in raw terms) and Arte and France 2 (both raw criticisms and critical density). These findings parallel the results of my conclusions that state-subsidized newspapers are just as or more critical of government and the dominant parties than the most commercial newspapers. Conversely, although there was a limited amount of investigative reporting conducted by any of the television news programs, U.S. commercial networks do more than other news programs.

Proximity to market pressures *does* seem to correlate closely with more dramatic, emotional images and less in-depth treatment of issues (as indicated by the shorter length of expert and other speaker interviews) in the more commercialized U.S. television news. Conversely, the relatively less commer-cially dominated French television news – including TF1 as well as France 2 and Arte – is more likely to give voice to diverse civil society groups, again, consistent with the tendency in French national newspapers. But, unlike its country's newspapers, television news in France is also quite populist, highlighting the voices of unaffiliated individuals even more than does U.S. television news. Arte Info most fully brings together these seemingly contradictory elements: 41 percent of those cited or interviewed on Arte represent civil society groups, while an additional 36 percent are unaffiliated individuals. This high emphasis on nongovernmental actors, both individual and collective, may in fact be Arte's way of navigating its French-German government sponsorship. Arte – and its audience – are committed to the pan-European project, as well as to multi-cultural internationalism more broadly (Schroeder 2005, 147).

By several measures, PBS offers the most multiperspectival, critical, and in-depth news coverage of immigration. This is a finding worth stressing. In the United States, critics of PBS abound, not only from the right but also from disappointed progressive policy scholars.[17] Although PBS falls short of the ideal "public sphere," as do all the media outlets examined in this study, it comes far closer than any of the commercial television news outlets and it rivals the best newspapers, especially in its explanatory journalism. At PBS, full expression of diverse, critical viewpoints is facilitated not only by its distance from market pressures, but also by the closest television equivalent to the French newspaper debate ensemble format, mixing in-depth news, commen-tary, and analysis. Conversely, the narrative format works against multiper-spectival news at the other TV news programs: one can see how attempts to incorporate multiple perspectives or "abstract political ideas" (Hallin and Mancini 1984, 845) would constitute inelegant, tangential disruptions to the unfolding of the story.

Finally, as with newspapers, high cultural capital of audience and lesser commercial pressures seem to coincide to produce similar discursive effects.

---

[17] See, e.g., Hoynes (1994), Aufderheide (2000), and Ouellette (2002).

Compared to all other channels, PBS and Arte are the least reliant on advertising and have the audiences highest in cultural capital (see Table 2.3). They also tend to offer the most multiperspectival, critical, and in-depth treatment of immigration.[18] In sum, does the medium matter? Yes, in that television news, even at its best, is generally less multiperspectival and critical than newspaper coverage; and yes, more positively, in that thoughtful interactive debate is made possible – although rarely realized, except on PBS – by the medium's technological affordances. On the other hand, the medium does not matter to the extent that the discursive effects of social class and commercialism transcend the technological vehicle. PBS's quality is at least in part a by-product of the demands of its culturally sophisticated audience. The medium matters, but nontechnological field factors matter as much or more.

[18] This study's findings contrast somewhat with James T. Hamilton's research that shows that, at least for American commercial television, it is not the audience that a media outlet has but rather the audience it desires that shapes content. Hamilton (2004) found that U.S. television news is mostly watched by men aged fifty and older, but that news producers target content toward eighteen- to thirty-four-year old women, whom they perceive to be more highly desired by advertisers. As a result of this drive, he shows, U.S. commercial television news has increased its proportion of human interest and light, entertaining news. It would be worth exploring further when and how actual versus desired audiences shape news content.

9

The Forces of Fields and the Forms of News

News is a complex co-production of the political, social scientific, and journalistic fields, and the substance of the mediated immigration debate changes along with economic or demographic shifts, new political alliances, and other contingent factors. This does not mean, however, as some would have it, that news simply mirrors social realities or that news production processes are chaotic or random. Patterns in the frames, speakers, images, and other features of news coverage accord with structural regularities of the fields that produce the coverage.

FIELD POSITION, LOGIC, AND STRUCTURE

In Chapter 2, I presented a threefold model of field-level influences: position, logic, and structure. Throughout this book, I have tried to show how field structures and dynamics have helped shape immigration news coverage in France and the United States. Here, I draw together these explanations. The journalistic field's position refers to its relation to other logics within the broader field of power, chiefly, nonmarket civic versus market power. The field's logic is the internal refraction of the field's societal position and the historical path by which it arrived there. Finally, the field's structure refers to the class hierarchies that shape relations between journalists and their sources, as well as between journalistic organizations and their audiences. I offer this field model not in opposition to the standard sociology of news but rather as a more comprehensive or "ample" framework for research. Todd Gitlin (1980, 251) once made the same claim on behalf of Gramscian hegemony. Certainly, field theory shares the same critical engagement: it is crucially concerned with how media often serve to reinforce dominant systems of power. Yet, compared to hegemony, the field framework offers the advantage of paying closer attention to distinctions in forms of power, how these may vary both within a society and cross-nationally, and how they might be mobilized for democratic purposes.

Journalistic fields in both countries are suspended between civic-cultural and market logics, with the particular balance of power established by the decisions (and nondecisions) of the state. This broad cross-national structural homology helps account for the broad discursive similarities in U.S. and French news coverage, such as the dominance in both countries of the public order and humanitarian frames, or of political elites as sources. In both countries, market incentives put a premium on conflict and drama, helping explain lesser attention being paid to positive hero frames or more complex, conceptual frames.

And yet, France and the United States are clearly not the same: the French and U.S. journalistic fields are not entirely homologous. The French government does more to promote civic-cultural over commercial ends. Because of a legal prohibition on being traded on the stock market, French newspapers are not subjected to the same degree of profit pressures that have beset American newspapers. Because they receive a certain proportion of their operating funds from government subsidies, all French newspapers are less reliant on advertising and the pressures that advertisers can exert to make news more consumer-friendly. In France, a strong public sector provides legitimacy to solidarity-oriented frames like national cohesion; in the United States, the dominance of the market assures the resonance of the good worker frame (at least when the economy is strong). State insulation from market forces in France also helps account for a lack of substantial convergence toward the "American" model, in either specific news content or form. Because some small noncommercial newspapers oriented wholly toward serious political and social issues are supported with public funds, the range of debate in the French public sphere is widened.

Although, as noted, investigative reporting of government abuses is slightly higher in the United States than in France, to be fair, it is not common in either country. Moreover, for a complex social phenomenon like immigration, arguably the most important task for journalism is to fully explain its causes and consequences in relation to national – and global – policies. To achieve this type of coverage, the findings in this study suggest that the state is not an impediment but rather a substantial contributor. Publicly subsidized media, in both France and the United States, consistently offer among the most ideologically diverse, critical, reasoned, and in-depth treatment of immigration in this study. Outside of PBS, the other relatively high-performing U.S. news media, such as the *Christian Science Monitor* and the *New York Times*, benefit from nonstate sources of largesse (a church, a founding family that treats the newspaper as a "trust") that serve as a buffer to market pressures.

The particular dynamics of journalistic practice are neither totally dependent nor independent of field position: they refract at the mezzo-level through the prism of tradition a given field's unique mix of market and nonmarket incentives and constraints. Although any given field features multiple logics of practice, I have tried to show that the dominant field logic is evident in the most commonly shared "form" of news that provides a template for the reporting, writing, and presentation of news. Distinctive news formats translate field position into journalistic practice and also provide a potential means to extend and elaborate journalistic professional autonomy. U.S. "narrative" journalism, as a form of serious (or light) entertainment, emerges in the context of advertiser pressures to attract the largest possible (high-consuming) audiences. French multigenre "debate" journalism, substantially funded by the state, serves the interests of political elites in a pluralist democracy seeking a relatively open forum through which to articulate their positions and mobilize their supporters.

French journalism provides a platform for civil society activists and scholars to speak in their own words, thus enriching and widening the public debate. Use of the debate ensemble format extends to mass market newspapers – such as the high-circulation *Le Parisien* – thus assuring that multiperspectival news is widely available in France. Conversely, American journalism's narrative storytelling lends itself to investigative reporting of problems with clear good guys and bad guys and provides the public with otherwise inaccessible glimpses of the immigrant experience. But the U.S. narrative approach also tends to individualize politics, diverting attention from the collective organizational work that sustains civil society, and it seems to be less well-equipped than French journalism to provide multiperspectival and in-depth critical news. Analysis of field position and logic helps explain why the French journalistic field can have both high internal pluralism (at individual newspapers) and high external pluralism (across the range of leading newspapers), against the expectations described by Hallin and Mancini (2004) that these two dimensions of pluralism should be generally opposed.

The role of the form of news in shaping these divergent U.S. and French outcomes is also evident when we compare newspapers and television. At first glance, echoing Hallin and Mancini's (1984) comparison of U.S. and Italian television almost three decades ago, a contemporary portrait emerges of U.S. media being simultaneously more elitist and populist, with the French media focused more on the political organizational sphere in between: civil society and political parties. However, this difference was most marked for newspapers in the two countries. French television news, both commercial and noncommercial, complicates this diagnosis. It was even more likely than U.S. TV news to emphasize "the man or woman on the street" in its coverage and was generally no more ideologically diverse. Why? Unlike in Hallin and Mancini's earlier study of Italian and U.S. television, there is less of a difference in the basic form of news in French and U.S. television. Narrative formats in both countries provide a better fit for individual profiles than the idea-driven debate ensemble format of French national newspapers (although it must be emphasized that on French TV news, narratives of individuals are almost always linked to narratives of collective action). The one exception to this seemingly "universal" television style is the American PBS NewsHour, whose news format most resembles the French newspaper multigenre style and which also tended to offer more multiperspectival and in-depth reasoned coverage than other television channels, French or American.

Finally, the internal structure of the field highlights the organizational dynamics of competition and class dynamics of journalist-audience and journalist-source relations as these vary across media outlets. Competition between reporting beats (Marchetti 2005) or between media outlets can shape coverage, sometimes accentuating differences. Other research, however, has shown how competition can also increase imitation, due to convergence in audience demographics among some outlets (Prior 2007) or the emergence of new mediating technologies (Boczkowski 2010). In the United States, the pushing aside of the labor beat by race- and ethnicity-oriented immigration reporters has probably helped reinforce the marginalization of the jobs and global economy frames. Competition between media outlets in France during the early 1980s may have played a role in *Libération*'s greater emphasis on cultural diversity. Over time, at least among the high-prestige national newspapers examined in this study, competition seems to homogenize more than differentiate in both countries (see Table 6.4).

Class demographics of audience surely influence the level of populism. In this study, unaffiliated individuals tend to make up the greatest proportion of speakers for those media outlets – both newspapers and television – with mass market demographics (percentage of high-income, high-education, and low-income audiences closest to the population as a whole). If PBS is distinct because of its funding and format, it is also different because its audience has a substantially higher level of education that that of other television channels. In general, media outlets with high cultural capital audiences tend to be the most multiperspectival, critical, and reasoned in a given national journalistic field: *Libération* for French newspapers, the *Christian Science Monitor* for American newspapers; PBS for American television, and to a certain extent, Arte for French television.

Likewise, class habitus dynamics surely play a role in accounting for the low level of attention accorded restrictionist groups, despite the fact that their views are often shared by a plurality or even majority of the general populace in both countries. Admittedly, part of the reason for the lesser attention seems to be resources: the immigrant rights groups are far better funded (either by the state or by major philanthropic organizations) than their restrictionist counterparts in both countries and benefit from the tacit support of businesses seeking cheap labor. However, restrictionist groups are also disadvantaged by the gap in income, education, and social status between their leaders and (especially) lower-middle-class members compared to elite national journalists. Immigrants, of course, are also often socially disadvantaged, but, as objects of sympathy, benefit from an upper-middle-class spirit of noblesse oblige. Habitus affinities may magnify the visibility and perceived legitimacy of pro-immigration groups and causes, whereas habitus disaffinities lessen the visibility and legitimacy of restrictionist groups and causes.

In short, my field analysis has confirmed substantial "internal" variations within national journalistic fields (Reese 2001, 178; Lemieux and Schmalzbauer 2000, 166). At the same time, the nation-state clearly remains an important demarcator of difference: across media sectors, consistent cross-national differences in form and content persist over time. Although field theory lends itself well to studies of audience-segmented media, my analysis of omnibus, mass market media hopefully offers at least a partial response to the important critiques of Hesmondhalgh (2006) and others regarding the framework's wider applicability.

My findings also complicate both the standard liberal and political economy predictions about the French and U.S. media. Countering liberal state-phobia, greater state intervention in the French case does not lessen the French media's critical, civic functioning; in fact, often the inverse is true. But also countering political economy's criticisms, the evidence of commercialism's negative effects on news coverage is mixed. In an ever more commercialized U.S. journalistic field, there has been an ideological narrowing as news has focused more on the dramatic and emotional public order and humanitarian frames. However, in both the United States and France, the institutional range of speakers has actually increased over time, and, although French newspapers still make room for more voices, U.S. newspapers have substantially closed the gap. It is important to note, however, that these findings are based on the performance of three leading prestige newspapers in each country: the *New York Times*, *Washington Post*, and *Los Angeles Times* in the United States, and *Le Monde*, *Libération*, and *Le Figaro* in France. Although commercial pressures have increased over time on these newspapers – especially in the United States – these are also organizations that self-consciously balance civic and commercial imperatives. Whether or not market "competition," as former *New York Times* editor Bill Keller once wrote, helps ensure quality journalism,[1] this study shows that commercial media (even the nonprestige titles) do indeed sometimes broaden or deepen the public debate. Based on the evidence presented in this book, I would simply suggest that tipping the balance in favor of nonmarket over market logics is likely to produce the most positive democratic outcomes.

Over time, it is far from self-evident from this study that Hallin and Mancini's "liberal" model is prevailing. Although the rise of narrative can be linked to an increasing market logic in the United States, this format has not won over a substantial number of converts in France. Conversely, U.S. news media – especially online, as I document later in this chapter – are adopting many elements of the French debate ensemble format. Such ongoing processes of cultural hybridization notwithstanding, preexisting tendencies in both countries persist. Within the two journalistic fields, I find little evidence of television's

---

[1] See Bill Keller, "Talk to the Newsroom," January 28, 2009 (http://www.nytimes.com/2009/01/30/business/media/02askthetimes.html?pagewanted=all): "Competition is, mostly, good for journalism. True, the scramble for readers' attention may contribute to tabloid sensationalism and press-pack feeding frenzies. But it also serves as a goad to aggressive reporting – and a check on the accuracy of our facts and analysis."

influence on newspapers. If indeed a privatized TF1 has transformed the French journalistic field, as Bourdieu has insisted, the transformation has not been toward a homogenization of the field but toward a greater distinction between newspaper and television journalistic practices.

Finally, this study has hopefully helped to refine our understanding of the dynamics and discursive effects of autonomy and heteronomy in fields of cultural production. As I have argued throughout, simply distinguishing between autonomy and heteronomy tells us little about what makes news discourse more or less multiperspectival, critical, and so on. Heteronomy per se is not a bad thing. Journalism dependent on civic-oriented foundations, beneficent publishing families, or government may be superior to other types of journalism in many respects, especially in addressing complexity or issues that lack obvious market appeal. Conversely, journalism dependent on the market may do a better job of illustrating the "human" impact of policies and trends and uncovering certain kinds of political malfeasance. Both kinds of journalism can make contributions; both have their blind spots. They are autonomous in some ways only because they are heteronomous in others. Heteronomy also varies in the extent to which it is self-limiting, whether through the publisher who delegates editorial power and permits dissenting views on the opinion pages or through the state that sets up legal and regulatory checks (Hallin and Mancini's "rational-legal authority") against temptations to politically instrumentalize public media.

But what of Bourdieu's ideal of autonomous cultural practice, somehow independent of all forms of heteronomy? Although some small, alternative media may come close to this ideal (even though dependent on a niche demographic paying audience or a generous philanthropist for survival), my concern here is not with this kind of autonomy of the margins.[2] In the French context, Bourdieu refers to a newspaper like *Le Monde* as the classic embodiment of professional autonomy, in which case its homologues in the United States would be the *New York Times* or the *Washington Post*. The autonomy of such high "symbolic capital" media outlets is in fact a delicate balancing act among civic, political, and market demands. Their virtue is that they are able to put substantial resources (more so in the U.S. case) behind their hybrid quest for professional excellence and market profitability. But they are not therefore superior in all politically relevant ways to other types of news media (Williams and Delli Carpini 2011), as this study has hopefully shown. In short, a singular autonomy-heteronomy dichotomy falls short of capturing the complexity of forms of journalism and their contributions to democracy. A pluralist journalistic field is best enabled by multiple forms of autonomy and heteronomy, rather than a single doxic professional model. If the French dominant "professional" form of

---

[2] This kind of autonomy is important but requires a different kind of research design to explore its social effects: for instance, a study of the circulation of ideas from the journalistic, political, artistic, and academic margins to various niche and omnibus publics.

news has less of a democratic deficit than the American model, it may be because of its relative lack of hegemonic ambition. Pluralism of speakers, ideologies, and styles is incorporated into the debate ensemble format. It is simultaneously a professional model and an antiprofessional model.

GOING BEYOND THE CASE STUDY: OTHER ISSUES, COUNTRIES, AND MEDIUMS

These findings are based on a single case study – a comparison of immigration news coverage in about twenty media outlets in two countries over a period stretching, in some instances, back to the 1970s. Because I focus on select peak media attention years across these four decades, it is possible that my findings may not apply as well to periods when immigration was only a minor issue. Across these peak media periods, it is clear that coverage varied in relation to changes in political contestation over the issue. At the same time, the fact that certain frames were consistently high across the dispersed years suggests that my findings are not idiosyncratic. Roberto Suro's (2008) massive Brookings Institution study examining *New York Times*, Associated Press, and CBS news coverage from 1980 to 2007 also found a consistently strong emphasis on "criminality" (public order frame) and a lack of attention to positive aspects of immigration (hero frames). Likewise, Suro's study found that coverage highlighted individual immigrants while paying short shrift, critical or otherwise, to business employers.

But what about other issues, countries, time periods, and mediums? The rising U.S. focus on the humanitarian frame and unaffiliated individuals accords with several studies that have shown an increasing human interest orientation in the news (Bogart 1989, 202–203; Rosenstiel, Forster, and Chinni 1998; Weldon 2008). Looking at U.S. national and regional newspaper coverage of social movement activism during presidential campaigns, Sarah Sobieraj (2011) finds similar tendencies to ignore, marginalize, or discredit activist groups. Sobieraj's examples mostly are of left-leaning groups; I find that the most disparaging media coverage is of the restrictionist "right" (although, for the immigration issue, the so-called right promotes economic left frames, so in this sense our findings are consistent). Similar to my study, Sobieraj (2011, 70) finds that the press tends to disempower activism by ignoring its organizational infrastructure, downplaying its substantive demands, dismissing structural arguments as inauthentic, and emphasizing instead personalities, personal histories, and the threat of disorder. What is important in my findings, however, is that it need not be this way. In France, journalistic accounts consistently link individual problems to civil society activism: this connection is not denied or denigrated but rather celebrated and promoted. The French case shows that media logics do indeed differ cross-nationally in democratically significant ways.

With other genres of news or on other specific policy issues, such as the environment, business, sexual harassment and discrimination, or national security, at least some findings might be different. Darras's (2005) comparison of French and U.S. political talk shows finds strong political field domination of the selection of interviewees in both countries, mitigating cross-national differences more evident in other segments of the two journalistic fields. Brossard, Shanahan, and McComas (2004, 371) find that the *New York Times* presents "more types of viewpoints on the issue of global warming than *Le Monde*." This difference with my findings may be a result of the particular national dynamics of the issue or the time period studied, as well as their focus on a single media outlet in each country. Our differences may also be related to comprehensiveness of measurement. In Brossard et al. (2004, 367), "themes" are measured but not analyzed in relation to ideological diversity; moreover, viewpoint diversity is only operationalized as a five-point scale of speaker types, not enough to make room for (potentially) discursively productive distinctions among branches of government, civil society segments, or other institutional fields.

In fact, many previous French-U.S. comparisons of different kinds of news coverage echo my findings. Several studies have been conducted on political campaign news. Gerstlé et al. (1991) find that, in 1988 campaign coverage, the U.S. national networks emphasized campaign strategies and poll rankings, whereas France's TF1 (shortly after being privatized) focused on distinguishing the positions of the various candidates and exploring topical issues raised in the campaigns. In a comparative study of election news coverage by national commercial and public television channels in Germany, the United Kingdom, and France, and national commercial channels in the United States, Frank Esser (2008, 412–425) finds that France 2's coverage is the most likely to focus on policy substance and that the U.S. commercial networks compress candidates' soundbites more severely than do the European channels (echoing my finding of shorter quotes in both U.S. newspapers and television). In his comprehensive study of French news coverage of the 2004 U.S. presidential election, Paul Adams (2007) discovers "restraint and balance" by the leading national newspapers, which concurs with my finding that even supposedly "partisan" newspapers like the conservative *Le Figaro* exhibit a high degree of internal pluralism. In Adams' assessment (p. 123): "The paper offered virtually every perspective from strong critique of the Bush administration to a defense of Bush policies, and a similarly broad spectrum of treatments of Kerry. *Le Figaro*'s 'Debates and Opinions' page was a remarkable source for powerful views of all kinds." Drawing on a random sample comparison of political news during the 1960s and 1990s in *Le Monde*, *Le Figaro*, and the *New York Times*, Dan Hallin and I show that the French newspapers offer more background context and more critical news coverage and provide a greater representation of diverse civil society viewpoints (Benson and Hallin 2007). Davidson's (2008) comparison of news coverage of media mergers in the French and U.S. press (including newsmagazines and regional newspapers) echoes this book's findings of a general lack of journalistic critical interrogation of business in both countries.

In this book, I do not pretend to have exhaustively accounted for the full diversity or complexity of French and American journalism.[3] It is certainly possible that one might arrive at different findings in a comparative study of small political or literary magazines, or blogs, or, for that matter, academic journals and books. However, many of the historical and social structural factors shaping mainstream journalism will also be at work in these other cultural fields.[4] At minimum, I hope that I have at least provided a fairly detailed portrait of one rather important sector of the French and U.S. journalistic fields, in the process helping to clear the fog of long-accumulated stereotypes.

More generally, the positive findings in this study about publicly funded media (newspapers and television) are supported by a growing body of international research. These studies show that public media tend to offer more in-depth, reasoned, ideologically diverse, and critical news coverage than their commercial counterparts. For example, Strömbäck and Dimitrova's (2006) comparison of Swedish and U.S. election news coverage showed that whereas the U.S. coverage tended to focus on the "horse race" and political strategies, the coverage of publicly funded Swedish newspapers tended to be more "issue-oriented, providing more interpretive reporting." Esser's (2008) multicountry study found "more extensive [election] coverage on public than commercial channels" and that the "toughest candidate interviews aired on the British channels," including the public BBC. A number of studies have demonstrated the consistently superior quality and independence of the BBC (Blumler and Gurevitch 2001, 390–397; Tunstall 2010).

Are European public media able to perform their critical democratic roles because of – or in spite of – government support? One study that looked at Swedish news reporting of local politics over time found that coverage actually became more critical beginning in the 1970s, around the time that government subsidies were enacted (Ekström, Johansson, and Larsson 2006). Of course, other factors have played a role, such as an increasing drive worldwide by journalists to "professionalize" during this period. Yet when Norwegian researchers directly compared subsidized and nonsubsidized newspapers in Norway, they found that "journalists working in subsidized newspapers

---

[3] Other U.S.-France comparative content analyses include Saguy (2003), Benson and Saguy (2005), Berkowitz and Eko (2007), Janssen, Kuipers, and Verboord (2008), and Hotchkiss (2010); other historical and institutional accounts are highlighted in Chapter 2.

[4] It may also be that different genres of journalism are produced to a certain extent by different types of media outlets in France and the United States. For example, the analytical and thematic approach of some national French newspapers is amply represented in U.S. political and literary magazines, and the political investigations of some U.S. national newspapers are pursued in France by its unique satirical weekly *Le Canard enchaîné* and, in recent years, by online news sites like Mediapart.fr. The crucial question, for democratic normative theory, then becomes the extent to which news and views circulate across media outlets and across field boundaries.

produce far more original news stories than journalists in non-subsidized newspapers" (Skogerbo 1997, 111), paralleling my findings of high-quality journalism even among the most highly subsidized French newspapers. In a classic 1980s international comparison of national television news programs, British media scholar Jay Blumler and colleagues (1986, 351) show that "broadcasting systems which are most dependent on advertising also schedule the narrowest range of programming." Recent research comparing publicly and privately owned television news in Denmark, Finland, the United Kingdom, and the United States by senior scholars James Curran, Shanto Iyengar, Anker Brink Lund, and Inka Salovaara-Moring (2009, 22), confirms and extends these findings, showing that "public service television gives greater attention to public affairs and international news, and thereby fosters greater [public] knowledge in these areas, than the market model." In this sophisticated study, which combines content analysis with survey research, Curran and colleagues demonstrate that public service television "encourages higher levels of news consumption and contributes to a smaller within-nation gap between the advantaged and disadvantaged." In a recent report on public media in fourteen leading democracies, Matthew Powers and I (Benson and Powers 2011) document numerous other examples of noncommercial media outperforming their commercial counterparts. Victor Pickard's (2011) critical synthesis of the literature arrives at many of the same conclusions.

In just the past five to ten years, the Internet has become an increasingly central platform for news media. Does that make this book only of historical interest? In fact, despite its focus on "old" print and broadcast media, this study can be useful for analyzing the new media landscape in a number of ways.

First, the field theoretical toolkit is eminently applicable to studying a range of types of cultural production. In various forms, it is being taken up by and productively used by numerous Internet and new media researchers.[5] As activists and policymakers increasingly seek to understand and potentially reshape complex media "ecosystems,"[6] this study provides a template for analyzing in detail a cross-section of an entire journalistic field, taking into account not only medium differences but also ownership, funding, and audience demographics. Second, my indicators of internal and external pluralism, criticism, image elements, and news generation and genres can be easily adapted for online media. Frame analysis has tended in the past to focus on documenting the specific content of media coverage on a case-by-case basis. This study is among the first to present ways of measuring generalizable properties of issue

---

[5] For recent online media research that draws on field theory, see Russell (2007), Davis (2007), Powers (2009), Compton and Benedetti (2010), Phillips (2010), Vos, Craft, and Ashley (2011), and Benson, Blach-Ørsten, Powers, Willig, and Vera Zambrano (2012). Robinson, Goddard, Parry, Murray, and Taylor (2010) usefully draw on field theory for their comprehensive study of British news media coverage of the 2003 Iraq invasion.

[6] See Napoli, Stonbely, Friedland, Glaisyer, and Breitbart (2012).

frames, such as frame diversity and frame concentration. Likewise, my challenge to Habermas's center-periphery model and my emphasis on the multiplicity of speakers linked to various institutional fields is not medium-specific. Third, one should not assume that technological and economic changes in the United States equally apply to other countries. As noted earlier, the financial decline of newspapers has been sharper in the United States than in much of Western Europe (Santhanam and Rosenstiel 2011).

Finally, despite their troubles, so-called legacy media outlets still have quite a lot of life in them: online, the well-established news media organizations often host the most viewed news websites (Hindman 2008). Mitchelstein and Boczkowski's (2009) comprehensive survey of online news research shows more continuity than change between the offline and online versions of leading news organizations. Hoffman (2006, 67) discovers a "startling" degree of "similarity" in news content between U.S. print and online newspapers. Barnhurst's (2002, 486; 2010, 563) content analyses of three U.S. newspapers in 2001 and 2005 show mostly similarities between print and online versions. Similarly, Finnemann and Thomasen (2005, 97–101) discover broad similarities in the page layout, specific news stories, and news formats of Danish print and online versions of the leading national newspapers. Quandt's five-country comparative study (2008, 735) finds little use of unique Internet capabilities by elite online newspapers, leading him to conclude that "online journalism ... is basically good old news journalism." My own recent collaborative research (Benson, Blach-Ørsten, Powers, Willig, and Vera Zambrano 2012) finds numerous continuities in the genres, authors, and topical foci of news in both print and online U.S., French, and Danish newspapers.

ASSESSING DEMOCRATIC QUALITIES AND QUANTITIES

Media scholars increasingly emphasize distinct democratic normative ideals and the differentiated capacity of various forms of journalism to achieve these ideals (Baker 2002; Ferree, Gamson, Gerhards, and Rucht 2002; Schudson 2008; Christians, Glasser, McQuail, Nordenstreng, and White 2009). Broadly speaking, these ideals can be captured in three democratic normative models: elitist, deliberative, and pluralist. The elitist model is rooted in the classic democratic elite theory associated with Walter Lippmann (1997) and the ideal of a "watchdog" press. The primary duties for the press are to examine the character and behavior of elected officials, to monitor closely their activities for corruption or incompetence, to critically analyze policy proposals, and to provide reliable, in-depth information about social problems. Whereas, in the elitist model, the press largely acts on behalf of the public, in the deliberative model, the press works alongside the public to "support reflection and value or policy choice" (Baker 2002, 148–149). In the deliberative model, mainstream media like the BBC and the *Washington Post* are not valued so much for their well-funded capacity to investigate as for their status as "inclusive, non-segmented media entities that support a search for general societal agreement on 'common goods'" (p. 149). The deliberative model provides a benchmark to evaluate both journalistically produced and non–journalistically produced discourse, including such aspects as civility, direct engagement of opposing viewpoints, and reasoned argumentation. Finally, the pluralist model emphasizes ideological diversity, popular inclusion, citizen empowerment and mobilization, and full expression through a range of communicative styles. It needs to be emphasized that, in each of these cases, the "debate" that occurs in this public sphere is largely "delegated" (Page 1996) rather than "direct" (although to a certain limited extent, the Internet is now facilitating greater direct interactions between journalists, delegated experts and spokespersons, and ordinary citizens [see, e.g., Adams 2007]).

With these three distinct models in mind, one can see that democracy encompasses a wide range of ideals, some of them potentially conflicting, and it would be difficult if not impossible for any single media outlet – or national media system – to adequately achieve all of them. Investigative journalism about immigration policies and their implementation is all too rare in both countries, but U.S. journalism does more to achieve this watchdog ideal. Conversely, the French press often does more to provide in-depth information and critically analyze policy, which are other important aspects of the elitist model. In relation to "procedural" measures of deliberation – such as news formats and genres, time or space for speakers to express their views, etc. – the French media are generally stronger. French immigration coverage generally comes closer to the pluralist ideal in terms of ideological diversity and citizen empowerment and mobilization, both at the level of the individual news organization (internal pluralism) and in relation to the media system as a whole (external pluralism). However, French pluralism is primarily institutional. When it comes to inclusion of unaffiliated individuals, U.S. media generally do a better job – with the notable exception of French television. Moreover, French TV news has the virtue of connecting individual problems to collective efforts to find policy solutions.

At the same time, both U.S. narrative and French debate ensemble formats have the potential to simplify or sensationalize the news – on the one hand as emotionally saturated melodrama, on the other as bold headline-hyped political theater. There also remain blind spots, even a kind of mystification, in immigration coverage in both countries. Although there certainly are public order and humanitarian problems associated with immigration in both countries, by emphasizing these frames so much the French and U.S. news media divert attention from other important aspects of immigration. Even if French newspapers do more to highlight the global economy frame, both media systems fall short of providing consistent critical and in-depth analyses of the economic causes and consequences of immigration. In this sense, the political economy critique of the capitalist media, even those outlets sheltered from market pressures, is all too accurate. Both media systems downplay what are arguably their greatest nation-specific problems. U.S. news media tend to ignore economic problems related to immigration – especially the jobs threat and inequalities arising from a neo-liberal global economy – even though these problems are substantial in the United States and probably cause more problems than in France. Conversely, over time, problems of racism have garnered less attention in the French media, even though there is growing evidence that France's largely "color-blind" education, employment, and housing policies are not working effectively to combat discrimination.

THE WAY FORWARD: IMPLICATIONS FOR REFORM

Journalists, like many other professionals, are understandably defensive about their reputation. They work hard and conscientiously, often under severe time pressures, to perform a public service. They are clearly not in it just for the money. Like academics, they belong to a kind of universal fraternity or sorority. In my interviews with journalists, I found that they were not eager to offer judgments on their colleagues. If anything, they tend to be harder on their national peers, whose failings they know well, than on their international counterparts. To the extent that I have praised French journalism, I would not be surprised if many French journalists do not share my assessment. Some American journalists may agree with my critical conclusions about their practices, but reject the idea that what happens in France has any relevance for the United States. What's more, whatever general patterns I have observed, there are always plenty of exceptions. The view from inside is not the same as the view from outside, which is not to say that the former is inherently superior to the latter. One's blind spots tend to be close at hand. And, ultimately, there may be disagreements on what is really important. As a sociologist and a concerned citizen, my ultimate concern is not the status of a profession but the health of democracy. In short, comparative research is inherently controversial, but even so, hopefully, worth the risk, if only to start a much-needed conversation about the varieties of journalism and the varieties of democracy.

With that said, I venture carefully into the territory of drawing lessons and suggesting reforms. The first reform concerns the need to expand and strengthen public media. Although the market is not antithetical to quality journalism, it seems clear from this study that the best journalism tends to be that with the most civic-cultural capital. Ideally, this capital ought to come from the democratic citizenry as a whole, through public subsidies. Philanthropy is an alternative, although not an adequate one either in the amount or duration of funding. In the absence of either public or philanthropic support, quality journalism tends to be financed by culturally elite audiences, either directly through high-cost subscriptions or indirectly through advertisers eager to reach them. As Herbert Gans commented to me when I presented him with my preliminary results, it is unfortunate "that for the most part multiperspectival journalism is to be found in media for the affluent and better educated, who probably need it least."[7] In similar fashion,

---

[7] Personal e-mail from Herbert J. Gans, January 26, 2010.

Patricia Aufderheide (2000, 96) has urged PBS to embrace a "public mandate that goes beyond niche marketing to the upper middle class." PBS's organizational and funding structures are far from ideal; they leave open the door to both partisan political and business influences. Ultimately, however, the championing of PBS by U.S. cultural elites may be what assures some minimal level of quality despite these ongoing pressures.

History is important: strong, publicly supported media in France and other Western European countries were built over many decades. If this helps explain why they remain resistant to commercialization, it also suggests that, lacking such a history, moving U.S. media in this direction will be difficult – although not impossible. The current economic crisis is clearly a "critical juncture," providing an opportunity for U.S. media policy to move in new directions. Journalists who want to improve their working conditions and capacity to produce quality work should support the efforts of progressive media policy reform groups like Free Press. Of course, the French and U.S. journalistic fields are each embedded in their respective fields of power, what some might label their "political cultures." But such an observation need not be linked to a resigned affirmation of the status quo. Rather, it suggests that change is more likely when it is linked to transformations in other fields.

Given that the forms of news are refractions of field position, it will be difficult to durably transform practice without changing broader structures of power. For example, in the United States, the long-term effects of the "public journalism" movement (Glasser 1999) have been limited in part because it took the commercial system as a given and did not challenge it. Public journalism's transformative potential was hollowed out by its accommodation to established power. However, if journalists agree that certain civic or professional goals are worth achieving, they may then be more willing to support the public policies needed to durably undergird these efforts.

My second set of recommendations concerns professional practices and reflexivity. One interesting finding of this study is that when American journalists cover civil society events their coverage is often just as multiperspectival as French news coverage. The difference, in part, is simply that civil society events make up a far larger proportion of immigration news coverage in France than in the United States. Some may argue that civil society protests and demonstrations are simply more common occurrences in France than in the United States. If so, this study's findings ought to be an incentive for both pro-immigration and restrictionist groups to redouble their efforts to organize the kinds of large-scale events that will most likely bring greater attention to their causes. And journalists should try harder to pay more consistent attention to such civil society activities. Yet qualitative aspects of civil society coverage are also important. If journalists characterize civil society as a random collection of individuals rather than as complex webs of organizations, they provide a misleading portrait and undermine mobilizing efforts. Journalists – especially editors who make decisions – also could be more reflexive and self-critical of the disadvantages as well as advantages of the narrative form of news. Narrative has become doxa in American journalism (it exists but is more contested in France): it is widely assumed that this is what news is and should be. Yet, in terms of what democracy needs, it may be that audiences don't actually need more stories that stress the human dimension. What they need is a way to connect the dots of causes and consequences. It's not a matter of having to eat one's broccoli, as Americans are fond of saying of any public-minded reform. No less of a small-d democrat than John Dewey felt that structural analysis could be interesting and entertaining too. Achieving this synthesis was for him the antidote to Walter Lippmann's pessimistic assumption that "what the press is it must continue to be." In Dewey's words:[8]

It is true that news must deal with events rather than with conditions and forces. It is true that the latter, taken by themselves, are too remote and abstract to make an appeal. Their record will be too dull and unsensational to reach the mass of readers. But there remains the possibility of treating news events in the light of a continuing study and record of underlying conditions. . . . If the word "sensational" can be used in a good sense, it may be said that a competent treatment of the news of the day, one based upon continuing research and organization, would be more sensational than present methods afford. To see underlying forces moving in and through events seemingly casual and disjointed will give a thrill which no report confined to the superficial and detached incident can give.

Indeed, since Dewey's time, American journalism has become much less event-centered (Barnhurst and Mutz 1997). On most days, half or more of the front page articles in the *New York Times* are *not* "breaking" event news (Weldon 2008). Immigration journalists in both the U.S. and France are clearly aware of the existence of social structures, as well as of persons and events, and actively attempt to "weave" these elements together into their "stories," just as does the best nonfiction or fiction. Yet, often, as I have tried to show with both qualitative and quantitative evidence, there seems to be a trade-off. Narrative journalism favors the compelling human interest drama to the detriment of any sustained structural analysis. Rather than embracing the "human interest narrative" as the best or inevitable formula for writing (and, clearly it has formulaic elements), journalists might push back and insist on the need to write more articles that try to get to the bottom of enduring debates of immigration's causes and effects.

It has been suggested to me by some American observers that, whatever the supposed intellectual virtues of the French press, the American press is ultimately more accessible and thus more influential. I am not sure that this point needs to be conceded. The French journalistic style, although often driven more by ideas than personalities, is not therefore "dry": the *événement* format sets a strict limit on the length of any given article and is liberally sprinkled with dramatic head-lines and photos. It provides its own dramatic mix of events and underlying conditions. This debate ensemble format represents an alternative response

---

[8] John Dewey, Review of *Public Opinion* by Walter Lippmann, *New Republic*, 30 (1922), p. 343.

to Dewey's challenge: instead of a single narrative-driven article, an image-saturated collage of news, opinions, analyses, interviews, and background factual dossiers that approach a given topic from multiple angles and perspectives. Perhaps a combination of narrative and multigenre approaches would come closest to fully achieving Dewey's ideal, but the particular quality as well as quantity of narratives also matters. In bringing together structure and agency, it is important to acknowledge collective as well as individual agency.

Media, of course, are only one factor that contribute to public opinion about immigration (or any other issue), and the precise influence of media is beyond the scope of this investigation. It remains an open question which kind of news is most likely to influence public policy making, and it is not self-evident that the French government's policies on immigration are any more enlightened than those currently in place in the United States. These and other connections between practices and forms of reporting and policy outcomes certainly deserve more attention. For the moment, I simply note the result of a recent Transatlantic Trends survey (funded by the German Marshall Fund and other international foundations), which seems to support the educational value of French multi-perspectival news coverage of immigration, including, as this study showed, a greater tendency to emphasize the global economic context of immigration. The Transatlantic Trends survey asked citizens in several immigrant-receiving nations what solution they favored to address the problem of illegal immigration. In France, the greatest percentage of respondents (44 percent) favored increasing development aid, whereas only 16 percent favored "reinforcing border controls." In contrast, in the United States, the greatest percentage (30 percent) favored reinforcing border controls, whereas only 16 percent favored increased development aid.[9]

Actually, there is some evidence that American journalism is increasingly branching out beyond narrative journalism. In the fall of 2010, *Arizona Republic* lead immigration reporter Dan Gonzalez spent several months researching a sixteen-page "Special Report on Global Immigration," organized around the themes of enforcement (Italy), integration (Germany), and amnesty (Spain). The original intention was to create lengthy narrative stories for each country that would attempt to, in a sense, do it all. But both for reasons of time and ease of communication, ultimately, the editors moved to a more multiarticle, multigenre, and multijournalist approach. As Gonzalez explained to me:[10]

When we came out [with this idea] we were going to do one story about [each country] . . . they were going to be stories that I went and reported and they were going to have real

    9 *Transatlantic Trends: Immigration* (2009), sponsored by The German Marshall Fund of the United States, The Lynde and Harry Bradley Foundation, Compagnia di San Paolo, Barrow Cadbury Trust, and Fundación BBVA, available at www.transatlantictrends.org.
    10 Daniel Gonzalez interview (2012). The expanded web version of the report presents information, images, and videos about immigration in twelve countries. See http://www.azcentral.com/news/global-immigration/.

people and immigrants [along with] policy and statistics – all woven into the stories. [But] when we sat down to plan out the story . . .. our [page] A1 editor said, you know what? It would be great if we took that theme and wrote a story that captured that theme from a global perspective. So for example: Amnesty. We would have the main story from Spain and what was happening in Spain but then we would [also] have a companion piece that was more policy oriented and that talked about the issue of amnesty from a global policy perspective . . . So that's when we enlisted [political reporter] Dan [Nowicki]. Although he didn't travel, he did these policy stories that could give this broader context.

Across the U.S. media landscape, other changes are afoot, closing the gap between American and various European styles of journalism. Interview tran-scripts are increasingly used in the *Los Angeles Times*, in both the opinion and news pages. Opinion columns are increasingly mixed with news reports and analyses in the news pages of the *New York Times* (Diamond 1994), and the *New York Times'* old Week in Review has been transformed into a "Sunday Review" that makes ample room for the voices of writers, artists, and research-ers alongside journalists.[11] With the Internet, notable in-depth articles about immigration become easily retrievable years after their first publication (as with the "Three Sisters" and "Remade in America" series mentioned in Chapter 3) and can also be linked to databases, maps, interactive graphics, expert debates, and other genres and types of information, analysis, and commentary.[12] NYTimes.com also now has a regular feature called "Room for Debate," in which "knowledgeable outsiders" are invited "to discuss major news events and other hot topics." For instance, on April 12, 2012, a debate on "How States Should Approach Immigration" included the perspectives of an immigration historian, various immigrant rights activists, and the director of a Texas restric-tionist organization, as well as 175 reader comments (see Figure 9.1).

Ultimately, achieving the ideals of in-depth, multiperspectival, and critical news involves editing as much as reporting. Its success rests at least partly on journalists' willingness to move off center-stage, to give up some of their long-held monopoly over access to the public sphere in order to make room for other voices. The reality is that in-depth, on-the-ground reports will continue to be few and far between as long as the Wall Street profit-maximizing model of owner-ship dominates U.S. professional journalism. Lacking substantial infusions of either private or public resources, the debate ensemble's "curating" approach may be one way journalism can deliver more democratic "bang for the buck."

Limitations or blindspots in news coverage related to class habitus of reporters may be the most difficult to amend. These kinds of suggestions inspire defensiveness. Most journalists feel that their professionalism helps them overcome any tendency toward special treatment, negative or positive, of

---

[11] See Arthur S. Brisbane, "Surrounded by Opinion, The Times Raises Its Voices," *The New York Times*, Sunday, July 3, 2011, p. 10 (Sunday Review).
[12] See the "Three Sisters" articles at http://www.nytimes.com/ref/us/three_sisters.html and the "Remade in America" series at http://projects.nytimes.com/immigration/.

FIGURE 9.1. NYtimes.com "Room for Debate," April 22, 2012. Reproduced with permission of *The New York Times*.

pro- or anti-immigration advocates. But this may be a case in which what is needed is less professionalism rather than more. One way to help achieve more multiperspectival news would be to self-consciously recruit journalists with diverse habitus (taking into account class background as much as or more than race/ethnicity or gender) and to loosen up news genre restrictions so that they have greater freedom to express their class-based perspectives.

When it comes to the most marginal groups, especially on the restrictionist right, at least some journalists feel that they are justified in ignoring or criticizing their views. Yet derision of immigration restrictionists is not simply a matter of marginalizing extremist hate groups that deserve to be marginalized. For one thing, not all supporters of immigration law enforcement or limits to immigration are nativists or racists. In addition, in many cases, restrictionist groups are expressing legitimate concerns about the effects of uncontrolled immigration that in previous periods were just as vociferously expressed by trade unions, political parties, environmentalists, university researchers, and newspaper editorial boards and columnists. These problems have not disappeared just because many mainstream groups no longer speak about them. To the extent that restrictionist groups blame immigrants, they are misguided; to the extent that they tap into public unease and concerns with neo-liberal globalization, of which immigration is one part, they are speaking truth to power. As Mabel Berezin (2009) shows for France, it is when these concerns are not heard that far right groups like the National Front are able to use scare tactics and misinformation for electoral gain. Journalists face a dilemma: how to raise legitimate issues that are mostly only being raised by marginalized restrictionist groups? One answer is for journalists to more proactively seek out respected but media-shy speakers to articulate these positions. Another answer is for more journalists – not only those writing on the opinion pages – to stop speaking only through their sources and to put forward the fundamental questions themselves, in their own voices.

Over the past several years, I have participated in several public forums in which immigration journalists have engaged in just this kind of critical reflection about their work. Prominent journalists, including some of whom I interviewed for this book, have written eloquent essays reflecting on their practice.[13] Certainly, many of the critiques I offer in this book are made by the journalists themselves. Nevertheless, I hope that my historical, cross-national research can offer some new ways of thinking about journalistic practices as they relate to diverse democratic aspirations. And because journalism is not only for journalists, I hope this book helps involve other democratic stakeholders in the conversation. Finally, any "advice" that I offer in this book applies to all of us involved in any form of knowledge production. If we want to widen and deepen the public debate, it's not enough to try to change our own individual practices. We also have to change the rules of the game.

---

[13] See, e.g., McDonnell (2011) and Bernstein (2011), both interviewed for this book, as well as other journalist-authored chapters in the same volume, and Harris (2012). See also Dell'Orto and Birchfield (2013).

Appendix A: Additional News Content Data

Online Appendix Tables

The following tables are available in an online appendix at http://rodneybenson. org/. Online Table (OT) numbers refer to chapter for which data are most relevant.

TABLE A.I. *Field Generation, Feature Genre, and Frames: Newspaper Core Samples, Combined 1970s–2000s*

Country/News Generation# (N = News packages)	Global Economy	Humanitarian	Racism	Cultural Diversity	Integration	Good Worker	Jobs	Public Order	Fiscal	National Cohesion
France										
Pol Field (n = 219)	23%	79%	43%	7%	13%	21%	14%	74%	15%	44%
	—	-.153**	—	—	—	—	—	—	.120*	.108*
CS Field (n = 113)	21%	95%	50%	10%	14%	12%	7%	68%	6%	32%
	—	.173**	—	—	—	-.109*	—	—	-.103*	—
Journ Field (n = 72)	44%	85%	50%	14%	15%	17%	10%	60%	8%	36%
	.186**	—	—	—	—	—	—	-.100*	—	—
Only Feature (n = 34)	—	—	—	—	—	—	—	—	—	-.134**
U.S.										
Pol Field (n = 267)	13%	63%	25%	4%	7%	23%	15%	72%	23%	5%
	—	-.179**	—	-.148**	-.185**	-.126**	—	.183**	—	-.206**
CS Field (n = 54)	11%	85%	44%	11%	20%	39%	19%	65%	28%	35%
	—	.117**	.141**	—	—	—	—	—	—	—
Journ Field (n = 162)	21%	77%	24%	12%	20%	33%	19%	51%	25%	13%
	.104*	.111*	—	.124**	.151**	—	—	-.190**	—	.271**
Only Feature (n = 185)	—	.098*	—	.142**	.158**	—	—	-.182**	—	—

Only significant bivariate correlations are shown. Percentages refer to proportion of news packages in which frame appeared.
Not included in this analysis are the handful of accident-generated news packages (5 in France, 3 in the U.S.). Feature articles are generally journalistic field-generated, but could also be generated by breaking news in the civil society or political fields (in which case the feature would provide less time-bound background for a time-sensitive topic).

* p < .05
** p < .01

TABLE A.2. *Immigration Frames in Individual French and U.S. Newspapers, 2002–2006 (Percentages Appearing in News Packages)*

Media Outlet (N News Packages)	Global Economy (%)	Humanitarian (%)	Racism/ Xenophobia (%)	Cultural Diversity (%)	Integration (%)	Good Worker (%)	Jobs (%)	Public Order (%)	Fiscal (%)	National Cohesion (%)
L'Humanité (63)	19	97	70	14	10	24	2	41	2	27
La Croix (56)	16	86	46	25	9	14	0	45	0	41
Libération (60)	38	92	37	12	20	28	8	57	7	40
Le Monde (60)	30	85	38	5	17	20	5	58	7	43
Le Figaro (48)	29	65	29	10	13	21	8	67	19	44
Les Echos (46)	18	73	44	7	9	40	2	49	7	18
Le Parisien (47)	2	81	30	28	13	9	4	53	11	38
France Averages	22	83	42	14	13	22	4	53	8	36
France High-Low Gap	36	32	41	23	11	31	8	26	19	26
C.S. Monitor (56)	11	73	29	14	13	29	29	71	27	18
L.A. Times (87)	11	80	20	11	6	37	14	69	11	20
N.Y. Times (68)	16	78	24	13	9	34	16	62	16	6
Wash. Post (81)	10	80	23	21	11	20	7	77	10	14
W.S. Journal (62)	5	58	24	16	3	42	8	66	10	8
USA Today (48)	6	67	23	21	6	29	19	75	19	15
Daily News (69)	0	78	16	6	7	19	1	36	0	6
U.S. Averages	8	73	23	15	8	30	13	65	13	12
U.S. High-Low Gap w/Daily News	16	22	13	15	10	23	28	41	27	14
New York Post (71)	1	54	10	7	4	15	1	41	4	4
U.S. High-Low Gap w/ New York Post	15	26	19	14	10	27	28	36	23	16

TABLE A.3. *Types of Speakers Cited in Individual French and U.S. Newspapers, 2002–2006 (Percentages of All Citations)*

Media Outlet (N Speakers Cited)	Executive/ Bureaucratic (%)	Judicial (%)	Center Legislative (%)	Center Parties (%)	Peripheral Parties (%)	Civil Society (%)	Business (%)	Individuals & Polls (%)	Foreign Organizations (%)
L'Humanité (667)	17	2	4	3	11	39	1	19	5
La Croix (884)	20	1	7	3	3	35	0	16	14
Libération (1,420)	18	2	5	5	5	34	1	21	9
Le Monde (857)	19	2	9	5	8	31	0	14	15
Le Figaro (744)	23	1	10	6	5	28	1	8	18
Les Echos (322)	29	0	3	6	2	25	4	4	26
Le Parisien (631)	30	2	2	5	3	23	2	31	3
France Averages	22	1	6	5	5	31	1	16	13
France High-Low Gap	13	2	8	3	9	16	4	27	23
C.S. Monitor (590)	20	1	11	1	0	40	4	19	4
L.A. Times (1,342)	20	3	13	2	0	23	5	29	6
N.Y. Times (1,005)	25	5	16	2	0	25	6	17	3
Wash. Post (936)	27	7	18	1	0	20	4	18	5
W.S. Journal (679)	23	4	9	1	0	24	16	20	5
USA Today (637)	20	3	19	1	0	30	6	21	5
Daily News (422)	25	6	7	0	0	19	6	38	1
U.S. Averages	23	4	13	1	0	26	7	23	3
U.S. High-Low Gap	7	6	12	2	0	21	12	21	6
New York Post (338)	33	5	17	1	0	11	2	31	1

Note: Civil Society combines the following speaker categories: Trade Unions, Religious, University/Research, Associations, Journalistic, and Arts and Entertainment.

TABLE A.4. *Balancing of Frames and Speakers by Individual French and U.S. Newspapers (Percentages of News Packages in which Frame Groups Appear)*[a]

Media Outlet (N News Packages)	Only Hero and/or Victim Frames (%)	Some Balance (Broad Balance)[b] (%)	Only Threat Frames (%)
France			
L'Humanité (63)	43	54 (27)	0
La Croix (56)	27	63 (27)	11
Libération (60/112)	29/25[c]	64/71 (37/38)	8/5
Le Monde (60/175)	24/21	68/73 (23/23)	8/5
Le Figaro (48/122)	12/9	62/73 (33/22)	25/18
Les Echos (46)	32	56 (24)	9
Le Parisien (47)	26	66 (15)	9
U.S.			
C.S. Monitor (56)	13	71 (32)	14
L.A. Times (87/205)	21/20	64/61 (29/23)	15/19
N.Y. Times (68/138)	22/20	67/62 (24/22)	10/16
Wash. Post (81/143)	16/20	73/67 (19/20)	10/11
W.S. Journal (62)	19	56 (27)	18
USA Today (48)	14	58 (33)	25
Daily News (69)	49	34 (9)	10
New York Post (71)	43	22 (4)	25

[a] Percentages may not add up to 100 because of rounding and because of news packages with no issue frames.
[b] Some Balance refers to packages in which a threat frame was paired with either a hero or victim frame; Broad Balance refers to packages mentioning at least one threat, hero, and victim frame.
[c] Percentages for all years combined are provided immediately after 2000s percentages for *New York Times, Washington Post,* and *Los Angeles Times* for U.S.; *Le Monde, Le Figaro,* and *Libération* (1980s–2000s) for France.

TABLE A.5. *Types of Speakers Cited in Individual French and U.S. Television News Programs, 2002–2006 (Percentages of All Citations)*

Media Outlet (N Total Speakers Cited)	Executive/ Bureaucratic (%)	Judicial (%)	Center Legislative (%)	Center Parties (%)	Peripheral Parties (%)	Civil Society (%)	Business (%)	Individuals & Polls (%)	Foreign Organizations (%)
TF1 (413)	24	1	2	1	1	31	2	35	3
France 2 (436)	21	1	2	2	4	28	0	39	3
French TV Core	23	1	2	2	3	30	1	37	3
Arte (297)	14	0	0	1	1	41	0	36	7
ABC (271)	26	3	9	1	0	20	3	33	4
CBS (324)	32	1	11	1	0	21	5	26	2
NBC (449)	36	2	14	1	0	19	4	22	3
U.S. TV Core	31	2	11	1	0	20	4	27	3
PBS (435)	21	1	24	2	0	28	7	13	3

TABLE A.6. *Immigration Frames in Individual French and U.S. Television News Programs, 2002–2006 (Percentages Appearing in News Packages)*

Media Outlet (N News Packages)	Global Economy (%)	Humanitarian (%)	Racism/ Xenophobia (%)	Cultural Diversity (%)	Integration (%)	Good Worker (%)	Jobs (%)	Public Order (%)	Fiscal (%)	National Cohesion (%)
TF1 (85)	6	64	15	7	21	7	1	29	2	12
France 2 (83)	11	66	14	4	23	5	1	29	5	7
French TV Core Average	9	65	15	6	22	6	1	29	4	10
Arte (58)	7	84	16	2	21	14	0	33	0	5
ABC (50)	14	58	8	6	14	18	2	52	8	4
CBS (54)	0	52	9	2	7	19	6	52	13	7
NBC (71)	3	35	15	1	13	18	4	62	6	6
U.S. TV Core Average	6	48	11	3	11	18	4	55	9	6
PBS (56)	13	43	18	7	21	39	16	64	16	12

Appendix B: Sources and Methods

This study draws on government, industry, and academic reports of news media funding, ownership, employment, and audiences; qualitative in-depth interviews with journalists, scholars, political officials, and immigration activists; and content analyses of newspaper and television news texts and images.

Media Organization Data

Newspaper Advertising and Audience Data (for Table 2.2)

U.S. advertising revenues (as a percentage of total revenues) are derived from newspaper companies' publicly available reports for 2006, which may include all newspapers owned by the company. Washington Post Co. percentage excludes income from its Kaplan educational division; Dow-Jones percentage excludes income from information services. *Christian Science Monitor* data are derived from a personal e-mail communication to the author from Susan Hackney, Marketing Director, *Christian Science Monitor*, June 23, 2008: in addition to advertising, 30 percent of *Monitor* revenues were from a church subsidy and 58 percent were from subscriptions and single-issue purchases. The *Daily News* figure of 53 percent is for 1997 and is derived from the *International Directory of Company Histories*, vol. 32 (St. James Press 2000), as posted on http://www.fundinguniverse.com/company-histories/New-York-Daily-News-Company-History.html (accessed October 8, 2008); more recent data are not publicly available.

French figures, except for *Les Echos*, are for 1990 (Albert 1990, 81). More recent, scattered data sources confirm continuity over time (Chaussebourg interview 2002; Mathien 2003; Charon 2005). Albert (2004, 98) does not provide percentage data for *Les Echos*, but he reports that in 2002 *Les Echos* and

La Tribune, the two French financial dailies, published the highest number of pages of advertising (3,601 and 2,966, respectively) and were ahead of *Le Figaro*'s 2,848 pages, which suggests that *Les Echos*'s proportion of funding from advertising may be roughly comparable to that of *Le Figaro*. Albert's 2002 data also shows continuity from 1990 in the relative amount of advertising for the major national newspapers: *Le Monde* followed *Le Figaro* with 2,532 pages, followed by *Le Parisien* with 1,462, *Libération* with 1,260, *La Croix* with 343, and *L'Humanité* with 246.

U.S. audience composition data are primarily from U.S. Audit Bureau of Circulations Reader Profiles, Scarborough Co. (courtesy of Kristi Brumlevee) and National Newspaper Association (courtesy of William Johnson), all 2006 reports with the exception of *USA Today*, which is from 2004. *Christian Science Monitor* figures are from roughly comparable 2007 Mediamark Research, Inc. (MRI) data, provided to the author by Susan Hackney of the *Monitor*. French audience data are from 2006 TNS-SOFRES–EPIQ French Newspaper Audience Composition Reports (information about *Le Parisien* includes national edition *Aujourd'hui en France*).

Index of Parity is calculated to compare newspaper audiences in each country relative to the general population of that country (100 = parity with general adult population). *Higher Education* = college degree or higher in U.S./any *enseignement supérieur* (any university education beyond the "bac," a post-high school degree awarded after passing a national examination) in France. (Household) *High Income* = >€60,000 in France/>$100,000 in U.S.; (Household) *Low Income* = <€12,000 in France/<$25,000 in U.S.; *Professional Occupation* = Census category "professional and related" in U.S./TNS-SOFRES–EPIQ categories *profession libérale* + *profession intermédiaire* in France. Although there are differences in how these categories are constructed, the core of both of these French and U.S. occupational groupings consists of professionals and other high "cultural capital" occupations including most doctors, lawyers, architects, teachers, clergy, librarians, and the like.

Television Audience Data (for Table 2.3)

Television audience composition data for France are for 2006 and were provided by Eurodata TV Worldwide/Médiamétrie, courtesy of Alexandra Brenkman and Jacques Braun (e-mails, October–December 2009). "CSP" (occupational-income) indexes, only available for France, are produced by contrasting TV audience data with INSEE All French public data presented in 2006 TNS-SOFRES–EPIQ French Newspaper Audience Composition Reports. Similar figures for the late 1990s are provided for TF1 and France 2 by Cotteret (2000, 216–217) and for Arte by Schroeder (2005). French age and audience size/percentage data are from 2006 Médiamétrie reports, provided to the author by Vincent Goulet, e-mail, December 2007. Arte 2007 audience/size data were provided by Arte employees to Jill Campaiola, on behalf of the author in January 2008.

Public Broadcasting Service (PBS) audience data are from the following sources: income (Nielsen Media Research, Public TV full day weekly "cume" average from Oct. 2008–Sept. 2009, reported in PBS 2010); education and age (July 2008–June 2009 survey data reported in PEJ 2010a State of the Media Report "Network TV Audience Trends"), and size of audience (2006 data in PEJ 2007 State of the Media Report "Network TV Audience Trends"). U.S. TV network news data are from the following sources: income (MRI spring 2002, cited in Papazian 2003, 223); education (2008–2009 data in PEJ 2010a State of the Media Report "Network TV Audience Trends"), age (2002 MRI data as cited in Papazian 2003, 223), and audience size and percentage of total audience (2006 data in PEJ 2007 State of the Media Report "Network TV Audience Trends"). Similar audience size and percentage figures for 2006 were provided by Rob Schlaepfer, CBS Evening News Research, in a November 14, 2007 e-mail.

High Income = annual household income of >$60,000 (PBS), >$75,000 (U.S. networks), and >€54,000 (all French TV); *Low Income* = annual household income <$20,000 (PBS), <$30,000 (U.S. networks), and <€14,400 (all French TV). *CSP+* refers to the "socio-political category" combining the relatively high-income job categories of artisan, businessperson, liberal professions, business manager (*cadres superieur*), and *profession intermédiaire*; *CSP−* refers to the "socio-political category" combining the relatively low-income French job categories of employee, qualified worker, nonqualified worker, and farmer. *Higher Education* = college degree or more (PBS, U.S. networks); bac + 2 or more (all France TV).

Interviews

Between 1997 and 2012, I conducted semistructured, in-depth interviews lasting 45 to 90 minutes with journalists, activists, and politicians in France and the United States. In addition, I observed page-one and other editorial meetings at several of the news organizations I studied (*Le Monde, Libération*, France 2, *Los Angeles Times, New York Times*). I also conducted many informational interviews with immigration scholars, especially in France (see acknowledgments). Although quotes from only a small portion of these interviews are included in the book, all of them informed and enriched my analysis.

My goal was to try to understand the journalistic field from the perspective of those inside it. Interview questions were focused on the following topical areas: personal educational and professional trajectory, organization of the immigration beat, definitions of good journalism, professional competitors, knowledge or interactions with readers or viewers, interactions with sources, and reconstructions of everyday practices (often via detailed discussions of specific recent articles) including generation of ideas, writing process, and editing. I used interviews in conjunction with other texts in which journalists reflected on their work, such as memoirs and articles for professional or trade journals, as well as other academic studies in which journalists were interviewed or observed. I do not claim to have constructed a random sample of all immigration reporters: rather, I attempted to speak to as many immigration reporters, former immigration reporters, and top editors as possible at a range of types of news organizations. Saturation served as a rough indicator of the adequacy of my sample: once I began to hear similar themes repeated by multiple interviewees working for the same type of media outlet or across a national field, I could have some confidence that these themes constituted part of the underlying logic of practice. I came away from these interviews with tremendous respect and admiration for the journalists: if I were in their shoes, working in the same conditions, I am sure I would have responded in much the same way – or at least aspired to similar standards of performance.

At the same time, this is a work of critical sociology. In contrast to Bruno Latour's actor-network theory, I do not privilege the insider account over the outsider perspective: both are needed. Individual action is always caught up in larger structures of power. Although I do not claim to have fully accounted for any particular individual's practices, I have sought to join journalists' accounts with other forms of data to identify patterned linkages between organizational structures, formats, and properties of news discourses. Normatively, as the central "mediating" field in democratic nation-states, journalism's purposes and aspirations can and should be interrogated by nonjournalists.

In sum, interviews – as well as my participation in various public forums with journalists – served as an important "reality" check on this research. These encounters helped me to always keep in mind the practical exigencies of journalistic work. My analysis nevertheless remains a view from the "outside." My explanations and my evaluations are not constrained by an insider journalistic framework. Through historical and cross-national comparative analysis, as well as democratic normative critique, I hope not only to show what journalists generally do, but how they might do things otherwise.

Selected On-the-Record Interviews

All interviews were conducted in person unless otherwise indicated. Titles are those held at the time of interview.

United States

Harry Bernstein, *Los Angeles Times* former labor reporter, March 1998, San Fernando Valley

Nina Bernstein, *New York Times* metro immigration reporter, June 2008, telephone interview

Bill Boyarsky, *Los Angeles Times* city editor, March 1998, Los Angeles

Martin Burns, PBS NewsHour producer, March 1998, Los Angeles

Larry Burroughs, *Orange County Register* managing editor, March 1998, Anaheim

Yvette Cabrera, Los Angeles *Daily News* reporter, March 1998, Los Angeles

Nancy Cleeland, *Los Angeles Times* reporter, March 1998, Anaheim

Suzanne Daley, *New York Times* Paris bureau chief, June 2002, Paris

Frank del Olmo, *Los Angeles Times* deputy editorial page editor, March 1998, Los Angeles

Paul Feldman, *Los Angeles Times* assistant metro editor, March 1998, Los Angeles

Lisa Fung, *Los Angeles Times* assistant business editor, March 1998, Los Angeles

Guillermo Garcia, *Orange County Register* reporter, March 1998, Anaheim

Ron Gonzales, *Orange County Register* reporter, March 1998, Anaheim

Daniel Gonzalez, *Arizona Republic* immigration reporter, May 2012, Phoenix

Saul Gonzalez, KCET/PBS producer, March 1998, Los Angeles

Rosalva Hernandez, *Orange County Register* reporter, March 1998, Anaheim

Marshall Ingwerson, *Christian Science Monitor* managing editor, May 2011, Boston

Clay Jones, *Christian Science Monitor* editorial page editor, May 2011, Boston

Jeffrey Kaye, PBS correspondent, March 1998, Los Angeles

Dianne Lindquist, *San Diego Union-Tribune* immigration reporter, March 1998, San Diego

Roberto Lovato, former Central American Resource Center director, March 1998, Los Angeles; March 2011, Boston

Alexandra Marks, *Christian Science Monitor* reporter, June 2008, telephone interview

Rubén Martínez, KCET/PBS (and former *LA Weekly* writer), March 1998, Claremont, CA

Patrick McDonnell, *Los Angeles Times* immigration reporter, March 1998, Los Angeles

Kathleen McElroy, *New York Times* digital editor, June 2011, New York

Ira Mehlman, Federation for American Immigration Reform Media Outreach Director, May 1995, telephone interview

David Poltrack, CBS Chief Research Officer, October 2007, New York

Julia Preston, *New York Times* national immigration reporter, July 2008, telephone interview

Alan Riding, *New York Times* cultural correspondent, June 2002, Paris

Rob Schlaepfer, CBS Evening News Research executive, October 2007, New York

Rich Simon, *Los Angeles Times* reporter, March 1998, Los Angeles

Frank Sotomayor, *Los Angeles Times* assistant metro editor, March 1998, Los Angeles

Glenn Spencer, Voice of Citizens Together founder, 1995, telephone interview

Jill Stewart, Los Angeles *New Times* (former *Los Angeles Times*) reporter, March 1998, Sherman Oaks, CA

Leo Wolinsky, *Los Angeles Times* managing editor, March 1998, Los Angeles

France

Mogniss Hamed Abdallah, Im'media director (immigration PR/film agency), March 1997, Paris

Pierre Allain, France 2 news editor and former political reporter, October 1998, Paris

Jean-Pierre Alaux, GISTI (immigrant legal rights group), October 1998

Nicolas Beau, *Le Canard Enchaîné* (formerly immigration/"second generation" reporter for *Le Monde* and *Libération*), March 1997, Paris

Jean-Michel Belorgey, Conseiller d'Etat (former PS deputé), Conseil d'Etat, September 1998, Paris

Philippe Bernard, *Le Monde* immigration reporter and editor, June 1997, Paris; November 2004, New York

Olivier Biffaud, *Le Monde* political reporter, October 1998, Paris

Gilles Bresson, *Libération* political reporter, October 1998, Paris

Bernard Brigouleix, *Le Monde* former political reporter (far right beat), October 1998, Paris

Véronique Brocard, *Télérama* (former *Libération* immigration reporter), February 1997, Paris

Hervé Brusini, France 2 (20 heures/8 p.m.) news director, May 1997, Paris

Anne Chaussebourg, *Le Monde* assistant managing editor, June 2002, Paris

Guilaine Chenu, France 2 political correspondent (former TF1 immigration reporter), May 1997, Paris

Jean-Michel Decujis, *Le Figaro* immigration reporter, June 1997, Paris

Abou Diarra, Club Diversité president, November 2009, Paris

Pascale Egré, *Le Parisien* (and former *L'Humanité*) immigration reporter, November 2009, telephone interview

Driss El Yazami, Génériques (former editor of *Sans Frontiére*, immigrant activist newspaper), July 1996, Paris; February 1997, Paris
Eric Favereau, *Libération* reporter, June 1997, Paris
Jean-François Fogel, *Le Monde* design consultant (former *Libération* assistant managing editor), June 2002, telephone interview
Franz-Olivier Giesbert, *Le Figaro* editor-in-chief, June 1997, Paris
Serge Halimi, *Le Monde Diplomatique* political editor, May 1998, Paris; June 2002, Paris.
Christine Herrero, FAS director (government agency responsible for immigrant integration), March 1997, Paris
Laurent Joffrin, *Libération* managing editor, June 1997, Paris
Eric Le Boucher, *Le Monde* assistant managing editor, June 2002, Paris
Antoine Lefèvre, TF1 political reporter, October 1998, Paris
Jean-Luc Mano, independent news producer (former TF1 and France 2 editor), May 1997, Paris
Christophe Nick, independent investigative reporter, June 1997, Paris
Amaury de Rochegonde, *Stratégies* media reporter, June 2002, Paris
Alain Rollat, *Le Monde* political reporter, October 1998, Paris
Jean-Jacques Rouche, *La Dépêche du Midi* reporter, March 2008, Toulouse
Dominique Simonnot, *Libération* immigration reporter, June 1997, Paris
Robert Solé, *Le Monde* assistant managing editor, June 2002, Paris
Michel Trillat, France 2 *société* editor, October 1998, Paris
Elise Vincent, *Le Monde* immigration reporter, April 2012, Minneapolis
Jean-Pierre Worms, former PS député, October 1998, Paris

Content Analysis

Peak Media Attention years were determined through word searches in Lexis-Nexis, Factiva, Proquest, Vanderbilt Television News Archives, and the French National Audiovisual Institute (INA) database, supplemented by previous over-time analyses of media attention to immigration conducted by other scholars, especially Bonnafous (1991) and Gastaut (2000) for France. Published subsequent to the completion of my research, peak media attention years identified by Suro (2008) for the years between 1980 and 2007 – 1986, 1994, 2006 – accord with mine. Sample years for the 1970s (1973 for France, 1974–75 for the United States) mark the first major contemporary upswing in media attention to immigration. Although only a few years over the thirty-two-year period were sampled, focusing on such critical discourse moments assures that the intensity and volume of the public debate are held relatively constant.

National average percentages reported in Chapters 3 and 4 equally weight all media outlets (for medium), newspaper and television coverage (for total media), and in some cases decade (for national media system): this procedure assures that no media outlet, medium, or time period dominates the aggregate totals.

For the U.S. sample, I searched for news items prominently mentioning variations of the root immigr* or alien* (the latter to capture the term "illegal aliens," used more commonly in the 1970s than now). For the French sample, in addition to searching for variants of immigr*, I searched for French-specific immigration-related terms *étranger*, *clandestin*, *sans papier*, *banlieue*, and *laïcité*. The latter two terms were added for the 2000s sample because I was finding that French news coverage increasingly referred to immigrant populations without using the term "immigrant." After a close reading of the texts, only those *banlieue* and *laïcité* articles focused on immigrant populations and not primarily on other social groups or aspects of urban problems or secularism were included in the sample; excluding articles found with these terms would have slightly reduced sample size, but would not have substantially changed overall findings. Like Bonnafous (1991, 18–21), I included news about "harkis" (Algerians who fought on the French side during Algeria's war for independence). Chavez (2001) distinguishes between refugees and immigrants, showing that they are treated quite differently in media coverage; given these differences, I generally did not include news about political refugees, except in those cases where the very "refugee" status of certain groups is being questioned and thus the debate is over whether to treat a certain group (e.g., Salvadorans, southeast Asians) in the same way as other immigrants. For the 2000s, two time periods in which media attention to immigration was high were *not* included because of their idiosyncratic character: 2001, especially from September 11 onward, and 2005, with the *banlieue* riots of November and December. The discursive effects of these events continued to reverberate in 2002 and 2006, and thus are captured in the sample (as are riots occurring in 1983 and 1991, or the many efforts to "crack down" on illegal immigration in both countries), but including the immediate periods of 9/11 and *banlieue* riot coverage could have overwhelmed the sample and made this more of a study of media attention to those particular events than an attempt to capture broader tendencies of news coverage.

News samples were constructed whenever possible from multiple data sources to ensure comprehensiveness. U.S. newspaper samples were gathered from Lexis-Nexis and Proquest searches for available years and otherwise from newspaper print indexes, supplemented by searches of microfilm collections. To assure rough equivalence of media outlet *n*'s, in some cases a random one-half to one-third selection of total evening news/page-one news packages were drawn for a given sample. French newspaper samples for 1973, 1983, and 1991 were assembled from lists provided by Bonnafous (1991), newspaper indexes when available, and exhaustive searches of the University of California-Berkeley's comprehensive microfilm collection. French 2002–2006 samples were assembled through systematic searches of Lexis-Nexis and Factiva. The U.S. TV news discourse sample was constructed from Lexis-Nexis transcripts and Vanderbilt Television News Archives online textual summaries; images were captured from DVDs of actual broadcasts provided by the Vanderbilt archives. For the French television news sample, I relied on the Institut National d'Audiovisuel's (INA) news program summaries and audio-visual collection. Image and word-for-word textual transcripts were created from onsite viewing of available sampled news packages. See Table B.1.

Frames, speakers, critical statements, images, and other news content elements were coded by several independent coders, including the author, after a period of training and test coding. A frame would be indicated by any empirical (or normative) reference to relevant aspects, whether made by a journalist or named or unnamed sources. Frames were only coded as binary variables

APPENDIX TABLE B.1. *News Content Samples*

	1970s All Core[a] Media	1980s All Core Media	1990s All Core Media	2000s All Core Media	2000s Extended Newspaper Sample[b]	2000s Extended TV News Sample[c]	2000s TV Image Sample
France							
News Packages	63	116	220	336	380	226	–
Frames[d]	169	301	621	811	1,130	383	–
Speakers	461	1,084	2,073	3,869	5,562	1,146	–
Images	–	–	–	–	–	–	6,126
United States							
News Packages	75	118	161	411	471	231	–
Frames	179	302	399	948	1,225	438	–
Speakers	494	1,070	1,725	4,319	5,662	1,479	–
Images	–	–	–	–	–	–	5,388

[a] All Core includes *Los Angeles Times, New York Times, Washington Post*, ABC, CBS, NBC for U.S., and *Le Figaro, Le Monde, Libération* (except for 1970s), France 2, and TF1 for France.
[b] In addition to core newspapers, Extended Newspaper Sample includes *Christian Science Monitor*, the (NY) *Daily News*, the *Wall Street Journal*, and *USA Today* (but not the *New York Post*) for U.S., and *Le Parisien/Aujourd'hui en France, La Croix, L'Humanité*, and *Les Echos* for France.
[c] In addition to core TV channels, Extended TV News Sample includes PBS for U.S. and Arte for France.
[d] All frames were coded for presence/absence in a news package. This figure refers to the number of news package in which a given frame is mentioned at least once, summed for all ten frames. Given that most news packages mention more than one frame, this figure will be greater than news packages.

(presence/absence in a news package); speakers were also coded for all specific speaker mentions. Critical statements were coded separately and were attributed to either the journalist-author or sources, but not specific types of sources.

Although TV transcripts were coded for frames, speakers, and the like in the same way as newspapers, a subsample of one-third of 2002–2006 U.S. and French TV news packages was also coded for images. An image was indicated by a unique camera angle; the number of images ranged from thirty to forty-five per television news package. Each unique image was digitally captured and subsequently coded.

Using random subsamples of 5–7 percent of the total samples, intercoder reliability using Holsti's method was calculated for frames, speakers, and critical statements at the level of the news package, as well as for images. Intercoder reliability (for pairs of coders, averaged across the three dyads) for frames ranged from .75 to 1.00 and averaged .89, and for speaker types ranged from .84 to 1.00 and averaged .92. Total number of criticisms in news packages ranged from 0 to 21: Pearson's R for Total Criticisms was .80 ($p < .001$). Holsti's reliability coefficient for presence/absence of types of criticism (administrative, character, truth, ideology, policy, and strategy) ranged from .76 to .94, and averaged .85; the coefficient for raw agreement, within one criticism, ranged from .79 to 1.00, and averaged .92. The reliability coefficient for presence/absence of targets of criticism (government, right, left, minor parties/civil society, business, and foreign) ranged from .72 to .96, and averaged .89; the coefficient for raw agreement, within one criticism, ranged from .80 to .98, and averaged .92. For image coding, intercoder agreement was .77 for topical depiction, .82 for action, .82 for scope (including closeups), and .88 for visible emotion, for an overall average of .82.

Appendix C: Immigration Context

What kind of "problem" is immigration – if indeed it is a problem at all? Social constructionists insist that "social problems" do not simply exist, out there in the "real world," but come to be understood as problematic through a process of discursive construction: in other words, various groups struggle to define some social phenomenon as problematic (or not) in various ways. However, this does not mean that there is not some social reality underlying this construction process (however tenuously or incompletely understood), as some so-called strict constructionists or postmodernists insist.[1] A "contextual" constructionist approach draws on official statistics, with some caution, as a baseline for comparison against social movement, political party, and media frames. I do not assume that academic research is necessarily and always valid, but there are a number of reasons to prefer it over popular, political, or journalistic discourse, notably the time and resources allocated to such research, the use of expert peer review, and the privileging of reasoned argumentation and systematic evidence

---

[1] In the sociological study of social problems, strict constructionists (e.g., Spector and Kitsuse 1977) decline to make empirical judgments about the validity of competing social constructions, refusing to privilege official or academic data, since these are also constructed. Contextual constructionists, among whom I count myself, would insist that one need not make overly strong objectivist claims about the precise nature of an empirical problem in order to engage with empirical research (Best 1989; Bilderback 1989; Gamson and Modigliani 1989). Although our understanding of the "social" is of course linguistically constructed, it is not simply and only discourse. As William Sewell (2005, 52) chides his fellow culturalists, "at the very time when particularly powerful changes in social and economic structures are manifested ever more insistently in our daily lives," it is curious indeed that so many academics "have ceased not only to grapple with such structures but even to admit their ontological reality."

over purely anecdotal impressions often prevalent in nonacademic discourses.[2] My object of analysis is this regard is not any particular social scientific study but, to the extent that it is possible to ascertain, the general consensus (with appropriate qualifications and caveats) across the entirety of the scientific field at a given historical moment. In what follows, I review the social scientific evidence about immigration as it relates to the following frames about immigration, roughly in order: cultural diversity, public order, integration versus national cohesion, fiscal, jobs, good worker, humanitarian, racism, and global economy. This review of the literature demonstrates the many broad similarities in French and U.S. immigration flows, costs, and benefits.

Both France and the United States historically have been among the leading migrant-receiving countries and, in raw terms, they remain among the top five worldwide. Until very recently, the percentage of French who were foreign born exceeded that in the United States. The French foreign-born population increased from 8 percent of total population in 1968 to 10 percent in 2006, whereas U.S. foreign-born population increased from 5 percent in 1970 to almost 13 percent in 2006, first officially surpassing France in the 2000 census (Fetzer 2000a: 161–166; INED 2011; MPI 2011).[3] Net migration (entries minus exits) increased in both countries during the period covered in this study: in the United States, from 660,000 (3.0 per 1,000 population) per year during the 1970s to 1.3 million (4.4 per 1,000 population) per year from 2000–2006; and in France, from 67,000 (1.3 per 1,000 population) per year during the 1970s to 144,000 (2.4 per 1,000 population) per year from 2000–2006 (MPI 2011). The estimated population of undocumented or illegal immigrants has also grown in both countries, although, again, more substantially in the United States than in France: in the U.S., from 3 million (1.3 percent of national population) in 1980 to 11.1 million (3.8 percent) in 2005; and in France, from 150,000 (0.3 percent of national population) in 1982 to 400,000 (0.7 percent) in 2005 (French Ministry of Social Affairs and National Solidarity 1984; Buffet 2006; Passel 2006; Schain 2008, 70).

In both countries, the proportion of non-European origin immigrants has increased substantially since the 1960s. In 1960, 75 percent of U.S. foreign-born residents were of European origin; by 2006, Europeans had fallen to just 12

---

[2] In this sense, I share Bourdieu's privileging of scientific knowledge, understood as a critical, reflexive enterprise. See Bourdieu and Wacquant (1992) and Bourdieu (1999).
[3] The French government does not directly provide data on foreign-born population. Following Fetzer (2000a), I calculate foreign-born population as the combined total of noncitizens and naturalized French citizens. See Grieco (2002) on the need to make these kinds of adjustments given cross-national differences in data categories.

percent of the foreign-born population. In contrast, South and Central Americans have risen from just 9 percent to 54 percent of the foreign-born population, and Asians rose during the same time period from 7 percent to 26 percent (MPI 2011). In France, from 1968 to 2007, North African nationality residents as a percentage of the foreigner population[4] increased from 24 to 29 percent, Asian nationality residents increased from 2 to 14 percent, and sub-Saharan African nationality residents increased from 1 to 12 percent (Weil 1991; INSEE 2007). Thus, although one group tends to dominate (North Africans in France; Latin Americans, and especially Mexicans, in the United States), there has been high, and even increasing, diversity in the national origins of immigrants in both countries.

Demographer Charles Hirschman (2005, 599–613) argues that "beyond population size, the most notable impact of immigration has been the broadening of the social and cultural diversity of the American population"; moreover, historically, first- and second-generation immigrants (along with other relatively marginalized populations, such as blacks, gays, Jews, etc.) have contributed disproportionately to the arts and have helped to "define 'Americanness' in novel ways." In France, as well, North and sub-Saharan African writers, musicians, and artists have become increasingly prominent in French popular as well as "high" culture (Tarr 2005; Hargreaves 2007). Thus, there is ample phenomenological evidence to support the cultural diversity frame.

Conversely, evidence for the public order frame is mixed. In the United States, illegal immigrants are accused of "bring[ing] crime to our communities" (George W. Bush); in France, the claim is made that "the more we have immigration, the more we'll have insecurity" (Jacques Chirac).[5] However, beyond the self-evident fact that illegal immigration itself is a crime (a civil offense, in most cases, in the United States), research consistently challenges any causal link between immigration and criminality. According to leading immigration sociologists Rubén Rumbaut and Walter Ewing (2007), research has consistently shown that incarceration rates "among young men are lowest for immigrants, even those who are the least educated and the least acculturated" and that this finding "holds true especially for the Mexicans, Salvadorans, and Guatemalans who make up the bulk of the undocumented

---

[4] These numbers do not include naturalized citizens.
[5] Transcript of President Bush's May 15, 2006, speech on immigration, *The New York Times*, "A Nation of Laws and Immigrants," May 16, 2006, p. 22; Quotation of Jacques Chirac in *Le Nouvel Observateur*, December 1990. "*Insécurité*," less directly linked to immigration, returned as a major theme of Chirac's 2002 presidential campaign (Terral 2004; Kuhn 2005). Many other politicians in both countries have used similar language.

population"; moreover, crime rates are lower than the national average in urban areas with high immigration populations, including cities along the U.S.-Mexico border (see also Lee, Martínez, and Rosenfeld 2001). French law does not allow any data on race or ethnicity to be collected, only distinguishing between "foreigners" and "citizens." Not including arrests for illegal entry or residence in France, foreigners made up about 11 percent of police arrests in 2000 and around 14 percent of the total prison population, approximately twice their proportion (about 6 percent) of the general population, percentages that have stayed relatively constant since the mid-1970s (Tournier 1997, 547–549; Mucchielli 2003, 38). Government research focusing on the period 1996 to 2005, a period of increasing violent crime rates, once again confirmed these historical patterns, showing that (despite public discourse to the contrary) foreigners were *not* disproportionately responsible for the *increase* in violent crime (Van Eeckhout 2007, 143–145). As in the United States, raw statistics do not take into account that foreigners (especially those of non-European origin) tend to be disproportionately male, young, and of low socioeconomic status, three of the chief indicators of increased participation in criminal activities; nor do they take into account the documented greater propensity of police to be suspicious of and to arrest non–European-appearing persons (Tournier 1997; Rumbaut and Ewing 2007).

The violent fall 2005 French riots by "immigrant youths" created a worldwide impression of rampant social unrest and attendant criminal behavior among the French immigrant or immigrant-origin population (Ossman and Terrio 2006; Snow, Vliegenthart, and Corrigall-Brown 2007; Russell 2007). In fact, rates of violent crime in poor French neighborhoods (generally far less ethnically homogeneous than in the United States[6]) are lower in France than in the United States, and the French riots of 2005 resulted in less bloodshed and property damage than comparable disturbances in the United States, such as the Los Angeles riots and looting in 1992, whose participants included Latino immigrants and their offspring as well as African Americans (Jacobs 2000; Hargreaves 2007, 68). In both countries, such violent outbursts, as well as everyday crime, are clearly related to poverty, opportunities, and expectations, rather than simply legal citizenship or resident status. Long-standing immigrant generational dynamics are also at work: whereas the first generation focuses on the relative improvement from the host country gained through the act of migration, the second generation finds that moving up from that first

---

[6] See Wacquant (1993) and Hargreaves (2007, 67).

rung of the social ladder will be very slow and difficult. This gap between high expectations and low social mobility may contribute to higher crime rates (relative to new immigrants) for low-income groups of recent immigrant origin (Roché 2001; Rumbaut and Ewing 2007, 5–10). Additional research in both France and the United States finds large differences in arrest and incarceration rates of foreign-origin youths (even controlling for country of origin of parents) from one locality to another, which suggests that "local contexts" of unemployment, segregation, and discrimination play the most important role in shaping patterns of delinquency (Portes and Rumbaut 1996; Mucchielli 2003, 51).

Although France's assimilationist "republican" tradition is often contrasted with American "multiculturalism," especially in France (Horowitz 1992; Benson and Saguy 2005), immigrants tend to be highly integrated in both countries. In the United States, the second and third generations of Central/South American-origin U.S. citizens are following the classic immigrant pattern of shifting toward either the sole or primary use of English (López 1982; Portes and Rumbaut 1996, 214–216; Bean and Stevens 2003, 256). Latino and other non-European immigrant groups also exhibit increasingly high rates of intermarriage across ethnic and racial lines, another oft-used indicator of sociocultural assimilation (Bean and Stevens 2003, 256). In France, immigration historian Gérard Noiriel (1996, 178) has termed the political debate around culture that emerged during the late 1980s – between living "with our differences" versus "reinforcing the Jacobin [assimilationist] model" – a "false paradigm" that singles out the "North African youth problem" when in fact the same process of immigrant adaptation over generations is at work that "has confronted French society in general for the past century." Indeed, research shows that, much as in America, the longer immigrants stay in France, the more likely they are to move up socioeconomically (even if progress may be slow for many), to intermarry, and to have fewer children, all indicators of integration or structural assimilation (INSEE 2003; Hargreaves 2007). Despite the active efforts of many sending countries to maintain the native language for the children of immigrants, the second generation, regardless of nation of origin, is almost universally fluent in French and prefers to speak French rather than the parental language (Hargreaves 1995, 193; Schain 2008). A direct comparative survey (Brouard and Tiberj 2005) of French of recent immigrant origin and other French citizens found that the two groups were almost equally likely (in both cases, more than 80 percent) to embrace the French principle of secularism (*laicité*).

In both countries, immigrants are accused of being a fiscal drain on the government (fiscal frame) and of lowering wages for low-income workers (jobs frame). U.S. research (Smith and Edmonston 1997; Fix and Passel 2002) has tended to show short-term net fiscal costs, especially at the local level, versus long-term gains at the national level (in part, because many illegal immigrants pay taxes for Social Security and Medicare benefits that they will never receive). This local-national mismatch in fiscal costs-benefits is one important factor fueling state and municipal anti-immigration initiatives in the United States (Schuck 2011, 85). French studies consistently show that, compared to French and other European Union (EU) citizens living in France, non-EU immigrants are more likely to receive family benefits, but less likely to receive medical and retirement benefits (Bernard 2002, 161–163; Boeri, Hanson, and McCormick 2002, 74). Whether immigrants impose net fiscal costs depends on many factors – including how much they pay in taxes and how likely they are to collect benefits. Reviewing the evidence across a range of "advanced economies," Rowthorn (2008, 560) concludes that the "positive contributions of some migrants are largely or wholly offset by the negative contributions of others" and that thus "there is no strong fiscal case for or against sustained large-scale immigration." As for negative effects on domestic worker wages, undocumented immigrants in France and the United States tend to work in the same kinds of employment sectors (construction, hotels, restaurants, domestic employment) (Hollifield 1994, 162); research in both countries *does* show that new immigrant workers, especially undocumented workers, have a dampening effect on wages for low-income workers,[7] although the size of these effects is debated.[8]

Economic gains from immigration are often touted in both countries. Research suggests, however, that such economic benefits are probably minimal and are at least partly redistributive in nature. Any "immigration surplus" positive effect on a national economy is dependent precisely on immigrants increasing total output while reducing labor costs, that is, wages.[9] The greatest gains are highly concentrated: the primary beneficiaries are those owners of businesses who hire low-wage, unskilled, and usually undocumented

---

[7] For the United States, see Huber and Espenshade (1997), Smith and Edmonston (1997), Friedberg (2007), and Swain (2007). In a review of the literature, Bean and Stevens (2003, 223) conclude: "immigration appears to worsen slightly the already precarious economic positions of African Americans, especially those with a high school education or less." Other U.S. research suggests that the greatest negative effects are felt by previous waves of illegal immigrants or recently legalized immigrants (Peri 2007, 14–15). For France, Dustmann and Glitz (2005) argue that negative wage effects for low-income workers are temporary.

[8] Harvard economist George Borjas, with an estimate of 5 percent for high school dropouts, is at the high end (Borjas 2001; 2003; 2006), and Smith and Edmonston (1997), with an estimate of 1–2 percent, are at the low end. In an online interview, economist Philip Martin estimates negative wage effects at 3 percent (Hanson and Martin 2006), although this amount is contested by some economists such as David Card (2005).

[9] As Borjas (2001, 90–96) famously put it, "No pain, no gain." See also Coppel, Dumont, and Visco (2001, 4) and Nannestad (2007).

immigrants, mainly in the restaurant and hotel industries, agriculture, construction, landscaping, and some manufacturing (Hanson and Martin 2006); in a more dispersed fashion, consumers of products and services provided by these industries may benefit from lower prices.

Many immigrants in both France and the United States are economically and socially marginalized (Sayad 1995; Ngai 2004), suffer violations of their basic human and political rights (Balibar, Chemillier-Gendreau, Costa-Lascoux, and Terray 1999; Kanstroom 2007; Wax 2008, 28–29), and are victims of racism or xenophobia (Gutiérrez 1995; Bleich 2003). It should be emphasized that not all immigrants are poor. Nevertheless, in both countries, immigrants, on average, tend to have less education, earn less, and suffer from more precarious working conditions than native residents (Portes and Rumbaut 2006; Schain 2008). Humanitarian problems of immigrants first became a French cause célèbre with the exposure during the late 1960s of the horrible living conditions in immigrant shanty-towns or *bidonvilles*; the proportion of immigrants owning housing and the quality of that housing still remain well below that of long-term French residents (Hargreaves 2007, 61–68). In 2005, French unemployment rates for immigrants and their children were substantially higher than those for the general population, although, as in the United States, there were important differences depending on country of origin. Immigrants and their adult children, aged twenty-five to fifty-nine, from North Africa, sub-Saharan Africa, and Turkey, had unemployment rates approaching 20 percent, whereas immigrant populations from Spain, Italy, and Portugal had unemployment rates on average of 6 percent (less than the 7 percent rate for all nonimmigrants) (Van Eeckhout 2007). As border enforcement has toughened in both the United States and across the EU, increasing numbers of migrants have died crossing the Arizona desert or the Mediterranean (Cornelius 2001; Spijkerboer 2007; Dunn 2009).

To what extent do immigrants suffer from xenophobia or racism? Support for immigration, per se, is at best "lukewarm" in both France and the United States: surveys measuring anti-immigration sentiment on a scale find the public in both countries squarely in the middle (Fetzer 2000b, 13). Immediately after the 9/11 attacks in New York, U.S. public attitudes about immigration in general and especially about illegal immigration – although not necessarily about individual immigrants – became more negative (Segovia and Defever 2010). At the same time, there is evidence that explicit prejudice or racist attitudes by white Americans against Hispanics have declined since the 1960s (Quillian 2006); likewise, in France, "bad opinions" of North Africans have declined over the same period.[10] In the United States, there is measurable discrimination against

---

[10] The percentage of French national survey respondents having a "bad opinion" of North Africans was 60 percent in 1966, 55 percent in 1974, 49 percent in 1991, 41 percent in 1993, 32 percent in

Hispanics in employment, wages, housing, and consumer and mortgage credit, although generally less than that faced by African Americans (Pager and Shepherd 2008). In France, lower education and skill levels surely play a role in the disproportionately high unemployment rates of Maghrebin immigrants and their offspring, yet as immigration scholar Alec Hargreaves (2007, 54) notes, "even when controlled comparisons were made with French nationals of identical age and skills, Maghrebis were almost twice as likely to be out of work, suggesting that they were the victims of discriminatory policies." Likewise, although a higher percentage of Portuguese workers than Southeast Asian workers lacked work qualifications, the unemployment rate among Southeast Asian workers was much higher (Hargreaves 2007, 54). Although ethnic quotas in housing were prohibited by the 1972 law on racial discrimination, research has demonstrated that ethnic discrimination in housing policies has continued to be rampant in France (Schain 1985, 176–182; Weil 1991, 249–256, 274–275; Hargreaves 2007, 185–186).

Racist or xenophobic violent actions or menaces against immigrants, sometimes dubbed "hate crimes," are a problem in both countries. Since the United States began systematically gathering data on hate crimes in 1992, the number of incidents reported against Hispanics has remained relatively steady at about 400 to 500 per year, out of a total of 7,000 to 10,000 per year. Blacks, gays and lesbians, and Jews have tended to be the most often victimized. In 2001, after the 9/11 attacks, anti-Islamic hate crimes briefly spiked, from 28 in 2000 to 481 in 2001, but by 2006 had declined to about 150 (FBI 2012). The Southern Poverty Law Center (2007) goes beyond the numbers to document the particularly heinous nature of many hate crimes against Latino immigrants. In France, racist or xenophobic violent actions or menaces against immigrants, especially North Africans and, increasingly, Muslims of any national origin or ethnicity, have gradually but steadily increased since the 1980s, from about 50 per year in 1980 and 1981, to between 200 and 300 during the early 1990s, to from 400 to 600 from 2001 to 2008.[11]

Finally, in both the United States and France, immigration has been part and parcel of the neo-liberal restructuring of the global economy that

---

1998, and 19 percent in 2003; this compares, for example, to 8 percent with a bad opinion of "African blacks" in 2003, down from 24 percent in 1991. See Gastaut (2000, 77–82); and "Le suivi du racisme et de l'antisemitisme en France: Sondage exclusif" CSA/Le Figaro, www. csa-fr.com, accessed February 25, 2010.

[11] See Commission nationale consultative des droits de l'homme (2009) for 1993–2008 data; see Aubry and Duhamel (1995, 238) for early 1980s data. Hargreaves (1995, 157) reports that Maghrebis accounted for 78 percent of those injured and 92 percent of those killed in attacks counted by state authorities as officially racist in nature between 1980 and 1993.

has occurred since the early 1970s, increasing job insecurity and income inequality for immigrant and nonimmigrant workers across developed as well as developing countries (Sassen 1999; Stiglitz 2003; Harvey 2005). Given its weaker welfare state, neo-liberal restructuring of the economy has had more far-reaching effects in the United States than in France. Just to give one indicator, the percentage of total national income (not including capital gains) controlled by the top 0.1 percent of the population was about the same in France and the United States in 1970 – about 2 percent; by 2005, this percentage had risen dramatically to 7.8 percent in the U.S., while remaining steady at about 2.5 percent in France (Alvaredo, Atkinson, Piketty, and Saez 2012).

Over the past four decades, all of these aspects of immigration have been discursively promoted at various times by governments, political parties, civil society groups, and academic experts. This is not to say that the rhetorical and policy playing field is even: in both the United States and France, the pro-immigration advocacy sector of civil society is much better funded and organized than its anti-immigration or restrictionist counterpart. In France, the budgets of immigrant rights groups like France Terre d'Asile (France Land of Asylum; €35 million), Amnesty International France (€15 million), Ligue des droits de l'homme (LDH, Human Rights League; €20 million), and Cimade (a long-established Protestant humanitarian organization; €7 million) together dwarf the €5 million budget of the National Front party, the main restrictionist voice in France. In the United States, the largest pro-immigration organizations such as the National Council of La Raza ($40 million), the American Civil Liberties Union (ACLU; $31 million), and the American Immigration Lawyers Association ($12 million) are better funded than the main restrictionist groups such as the Federation for American Immigration Reform ($8 million), U.S. English ($5 million), and Numbers USA ($3 million).[12] On the other hand, despite their smaller paid staffs and budgets, restrictionist groups have tried to use the power of mobilized citizens and public opinion, as expressed in surveys, to advance their causes. Governments and the political opposition, with an eye on the next election, have not infrequently been the direct or indirect allies of restrictionist politics and policies. Table C.1 provides a chronology of the key political events in the French and U.S. national immigration policy debates since the 1970s.

---

[12] Numbers are from organization websites. See Online Appendix for a complete listing of founding, membership, budgets, and funding sources of a cross-section of the major immigration-related civil society organizations in both countries.

TABLE C.1. *Immigration Politics Chronology for France and the United States*

	France	United States
1970s	1972: Protests against restrictive Marcellin-Fontanet law 1973: Ordre Nouveau protest against uncontrolled immigration 1974: President Giscard d'Estaing ends worker immigration	1972–1974: UFW pickets against illegal immigrant "strikebreakers" 1974: U.S. Attorney General Saxbe warns of national crisis 1975: Under pressure, UFW drops campaign against illegal immigrant workers 1979: Founding of FAIR
1980s	1981: Socialist president Mitterrand elected, legalizes immigrant associations 1983: *Marche des beurs* "for equality of rights"; National Front wins local elections in Dreux 1984: Founding of antiracism group SOS-Racisme 1986: Pasqua law immigration restrictions 1989: First "Headscarves" affair prompts discussion of "*laïcité*"; Formation of "High Council on Integration"	1982: MALDEF victory in *Plyler vs. Doe* Supreme Court case establishes right of undocumented immigrant children to public school education; Founding of immigrant rights organization National Immigration Forum 1983: Founding of U.S. English 1986: Passage of English-only Proposition 63 in California; U.S. IRCA legislation legalizes millions of immigrants and creates (unenforced) penalties for employers who hire illegal immigrants
1990s	1991: *Banlieue* riots in Sartrouville and Mantes-la-Jolie; Socialist Prime Minister Edith Cresson proposes "charter airflights" to deport illegal immigrants 1996: *Sans papiers* occupation of St. Bernard church in Paris 1998: Bruno Megret splits from National Front, forming MNR party	1990: Light Up the Border anti-illegal immigration protests in southern California 1994: NAFTA treaty with Mexico contributes to increasing immigration to U.S. 1994: Proposition 187 passes in California 1996: U.S. welfare reform bill lessens benefits for legal immigrants 1997: Founding of restrictionist Numbers USA
2000s	2002: Le Pen defeats socialist Lionel Jospin to earn spot on second presidential ballot 2003–04: Second "headscarves affair"; passage of law banning "ostentatious" religious symbols in secondary schools 2005: Widespread *banlieue* riots 2006: Protests against Sarkozy "*immigration choisie*" bill and deportations of *sans papier* children	2000: AFL-CIO drops support for employer sanctions; Restrictionist Proposition 200 passes in Arizona; Founding of group Humane Borders 2004: Minuteman (anti-illegal immigration) Project 2005: Republican-sponsored Resolution 4473, making illegal immigration a felony, passes House of Representatives 2006: Massive pro-immigrant protests against HR 4473 across U.S.

FAIR, Federation for American Immigration Reform; IRCA, Immigration Reform and Control Act; MALDEF, Mexican American Legal Defense and Educational Fund; MNR, National Republican Movement (France); NAFTA, North American Free Trade Association; UFW, United Farm Workers

References

Adams, Paul C. 2007. *Atlantic Reverberations: French Representations of an American Presidential Election*. Aldershot, UK: Ashgate.

Aeschimann, Eric. 2007. *Libération et ses fantômes*. Paris: Seuil.

Albert, Pierre. 1990. *La presse française*. Paris: La Documentation française.

Albert, Pierre. 1998. *La presse française*. Paris: La Documentation française.

Albert, Pierre. 2004. *La presse française*. Paris: La Documentation française.

Alexander, Jeffrey C. 1981. "The mass news media in systemic, historical and comparative perspective." In E. Katz and T. Szecsko, eds., *Mass Media and Social Change*, 17–51. Beverly Hills, CA: Sage.

Alexander, Jeffrey C., and Philip Smith. 1993. "The discourse of American civil society: A new proposal for cultural studies." *Theory and Society* 22, 151–207.

Altheide, David L. 1987. "Format and symbols in TV coverage of terrorism." *International Studies Quarterly* 31, 161–176.

Altheide, David L., and Robert P. Snow. 1979. *Media Logic*. Thousand Oaks, CA: Sage.

Alvaredo, Facundo, Tony Atkinson, Thomas Piketty, and Emmanuel Saez. 2012. The World Top Incomes Database. Available at http://g-mond.parisschoolofeconomics.eu/topincomes/. Accessed May 9, 2012.

Anderson, C.W. 2013. *Rebuilding the News*. Philadelphia: Temple University Press.

Anderson, Simon P. 2005. "Regulation of television advertising." Working Paper, Department of Economics, University of Virginia. Available at: http://www.virginia.edu/economics/Workshops/papers/anderson/tvadrego81705.pdf. Accessed April 19, 2010.

Asline, Jacques. 1990. *La Bataille du 20 Heures: Quarante ans de journaux télévisés*. Paris: Acropole.

Aubry, Martine, and Olivier Duhamel. 1995. *Petit dictionnaire pour lutter contre l'extrême droite*. Paris: Seuil.

Aufderheide, Patricia. 1990. "After the Fairness Doctrine: Controversial broadcast programming and the public interest." *Journal of Communication* 40(30), 47–72.

Aufderheide, Patricia. 2000. *The Daily Planet: A Critic on the Capitalist Culture Beat*. Minneapolis: University of Minnesota Press.

Auletta, Ken. 1992. *Three Blind Mice: How the TV Networks Lost Their Way*. New York: Vintage Books.

Bacon, David. 2008. *Illegal People: How Globalization Creates Migration and Criminalizes Immigrants*. Boston: Beacon Press.

Bagdikian, Ben H. 1992. *The Media Monopoly*, 4th edition. Boston: Beacon Press.

Bagdikian, Ben H. 2004. *The New Media Monopoly*. Boston: Beacon Press.

Baker, C. Edwin. 1994. *Advertising and a Democratic Press*. Princeton: Princeton University Press.

Baker, C. Edwin. 2002. *Media, Markets, and Democracy*. Cambridge, UK: Cambridge University Press.

Baker, C. Edwin. 2007. *Media Concentration and Democracy: Why Ownership Matters*. Cambridge, UK: Cambridge University Press.

Balibar, Étienne, Monique Chemillier-Gendreau, Jacqueline Costa-Lascoux, and Emmanuel Terray. 1999. *Sans-papiers: l'archaïsme fatal*. Paris: Editions la Découverte.

Balle, Francis. 2001. *Médias et sociétés*, 10th edition. Paris: Montchrestien.

Barbrook, Richard. 1995. *Media Freedom: The Contradictions of Communications in the Age of Modernity*. London: Pluto Press.

Barnhurst, Kevin G. 2002. "News geography & monopoly: the form of reports on U.S. newspaper internet sites." *Journalism Studies* 3(4), 477–489.

Barnhurst, Kevin G. 2010. "The form of reports on US newspaper Internet sites: an update." *Journalism Studies* 11(4), 555–566.

Barnhurst, Kevin G., and Diana Mutz. 1997. "American journalism and the decline in event-centered reporting." *Journal of Communication* 47(4), 27–53.

Barnhurst, Kevin G., and John Nerone. 2001. *The Form of News: A History*. New York: Guilford Press.

Barnouw, Erik. 1977. *Tube of Plenty: The Evolution of American Television*. New York: Oxford University Press.

Battegay, Alain, and Ahmed Boubeker. 1993. *Les Images publiques de l'immigration*. Paris: CIEMI L'Harmattan.

Baumgartner, Frank. 1996. "Public interest groups in France and the United States." *Governance* 9(1), 1–22.

Bean, Frank D., and Gillian Stevens. 2003. *America's Newcomers and the Dynamics of Diversity*. New York: Russell Sage Foundation.

Becker, L. B., T. Vlad, J. Prine, J. Huh, A. Punathambekar, T. Drake, G. Daniels, and G. M. Kosicki. 2001. Annual survey of journalism and mass communication enrollments. Report presented at the annual convention of the AEJMC, Washington, D.C.

Beckett, Katherine. 1996. "Culture and the politics of signification: the case of child sexual abuse." *Social Problems* 43, 57–76.

Behr, Edward. 1993. "L'ami américain: si je racontais *Libération*." *Libération*, June 5–6, p. 20.

Bennett, W. Lance. 1990. "Toward a theory of press-state relations in the United States." *Journal of Communication* 40(2), 103–125.

Bennett, W. Lance. 2011. *News: The Politics of Illusion*, 9th edition. New York: Pearson-Longman.

Bennett, W. Lance, Regina G. Lawrence, and Steven Livingston. 2007. *When the Press Fails: Political Power and the News Media from Iraq to Katrina*. Chicago: University of Chicago Press.

Benoît, Jean. 1980. *Dossier E comme esclaves*. Paris: Alain Moreau.

Benson, Rodney. 1999. "Field theory in comparative context: a new paradigm for media studies." *Theory and Society* 29, 463–498.

Benson, Rodney. 2003. "Commercialism and critique: California's alternative weeklies." In J. Curran and N. Couldry, eds., *Contesting Media Power: Alternative Media in a Networked World*, 111–127. Lanham, MD: Rowman and Littlefield.

Benson, Rodney. 2004. "La fin du *Monde*? Tradition and change in the French press." *French Politics, Culture & Society* 22(1), 108–126.

Benson, Rodney. 2005. "Mapping field variation: journalism in France and the United States." In R. Benson and E. Neveu, eds., *Bourdieu and the Journalistic Field*, 85–112. Cambridge, UK: Polity.

Benson, Rodney. 2006. "News media as a 'journalistic field': what Bourdieu adds to new institutionalism, and vice versa." *Political Communication* 23(2), 187–202.

Benson, Rodney. 2008. "Normative theories of journalism." In W. Donsbach, ed., *The Blackwell International Encyclopedia of Communication*, 2591–2597. New York: Blackwell.

Benson, Rodney. 2010a. "American journalism and the politics of diversity." In R. A. Lind, ed., *Race/Gender/Media: Considering Diversity Across Audiences, Content, and Producers*, 2nd ed., 333–340. London: Allyn & Bacon.

Benson, Rodney. 2010b. "What makes for a critical press? A case study of French and U.S. immigration news coverage." *International Journal of Press/Politics* 15(1), 3–24.

Benson, Rodney, and Daniel C. Hallin. 2007. "How states, markets and globalization shape the news: the French and U.S. national press, 1965–1997." *European Journal of Communication* 22 (1), 27–48.

Benson, Rodney, and Matthew Powers. 2011. *Public Media and Political Independence*. Washington, DC: Free Press. Available online at: http://www.freepress.net/blog/11/02/10/public-media-and-political-independence-lessons-future-journalism-around-world

Benson, Rodney, and Abigail C. Saguy. 2005. "Constructing social problems in an age of globalization: a French-American comparison." *American Sociological Review* 70(2), 233–259.

Benson, Rodney, Mark Blach-Ørsten, Matthew Powers, Ida Willig, and Sandra Vera Zambrano. 2012. "Media systems online and off: the form of print and online news in the United States, France, and Denmark." *Journal of Communication* 62(1), 21–38.

Berezin, Mabel. 2009. *Illiberal Politics in Neo-Liberal Times: Culture, Security and Populism in the New Europe*. Cambridge, UK: Cambridge University Press.

Berg, Justin Allen. 2009. "White public opinion toward undocumented immigrants: threat and interpersonal environment." *Sociological Perspectives* 52(1), 39–58.

Berkowitz, Dan, and Lyombe Eko. 2007. "Blasphemy as sacred rite/right." *Journalism Studies* 8(5), 779–797.

Bernard, Philippe. 2002. *Immigration: le défi mondial*. Paris: Gallimard.

Berning, Nora. 2010. "The cultural television Channel Arte and the (non-)existence of a cross-border Franco-German public sphere." *Web Journal of French Media Studies* 8, 1–14.

Bernstein, Nina. 2011. "The making of an outlaw generation." In M. M. Suárez-Orozco, V. Louie, and R. Suro, eds., *Writing Immigration*, 23–43. Berkeley: University of California Press.

Berthaut, Jérôme, Eric Darras, and Sylvain Laurens. 2009. "Pourquoi les faits-divers stigmatisent-ils?" *Réseaux* 157–158, 89–125.

Best, Joel. 1989. "Extending the constructionist perspective: An introduction – and a conclusion." In J. Best, ed., *Images of Issues*, 243–253. New York: Aldine de Gruyter.

Bilderback, Loy. 1989. "'A greater threat than the Soviet Union': Mexican immigration as social problem." In J. Best, ed., *Images of Issues*, 223–241. New York: Aldine de Gruyter.

Bird, Elizabeth, ed. 2010. *The Anthropology of News & Journalism: Global Perspectives*. Bloomington: Indiana University Press.

Blatt, David. 1997. "Immigrant politics in a republican nation." In A. G. Hargreaves and M. McKinney, eds., *Post-Colonial Cultures in France*, 40–55. London: Routledge.

Bleich, Erik. 2003. *Race Politics in Britain and France: Ideas and Policymaking since the 1960s*. Cambridge, UK: University of Cambridge Press.

Blin, Frédéric. 2002. "Les sécretaries de rédaction et les éditeurs de *Libération*." *Réseaux* 111, 165–190.

Bloemraad, Irene, Kim Voss, and Taeku Lee. 2011. "The Protests of 2006: What Were They, How Do We Understand Them, Where Do We Go?" In K. Voss and I. Bloemraad, eds., *Rallying for Immigrant Rights*, 3–43. Berkeley: University of California Press.

Blumler, Jay G., Malcolm Brynin, and T. J. Nossiter. 1986. "Broadcasting finance and programme quality: an international review." *European Journal of Communication* 1(3), 343–364.

Blumler, Jay G., and Michael Gurevitch. 2001. "'Americanization' reconsidered: U.K.-U.S. campaign communication comparisons across time." In W. L. Bennett and R. M. Entman, eds., *Mediated Politics*, 380–403. Cambridge, UK: Cambridge University Press.

Boczkowski, Pablo J. 2004. *Digitizing the News: Innovation in Online Newspapers*. Cambridge, MA: MIT Press.

Boczkowski, Pablo J. 2010. *News at Work: Imitation in an Age of Information Abundance*. Chicago: University of Chicago Press.

Boeri, Tito, Gordon Hanson, and Barry McCormick. 2002. *Immigration Policy and the Welfare System*. Oxford: Oxford University Press.

Bogart, Leo. 1989. *Press and Public: Who Reads What, When, Where, and Why in American Newspapers*. Hillsdale, NJ: Lawrence Erlbaum Associates.

Bonnafous, Simone. 1991. *L'Immigration prise aux mots: Les immigrés dans la presse au tournant des années 80*. Paris: Éditions Kimé.

Borjas, George J. 2001. *Heaven's Door: Immigration Policy and the American Economy*. Princeton: Princeton University Press.

Borjas, George J. 2003. "The labor demand curve is downward sloping: reexamining the impact of immigration on the labor market." *Quarterly Journal of Economics* 118, 1335–1374.

Borjas, George J. 2006. Immigration in high-skill labor markets: the impact of foreign students on the earnings of doctorates (March). NBER Working Paper No. W12085.

Boudana, Sandrine. 2010a. *Journalistic Objectivity as a Performance: Construction of a Model of Evaluation and Application to the Case of the French Press Coverage of the Second Intifada*. Ph.D. Dissertation, Humanities and Social Sciences, Hebrew University.

Boudana, Sandrine. 2010b. "On the values guiding the French practice of journalism: Interviews with thirteen war correspondents." *Journalism* 11(3), 293–310.

Bourdieu, Pierrre. 1979. "Public opinion does not exist." In A. Mattelart and S. Siegelaub, eds., *Communication and Class Struggle*, 124–130. New York: International General.

Bourdieu, Pierre. 1984. *Distinction*. Cambridge, MA: Harvard University Press.

Bourdieu, Pierre. 1993. *The Field of Cultural Production.* New York: Columbia University Press.

Bourdieu, Pierre. 1995. *The Rules of Art.* Stanford: Stanford University Press.

Bourdieu, Pierre. 1998. *On Television.* New York: New Press.

Bourdieu, Pierre. 1999. "Understanding." In P. Bourdieu, ed., *The Weight of the World,* 607–626. Cambridge, UK: Polity.

Bourdieu, Pierre. 2000. "Libé vingt ans après." *Actes de la recherches en sciences sociales* 101–102, 39.

Bourdieu, Pierre. 2005. "The political field, the social science field, and the journalistic field." In R. Benson and E. Neveu, eds., *Bourdieu and the Journalistic Field,* 29–47. Cambridge, UK: Polity.

Bourdieu, Pierre, and Hans Haacke. 1995. *Free Exchange.* Cambridge, UK: Polity.

Bourdieu, Pierre, and Loïc Wacquant. 1992. *An Invitation to Reflexive Sociology.* Chicago: University of Chicago Press.

Bourdon, Jérôme. 1994. "Alone in the desert of 50 million viewers: audience ratings in French television." *Media, Culture & Society* 16, 375–394.

Bowen, John R. 2007. *Why the French Don't Like Headscarves: Islam, the State, and Public Space.* Princeton: Princeton University Press.

Branton, Regina, and Johanna Dunaway. 2008. "English- and Spanish-language media coverage of immigration: a comparative analysis." *Social Science Quarterly* 89(4), 1006–1022.

Branton, Regina, and Johanna Dunaway. 2009. "Slanted newspaper coverage of immigration: the importance of economics and geography." *The Policy Studies Journal* 37(2), 257–273.

Brigouleix, Bernard. 1977. *L'Extrême Droite en France.* Paris: Fayolle.

Broersma, Marcel J., ed. 2007. *Form and Style in Journalism. European Newspapers and the Representation of News, 1880–2005.* Dudley, MA: Peeters

Brossard, Dominique, James Shanahan, and Katherine McComas. 2004. "Are issue-cycles culturally constructed? A comparison of French and American coverage of global climate change." *Mass Communication & Society* 7(3), 359–377.

Brouard, Sylvain, and Vincent Tiberj. 2005. *Français comme les autres?* Paris: CEVIPOF.

Buffet, François-Noël (rapporteur). 2006. "Sénat Rapport de la commission d'enquête sur l'immigration clandestine." Paris: *Journal officiel* (April 7).

Buzzi, Paul. 1994. "Le Front national: entre national-populism et idéologie d'extrême-droite." In P. Bréchon, ed., *Le discours politique en France: Evolution des idées partisanes,* 15–36. Paris: La Documentation française.

Calavita, Kitty. 1996. "The new politics of immigration: 'balanced-budget conservatism' and the symbolism of Proposition 187." *Social Problems* 43(3), 284–305.

Calhoun, Craig. 1992. "Introduction." In C. Calhoun, ed., *Habermas and the Public Sphere,* 1–50. Cambridge, MA: MIT Press.

Card, David. 2005. "Is the new immigration really so bad?" *Economic Journal* 115(506), 300–323.

Carey, James W. 1995. "The press, public opinion, and public discourse." In T. L. Glasser and C. T. Salmon, eds., *Public Opinion and the Communication of Consent.* New York: Guilford Press.

Castells, Manuel. 1997. *The Power of Identity; The Information Age: Economy, Society, and Culture* (Vol. 2). Oxford: Blackwell.

Chalaby, Jean K. 1996. "Journalism as an Anglo-American invention: a comparison of the development of French and Anglo-American journalism, 1830s–1920s." *European Journal of Communication* 11, 303–326.

Chalaby, Jean K. 2002. *The de Gaulle Presidency and the Media: Statism and Public Communications*. New York: Palgrave MacMillan.

Chalaby, Jean K. 2004. "Scandal and the Rise of Investigative Reporting in France." *American Behavioral Scientist* 47(9), 1194–1207.

Chalaby, Jean K. 2005. "French political communication in a comparative perspective: the media and the issue of freedom." *Modern & Contemporary France* 13(3), 273–290.

Champagne, Patrick. 1990. *Faire l'Opinion*. Paris: Les Editions de Minuit.

Champagne, Patrick. 2005. "The double dependency: the journalistic field between politics and markets." In R. Benson and E. Neveu, eds., *Bourdieu and the Journalistic Field*, 48–63. Cambridge, UK: Polity.

Champagne, Patrick, and Dominique Marchetti. 2005. "The contaminated blood scandal: reframing medical news." In R. Benson and E. Neveu, eds., *Bourdieu and the Journalistic Field*, 113–134. Cambridge, UK: Polity.

Chaniac, Régine, ed. 2009. *L'Audience*. Paris: CNRS.

Chaplin, Tamara. 2007. *Turning on the Mind: French Philosophers on Television*. Chicago: University of Chicago Press.

Chapman, Herrick, and Laura L. Frader, eds. 2004. *Race in France*. New York: Berghahn Books.

Charles, Christophe. 2004. *Le siècle de la presse: 1830–1939*. Paris: Seuil.

Charon, Jean-Marie. 1991. *La presse en France de 1945 à nos jours*. Paris: Seuil.

Charon, Jean-Marie. 1996. *La presse quotidienne*. Paris: La Découverte.

Charon, Jean-Marie. 2003. "Journalist training in France." In R. Fröhlich and C. Holtz-Bacha, eds., *Journalism Education in Europe and North America: An International Comparison*, 139–167. Cresskill, NJ: Hampton Press.

Charon, Jean-Marie. 2005. *La presse quotidienne*. Paris: La Découverte.

Chavez, Leo R. 2001. *Covering Immigration*. Berkeley: University of California Press.

Chavez, Leo R. 2008. *The Latino Threat*. Stanford: Stanford University Press.

Chomsky, Aviva. 2007. *'They Take Our Jobs!' and 20 Other Myths about Immigration*. Boston: Beacon Press.

Chong, Dennis, and James N. Druckman. 2007. "Framing theory." *Annual Review of Political Science* 10, 103–126.

Christian Science Monitor. 2008. "About the Monitor." Available at: http://www.csmonitor.com/aboutus/about_the_monitor.html. Accessed March 6, 2008.

Christians, Clifford G., Theodore L. Glasser, Denis McQuail, Kaarle Nordenstreng, and Robert A. White. 2009. *Normative Theories of the Media*. Urbana: University of Illinois Press.

Clark, Priscilla Parkhurst. 1987. *Literary France: The Making of a Culture*. Berkeley: University of California Press.

Clayman, Steven E., and Ann Reisner. 1998. "Gatekeeping in action: editorial conferences and assessments of newsworthiness." *American Sociological Review* 63, 178–199.

Clément, Jérôme. 2011. *Le choix d'Arte*. Paris: Bernard Grasset.

Collins, Ronald K. L. 1992. *Dictating Content: How Advertising Pressure Can Corrupt a Free Press*. Washington, DC: Center for the Study of Commercialism.

Collovald, Annie. 2001. "Des désordres sociaux aux violences urbaines. La dépolitisation du débat sur l'immigration." *Actes de la recherche en sciences sociales* 136–137, 104–113.

Commission nationale consultative des droits de l'homme. 2009. Annual Report [2008]. Paris: La Documentation française.

Compton, James R., and Paul Benedetti. 2010. "Labour, new media, and the institutional restructuring of journalism." *Journalism Studies* 11(4), 487–499.

Conniff, Ruth. 1993. "The war on aliens: the right calls the shots." *The Progressive* (October): 22–29.

Connor, Roger. 1986. "Re: quo vadis." Internal Memorandum. Federation for American Immigration Reform. Washington, DC.

Cook, Timothy E. 1998. *Governing with the News: The News Media as a Political Institution*. Chicago: University of Chicago Press.

Cooper, Ann 1986. "Immigration reformer stirs the melting pot." *National Journal*. May 17.

Coppel, Jonathan, Jean-Christophe Dumont, and Ignazio Visco. 2001. "Trends in immigration and economic consequences." Economics Department Working Paper No. 284, OECD.

Cornelius, Wayne A. 2001. "Death at the border: efficacy and unintended consequences of U.S. immigration control policy." *Population and Development Review* 27 (4), 661–685.

Cotteret, Jean-Marie. 2000. *La magie du discours: Précis de rhétorique audiovisuelle*. Paris: Michalon.

Cottle, Simon. 1995. "The production of news formats: determinants of mediated public contestation." *Media, Culture & Society* 17, 275–291.

Cowan, Geoffrey, and David Westphal. 2010. *Public Policy and Funding the News*. Los Angeles: USC Annenberg School.

Craig, Ann L. 1981. "Mexican immigration: changing terms of the debate in the United States and Mexico." Working Paper, Program in United States-Mexican Studies, University of California, San Diego, La Jolla, CA.

Cranberg, Gilbert, Randall P. Bezanson, and John Soloski. 2001. *Taking Stock: Journalism and the Publicly-Traded Newspaper Company*. Ames: Iowa State University Press.

Crawford, James. 1992. *Hold Your Tongue: Bilingualism and the Politics of 'English Only.'* New York: Addison-Wesley.

Crossley, Nick. 2004. "On systematically distorted communication: Bourdieu and the socio-analysis of publics." *Sociological Review* 52, 88–112.

CSA [Conseil supérieur de l'audiovisuel]. 2000. *Bilan de la société privée TF1*. Paris: CSA.

Curran, James. 2011. *Media and Democracy*. London: Routledge.

Curran, James, Shanto Iyengar, Anker Brink Lund, and Inka Salovaara-Moring. 2009. "Media system, public knowledge and democracy: a comparative study." *European Journal of Communication* 24(5), 5–26.

D'Angelo, Paul, and Jim A. Kuypers, eds. 2010. *Doing News Framing Analysis: Empirical and Theoretical Perspectives*. New York: Routledge.

Darnton, Robert. 1975. "Writing news and telling stories." *Daedalus* 104, 175–194.

Darras, Eric. 2005. "Media consecration of the political order." In R. Benson and E. Neveu, eds., *Bourdieu and the Journalistic Field*, 156–173. Cambridge, UK: Polity.

Davidson, Roei. 2008. "'An insider's game': framing media mergers in France and the United States." *Gazette* 68(4), 331–346.

Davis, Aeron. 2007. *The Mediation of Power*. London: Routledge.

Delgado, Hector L. 1993. *New Immigrants, Old Unions: Organizing Undocumented Workers in Los Angeles*. Philadelphia: Temple University Press.

Dell'Orto, Giovanna, and Vicki L. Birchfield, eds. 2013. *Reporting at the Southern Borders*. London: Routledge.

Delporte, Christian. 1999. *Les journalistes en France 1880–1950: Naissance et construction d'une profession*. Paris: Seuil.

Dennis, Everette E. 2004. "A free and subsidized press? – The European experience with newspaper subsidies and other government interventions." Paper prepared for 2004 Breaux Symposium, March 19–20, Louisiana State University.

Derieux, Emannuel. 2001. *Droit des médias*. Paris: Dalloz.

De Tarlé, Antoine. 1980. "The press and the state in France." In A. Smith, ed., *Newspapers and Democracy: International Essays on a Changing Medium*, 127–148. Cambridge, MA: MIT Press.

Deuze, Mark. 2007. *Media Work*. Cambridge, UK: Polity.

Devillard, Valérie, Marie-Françoise Lafosse, Christine Leteinturier, Jean-Pierre Marhuenda, and Rémy Rieffel. 1992. *Les journalistes français en 1990: Radiographie d'une profession*. Paris: La Documentation française.

Devillard, Valérie, Marie-Françoise Lafosse, Christine Leteinturier, and Rémy Rieffel. 2001. *Les journalists français à l'aube de l'an 2000: Profils et parcours*. Paris: La Documentation française.

Diamond, Edwin. 1994. *Behind the Times: Inside the New New York Times*. New York: Villard.

DiMaggio, Paul, and Kristen Stenberg. 1985. "Conformity and diversity in American resident theaters." In J.H. Balfe and M.J. Balfe, eds., *Art, Ideology, and Politics*, 116–139. New York: Praeger.

DiMaggio, Paul J., and W.W. Powell. 1991. "Introduction." In W.W. Powell and P.J. DiMaggio, eds., *The New Institutionalism in Organizational Analysis*, 1–38. Chicago: University of Chicago Press.

Dionne, E.J., Jr. 2008. "Migrating attitudes, shifting opinions: the role of public opinion in the immigration debate." In R. Suro, ed., *A Report on the Media and the Immigration Debate*. Washington, DC: Brookings Institution.

Dowd, Timothy J., Kathleen Liddle, Kim Lupo, and Anne Borden. 2002. "Organizing the musical canon: the repertoires of major U.S. symphony orchestras, 1842 to 1969." *Poetics* 30, 35–61.

Downie, Leonard, Jr., and Michael Schudson. 2009. "The reconstruction of American journalism." *Columbia Journalism Review*, published online October 19. Available at: http://www.cjr.org/reconstruction/the_reconstruction_of_american.php?page=all

Dunaway, Johanna, Marisa A. Abrajano, and Regina P. Branton. 2007. "Agenda setting, public opinion, and the issue of immigration reform." Center for Comparative Immigration Studies Working Paper 162, University of California, San Diego.

Dunn, Timothy J. 2009. *Blockading the Border and Human Rights*. Austin: University of Texas Press.

Dustmann, Christian, and Albrecht Glitz. 2005. *Immigration, Jobs and Wages: Theory, Evidence and Opinion*. London: Centre for Economic Policy Research.

Duval, Julien. 2005. "Economic journalism in France." In R. Benson and E. Neveu, eds., *Bourdieu and the Journalistic Field*, 135–155. Cambridge, UK: Polity.

Ekström, Mats, Bengt Johansson, and Larsåke Larsson. 2006. "Journalism and local politics: a study of scrutiny and accountability in Swedish journalism." *Journalism Studies* 7(2), 292–311.

Entman, Robert M. 1993. "Framing: toward clarification of a fractured paradigm." *Journal of Communication* 43, 51–58.

Entman, Robert M. 2004. *Projections of Power: Framing News, Public Opinion, and U.S. Foreign Policy.* Chicago: University of Chicago Press.

Entman, Robert M. 2006. "Punctuating the homogeneity of institutionalized news: abusing prisoners at Abu Ghraib versus killing civilians at Fallujah." *Political Communication* 23, 215–224.

Entman, Robert M. 2012. *Scandal and Silence: Media Responses to Presidential Misconduct.* Cambridge, UK: Polity.

Epstein, Edward Jay. 1973. *News from Nowhere: Television and the News.* New York: Random House.

Espenshade, Thomas J., and Katherine Hempstead. 1995. "Contemporary American attitudes toward U.S. immigration." *International Migration Review* 30, 535–570.

Esser, Frank. 1998. "Editorial structures and work principles in British and German newsrooms." *European Journal of Communication* 13, 375–405.

Esser, Frank. 2008. "Dimensions of political news cultures: sound bite and image bite news in France, Germany, Great Britain, and the United States." *Press/Politics* 13(4), 401–428.

Etats généraux de la presse écrite. (2009). Available at: http://www.etatsgenerauxdelap resseecrite.fr/home/index.php. Accessed October 13, 2010.

Ettema, James S., and Theodore L. Glasser. 1998. *Custodians of Conscience: Investigative Journalism and Public Virtue.* New York: Columbia University Press.

Eveno, Patrick. 2001. *Le journal Le Monde: une histoire d'indépendance.* Paris: Editions Odile Jacob.

Eveno, Patrick. 2003. *L'argent de la presse française des années 1820 à nos jours.* Paris: Editions du CTHS.

Eveno, Patrick. 2004. "Du l'organe du Parti au journal d'opinion: *L'Humanité*, une entreprise politique." In C. Delporte, C. Pennetier, J-F. Sirinelli, and S. Wolikow, eds. *L'Humanité de Jaurès à nos jours*, 199–228. Paris: Nouveau Monde.

Eveno, Patrick. 2008. *La presse quotidienne nationale: fin de partie ou renouveau?* Paris: Vuibert.

FAIR. 1993. Federation for American Immigration Reform Annual Report. Washington, DC.

Favell, Adrian. 1998. *Philosophies of Integration: Immigration and the Idea of Citizenship in France and Britain.* New York: St. Martin's Press.

FBI. 2012. U.S. Federal Bureau of Investigation Uniform Crime Reports: Hate Crimes, Reports 1995–2006. Available at: http://www.fbi.gov/about-us/cjis/ucr/ucr/.

FCC. 2010. "About the FCC [Federal Communications Commission]." Available at: http://transition.fcc.gov/aboutus.html. Accessed April 18.

Feldblum, Miriam. 1993. "Paradoxes of ethnic politics: the case of Franco-Maghrebis in France." *Ethnic and Racial Studies* 16(1), 52–74.

Fenton, Natalie, ed. 2010. *New Media, Old News.* London: Sage.

Ferenczi, Thomas. 1993. *L'invention du journalisme en France.* Paris: Plon.

Fernández, Celestino, and Lawrence R. Pedroza. 1981. "The border patrol and news media coverage of undocumented Mexican immigration during the 1970s." Working Paper, Mexican American Studies & Research Center, University of Arizona, Tucson.

Ferree, Myra Marx, William Anthony Gamson, Jürgen Gerhards, and Dieter Rucht. 2002. *Shaping Abortion Discourse: Democracy and the Public Sphere in Germany and the United States.* Cambridge, UK: Cambridge University Press.

Fetzer, Joel S. 2000a. *Public Attitudes toward Immigration in the United States, France, and Germany.* Cambridge, UK: Cambridge University Press.

Fetzer, Joel S. 2000b. "Economic self-interest or cultural marginality? Anti-immigration sentiment and nativist political movements in France, Germany and the USA." *Journal of Ethnic and Migration Studies* 26(1), 5–23.

Finnemann, N. O., and B. H. Thomasen. 2005. "Denmark: multiplying news." In R. Van der Wurff and E. Lauf, eds., *Print and Online Newspapers in Europe*, 91–103. Amsterdam: Het Spinhuis Publishers.

Fishman, Mark. 1980. *Manufacturing the News.* Austin: University of Texas Press.

Fix, Michael, and Jeffrey Passel. 2002. "The scope and impact of welfare reform's immigrant provisions." Urban Institute Discussion Paper 02–03.

Fligstein, Neil. 1990. *The Transformation of Corporate Control.* Cambridge, MA: Harvard University Press.

Frank, Thomas. 2002. *One Market Under God.* New York: Vintage.

Freedman, Des. 2008. *The Politics of Media Policy.* Cambridge, UK: Polity.

Freeman, Gary P. 1979. *Immigrant Labor and Racial Conflict in Industrial Societies: The French and British Experience 1945–1975.* Princeton: Princeton University Press.

Freiberg, J. W. 1981. *French Press: Class, State, and Ideology.* New York: Praeger.

French Ministry of Social Affairs and National Solidarity. 1984. "The employment market and immigrants in an irregular situation: lessons from the recent legalization exercise in France." *International Migration Review* 18(3), 558–578.

Friedberg, Rachel M. 2007. "Testimony before the U.S. House of Representatives Committee on the Judiciary, Subcommittee on Immigration, Citizenship, Refugees, Border Security, and International Law: Hearing on the U.S. Economy, U.S. Workers, and Immigration Reform." May 3.

Friedman, Paul. 2012. "Weighing anchors." *Columbia Journalism Review* (July/August), 14–20.

Gamson, William A. 1992. *Talking Politics.* Cambridge, MA: Harvard University Press.

Gamson, William A., and Andre Modigliani. 1989. "Media discourse and public opinion on nuclear power: a constructionist approach." *American Journal of Sociology* 95, 1–37.

Gandy, Oscar H., Jr. 1992. "Public relations and public policy." In E. Toth and R. Heath, eds., *Rhetorical and Critical Approaches to Public Relations*, 131–163. Hillsdale, NJ: Lawrence Erlbaum.

Gans, Herbert J. 1979. *Deciding What's News.* New York: Random House.

Gans, Herbert J. 1995. *The War Against the Poor.* New York: Basic Books.

Gans, Herbert J. 2003. *Democracy and the News.* Oxford: Oxford University Press.

Gans, Herbert J. 2005. *Deciding What's News*, 2nd ed. Evanston, IL: Northwestern University Press.

García, Mario T., ed. 1995. *Rubén Salazar, Border Correspondent: Selected Writings, 1955–1970.* Berkeley: University of California Press.

Garnham, Nicholas. 2000. *Emancipation, the Media, and Modernity.* New York: Oxford University Press.

Gastaut, Yvan. 2000. *L'immigration et l'opinion en France sous la Ve République.* Paris: Seuil.

Gatien, Emannuelle. 2007. "Excellence journalistique et institutionnalisation du journalisme: L'exemple du prix Albert Londres." Unpublished Working Paper, Institut d'Etudes Politiques de Toulouse.

Gerstlé, Jacques, Dennis K. Davis, and Olivier Duhamel. 1991. "Television news and the construction of political reality in France and the United States." In L.L. Kaid, J. Gerstlé, and K.R. Sanders, eds., *Mediated Politics in Two Cultures: Presidential Campaigning in the United States and France*, 119–143. New York: Praeger.

Gilchrist, Jim, and Jerome R. Corsi. 2006. *Minutemen: The Battle to Secure America's Borders.* Los Angeles: World Ahead Publishing.

Ginsberg, Benjamin. 1986. *The Captive Public: How Mass Opinion Promotes State Power.* New York: Basic.

Gitlin, Todd. 1980. *The Whole World is Watching.* Berkeley: University of California Press.

Glasser, Theodore L. 1992. "Professionalism and the derision of diversity: the case of the education of journalists." *Journal of Communication* 42 (2), 131–140.

Glasser, Theodore L., ed. 1999. *The Idea of Public Journalism.* London: Guilford Press.

Golding, Peter, and Graham Murdock. 2000. "Culture, communications, and political economy." In J. Curran and M. Gurevitch, eds., *Mass Media and Society*, 3rd ed., 70–92. London: Arnold.

Gonzalez, Juan. 2001. *Harvest of Empire.* New York: Penguin.

Gottlieb, Robert, and Irene Wolt. 1977. *Thinking Big: The Story of the Los Angeles Times, Its Publishers and Their Influence on Southern California.* New York: G.P. Putnam's Sons.

Graber, Doris. 1988. *Processing the News.* New York: Longman.

Greenhouse, Stephen. 2008. *The Big Squeeze: Tough Times for the American Worker.* New York: Knopf.

Greenwald, Marilyn, and Joseph Bernt. 2000. *The Big Chill: Investigative Reporting in the Current Media Environment.* Ames: Iowa State University Press.

Grieco, Elizabeth. 2002. "Defining 'foreign born' and 'foreigner' in international migration statistics." From Migration Policy Institute. Available at: http://www.migrationinformation.org/Feature/print.cfm?ID=34. Accessed February 1, 2008.

Grueskin, Bill, Ava Seave, and Lucas Graves. 2011. *The Story So Far: What We Know About the Business of Digital Journalism.* New York: Columbia Journalism School.

Guiraudon, Virginie. 2000. *Les politiques d'immigration en Europe: Allemagne, France, Pays- Bas.* Paris: L'Harmattan.

Guisnel, Jean. 2003. *Libération, la biographie.* Paris: La Découverte.

Gutiérrez, David G. 1995. *Walls and Mirrors: Mexican Americans, Mexican Immigrants and the Politics of Ethnicity.* Berkeley: University of California Press.

Habermas, Jürgen. 1989. *The Structural Transformation of the Public Sphere.* Cambridge, MA: MIT Press.

Habermas, Jürgen. 1996. *Between Facts and Norms.* Cambridge, MA: MIT Press.

Habermas, Jürgen. 2006. "Political communication in media society: does democracy still enjoy an epistemic dimension?" *Communication Theory* 16, 411–426.

Halimi, Serge. 2005. *Les nouveaux chiens du garde.* Paris: Raisons d'Agir.

Hall, Stuart, Chas Critcher, Tony Jefferson, Tony Clarke, and Brian Roberts. 1978. *Policing the Crisis.* New York: Holmes & Meier Publishers.

Hallin, Daniel C. 1986. *'The Uncensored War': The Media and Vietnam*. New York: Oxford University Press.

Hallin, Daniel C. 1994. *We Keep America on Top of the World: Television journalism and the public sphere*. London: Routledge.

Hallin, Daniel C. 1996. "Commercialism and professionalism in the American News Media." In J. Curran and M. Gurevitch, eds., *Mass Media and Society*, 2nd ed., 243–262. London: Arnold.

Hallin, Daniel C., and Paolo Mancini. 1984. "Speaking of the president: political structure and representational form in U.S. and Italian television news." *Theory and Society* 13, 829–850.

Hallin, Daniel C., and Paolo Mancini. 2004. *Comparing Media Systems*. Cambridge, UK: Cambridge University Press.

Hallin, Daniel C., and Paolo Mancini. 2012. *Comparing Media Systems Beyond the Western World*. Cambridge, UK: Cambridge University Press.

Hamilton, James T. 2004. *All the News That's Fit to Sell: How the Market Transforms Information into News*. Princeton: Princeton University Press.

Hanitzsch, Thomas. 2007. "Deconstructing journalism culture: toward a universal theory." *Communication Theory* 17, 367–385.

Hanitzsch, Thomas. 2011. "Populist disseminators, detached watchdogs, critical change agents and opportunist facilitators: Professional milieus, the journalistic field and autonomy in 18 countries." *The International Communication Gazette* 73(6), 477–494.

Hanson, Gordon, and Philip Martin. 2006. "Econoblog: immigration's costs – and benefits," Wall Street Journal Online, June 26. Available at: http://online.wsj.com/public/article/SB11510094830578794O-tA5PPoYa_9UoAlXBQQhnaDyMIYc_200 60725.html?mod=tff_main_tff_top

Hargreaves, Alec G. 1992. "Ethnic minorities and the mass media in France." In R. C. and N. Hewitt, eds., *Popular Culture and Mass Communication in Twentieth-Century France*, 165–180. Lampeter, UK: Edwin Mellen Press.

Hargreaves, Alec G. 1995. *Immigration, 'Race' and Ethnicity in Contemporary France*. London: Routledge.

Hargreaves, Alec G. 2004. "Half-measures: anti-discrimination policy in France." In H. Chapman and L. L. Frader, eds., *Race in France*, 227–245. New York: Berghahn Books.

Hargreaves, Alec G. 2007. *Multi-Ethnic France*. London: Routledge.

Harris, Janet. 2012. "Reporting migration – a journalist's reflection on personal experience and academic critique." In K. Moore, B. Gross, and T. Threadgold, eds., *Migrations and the Media*, 253–268. New York: Peter Lang.

Hart, Jack R. 1981. *The Information Empire: The Rise of the Los Angeles Times and the Times Mirror Corporation*. Washington, DC: University Press of America.

Harvey, David. 2005. *A Brief History of Neoliberalism*. Oxford: Oxford University Press.

Hasty, Jennifer. 2005. *The Press and Political Culture in Ghana*. Bloomington: Indiana University Press.

Heider, Don, ed. 2004. *Class and News*. Lanham, MD: Rowman and Littlefield.

Herbst, Susan. 1995. *Numbered Voices: How Opinion Polling has Shaped American Politics*. Chicago: University of Chicago Press.

Herman, Edward S., and Noam Chomsky. 1988. *Manufacturing Consent: The Political Economy of the Mass Media*. New York: Pantheon.

Hesmondhalgh, David. 2006. "Bourdieu, the media and cultural production." *Media, Culture & Society* 28(2), 211–231.

Hess, Stephen. 1981. *The Washington Reporters*. Washington, DC: Brookings Institution.

Hilgartner, Stephen, and Charles L. Bosk. 1988. "The rise and fall of social problems: a public arenas model." *American Journal of Sociology* 94, 53–78.

Hindman, Matthew. 2008. *The Myth of Digital Democracy*. Princeton: Princeton University Press.

Hirschmann, Charles. 2005. "Immigration and the American century." *Demography* 42(4), 595–620.

Hoffman, L. H. 2006. "Is internet content different after all? A content analysis of mobilizing information in online and print newspapers." *Journalism & Mass Communication Quarterly* 83(1), 58–76.

Hollifield, James F. 1994. "Immigration and republicanism in France: the hidden consensus." In W. Cornelius, P. Martin, and J. Hollifield, eds., *Controlling Immigration*, 143–175. Stanford: Stanford University Press.

Horowitz, Donald. 1992. "Immigration and group relations in France and America." In D. Horowitz and G. Noiriel, eds., *Immigrants in Two Democracies: French and American Experience*, 3–35. New York: NYU Press.

Horowitz, Donald, and Gérard Noiriel, eds. 1992. *Immigrants in Two Democracies: French and American Experience*. New York: NYU Press.

Hotchkiss, Nicole. 2010. "Globalizing security? Media framing of national security in France and the United States from the Cold War through 11 September." *International Journal of Comparative Sociology* 51(5), 366–386.

Howard, A.E. Dick. 1989. "The press in court." In P. S. Cook, D. Gomery, and L. W. Lichty, eds., *American Media: The Wilson Quarterly Reader*, 73–80. Washington, DC: Wilson Center Press.

Hoynes, William. 1994. *Public Television for Sale: Media, the Market, and the Public Sphere*. Boulder, CO: Westview Press.

Hubé, Nicolas. 2004. "La conférence de rédaction du *Monde*: Une approche ethnographique de l'élaboration de la 'Une'" In J.-B. Legavre, ed., *La presse écrite: objets délaissés*, 191–209. Paris: L'Harmattan.

Hubé, Nicolas. 2008. *Décrocher la 'Une'*. Strasbourg: Presses Universitaires de Strasbourg.

Hubé, Nicolas, and Nicolas Kaciaf. 2006. "Les page 'société' ou les pages 'politiques' en creux: Retour sur des conflits de bon voisinage." In I. Chupin and J. Nollet, eds., *Les frontières journalistiques*, 189–212. Paris: L'Harmattan.

Huber, Gregory A., and Thomas J. Espenshade. 1997. "Neo-Isolationalism, Balanced - Budget Conservatism, and the Fiscal Impacts of Immigrants." *International Migration Review* 31, 1031–1054.

Hughes, Sallie. 2006. *Newsrooms in Conflict: Journalism and the Democratization of Mexico*. Pittsburgh: University of Pittsburgh Press.

Hunter, Mark. 1997. *Le journalisme d'investigation*. Paris: Presses Universitaires de France.

INED. 2011. "Population selon la nationalité." Available at: http://www.insee.fr/fr/themes/tableau.asp?reg_id=0&ref_id=nattefo2131&id=339. Accessed August 25.

INSEE. 2003. "La fécondité des étrangères en France diminue," *La société française: Données sociales 1993*, 46–53. Paris: Insee.

INSEE. 2007. Étrangers selon leur nationalité. Available at INED (Institut nationale d'études démographiques) website: http://www.ined.fr/en/pop_figures/france/immigrants_foreigners/immigrantsforeigners1982/. Accessed August 25.

Iskander, Natasha. 2007. "Informal work and protest: undocumented immigrant activism in France, 1996–2000." *British Journal of Industrial Relations* 45 (2), 309–334.

Iyengar, Shanto. 1991. *Is Anyone Responsible? How Television Frames Political Issues*. Chicago: University of Chicago Press.

Jackall, Robert, and Janice M. Hirota. 2000. *Image Makers*. Chicago: University of Chicago Press.

Jacobs, Ronald N. 2000. *Race, Media, and the Crisis of Civil Society*. Cambridge, UK: Cambridge University Press.

Jacobs, Ronald N., and Eleanor Townsley. 2011. *The Space of Opinion*. Oxford: Oxford University Press.

Janssen, Susanne, Giselinde Kuipers, and Marc Verboord. 2008. "Cultural globalization and arts journalism: the international orientation of arts and culture coverage in Dutch, French, German, and U.S. newspapers, 1955 to 2005." *American Sociological Review* 73, 719–740.

Jarvis, Jeff. 2009. *What Would Google Do?* New York: Harper Business.

Jasperson, Amy E., and Mansour O. El-Kikhia. 2003. "CNN and al Jazeera's media coverage of America's war in Afghanistan." In P. Norris, M. Kern, and M. Just, eds., *Framing Terrorism*, 114–132. New York: Routledge.

Joffrin, Laurent. 1992. *La régression française*. Paris: Seuil.

John, Richard R. 1995. *Spreading the News*. Cambridge, MA: Harvard University Press.

Juhem, Philippe. 1999. "La participation des journalistes à l'emergence des mouvements sociaux." *Reseaux* 98 (17), 121–152.

Juhem, Philippe. 2001. "Alternances politiques et transformations du champ de l'information en France après 1981." *Politix* 14(56), 185–208.

Kanstroom, Daniel. 2007. *Deportation Nation*. Cambridge, MA: Harvard University Press.

Kaplan, Richard L. 2002. *Politics and the American Press: The Rise of Objectivity, 1865–1920*. Cambridge, UK: Cambridge University Press.

Katz, Elihu. 1989. "Journalists as scientists: notes toward an occupational classification." *The American Behavioral Scientist* 33 (2), 238–246.

Kendall, Diana. 2011. *Framing Class*, 2nd ed. Lanham, MD: Rowman and Littlefield.

Kennedy, Dan. 2009. "Second Life: After 100 years as a daily, the *Christian Science Monitor* reinvents itself for the Internet Age." *CommonWealth* (Winter), 37–42.

Keogan, Kevin. 2002. "A Sense of place: the politics of immigration and the symbolic construction of identity in Southern California and the New York metropolitan area." *Sociological Forum* 17 (2), 223–253.

Kim, Sei-hill, John P. Carvalho, Andrew G. Davis, and Amanda M. Mullins. 2011. "The view of the border: news framing of the definition, causes, and solutions to illegal immigration." *Mass Communication and Society* 14(3), 292–314.

Kirtley, Jane E. 2005. "Legal evolution of the government – news media relationship." In G. Overholser and K. H. Jamieson, eds., *The Press*, 277–283. Oxford: Oxford University Press.

Klinenberg, Eric. 2005. "Convergence: news production in a digital age." *The ANNALS of the American Academy of Political and Social Science* 597, 48–64.

Klinenberg, Eric. 2007. *Fighting for Air*. New York: Metropolitan Books

Krause, Monika. 2011. "Reporting and the transformations of the journalistic field: U.S. news media, 1890–2000." *Media, Culture, & Society* 33(1), 89–104.

Krauss, Ellis. 2000. *Broadcasting Politics in Japan: NHK and Television News*. Ithaca, NY: Cornell University Press.

Kuhn, Raymond. 1995. *The Media in France*. London: Routledge.

Kuhn, Raymond. 2005. "'Be very afraid': Television and L'Insécurité in the 2002 French presidential election." *European Journal of Communication* 20(2), 181–198.

Kuhn, Raymond. 2010. "Public service television in Sarkozy's France." Paper presented to RIPE@2010: Public Service Media After the Recession, September 8–11, London.

Kurtz, Howard. 2007. *Reality Show: Inside the Last Great Television News War*. New York: Free Press.

Kwong, Peter. 1997. *Forbidden Workers: Illegal Chinese Immigrants and American Labor*. New York: New Press.

Lamont, Michèle. 2000. *The Dignity of Working Men: Morality and the Boundaries of Race, Class, and Immigration*. Cambridge, MA: Harvard University Press.

Lamont, Michèle. 2004. "Immigration and the salience of racial boundaries among French workers." In H. Chapman and L. L. Frader, eds. *Race in France*, 141–161. New York: Berghahn Books.

Lamont, Michèle, and Laurent Thévenot, eds., 2000. *Rethinking Comparative Cultural Sociology: Repertoires of Evaluation in France and the United States*. Cambridge, UK: Cambridge University Press.

Lanahan, David. 2008. "Secrets of the city: what The Wire reveals about urban journalism." *Columbia Journalism Review* (January/February).

Lapinski, John S., Pia Peltola, Greg Shaw, and Alan Yang. 1997. "The polls – trends: immigrants and immigration." *Public Opinion Quarterly* 61, 356–383.

Lawrence, Regina. 2000. *The Politics of Force: Media and the Construction of Police Brutality*. Berkeley: University of California Press.

Le Bohec, Jacques. 2004a. *L'implication des journalists dans le phenomene Le Pen*, Vol. I. Paris: L'Harmattan.

Le Bohec, Jacques. 2004b. *Les interactions entre les journalists et J.-M. Le Pen*, Vol. 2. Paris: L'Harmattan.

Lecomte, Monica. 1999. *Television broadcasting in contemporary France and Britain*. Berghahn Books.

Lee, Matthew T., Ramiro Martínez, Jr., and Richard B. Rosenfeld. 2001. "Does immigration increase homicide? Negative evidence from three border cities." *Sociological Quarterly* 42(4), 559–580.

Lemert, James. 1984 "News context and the elimination of mobilizing information: an experiment." *Journalism Quarterly* 61(2), 243–249.

Lemieux, Cyril. 2000. *Mauvaise presse*. Paris: Éditions Métailié.

Lemieux, Cyril. 2001. "Heurs et malheurs du journalisme d'investigation en France." In C. Delporte, M. Palmer, and D. Ruellan, eds., *Presse à scandale, scandale de presse*, 85–96. Paris: L'Harmattan.

Lemieux, Cyril. 2004. "De certaines différences internationales en matière de pratiques journalistiques: comment les décrire, comment les expliquer?" In J.-B. Legavre, ed., *La presse écrite: objets délaissés*, 29–50. Paris: L'Harmattan.

Lemieux, Cyril, and John Schmalzbauer. 2000. "Involvement and detachment among French and American journalists: to be or not to be a 'real' professional." In M. Lamont and L. Thévenot, eds., *Rethinking Comparative Cultural Sociology*, 148–169. Cambridge, UK: Cambridge University Press.

Leonard, Thomas C. 1986. *The Power of the Press: The Birth of American Political Reporting*. Oxford: Oxford University Press.

Levy, David. 2010. "PSB policymaking in comparative perspective: the BBC Charter Review process and the French Commission pour la nouvelle télévision publique." Paper presented to RIPE@2010: Public Service Media After the Recession, September 8–11, London.

Levy, David, and Rasmus Kleis Nielsen, eds. 2011. *The Changing Business of Journalism and Its Implications for Democracy*. Oxford: Reuters Institute for the Study of Journalism.

Lippmann, W. 1997 [1922]. *Public Opinion*. New York: Free Press.

Lochard, Guy. 2005. *L'information télévisée*. Paris: Clemi-INA-Vuibert.

López, David. 1982. *The Maintenance of Spanish Over Three Generations in the United States*. Los Alamitos, CA: National Center for Bilingual Research.

Lowrey, Tina M., L.J. Shrum, and John A. McCarty. 2005. "The future of television advertising." In A. Kimmel, ed., *Marketing Communication: Emerging Trends and Developments*, 113–132. New York: Oxford University Press.

Lubbers, Marcel, and Peer Scheepers. 2002. "French Front National voting: a micro and macro perspective." *Ethnic and Racial Studies* 25(1), 120–149.

Lunby, Knut. 2009. "Media logic: looking for social interaction." In K. Lunby, ed., *Mediatization*, 101–119. New York: Peter Lang.

Mancini, Paolo. 2000. "Political complexity and alternative models of journalism: The Italian case." In J. Curran and M-J. Park, eds., *De-Westernizing Media Studies*, 265–278. London: Routledge.

Marchetti, Dominique. 2000. "Les révélations du 'journalisme d'investigation.'" *Actes de la recherche en sciences sociales* 131(1), 30–40.

Marchetti, Dominique. 2005. "Sub-fields of specialized journalism." In R. Benson and E. Neveu, eds., *Bourdieu and the Journalistic Field*, 64–82. Cambridge, UK: Polity.

Marchetti, Dominique, and Denis Ruellan. 2001. *Devenir Journalistes: Sociologie de l'entrée sur le marché du travail*. Paris: La Documentation française.

Marthaler, Sally. 2008. "Nicolas Sarkozy and the politics of French immigration policy." *Journal of European Public Policy* 15(3), 382–397.

Martin, John Levi. 2003. "What is field theory?" *American Journal of Sociology* 109, 1–49.

Massey, Douglas S. 1998. "March of folly: U.S. immigration policy under NAFTA." *American Prospect* 9(37), 22–33.

Mathien, Michel. 2003. *Economie générale des médias*. Paris: Ellipses.

Mazzolini, G. 1987. "Media logic and party logic in campaign coverage: the Italian general election of 1983." *European Journal of Communication* 2(1), 55–80.

McChesney, Robert W. 1993. *Telecommunications, Mass Media and Democracy: The Battle for the Control of U.S. Broadcasting, 1928–1935*. New York: Oxford University Press.

McChesney, Robert W. 2000. *Rich Media, Poor Democracy*. New York: New Press.

McChesney, Robert W., and John Nichols. 2010. *The Death and Life of American Journalism*. New York: Nation Books.

McCombs, Maxwell. 2004. *Setting the Agenda*. Cambridge, UK: Polity.

McDonnell, Patrick. 2011. "Covering immigration: from stepchild beat to newsroom mainstream." In M.M. Suárez-Orozco, V. Louie, and R. Suro, eds., *Writing Immigration*, 90–101. Berkeley: University of California Press.

McGowan, William. 2002. *Coloring the News*. San Francisco: Encounter Books.

Miège, Bernard, ed. 1986. *Le J.T.: Mise en scène de l'actualité à la télévision*. Paris: La Documentation française.

Mitchelstein, Eugenia, and Pablo Boczkowski. 2009. "Between tradition and change: A review of recent research on online news production." *Journalism* 10(5), 562–586.

Molotch, Harvey, and Marilyn Lester. 1974. "News as purposive behavior: on the strategic use of routine events, accidents, and scandals." *American Sociological Review* 39, 101–112.

Monforte, Pierre. 2009. "Social movements and Europeanization processes: the case of the French associations mobilizing around the asylum issue." *Social Movement Studies* 8(4), 409–425.

Morris, J. 2005. "The Fox News factor." *Press/Politics* 10, 56–79.

MPI. 2011. "Country: United States." Migration Policy Institute comparative data. Available at: http://www.migrationinformation.org/datahub/countrydata/country.cfm. Accessed August 25, 2011.

M'Sili, Marine. 2000. *Le Fait divers en République*. Paris: CNRS.

Mucchielli, Laurent. 2003. "Délinquance et immigration en France: un regard sociologique." *Criminologie* 36(2), 27–55.

Muhlmann, Geraldine. 2008. *A Political History of Journalism*. Cambridge, UK: Polity.

Murschetz, Paul. 1998. "State Support for the Daily Press in Europe: A Critical Appraisal." *European Journal of Communication* 13(3), 291–313.

Nannestad, Peter. 2007. "Immigration and welfare states: A survey of 15 years of research." *European Journal of Political Economy* 23, 512–532.

Napoli, Philip, Sarah Stonbely, Lew Friedland, Tom Glaisyer, and Joshua Breitbart. 2012. *Understanding Media Diversity Using Media Ecosystem Analysis*. Washington, DC: New America Foundation.

Nel, Noël. 1988. *A Fleurets Mouchetés: 25 ans de débats télévisés*. Paris: La Documentation française.

Neveu, Erik. 2009. *Sociologie du journalisme*. Paris: La Découverte.

Newspaper Association of America. 2001. *Circulation Facts, Figures and Logic*. Accessed via Internet, April 2004.

Ngai, Mae M. 2004. *Impossible Subjects: Illegal Aliens and the Making of Modern America*. Princeton: Princeton University Press.

Nielsen, Rasmus Kleis, and Geert Linnebank. 2011. *Public Support for the Media: A Six-Country Overview of Direct and Indirect Subsidies*. Oxford, UK: Reuters Institute for the Study of Journalism.

Noah, Timothy. 2012. *The Great Divergence: America's Growing Inequality Crisis and What We Can Do about It*. New York: Bloomsbury Press.

Noiriel, Gérard. 1996. *The French Melting Pot: Immigration, Citizenship and National Identity*. Minneapolis: University of Minnesota.

Noiriel, Gérard. 2007. *Immigration, antisémitisme et racisme en France*. Paris: Fayard.

O'Connor, Karen, and Lee Epstein. 1988. "A legal voice for the Chicano community: the activities of the Mexican-American Legal Defense and Educational Fund, 1968–1982." In F. C. Garcia, ed., *Latinos and the Political System*, 255–268. Notre Dame: University of Notre Dame Press.

Oliver, Pamela E., and Daniel J. Myers. 1999. "How events enter the public sphere: conflict, location, and sponsorship in local newspaper coverage of public events." *American Journal of Sociology* 105(1), 38–87.

Open Society Institute. 2005. *Television Across Europe: Regulation, Policy and Independence.* Available at: http://www.soros.org/initiatives/media/articles_publica tions/publications/eurotv_20051001

Opportunity Agenda, The. 2010. *California Public Discourse on Immigration: A Scan of Print Media Coverage and Public Opinion in 2008–2009.* Available at: http://opportu nityagenda.org/media_analysis_california_public_discourse_immi gration_2009.

O'Shea, James. 2011. *The Deal from Hell: How Moguls and Wall Street Plundered Great American Newspapers.* New York: PublicAffairs.

Ossman, Susan, and Susan Terrio. 2006. "The French riots: questioning spaces of surveillance and sovereignty." *International Migration* 44 (2), 5–19.

Ouellete, Laurie. 2002. *Viewers Like You? How Public TV Failed the People.* New York: Columbia University Press.

Padioleau, Jean G. 1985. *Le Monde et le Washington Post.* Paris: Presses Universitaires de France.

Page, Benjamin. 1996. *Who Deliberates? Mass Media in Modern Democracy.* Chicago: University of Chicago Press.

Pager, Devah, and Hana Shepherd. 2008. "The sociology of discrimination: racial discrimination in employment, housing, credit, and consumer markets." *Annual Review of Sociology* 34, 181–209.

Palmer, Michael B. 1994. "Les héritiers de Théophraste." In J.-F. Lacan, M. Palmer, and D. Ruellan, eds., *Les Journalistes.* Paris: Syros.

Palmeri, Hélène C., and Willard R. Rowland, Jr. 2011. "Public television in a time of technological change and socioeconomic turmoil: the cases of France and the United States, part I." *International Journal of Communication* 5, 1082–1107.

Papazian, E., ed. 2003. *TV Dimensions 2003.* New York: Media Dynamics, Inc.

Paracuellos, Jean-Charles. 1993. *La télévision: clefs d'une économie invisible.* Paris: La Documentation française.

Passel, Jeffrey S. 2006. "The size and characteristics of the unauthorized migrant population in the U.S." Pew Hispanic Center Research Report, March 7. Available at: http://pewhispanic.org/files/reports/61.pdf.

PBS (Public Broadcasting Service). 2010. "PBS: An Overview." Available at: http://www. pbs.org/aboutpbs/aboutpbs_corp.html. Accessed April 22, 2010.

Péan, Pierre, and Christophe Nick. 1997. *TF1: un pouvoir.* Paris: Fayard.

Pedelty, Mark. 1995. *War Stories.* London: Routledge.

PEJ. 2007. (Project for Excellence in Journalism). *The State of the News Media: An Annual Report on American Journalism.* Available at: http://www.stateofthenewsmedia.org

PEJ. 2010a. (Project for Excellence in Journalism). *The State of the News Media: An Annual Report on American Journalism.* Available at: http://www.stateofthenewsmedia.org

PEJ. 2010b. "Who Owns the News Media" Profile of Public Broadcasting Service. Available at: http://www.stateofthemedia.org/2010/media-ownership/. Accessed April 18.

Peri, Giovanni. 2007. "How immigrants affect California's employment and wages." *California Counts: Population Trends and Profiles* 8(3), 1–19.

Perrier, J-C. 1994. *Le roman vrai de Libération.* Paris: Juilliard.

Peterson, Richard, and Roger Kern. 1996. "Changing highbrow taste." *American Sociological Review* 61(5), 900–907.

Pettigrew, Thomas F., Ulrich Wagner, and Oliver Christ. 2007. "Who opposes immigration? Comparing German with North American findings." *Du Bois Review* 4(1), 19–39.

Phillips, Angela. 2010. "Old sources: new bottles." In N. Fenton, ed., *New Media, Old News*, 87–101. London: Sage.

Picard, Robert G. 2005. "Money, media, and the public interest." In G. Overholser and K. H. Jamieson, eds., *The Press*, 337–350. Oxford: Oxford University Press.

Pickard, Victor. 2011. "Can government support the press? Historicizing and internationalizing a policy approach to the journalism crisis." *The Communication Review* 14, 73–95.

Pickard, Victor, Josh Stearns, and Craig Aaron. 2009. "Saving the news: toward a national journalism strategy." Washington, DC: Free Press Policy Report.

Portes, Alejandro. 1999. "Models and realities: the consequences of immigration." *Contemporary Sociology* 28(4), 387–390.

Portes, Alejandro, and Rubén G. Rumbaut. 1996. *Immigrant America: A Portrait.* Berkeley: University of California Press.

Portes, Alejandro, and Rubén G. Rumbaut. 2006. *Immigrant America: A Portrait,* 3rd edition. Berkeley: University of California Press.

Porto, Mauro. 2007. "Frame diversity and citizen competence." *Critical Studies in Media Communication* 24, 303–321.

Postman, Neil. 2005. *Amusing Ourselves to Death.* New York: Penguin.

Poulet, Bernard. 2003. *Le pouvoir du Monde.* Paris: La Découverte.

Powell, Walter W. 1991. "Expanding the scope of institutional analysis." In W. W. Powell and P. J. DiMaggio, eds., *The New Institutionalism in Organizational Analysis,* 183–203. Chicago: University of Chicago Press.

Powers, Matthew. 2009. "Forms of power on/through the Web." *Journalism Studies* 10(2), 268–280.

Preston, Julia, and Samuel Dillon. 2004. *Opening Mexico: The Making of a Democracy.* New York: Farrar, Straus, and Giroux.

Prior, Markus. 2007. *Post-Broadcast Democracy.* Cambridge, UK: Cambridge University Press.

Quandt, Thorsten. 2008. "(No) news on the World Wide Web?" *Journalism Studies* 9(5), 717–738.

Quillian, Lincoln. 2006. "New approaches to understanding racial prejudice and discrimination." *Annual Review of Sociology* 32, 299–328.

Ramonet, Ignacio. 2001. "*Le Monde,* la Bourse et nous." *Le Monde Diplomatique,* December.

Rawolle, Shaun, and Bob Lingard. 2010. "The mediatization of the knowledge based economy: An Australian field based account." *Communications* 35, 269–286.

Reese, Stephen D. 2001. "Understanding the global journalist: a hierarchy-of-influences approach." *Journalism Studies* 2(2), 173–187.

Reese, Stephen D., Oscar H. Gandy, Jr., and August E. Grant, eds. 2003. *Framing Public Life.* Mahwah, NJ: Lawrence Erlbaum.

Rieffel, Rémy. 1984. *L'Elite des journalistes.* Paris: Presses Universitaires de France.

Rigoni, Isabelle, ed. 2007. *Qui a peur de la télévision en couleurs? La diversité culturelle dans les médias.* Paris: Aux lieux d'être.

Rimbert, Pierre. 2005. *Libération de Sartre à Rothschild.* Paris: Raisons d'Agir.

Roberts, Gene, and Hank Klibanoff. 2006. *The Race Beat.* New York: Knopf.

Robertson, Lori. 2000. "Reporters who know the business." *American Journalism Review* 22 (December).

References

Robinson, Piers, Peter Goddard, Kate Parry, Craig Murray, and Philip M. Taylor. *Pockets of resistance: British news media, war and theory in the 2003 invasion of Iraq.* Manchester, UK: Manchester University Press.

Roché, Sebastian. 2001. *La délinquance des jeunes: Les 13–19 ans racontent leurs délits.* Paris: Seuil.

Rodríguez, Olga. 1977. *The Politics of Chicano Liberation.* New York: Pathfinder Press.

Rohlinger, Deana A. 2007. "American media and deliberative democratic processes." *Sociological Theory* 25(2), 122–148.

Rollat, Alain. 1985. *Les hommes de l'extrême droite: Le Pen, Marie, Ortiz et les autres.* Paris: Calmann-Lévy.

Rollat, Alain, and Edwy Plenel. 1992. *La République menacée: dix ans d'effet Le Pen.* Paris: Editions Le Monde.

Rosenstiel, Tom, Stacy Forster, and Dante Chinni. 1998. "Changing definitions of news: a look at the mainstream press over 20 years." *Report for the Project for Excellence in Journalism,* Washington, DC.

Rowthorn, Robert. 2008. "The fiscal impact of immigration on the advanced economies." *Oxford Review of Economic Policy* 24(3), 560–580.

Ruellan, Denis. 1993. *Le professionalisme du flou: identité et savoir-faire des journalistes français.* Grenoble: Presses Universitaires de Grenoble.

Ruffin, François. 2003. *Les petits soldats du journalisme.* Paris: Les Arènes.

Rumbaut, Rubén, and Walter A. Ewing. 2007. "The myth of immigrant criminality." Published online by the Social Science Research Council, May 23, 2007. Available at: http://borderbattles.ssrc.org. Accessed January 16, 2008.

Runciman, W. R. 1989. *Treatise on Social Theory,* Vol. 2. Cambridge, UK: Cambridge University Press.

Russell, Adrienne. 2007. "Digital communication networks and the journalistic field: the 2005 French riots." *Critical Studies in Media Communication* 24(4), 285–302.

Ryan, Charlotte. 1991. *Prime Time Activism.* Boston: South End Press.

Saguy, Abigail C. 2003. *What is Sexual Harassment? From Capitol Hill to the Sorbonne.* Berkeley: University of California Press.

Saïtta, Eugénie. 2005. "*Le Monde,* vingt ans après." *Réseaux* 131, 191–225.

Samuelson, F. M. 1979. *Il était une fois Libération.* Paris: Seuil.

Santa Ana, Otto. 1999. "'Like an animal I was treated': anti-immigrant metaphor in U.S. public discourse." *Discourse & Society* 10(2), 191–224.

Santhanam, Laura Houston, and Tom Rosenstiel. 2011. "Why U.S. newspapers suffer more than others." The State of the News Media 2010. Available at: http://stateofthe media.org/2011/mobile-survey/international-newspaper- economics/.

Sassen, Saskia. 1999. *Globalization and Its Discontents.* New York: New Press.

Sayad, Abdelmalek. 1995. *Un Nanterre algérien, terre de bidonvilles.* Paris: Ed. Autrement.

Schain, Martin A. 1985. "Immigrants and politics in France." In J. S. Ambler, ed., *The French Socialist Experiment,* 166–190. Philadelphia: Institute for the Study of Human Issues.

Schain, Martin A. 2008. *The Politics of Immigration in France, Britain, and the United States.* New York: Palgrave Macmillan.

Scheufele, Dietram A. 1999. "Framing as a theory of media effects." *Journal of Communication* 49, 103–122.

Schiller, Dan. 1981. *Objectivity and the News*. Philadelphia: University of Pennsylvania Press.

Schiller, Herbert. 1991. "Not yet the post-imperialist era." *Critical Studies in Mass Communication* 8, 13–28.

Schneider, Mark A. 2001. "Does culture have inertia?" *Culture* (Newsletter of the Sociology of Culture Section of the American Sociological Association) 15, 3.

Schroeder, Michael. 2005. "Who are the viewers of Arte?" In M. Meyer, ed., *Educational Television: What do People Want?*, 143–154. Luton, UK: John Libbey Media.

Schuck, Peter H. 2011. "Some observations about immigration journalism." In M. M. Suárez-Orozco, V. Louie, and R. Suro, eds., *Writing Immigration*, 73–89. Berkeley: University of California Press.

Schudson, Michael. 1978. *Discovering the News*. New York: Basic Books.

Schudson, Michael. 1989. "How culture works: perspectives from media studies on the efficacy of symbols." *Theory and Society* 18(2), 153–180.

Schudson, Michael. 1995. *The Power of News*. Cambridge, MA: Harvard University Press.

Schudson, Michael. 2005. "Autonomy from what?" In R. Benson and E. Neveu, eds., *Bourdieu and the Journalistic Field*. Cambridge, UK: Polity Press.

Schudson, Michael. 2008. *Why Democracies Need an Unlovable Press*. Cambridge, UK: Polity Press.

Schudson, Michael. 2011. *The Sociology of News*. New York: W.W. Norton.

Sedel, Julie. 2004. "La nouvelle formule du *Monde*: Contribution à une etude des transformations du fonctionnement journalistique." *Questions de communication* 6, 299–315.

Sedel, Julie. 2009. *Les médias et la banlieue*. Lormont, France: Le Bord de l'Eau-INA.

Segovia, Francine, and Renatta Defever. 2010. "The polls – trends: American public opinion on immigrants and immigration policy." *Public Opinion Quarterly* 74(2), 375–394.

Serrin, William. 1992. "Labor and the mainstream press: the vanishing labor beat." In S. Pizzigati and F. J. Solowey, eds., *The New Labor Press: Journalism for a Changing Union Movement*, 9–18. Ithaca: Cornell University Press.

Sewell, William H., Jr. 2005. *Logics of History: Social Theory and Social Transformation*. Chicago: University of Chicago Press.

Shoemaker, Pamela J., and Akiba A. Cohen. 2006. *News Around the World*. New York: Routledge.

Shoemaker, Pamela J., and Stephen D. Reese. 1996. *Mediating the Message: Theories of Influence on Mass Media Content*. New York: Longman.

Shorenstein, Stuart Alan, and Lorna Veraldi. 1989. "Does public television have a future?" In P. S. Cook, D. Gomery, and L. W. Lichty, eds., *American Media: The Wilson Quarterly Reader*, 229–242. Washington, DC: Wilson Center Press.

Siebert, Fred S., Theodore Peterson, and Wilbur Schramm. 1956. *Four Theories of the Press*. Urbana: University of Illinois Press.

Silverman, Maxim. 1992. *Deconstructing the Nation: Immigration, Racism and Citizenship in Modern France*. London: Routledge.

Silvestre, Charles. 1996. "Ivan Levaï n'en finit pas de passer la presse en revue." *L'Humanité*. November 16.

Siméant, Johanna. 1998. *La cause des sans papiers*. Paris: Presse de Sciences Po.

Siracusa, Jacques. 2001. *Le JT, machine à decrier: Sociologie du travail des reporters à la television*. Brussels: De Boeck Université-INA.

Skerry, Peter. 1993. *Mexican Americans: The Ambivalent Minority*. Cambridge, MA: Harvard University Press.

Skogerbø, Eli. 1997. "The press subsidy system in Norway." *European Journal of Communication* 12(1), 99–118.

Skrentny, John David, ed. 2001. *Color Lines: Affirmative Action, Immigration, and Civil Rights Options for America*. Chicago: University of Chicago Press.

Smith, James P., and Barry Edmonston, eds. 1997. *The New Americans: Economic, Demographic and Fiscal Effects of Immigration*. Washington, DC: National Academy Press.

Snow, David A., and Robert D. Benford. 1988. "Ideology, frame resonance, and participant mobilization." *International Social Movement Research* 1, 197–217.

Snow, David A., Rens Vliegenthart, and Catherine Corrigall-Brown. 2007. "Framing the French riots: A comparative study of frame variation." *Social Forces* 86(2), 385–415.

Sobieraj, Sarah. 2011. *Soundbitten: The Perils of Media-Centered Political Activism*. New York: NYU Press.

Solé, Robert. 1988. "Le journaliste et l'immigration." (An interview with Jacqueline Costa-Lascoux). *Revue Européenne des Migrations Internationales* 1–2, 157–165.

Soulages, Jean-Claude. 1999. *Les Mises en scène visuelles de l'information: Étude comparée France, Espagne, États-Unis*. Paris: INA-Nathan.

Southern Poverty Law Center. 2007. "Hate crimes against Latinos rising nationwide." In *Intelligence Report* (Brentin Mock), 128. Available at: http://www.splcenter.org/get-informed/intelligence-report/browse-all-issues/2007/winter/immigration-backlash

Sparrow, Bartholomew H. 1999. *Uncertain Guardians: The News Media as a Political Institution*. Baltimore, MD: Johns Hopkins University Press.

Spector, Malcolm, and John I. Kitsuse. 1977. *Constructing Social Problems*. Menlo Park, NJ: Cummings.

Spijkerboer, Thomas. 2007. "The human costs of border control." *European Journal of Migration and Law* 9, 127–139.

Squires, James D. 1993. *Read All About It! The Corporate Takeover of America's Newspapers*. New York: Random House.

Stanger, Ted. 2003. *Sacrés Français: Un Américain nous regarde*. Paris: Michalon.

Starr, Paul. 2004. *The Creation of the Media*. New York: Basic Books.

Stiglitz, Joseph E. 2003. *Globalization and its Discontents*. New York: W.W. Norton.

Streeter, Thomas. 1996. *Selling the Air*. Chicago: University of Chicago Press.

Strömbäck, Jesper, and Daniela V. Dimitrova. 2006. "Political and media systems matter: a comparison of election news coverage in Sweden and the United States." *Press/Politics* 11(4), 131–147.

Suro, Roberto. 2008. "The triumph of no: how the media influence the immigration debate." In R. Suro, ed., *A Report on the Media and the Immigration Debate*, 1–47. Washington, DC: Brookings.

Swain, Carol M. 2007. "The Congressional Black Caucus and the impact of immigration on African American unemployment." In Carol Swain, ed., *Debating Immigration*, 175–188. Cambridge, UK: Cambridge University Press.

Taguieff, Pierre-André. 1988. *La Force du préjugé*. Paris: La Découverte.

Tanton, John. 1986. "FAIR: Quo vadis." Internal Memorandum. Federation for American Immigration Reform. Washington, DC.

Tarr, Carrie. 2005. *Reframing Difference: Beur and Banlieue Filmmaking in France*. New York: Manchester University Press.

Tasini, Jonathan. 1990. "Lost in the margins: labor and the media." *Extra!* 3(7).

Taylor, Charles. 1990. "Modes of civil society." *Public Culture* 3(1), 95–118.

Teitelbaum, Michael S. 2006. "Immigration: the opinion gap." *Christian Science Monitor*, April 17.

Terral, Julien. 2004. *L'insécurité au journal télévisé*. Paris: L'Harmattan.

Thibau, Jacques. 1996. *Le Monde 1944–1996*. Paris: Plon.

Thogmartin, Clyde. 1998. *The National Daily Press of France*. Birmingham, AL: Summa Publications.

Thomas, Elaine R. 2006. "Keeping identity at a distance: Explaining France's new legal restrictions on the Islamic headscarf." *Ethnic and Racial Studies* 29(2), 237–259.

Thomas, Ruth. 1976. *Broadcasting and Democracy in France*. Philadelphia: Temple University Press.

Tilly, Charles. 1986. *The Contentious French*. Cambridge, MA: Harvard University Press.

Tournier, Pierre. 1997. "Nationality, crime, and criminal justice in France." *Crime and Justice* 21, 523–551.

Tuchman, Gaye. 1978. *Making News*. New York: Free Press.

Tunstall, Jeremy. 2010. "The BBC and UK public service broadcasting." In P. Iosofidis, ed., *Reinventing Public Service Communication*, 145–157. London: Palgrave Macmillan.

Tunstall, Jeremy, and David Walker. 1981. *Media Made in California*. Oxford: Oxford University Press.

Turow, Joseph. 1997. *Breaking Up America*. Chicago: University of Chicago Press.

Underwood, Doug. 1995. *When MBAs Rule the Newsroom*. New York: Columbia University Press.

U.S. Census Bureau. 2003. "Educational attainment in the United States: 2003." *Current Population Reports*, P20–550 (Nicole Stoops).

Usher, Nikki, and Michelle D. Layser. 2010. "The quest to save journalism: a legal analysis of new models for newspapers from nonprofit tax-exempt organizations to L3Cs." *Utah Law Review* 4, 1315–1371.

Utard, Jean-Michel. 2008. "Du 8 ½ à Arte info: le quotidien d'une rédaction binationale." In M-F. Lévy and M-N. Sicard, eds., *Les lucarnes de l'Europe*. Paris: Publications de la Sorbonne.

Van Eeckhout, Laetitia. 2007. *L'immigration*. Paris: La Documentation française.

Veugelers, Jack, and Michèle Lamont. 1991. "France: Alternative Locations for Public Debate." In R. Wuthnow, ed., *Between States and Markets: The Voluntary Sector in Comparative Perspective*, 125–156. Princeton: Princeton University Press.

Vos, Tim, Stephanie Craft, and Seth Ashley. 2011. "New media, old criticism: bloggers' press criticism and the journalistic field." *Journalism* (October), 1–19.

Wacquant, Loïc J.D. 1993. "Urban outcasts: stigma and division in the black American Ghetto and the French urban periphery." *International Journal of Urban and Regional Research* 17(3), 366–383.

Wahl-Jorgensen, Karin. 2012. "The strategic ritual of emotionality: a case study of Pulitzer Prize-winning articles." *Journalism* 14, 1–17.

Waisbord, Silvio. 2000. *Watchdog Journalism in South America: News, Accountability, and Democracy*. New York: Columbia University Press.

Waldman, Steven. 2011. *The Information Needs of Communities*. Washington, DC: Federal Communications Commission.

WAN (World Association of Newspapers). 2007. *World Press Trends*. Paris: World Association of Newspapers and ZenithOptimedia.

Watts, Julie. 2002. *Immigration Policy and the Challenge of Globalization*. Ithaca: Cornell University Press.

Wauters, Corentin. 2009. "State aid and 10 commandments to revive the French press." European Journalism Centre (published on July 6, 2009). Available at: http://www.ejc.net/magazine/article/state_aid_and_10_commandments_to_revive_french_press/

Wax, Steven T. 2008. *Kafka Comes to America*. New York: Other Press.

Weaver, David H. 2003. "Journalism education in the United States." In R. Fröhlich and C. Holtz-Bacha, eds., *Journalism Education in Europe and North America: An International Comparison*, 49–64. Cresskill, NJ: Hampton Press.

Weaver, David H., Randal A. Beam, Bonnie J. Brownlee, Paul S. Voakes, and G. Cleveland Wilhoit. 2007. *The American Journalist in the 21st Century*. Mahwah, NJ: Lawrence Erlbaum.

Weil, Patrick. 1991. *La France et ses étrangers*. Paris: Gallimard.

Weldon, Michele. 2008. *Everyman News*. Columbia: University of Missouri Press.

Wessler, Hartmut. 2008. "Investigating deliberativeness comparatively." *Political Communication* 25, 1–22.

White, Hayden. 1981. "The value of narrativity in the representation of reality." In J. T. Mitchell, ed., *On Narrative*. Chicago: University of Chicago Press.

Wihtol de Wenden, Catherine. 1988. *Les immigrés et la politique*. Paris: Presses de la Fondation Nationale des Sciences Politiques.

Wihtol de Wenden, Catherine, and Rémy Leveau. 2001. *La beurgeoisie: Les trois âges de la vie associative issue de l'immigration*. Paris: CNRS Editions.

Williams, Bruce A., and Michael X. Delli Carpini. 2011. *After Broadcast News: Media Regimes, Democracy, and the New Information Environment*. Cambridge, UK: Cambridge University Press.

Williams, Raymond. 2003 [1974]. *Television: Technology and Cultural Form*. London: Routledge Classics.

Wolff, Michael. 2010. *The Man Who Owns the News: Inside the Secret World of Rupert Murdoch*. New York: Broadway Books.

Zolberg, Aristide R. 2006. *A Nation by Design: Immigration Policy in the Fashioning of America*. New York: Russell Sage Foundation.

Index

Index

Other Books in the Series (continued from page iii)

Daniel C. Hallin and Paolo Mancini, eds., *Comparing Media Systems Beyond the Western World*

Robert B. Horwitz, *Communication and Democratic Reform in South Africa*

Philip N. Howard, *New Media Campaigns and the Managed Citizen*

Ruud Koopmans and Paul Statham, eds., *The Making of a European Public Sphere: Media Discourse and Political Contention*

L. Sandy Maisel, Darrell M. West, and Brett M. Clifton, *Evaluating Campaign Quality: Can the Electoral Process Be Improved?*

Pippa Norris, *Digital Divide: Civic Engagement, Information Poverty, and the Internet Worldwide*

Pippa Norris, *A Virtuous Circle: Political Communications in Postindustrial Society*

Adam F. Simon, *The Winning Message: Candidate Behavior, Campaign Discourse*

Daniela Stockmann, *Media Commercialization and Authoritarian Rule in China*

Bruce A. Williams and Michael X. Delli Carpini, *After Broadcast News: Media Regimes, Democracy, and the New Information Environment*

Gadi Wolfsfeld, *Media and the Path to Peace*

CPSIA information can be obtained at www.ICGtesting.com
Printed in the USA
BVOW05s0917240714

360319BV00002B/189/P